# FRONTIER RELIGION

# FRONTIER RELIGION

## MORMONS AND AMERICA
## 1857–1907

*Konden Smith Hansen*

THE UNIVERSITY OF UTAH PRESS
SALT LAKE CITY

Copyright © 2019 by The University of Utah Press. All rights reserved.

 The Defiance House Man colophon is a registered trademark of The University of Utah Press. It is based on a four-foot-tall Ancient Puebloan pictograph (late PIII) near Glen Canyon, Utah.

Library of Congress Cataloging-in-Publication Data

Names: Smith, Konden Rich, author.

Title: Frontier religion : Mormons and America, 1857-1907 / Konden Smith Hansen.

Description: Salt Lake City : The University of Utah Press, [2019] | Includes bibliographical references. |

Identifiers: LCCN 2018048206 (print) | LCCN 2018049740 (ebook) | ISBN 9781607816898 | ISBN 9781607816881 (cloth : alk. paper)

Subjects: LCSH: Church of Jesus Christ of Latter-day Saints—United States—History. | Mormon Church--United States—History. | Church of Jesus Christ of Latter-day Saints—Public relations—West (U.S.)—History. | Mormon Church—Public relations—West (U.S.)—History. | Religion and culture—West (U.S.)

Classification: LCC BX8611 (ebook) | LCC BX8611 .S675 2019 (print) | DDC 289.3/7309034—dc23

LC record available at https://lccn.loc.gov/2018048206

Chapter 5 republished with permission of ABC-CLIO from *Mormons in Popular Culture*, Volume 2, edited by J. Michael Hunter, 2013. Permission conveyed through Copyright Clearance Center, Inc.

Errata and further information on this and other titles available online at UofUpress.com

Printed and bound in the United States of America.

*Dedicated to Val Avery, whose mentorship helped shape the initial formations of this book, and Moses Moore, without whom this book would not have been possible.*

# CONTENTS

# ACKNOWLEDGMENTS

N O BOOK EMERGES outside of its own context, and as part of the context of this book, there have been many mentors, colleagues, family, and friends who have played an important role. First and foremost, Moses Moore at Arizona State University has served as an important mentor, who taught me over the years how to see the complex workings of American religious history, and has offered important and detailed critique, insight, and encouragement. More than anyone else, Moses provided important guidance in learning both how to discern the historical record and what it meant to be a historian myself. At Arizona State University I benefited from the brilliance and kind collegiality of those in the departments of Religious Studies, History, and Philosophy, all of whom read parts or the entirety of this manuscript and who offered helpful ideas and opened up new questions. These are Tisa Wenger, Tracy Fessenden, Daniel Ramirez, Richard Wentz, Joel Gereboff, Stephen Mackinnon, Peter de Marneffe, Peter Iverson, and Linell Cady. It is with gratitude to them and other professors for the formation of many of the ideas and attitudes that aided my journey and motivation into the historian's craft. The several workshops at Arizona State University under James Foard and the several grad students who took part in them offered an important space in which to present and have critiqued many of the ideas in this book. The grants and financial support of the Religious Studies Department have also been greatly appreciated.

My first introduction to American religious and Mormon history was under the mentorship of Valeen Avery at Northern Arizona University, who quickly became a friend and mentor, and whose own adventures in Mormon history presented an important background for my own approach to and interest in religious historiography. Richard Wentz also sits as a mentor of great influence on me and how I came to approach historical records and historical inquiry. Both he and Val are greatly missed. As a new grad student, I remember asking Richard about Thanksgiving and whether or not there were any historical records that upheld is historicity. Richard's response was provocative: "Perhaps a more constructive question would have to do with why Thanksgiving has been so important that we needed it to have happened?" "Why do we retell this story when so many other stories get ignored?" These questions took time to sink in, but their insight framed much of my own historical inquiry and many of the questions I asked throughout this book.

There were many mentors and friends who aided and offered support to this work and who broadened and challenged my initial parochial and often naive interests and assumptions. There are too many to name, but these are a few who had a particularly profound impact on me that directly related to the bringing forth of this book: Bruce Sullivan, Scott Reese, Michael Amundson, Peter van der Loo, Beau Seegmiller, Brandon Cleworth, David Howlett, Doe Daughtrey, Marcos Cabrera Geserick, Armand Mauss, Matthew Garrett, Ann Wertman Stegner, Brett Hendrickson, Joel Stoker, Charles Barfoot, Curtis M. Hinsley, Richard E. Turley, Richard Bushman, Kathleen Flake, James B. Allen, R. Laurence Moore, Andrea Radke-Moss, Reid Neilson, D. Michael Quinn, and Christopher Smith. There are others whose names I know I've left out but who equally deserve recognition. As part of this, sections and chapters of this work greatly benefited from important feedback I received from presentations at the American Academy of Religion, the Religion in the American West group at the American Academy of Religion, the Mormon History Association, the Western Conference for the Study of Religion, and the Conference of the Claremont Mormon Studies Student Association.

To the individuals and organizations that offered their time, finances, or help, thank you. My thanks in particular to Ben Park who offered important "secret documents" at a time of need; Joe Geisner who time and again generously shared key documents and insight pertaining to this book; and Michael Paulos who has been a good friend and has offered important critique over parts of the manuscript as well as encouragement. Special thanks to the interlibrary loans department at Arizona State University and the University of Arizona, whose work often goes unnoticed. Jennifer Nichols of the University of Arizona library has opened her office to me in my search for certain hard-to-find documents. Megan Badger has lent her expertise and opinion. There are other institutions that have provided valuable service and generous funding to the furtherance of academic research and publishing, all of whom I am grateful to: the Library of Congress, the Bancroft Library at UC Berkeley, the Chicago History Museum, the Chicago Public Library, the Hayden Library at Arizona State University, the General Research Division at the New York Public Library, the Illinois Newspaper Project of the University of Illinois at Urbana-Champaign, the Metropolitan Museum of Art, the Main Library at the University of Arizona, and the Provost Author Support program through Faculty Affairs at the University of Arizona. This list is not comprehensive.

There were, of course, the many "blind reviewers" to whom I offer my highest gratitude, as well as those whose names I do know, such as Lavina Fielding Anderson, Klaus Hansen, James Badger, and Leslie Chilton. I feel a special level of gratitude to both Lavina and Klaus, for not only their willingness to read and offer helpful suggestions on the entirety or portions of my manuscript, but also for their friendship and generosity. On top of this, Leslie has been a generous and thorough reviewer of this manuscript through many drafts and editions over the years. Her help has been most profound. I also owe deep gratitude to James for his willingness to read and critique this manuscript, and to Karen Seat at the University of Arizona for providing an academic setting in which I could finalize this book. And of course, John Alley and Thomas Krause and others at the University of Utah Press who have been key in pushing this forward to publication.

I also acknowledge the many students and colleagues at Northern Arizona University, Arizona State University, Glendale Community College, and now the University of Arizona for the many times I slipped in ideas from this work as a way of feeling them out. To all of you, thanks for listening, challenging, and sometimes bringing new ideas and images to my attention, some of which informed aspects of this book. And, of course, Mary Hansen Smith for enduring me and the overly drawn-out existence of this work. Many points throughout the book have been the result of our many late-night conversations.

# INTRODUCTION

For early Protestant historian Philip Schaff, Mormonism represented "one of the unsolved riddles of the modern history of religion." Perhaps among the more puzzling questions about Mormon history has to do with the disjointed and even contradictory link between nineteenth- and twentieth-century Mormonism. "It is as if there were two Latter-day Saint churches," noted historian Kathleen Flake, "not one." The question of Mormonism's identity as "American" is related and equally complex, or as R. Laurence Moore quipped, "highly schizophrenic." Historian Sydney Ahlstrom concluded, "One cannot even be sure if the object of our consideration is a sect, a mystery cult, a new religion, a church, a people, a nation, or an American subculture; indeed, at different times and places it is all of these." The study of Mormon history is full of complications and ironies that make it both fascinating and widely relevant. While this book focuses on Mormon history, it looks at interactions with Protestantism, and how both traditions and their relationships were connected to larger trajectories in the history of American religion and the American nation-state, especially its growing secularization. Indeed, the confusing and even contradictory puzzle pieces of Mormonism are parts of a more complicated national puzzle, with a locus on the American frontier, which affected Protestantism as well. Nowhere was this more apparent than in the simultaneous inclusion and exclusion of Mormonism at the Chicago World's Columbian Exposition in 1893, where an expansion of secular religious toleration benefited Mormonism but also provided a way to constrict it, creating clear boundaries to that toleration.

The World's Fair in Chicago positioned America and the American West as a leading player in world innovation and scientific progress at the beginning of the modern era. Earlier world's fairs had piqued international interest, most famously in the great European cities of London in 1851 and Paris in 1889, but Chicago's exposition, its structure, and its location in what was still seen as a recently emergent American West generated unprecedented interest. In a uniquely American push, many Protestants anticipated that this first fair to include a Parliament of Religions would provide an essential key to unlocking Christian public influence, not just in America, but in the world. Such Christian idealism had been powerfully connected to American politics and frontier culture throughout earlier decades, but at the fair it became a complicated and troubled source of inspiration for the modern nation-state. Considering common anxieties over the public relevance of religion, it was not surprising that Mormons were excluded from participating in the Parliament; that served as a reminder that the Mormon religion was both irrelevant and indecent, unsuited to the Parliament's public exhibition of "true religion." What was remarkable, however, was the simultaneous acceptance and even popular celebration of Mormons at the more secular parts of the World's Fair. This reflected the emergence of a new way of thinking about the American West, together with a new dynamic concerning religious diversity and its increased value within American society.

To better understand this disparity, it is important to place Mormon-American relations within a broad revolutionary shift in American culture toward secularism and to see how this shift influenced popular responses to religious minority groups. This book begins by looking at a critical theme of this shift, that is, the frontier's connection to the ideal among both Mormons and Protestants of a kingdom of God. How that ideal evolved among these groups in relationship to power within the United States connects their history to American history in the latter half of the nineteenth century. Rather than being just a vague theological abstraction, the kingdom of God ideal as contested on the frontier brokered the relationship between religion and American identity and political practice. As Protestants throughout the nineteenth century denied that Mormonism had a part to play in the kingdom of God, the resulting negative engagements played a part in the larger conversation about what religion was and where it fit within the American republic and the acceptable characteristics of American society. In recognizing that these opposing Christian worlds were not so far apart in the inspiration they pulled from the frontier, their shared visions of Christ's impending rule in America, or their configurations of what religious influence should look like in a secular world, we can perceive a type of coresponsibility over what would come to be religion's place (and non-place) in American society. Though often studied as separate events, the Utah War of 1857–1858, the antipolygamy crusades of the 1870s and 1880s, the World's Fair and its Parliament of Religions in 1893, and the Reed Smoot hearings from 1904 to 1907 taken together showcase how Americans understood themselves in relation to their country, their religions, and each other. It becomes clear that the intellectual and political patterns that played key roles in transforming Mormonism at the end of the nineteenth century also affected Protestantism.

In following the early intellectual and institutional relationships Mormons and Protestants had with American identity and political practice, part I herein, "Kingdoms in Definition," describes the kingdom of God ideal as employed on the American western frontier by both Mormons and Protestants. In important ways, the frontier, with its own myths and rituals, functioned like a religion, intensely informing an American vision of Christianity that became markedly different from that of Europe. Though it embodied and grew out of this frontier faith, Mormonism also provided a useful foil during the Utah War and the antipolygamy crusades, by which Americans could exclude irreligion and thus define the nation, as affected by the frontier, as a purified, righteous kingdom and redeemer nation, preparing for the coming of Christ and His imminent thousand-year earthly reign. A study of the contentious history between Protestants and Mormons suggests they had similar though competing visions of the frontier as it related to the kingdom. They would therefore potentially suffer the same theological dislocations in an increasingly secularized future. The struggle between their visions reveals not only the vitality of religious power in nineteenth-century America but also weaknesses that began to make this power untenable in an era that was developing secular mythologies and supportive elites. In part II, "Kingdoms in Transition," these growing cracks in religious strength are revealed in intellectual, social, economic, and political developments that began to sever America's traditional religious and political networks, to dismantle old religious ideals, and to promote new ones that upheld religious tolerance and favored pluralism. The significance of the frontier did not disappear with these modern-secular ideas, but instead retained its religious potency, becoming enshrined in more secular ways in the American intellectual and popular consciousness. As shown throughout these chapters, the emergence of the secular was seldom a clear separation from the religious, and in many ways continued to comfortably navigate between both. However, the impact that this modern-secular shift had upon the nation was dramatic, presenting new contradictions and challenges to earlier concerns regarding the relationship religion held with the state. In the wake of the cracks, which were manifested in the discussions and tensions at the World's Fair of 1893 and in the national four-year congressional contestation of the Senate seat of Mormon apostle Reed Smoot, Mormonism found an acceptance that would have been inconceivable a few decades earlier. Yet, both Mormons and Protestants found themselves needing to articulate their relevance in a new, secularized era and thereby came to redefine their shared vision of religious influence relative to the modern nation-state.

The Protestant-Mormon conflict spanning half a century not only led to Mormonism's transition into modernity but also was a key factor in the creation of that modernity. The conflict hinted at a disagreement about the meaning of America that would continue, though, in an era of increased secularity and modernity. Mormonism's late acceptance into the American polity due to changes in the Protestant idea of religion and the impact of growth in the American West helps clarify the development of our modern understanding of religious pluralism and religious liberty. Still, pluralism remained limited as modern America retained exclusionary ideas of the relationship of religion to the state, which had been fashioned in relation to both Mormon and Protestant responses to the frontier, as it inspired their contesting projections of the kingdom of God.

What did it mean—and what does it mean—to be American and religious within a religiously plural society? Did embracing one imply the surrender of the other? How did religious minority groups navigate between new trends toward secularism and the demands of tradition?

How did these encounters affect the meaning of terms such as *religious* and *secular*? What became of individual and group agency in light of larger and more powerful cultural forces for change? Did minority groups retain their significance in this larger national narrative, or did they become mere bit players in the larger picture of American progress and development? The answers to these questions have implications for Mormons and Protestants and how they each perceive their past. Both minorities and majorities had to redefine their roles within American society as our social and political institutions grew more secular, scientific, and pluralistic. It is important to recognize, however, that secularization does not equal loss of religious faith or even imply abandonment of the old religious vision of the frontier, nor that religious players ceased to exist. Instead, as articulated by Charles Taylor, secularization increased the options for how Americans could express themselves and the myths and stories they adopted and employed.

This book joins a larger discussion in religious studies surrounding the question of religion and its relation to the secular and how those rubrics inform American religious historiography. The term *religion* itself has become a messy point of debate, concerning both its usefulness as an analytical category and the impossibility of removing it from its theological and academic origins. The term *secular* has similarly defied easy academic categorization, though often serving as the opposite of what is meant by religion, with the latter being private, emotional and other-worldly, while the other is public, rational and this-worldly. As has been argued by others, both categories are mere ideological constructs, formulated in their own set of parochial, modern-western values that similarly do not open themselves up for critique. Tisa Wenger, however, argues for their usefulness, as both first- and second-order categories: On the one hand, such terms provide meaning to those practicing religion and become part of an intersecting discourse between courts, legal codes, popular literature, world fairs, senate chambers, and so on. On the other hand, religion stands as a cultural category, similar to art, politics, tradition, and culture itself, that allows for comparison across time. Though I define my use of *religion* as an academic category in the beginning of chapter 1, I also adhere in this work to the rough contours of these terms' evolving meaning to those I study, and I explore how the interactive defining of these terms constructed relations of power and infused these relations with meaning and morality that was wrongly conceived to be both universal and timeless. The significance of this is that it is here, within this encounter between Mormons and Protestants and the terms religion and secular, that the meaning of America and its normative narrative of religious liberty took shape.

As an important contribution to the shift between religious and secular ideologies in formulating an American identity, recent Johns Hopkins graduate Frederick Jackson Turner in 1893 provided a usable framing of the American past and its relation to an imagined American character in what became known by later historians as the Frontier Thesis. Presented before the American Historical Association at the World's Fair on July 12, 1893, Turner dissolved an earlier historiographical storyline of Providential progress furthered by Protestant church historians. It conflated national piety with national health and progress. Turner instead argued that it was not God, heroic individuals, or even the religious institutions of Europe that explained America's unique national self and destiny, but rather the daunting expanse of America's ostensibly free and open wilderness, which he asserted had only now been tamed. Rather than serving as a geographic place for Turner, the frontier stood as a type of institution itself, an institution that Americanized citizens and made them hardworking, democratic, and liberty loving. This new secular mythology of an imagined American character rooted in the mythical space of the western frontier soon became a central theme in the later story of Mormon-Protestant encounters. Such encounters provided the path in which Mormonism successfully engaged the modern world, but they also helped provide an emotional and intellectual framework in which the modern world could discern, on an empirical level, what it now meant to be American.

In marking a critical historiographical turning point that remained unquestioned for over three decades and that continued to dominate American history for several more, Turner's progressive model provided a paradigm for the social sciences in ways like what Darwin's theory of organic evolution did for the physical sciences. Certainly, embodying the conservative progressivism of the Chicago World's Fair and its anti-European tone, Turner's Frontier Thesis gave American historians and the nation's other intellectuals a new point of reference. It explained the emergence of what historians considered a uniquely American character and transformed the providential account of America's destiny from that of a Protestant-European story of the English Reformation and the Puritan covenant to that of the natural outcome of America's frontier environment, all the while maintaining the Protestant sense of racial and national exceptionalism and destiny. Indeed, however redesigned his frontier faith, Turner solidified and again made relevant for America's intellectuals the frontier as the mythic origin of the true American spirit and the base point for America's future. The frontier hypothesis worked largely because it already had. Turner was as much a prophet-reformer of the old frontier religion as he was a historian, saving the old message through endowing it with new, modern relevance.

This geographic and ideological shift as heralded by Turner did not just mark an important point of departure from traditional American historiography (which often focused on religion, individuals, and institutions, as well as theoretical and theological speculation), it delivered a new and uniquely American triumphant national identity. Serving as an important bridge between the two sections of this book, this reformed frontier narrative and its message demonstrated the power the frontier religion had in the minds of many Americans as they navigated their way toward realization of the American ideal. Later historians have criticized the more celebratory strains of progress in Turner's model, recognizing his history as a type of conservative nationalism that was more interested in addressing contemporary needs of industrialization than in better understanding the past. Turner's Frontier Thesis represented, in new form, a familiar anxiety over the frontier, which cast its shadow on what it meant to be as well as how one came to be "truly American."

Turner's narrative, in customary fashion, credited "English-speaking white men" for the greatness of the country, thereby rendering American diversity less salient, limiting it to a mere supportive role, even in an era of increased religious pluralism. Turner's model thus excluded more than it included, leaving out women as well as a host of racial minorities, as it emphasized a bleached, homogeneous mythology of the American frontier and its role in defining the country. Turner was innovative for the new, more scientific discipline of history, and the Frontier Thesis was intended not so much to uphold the status quo as to accurately describe, justify, and improve existing institutions. In this attempt to sustain but improve what then was, Turner's thesis was consistent with the evolutionary model of the emergent social sciences, powerfully linking historiography with them and their reliance on Darwinian evolution. Such social evolutionary thinking predicted important, dynamic intellectual, social, and political developments for the growing nation, in a way that fed a hunger for reassurance of America's noble destiny and identity. Mormons, living on the frontier in a dynamic age, could anticipate a place in this new national drama. Turner's frontier model was successful not because it was historically accurate but because it provided easily grasped coherence at a time of great cultural incoherence; this was not a dismantling of old religious myths for the sake of secular science, but rather the replacement of one myth with another.

An important aspect of myths is that they not only provide orientation and coherence but also establish power and authority. Though Turner's Frontier Thesis was largely silent on the question of religion, this study demonstrates that it was an important site of both colonial control and the formation of American institutions. In her studies on Pueblos in the early twentieth century and their struggles over religious liberty in the United States, Wenger contended that, like Hinduism, Native American religion became an acceptable component of American diversity only as it was redefined to fit the historical, colonial, and implicitly Christian usage of the term *religion* itself. Spencer Fluhman observed that Protestants defined the term partly through their "public condemnations of what Mormonism was," thus making all the more ironic the Mormon attempt to gain national acceptance by asserting the identity of a religion. Recognizing Mormonism's adoption of a later definition of *religion* as separate from national and local structures of power, this work explores the historical implications of these American intellectual and cultural shifts for Mormons and Protestants, against the backdrop of Turner's thesis. One outcome was to normalize modern understanding of religion and its relation to the state, which would later redefine the national image of Mormonism, together with Mormonism's self-image.

This understanding of the frontier and religion is key in charting the shift that underlined the simultaneous rejection and celebration of Mormonism at the World's Fair while also undermining a broader sense of religious tolerance. As will be seen, Mormonism's transformation from "anti-American" to "quintessentially American" encouraged new formations of power in America. The newly expressed ideals of American religious pluralism justified as moral and necessary the suppression of behaviors, religious practices, and beliefs that had been deemed unacceptable or not properly religious. Even Protestants found themselves victims of a new dichotomy of irrational religion and the rational secular state at the beginning of the twentieth century, a dichotomy that they themselves helped create in their long fight against religious diversity and secularization.

The intent of this book is not to provide a comprehensive comparison or analysis of these shifts, but rather to provide a broad perspective to rethink the traditional narratives and to highlight points of historical neglect. As a cursory review of the literature suggests, an important area of neglect has been the shared world of Mormons and Protestants, which in consequence has reductively left the former seeming parochial and the latter exclusionary. A broad reexamination of religious pluralism and religious liberty in North America allows us to question and reopen what many historians and students of Mormon history and American religion presume is a closed matter—namely, that broad religious liberty necessarily existed, and that religious pluralism was necessarily liberal and a natural evolutionary outcome of modernity. Gender and ethnic and racial presumptions and challenges play a part in these dynamics, together with broader cultural and environment influences, but in order not to distract from my larger inquiry into religious diversity, progressivism, and the shifting relationship between religion and the state, I have sought to limit my inquiry. In seeking not to be conclusive but instead thematic, my focus is to suggest that if this grand American experiment of religious liberty is to retain its relevance within America's ever-expansive and diverse citizenry, then it is essential to reevaluate and better understand the moral and religious contexts in which it came to be, so as to reevaluate and reimagine what it now is and can yet be.

# PART I

## KINGDOMS IN DEFINITION

# CHAPTER 1

## *Frontier Religion and the American Kingdom of God*

And now, Jehovah God, thou who by long ages of watch and discipline, didst make of thy servant Abraham a people, be thou the God also of this great nation. Remember still its holy beginnings, and for the fathers' sakes, still cherish and sanctify it. Fill it with thy Light and thy Potent Influence, till the glory of thy Son breaks out on the western sea, as now upon the eastern, and these uttermost parts, given to Christ for a possession, become the bounds of a new Christian Empire, whose name the believing and the good of all people shall hail as a name of hope and blessing!

—Congregational Minister Horace Bushnell

To count something as a religion, it is not essential that it include a belief in God, or even that it represent a recognized system of ethics or belief in an afterlife. It also doesn't rely on feelings of absolute dependence with some otherworldly or transcendent power. While there are many ways to define religion, I define it here as a cultural system or structure that connects individuals and communities, reflected by specific beliefs, myths, and practices, to what is determined to be sacred, Absolute, or otherwise set apart from "ordinary life." In the broadest sense, philosopher William James described religion as consisting of "the belief that there is an unseen order, and that our supreme good lies in harmoniously adjusting ourselves thereto."[1] These adjustments come through many mediums, including calling on divine beings, engaging metaphysical powers, telling stories, visiting auspicious geographical sites, and experiencing transcendent emotional states. Stories that reveal insight into this unseen order are called myths, while rituals are those repetitive actions that connect people to it and make it feel real. Symbols provide the transcendent language or visuals through which stories, events, and actions prompt individuals and groups to reflect on this unseen order. In a related way, anthropologist Clifford Geertz defined religion as a "system of symbols" that establish powerful moods and motivations, which formulate strong conceptions of a "general order of existence" that feel realistic. Similar to Paul Tilich's more vague definition of religion, Americanist Richard Wentz explained religion as "the way in which people strive to discern ultimate order and meaning in the course of existence."[2]

The American frontier as imagined in the minds of nineteenth-century Americans stood as a type of religious institution, complete with its own particular beliefs, myths, and practices that oriented much of the country toward a general "unseen order" of existence—an order that united an older millenarian anxiety with that of a newly imagined political ideal. This frontier system, though imagined, felt real, and in very real ways represented a critical key toward discerning ultimate order and meaning in what it meant to be American. Paul Reeve added that the selection of this frontier space, its naming, together with the ritualized retelling of its founding, offered important "transtemporal functions" that positioned Mormons and American frontier settlers "in time and space and defined its worldview."[3] As a sacred geographic system, the frontier opened the doors to an extrabiblical revelation that brought humanity into contact with God's work in the last days, a human-divine relationship that cultivated a shared responsibility over the construction of God's kingdom on earth.

The kingdom of God ideal as connected to this frontier mythology represents an intrinsic yet neglected aspect of American history, often hidden just below the surface of more general and temporal statements of progress and civilization. In impressive ways, mental formulations of the frontier unleashed an anxiety over what it meant to be civilized and progressive, inspiring not just hopes of what could be gained through the experience of the American frontier, but also great concerns over what could be lost. This was not just for Protestants, as Mormonism reached its fullest expression through the conflation of the kingdom and this frontier faith, seeing them together as a type of revelation into the actualizing of Christ's imminent kingdom and anticipated thousand-year reign on earth. For Mormons, the American frontier and its attendant popular myths played a decisive role in fashioning a peculiar and chosen people, requiring the emigration and building of Mormon settlements that took them forward to the ancient, and—quite literally—original location of the Garden of Eden on the western edge of the frontier in the 1830s: Jackson County, Missouri. Not only would this frontier faith help produce and grant unprecedented success to new religious movements like Mormonism, but this new wilderness-trained gospel transformed how many Americans looked at religion, coming to even affect in important ways how society and political policy were impacted.

This frontier vision of the kingdom originated in less-developed ways in North America with the Puritans, was advanced and extended by the later Protestant evangelical revivalist movements, and by 1830 had become a central ideal for many American Protestants, the leading American identity of the time. As a child of the enchanted frontier of both folk religion and Methodism, Joseph Smith enlisted this popular frontier rhetoric and projected in 1829 that a "marvelous work" was "about to come forth" in America, and by the end of his life in 1844, Smith had sealed this important link between the frontier and the kingdom in ways that connected both the ecclesiastical and political even more deeply than had the Puritans before. A frontier religion itself, Mormonism, or the Church of Christ—later called the Church of Jesus Christ of Latter-day Saints—brought forth various revelations that indicated that new things were emergent on the frontier in the "latter days." The last days, then, were *right now*, effectively encoding into the Mormon message these central hopes and beliefs of the American frontier. Smith's brilliance was in his embrace and expansion of these already felt frontier anxieties as part of the larger democratizing and innovative spirit of early American evangelical revivalism.[4] Although soon departing from the larger Christian community due to more radical economic, social, sexual, and civic doctrines as introduced by Smith, Mormonism represented part of the religious fabric of antebellum America—a fabric partially woven by the concept of the frontier which had influenced and continued to influence America's religious and social vision of itself.[5]

As Americans engaged these new contradictory theocratic and democratizing dynamics of religion in the early years of the nation, the separation of church and state remained blurred and the question of disestablishment remained contentious. For many American Protestants in the antebellum period, visions of Christ's kingdom and His future reign on earth were synonymous with this emergent Christian expansionism, or, as prominent Congregationalist minister Horace Bushnell anticipated, "a new Christian empire."[6] While religious piety and civic obligation had long been synonymous for American Protestants, as initiated by the Puritans and other settlers, Protestants and others in the new nation moved to reconcile themselves with new trends toward disestablishment and the new and seemingly contradictory philosophy of religious liberty and separation that many believed to be unique influences of the frontier. With freedom of religion described as a "lively experiment," Protestant Americans, aided by a weak antebellum federal government that encouraged strong and efficient individual and voluntary response to perceived national issues and crises, such as the open space of the frontier, orchestrated a sophisticated and organized response to these new trends. Achieving unprecedented public support through a series of evangelical revivals, these trends preserved and even furthered Protestant privilege, whose public social efforts were seen as a type of higher expression of citizenship within Christ's heavenly kingdom, allowing individual efforts to transcend any single Protestant denomination.

In the heart of these concerns and actions was the mythologized American Western wilderness, or frontier religion. It was within these mental configurations of the frontier that new American institutions and characteristics were being raised and shaped, including, of course, religion and civic theology which sought the progression of society and its associated earthly reign of Christ. Though the Mormon experience on the frontier would solidify a more centralized theocratic system of authority and obedience for the building of the Mormon kingdom of God, the genius of the "frontier spirit" or mentality for American Protestants was that it encouraged and even demanded religious individuals across denominational lines to get involved and work together.[7] This involvement included volunteer associations and reform societies and thus directed and fashioned the Protestant ideal of the kingdom of God as a powerful social and political reality.

As an important context for these realities, this kingdom ideal took shape on the frontier, impacting both Protestantism and Mormonism in profound ways. The complex relationships that emerged within both groups to American religious diversity and its influence on the evolving sense of a particular national identity became central to this shared story. As part of this significance, Protestants and Mormons alike tapped into the nation's fluid and innovative dynamic between religion and the state, together helping to create for their own people an overwhelming vision of divine "chosen-ness" and benevolent motivation that colored their responses to each other and how each would look at the formations of national and state government. The developing idea of the American frontier as related to the evolving sense of the kingdom informed the political arrangements of Protestant and Mormon groups alike. Such arrangements on the local and national level represented an essential component of these groups' growing perceptions of America as a "religious Christian nation." Though these themes will be challenged and transformed in Part II of this book, they demonstrate an essential cultural backdrop for Part I, as well as the contours in which the latter half of this book takes shape.

## FRONTIER RELIGION AND THE AMERICAN KINGDOM OF GOD

The relation of religion to the civil state in the United States during the nineteenth century was both unique and innovative within the history of global Christianity, and was further made unique by taking place in a culture which generally defined itself and its institutions by way of the frontier, a concept long mythologized in the American mind and later theorized by Frederick Jackson Turner. Turner's famed Frontier Thesis argued that until 1890, American history was largely that of the colonization of the Great West, a colonization movement marked by the provision and cultivation of "free land," the "continuous recession of the wild frontier," and "the advance of the American settlement westward."[8] In determining the importance of the American frontier, the implications of Turner's thesis had less to do with conquering geography than with the product that that process created—the American. As such, although

Turner himself posited his thesis within the scientific rules of empirical records, his thesis instead rested within the realm of myth and fantasy about a particular conservative ideal for America. Offering one of the first real critiques of Turner, Henry Nash Smith positioned Turner as coming out of these earlier myths of the frontier, establishing as scientific fact earlier religious assumptions. The almost universal appeal Turner enjoyed had much to do with the cultural familiarity of his ideas, displaying in his hypothesis "an echo in ideas and attitudes already current."[9] The Frontier Thesis, then, was not about some vague theoretical force that made America exceptional above all other countries, but instead stood as an already imagined invisible, yet real and now scientifically visible force that taught Americans how to act and think about themselves, the growth of their institutions, and the direction of their national destiny. Turner's attempt to illuminate these early held forces of the frontier was not a first, but rather stands on the shoulders of an entire century of intellectual and mythical thought that viewed the American frontier as a place of promise and rebirth, where invisible forces became visible and the struggles against darkness and disorder came to light.

Turner's focus on the frontier can be traced back to other observers of the American republic. In 1834, Presbyterian minister and historian Robert Baird theorized that the idea of the frontier stood as an abstract and invisible force that not only modified individual behavior but fashioned and made visible a particular "American character" and thus informed its laws and institutions. This character could thus be "readily enumerated; and they are all created by the peculiar circumstances in which the people have been placed in that new world," being specifically noted for their independence of mind and action, a spirit of adventure, and an apparent roughness and even rudeness of manners. Owing much to their "remote [Puritan] ancestors," this new "frontier race" had developed as a consequence of the forces of the frontier's new political and religiously synched institutions that Baird had expressed as likely not contemplated by "the founders of our country."[10] This unique situation and character development was also noted by French traveler Alexis de Tocqueville who described the frontier as "the means" in which Americans were to remain free. Their European ancestry may have given them a love of equality and freedom, but it was "Nature herself," or a "boundless continent," that "favors the cause of the people."[11] Similarly, magazine editor Edwin L. Godkin attributed America's unique political arrangements with religion as a product of the invisible forces of the frontier, which instilled characteristics of independence, equality, individualism, and a visible and powerful work ethic. Democratic governance, capitalism, and the experiment of religious liberty were thus natural products of the frontier. Obstructions to this "rational progress," continued Godkin, were merely the fault of newness, whose "great remedy is time."

The progressive forces of the frontier were both lineal and assured, revealing the imposition of morality as a geographic direction and racial imperative. Thus, in a type of geographically linked inevitable progressive timetable, Americans optimistically experimented with new relations between religion, economy, and politics in ways that overcame the presumed chaos and savagery of the frontier, ways that also originated in the premise of a weak but idealized government and a powerful sense of racial and religious supremacy and national destiny. Godkin continued that these frontier-inspired characteristics were the source of "national greatness" and the nation's "only sure and lasting foundation."[12] Literature of the late nineteenth and early twentieth centuries romanticized these frontier-American ideals into both real and fictional characters, such as Kit Carson, William F. ("Buffalo Bill") Cody, and Davy Crockett, whose frontier heroics could be as much fantasy as reality.[13] Thus Toqueville, Baird, and Godkin, together with the imagined feats of brave frontier men in popular American literature, helped to evolve the popular vision and even myth of the frontier, giving it meaning that justified current experimentations in democratic governance and religion, in ways that were true to both the religio-political intentions of the past and current visions of a brave, free, white, patriarchal, glorious, and individualistic future.

These new dynamics that linked the frontier to these "American" characteristics profoundly affected the relationship between church and state in America, creating, as Protestant theologian and historian Philip Schaff writes, "something wholly new." This "kingdom talk" of newness echoes back to the early days of the Protestant Reformation where Protestants were not simply protesting against the corruptions of the Roman Catholic Church, but more importantly pro-testifying of this kingdom of God as a revolution among the saints, inaugurated at Jesus's birth, but now being fulfilled through their very own Reformation. That "something wholly new" was happening in America brings us to the Protestant Puritan heritage itself, becoming even more profound following the American Revolution and its perceived new potentials for how church and state were to be arranged.

This "something new" as conceived by nineteenth-century Protestants did not fully reside in the concept of the separation of religion and the state as modeled by earlier Enlightenment rationalists, most famously Thomas Jefferson and James Madison in the late eighteenth century. Rather, this newness celebrated by Schaff and other Americans came from linking this American dynamic to that of the Protestant movement that saw religion in America as finalizing the European Reformation, and culminating in God's literal reign on Earth—made uniquely real with the new American frontier environment and national context.[14] Earlier British colonists like the Puritans did not imagine this Christian revolution by way of Christ's imminent or even millennial return as would later millenarians, but instead, they understood Christ's rule and kingdom to have been already enacted. They were not anticipating the "latter days," but rather were tapping into the eternal sovereignty of Christ that governed what already was, and which they needed to submit to. The Puritans did not anticipate this "something new" as an end to the corrupt world, but instead the bringing forth of new opportunities to actualize this spiritual revolution begun with the Reformation through the enforcement of new religious codes and biblical laws, which their geographic separation in America made possible. With the new possibilities brought on by the American Revolution, frontier expansion, and the attendant evangelical revivals, this "something new" by the time of Schaff in the early to mid-nineteenth century had new reference to a recrafted civil contract. This new contract linked together religion and the state in a way that expanded this earlier idea of the sovereignty of Christ, through the efforts of "awakened" individuals to a new literal kingdom of God in America.[15]

In light of these new developments in America, historian Ernest Tuveson, in his examination of how Americans perceived the European agenda as culminating on the frontier, explained that American Protestants looked to Daniel's apocalyptic visions and St. John's Revelation as having real-world application and significance for the new nation. It was more than "an allegory of the spiritual order: there is, God has promised, an actual historical kingdom of God to be expected, one inhabited by persons in mortal flesh."[16] The Puritan notion of the kingdom that "already was" had evolved by the nineteenth century to include the idea that the millennium, or thousand-year reign of Christ on earth, was "soon to be." These new millenarian ideas suggest a new school of theological thought that informed a unique American theology, which made the most sense in this new and unique American frontier context. Informed by this same religious and political environment, Mormon apostle John Taylor argued that the anticipated kingdom of Christ that was to unfold in the American frontier wilderness was to become manifest in more visible and tangible ways than earlier imagined. The reign and sovereignty of Christ was no "aerial phantom," remarked Taylor, but "a substantial reality. It will be established as before said, on a literal earth, and will be composed of literal men, women, and children."[17] As Turner would later project, the frontier environment had important implications in how Americans fashioned new political boundaries and institutions, however much he and his successors underappreciated the role of religion as part of those creative energies. Prior to Turner, Americans understood this ideal of the kingdom as retained from European roots and sources, but also imagined a significant role for the frontier and its call for individual effort in that equation.

The ideal of the kingdom, possessed by both Calvinist Protestants and Mormons (not to mention others such as the Millerites, Oneidas, Campbellites, Quakers, etc.), reaches back to a shared New England Puritan heritage, which united together and evolved with American expansion an interpretive lens of America's national destiny with that of God's holy writ. The frontier wilderness, one of the most pervasive and meaningful aspects of the American landscape, helped shape early American thought, as well as assist in the clash—and the integration— of European Calvinist philosophy and an emergent republican political philosophy. The frontier was almost a type of independent scripture or revelation itself, revealing the workings of God in the true meaning of historical action.

The first European settlers on the eastern American seaboard were literally on a frontier of the British Empire, as well as symbolically on and engaging in a frontier of theological beliefs and development.

They were largely informed by their readings of the Old Testament and its sense of divine involvement in the affairs of civil governments. In renouncing the legal and religious structures of England, early Calvinist colonists took up those of Moses, and in the words of Ahlstrom, were determined "to make God's revealed Law and the historical example of Israel an explicit basis for ordering the affairs of men in this world."[18] With the birth of the new nation, influential figures like President Ezra Stiles Ely of Yale University helped to weave these early sentiments together into the new national fabric, proclaiming in 1791 that the new nation was indeed "God's American Israel," thereby upholding anew the old Puritan covenant motif of chosen land/chosen people—and Ely was not alone in his vision.[19] "The Canaanite was in the land," described Rev. Leonard Bacon, eminent nineteenth-century pastor of a prominent Congregationalist church in New Haven. As it was in the biblical deserts of Canaan, God's new Israel was charged with the holy calling to protect their children and servants against the country's inherent "barbarian vices" and "heathenish and hideous superstitions," most prominently displayed on the frontier.[20] American writers and Protestant historians conflated with ease their own nation's pilgrim wanderings in the American wilderness with those of Abraham and Moses, bridging together not just the deserts of Sinai and Canaan with those of America, but also its indigenous inhabitants with those of Canaan, whom God commanded Israel to destroy—thereby marking both the Native American and the frontier with deep religious symbolism and expediency.

Nineteenth-century historians and poets celebrated this sacred drama of the wilderness as both a reenactment of the biblical narrative and an important reference point for the inevitability of the kingdom that was to come. Nineteenth-century poet Walt Whitman wrote of the frontier and its American pioneers as offering a rebirth unique to world history—one that God was using to restore man's lost harmony with nature, and that opened a new era that served to prelude a unified world with global peace.[21] Though encouraging a level of isolationism, this "garden myth," as historian Henry Nash Smith labeled it, had a powerful effect over American perceptions and imaginations, setting up something euphoric and even divine about the actual environment of the Western frontier and godly about those who settled it. Like the Garden of Eden, as Nash continued, the American garden (and thus the rural agriculturalist profession) was linked to God, leading Americans to imagine the effects of settling this geography as inspiring cultural and social progress, making people smart, healthy, beautiful, and prone to excelling in art, music, intellect, and virtue. The American garden was thus the school for virtue for the nation, where raising children on a farm was closer not only to nature, but to God. At the same time, every garden is threatened by its snakes—meaning those dangerous and sadistic forces that cannot be civilized but must be destroyed.[22] The central feature of this garden myth was not that it brought great promise of progress and civilization, but that it distinguished such great accomplishments through that of its opposite—barbarism.

Early colonists "expatriated themselves from the old world," wrote Presbyterian minister and historian Robert Baird, "not merely to find liberty of conscience in the forests of the new, but that they might extend the kingdom of Christ, by founding States where the truth should not be impeded by the hindrances that opposed its progress elsewhere." Europe may have been the Egypt in which the sacred story of redemption began, but it was now in the forests of America that the Promised Land and fulfillment of the long-sought spiritual revolution was imagined. In ways that reassured nineteenth-century realities, Baird explained that these colonists, in their drive to build the same kingdom Baird had committed himself to, "just exchanged what they considered a worse than Egyptian bondage, for a Canaan inhabited by the heathen, whom they were soon compelled to 'drive out.'"[23]

With all its challenges, the great American wilderness conjured up the idea of a "new Adam in a new Eden," offering Americans, noted one historian, "mankind's great second chance." Much had changed conceptually and geographically from the day of the first colonies and those of the new republic, but the original vision of the American kingdom, as popularized, transformed, and democratized during the great evangelical revivals of the eighteenth and nineteenth centuries, now became explicit affirmation in the law and custom of the new states.[24] Without exaggeration, remarked Baird, America's "public institutions still carry the stamp of their origin," and "the monuments of the fathers are yet standing." Far from idealizing Jefferson and Madison's "separation" ideal, nineteenth-century American Protestantism had become, "though without establishments and with equal liberty to men's conscience," "the religion of the laws and of the government."[25] Expressing an explicit connection to these earlier Puritans and their visions of the kingdom, which he now dedicated his research to, Baird emphasized the "solid remains" that reaffirmed America's continued "chosen" nature— which coordinated with the vision of the expanding frontier and its auspicious character, and which was being swiftly transformed into states and territories that required governance.

Prior to a federal Constitution and the efforts of Virginia representative James Madison, who would seek to separate religion from federal power, Protestants went on to lead the creation of theocratic-styled jurisprudence and its associated laws for their own individual states. Though Catholics understood the kingdom in terms of the political rule of ecclesiastical authorities, Protestants instead pushed for the political rule of the saints, meaning those whose hearts have been sanctified and are now part of the invisible church or kingdom of Christ. In 1776, Pennsylvania established religion as a critical aspect of the state and guaranteed religious liberty and civil rights only to those who professed to believe in God.[26] With an early sense of American pride, author Stephen Colwell wrote about a number of state constitutions that emerged in the 1770s and 1780s that either retained ancient charters of Puritan origin or otherwise acknowledged Christianity as the "privileged religion": New Hampshire, Massachusetts, Connecticut, and New Jersey all "expressly recognized Protestant Christianity," and as such "rightly" excluded from the state "infidels and unbelievers" in hopes of preserving the sanctity of the scriptures within American public and private life.[27] Baird noted that it was "certainly a mistake" to assume that since the national Constitution did not mention Christianity "that the general government can do nothing whatever to promote religion," pointing out that not only were Sabbath laws recognized by these states but that they were observed "to a degree rarely witnessed in other countries." Protestants were early on defining the American experiment of religious liberty as not meaning to "prostrate humanity," nor "much less advance Mahomedanism, or Judaism, or infidelity," but instead intended to check the "rivalry among Christian sects."[28]

As understood by Puritans, liberty belonged to Christ alone, and could be understood only through the Bible and found only in God's kingdom, with which these early states sought to align themselves. In speaking of liberty, citizens were to concern themselves with duties and obedience to these laws, rather than individual conscience and freedoms that challenged them. Unlike what Jefferson hoped, religion in nineteenth-century America was not a private affair, but rather that of the state. Beyond the old Protestant cliché that early British colonists came to America looking for liberty of conscience, a more profound point behind the initial hope and inward zeal of America's first Puritan leaders was, according to historian Vernon Parrington, "to set up a Kingdom of God on earth."[29] Within these newly formed state governments under a larger but weak federal government, Protestants

FIGURE 1.1. "Camp Meeting of the Methodists in North America," by Jacques Gerard Milbert, 1819. M. Dubourg, engraver. The great American revivals of the early nineteenth century transformed how many Americans thought about themselves, their nation, and their religion. These revivals helped link the ideal of the kingdom with world renewal and millennialism. Individual religious enthusiasm, as portrayed by the person lying on the ground, helped unite Protestants together into a larger, nondenominational psychological and social coherence that reinvented the meaning of "the people" in American religion and politics. Courtesy of the Library of Congress.

perceived themselves as continuing the religiously inspired principles and impulse of their Puritan ancestors, thereby taking part within and fulfilling the earlier visions of the European Reformation and the newly articulated kingdom ideal as presented in the new American frontier environment.

## REDEFINING RELIGIOUS DISESTABLISHMENT

However, religious disestablishment did come, directed by the efforts of Thomas Jefferson, whom Robert Baird referred to as the "arch infidel," and his Virginia colleague James Madison, with Massachusetts and the Congregationalist Church, site of the first Puritan colonies, holding out until 1833.[30] For Congregationalist minister and Yale president Timothy Dwight (1752–1817), "the first duty of a ruler, and the first concern of a virtuous ruler, is the support of religion," by which was always understood to be that of the Protestant variety.[31] But disestablishment now threatened this Puritan kingdom ideal that Protestants now sought to repeat on the national level, thereby complicating how Christians were to approach their new government. Lyman Beecher, Dwight's ministerial successor and organizer of the New England religious awakenings in the first part of the nineteenth century, articulated best the fears—as well as the new hopes—of many Protestant ministers during this period of national identification, and reidentification and innovative participation in religious and political matters.[32] The evangelical awakenings had not just represented an awakening to the importance of religion in society, but also that of a national self-identity and the relation of religion to that identity. In reflecting upon the 1818 disestablishment of religion in Connecticut, Beecher despaired that "the injury done to Christ" was "irreparable," and confessed that "for several days I suffered what no tongue could tell." However, after further thought, he went on to explain that religious disestablishment was "the best thing that ever happened to the state of Connecticut."[33] Rather than Christianity losing power, it gained, as it could now unhesitatingly link arms with this new political and philosophical conception of disestablishment and separation in ways that were both potent and invisible, thereby linking together the post-Revolutionary understanding of religious liberty to that of the old-kingdom ideal of obedience.[34] Rather than ministers having "lost their influence; the fact is, they have gained. By voluntary efforts, societies, missions, and revivals, they exert a deeper influence than ever they could by queues, and shoe-buckles, and cocked hats, and gold-headed canes."[35] Rather than an attack on Christian influence, disestablishment was a new revelation into the power of the kingdom and the true meaning behind the invisible kingdom of Christ that visible churches were seeking to reflect.

With disestablishment, individual Christians were enabled and even encouraged through these new voluntary networks to bring forth a more efficient "moral establishment" that imposed a particular Christian morality and benevolence on American law.[36] As part of his argument over the democratization of American Christianity, Nathan Hatch points to frontier revivals of the early nineteenth century as part of a larger class struggle over social and religious authority. As he put it, frontier revivals inspired individuals on a popular level to embrace religion, to think, to interpret, and to organize for themselves, thus empowering individual conscience among the popular classes in early nineteenth-century America. Through these revivals, new cultural trends looked for God in individual souls and revival trends, rather than traditional church structures like those in Boston and educated clergymen such as Beecher. However threatening to the status of traditional elitist clergy, Lyman Beecher also shows us that these revolutionary shifts in religion and American governance were in a major way part of an active and purposeful ideological restructuring of what elites like Beecher understood the kingdom of Christ to be as it faced disestablishment.[37]

Beecher continued to support religious restrictions on individual citizens based upon biblical law, but not as imposed by clergy and politician, but instead those of individual Christian citizens of the kingdom itself. The kingdom no longer belonged to the church or the state, but was rather an individual possession, making it more real and potent in the lives of individuals and their effect on the state. Often expressed in the religious life of Protestants as the "priesthood of all believers," the words of early revivalist George Whitefield that the reason American Protestants didn't need a pope was "because we love to be popes ourselves, and set up our own experience as a standard to others," gained new insight with Beecher and his Boston church—once the capital of the Puritan commonwealth.[38]

As Beecher now understood, disestablishment did not discourage these earlier theocratic leanings and ambitions, but gave them a new and more efficient methodology that only encouraged its further utilization within American politics and religion. Colwell noted, several decades into disestablishment, that Christianity in the United States enjoys "advantages here never before accorded to it by accident or by power." Kenneth Scott Latourette celebrated the nineteenth century as "the great century," for "never had [Christianity] exerted so wide an influence upon the human race." As a legally protected and even privileged majority, Protestants wielded the resulting power in the new nation "at their pleasure."[39] Believing religious liberty to be dependent upon a strict wall of separation, Jefferson charged such arrangements as a type of Christian "conspiracy"; it was Beecher and this higher kingdom ideal, however, rather than Jefferson and his Enlightenment understanding of private faith, that defined how most nineteenth-century Protestants came to understand the ideal of religious liberty and disestablishment and its relation to the church and kingdom.[40]

Beecher was instrumental in promoting and reaffirming this earlier Puritan ideal of the American kingdom, which now had achieved a new democratized status as part of these new national developments. Even though he had earlier criticized famed American revivalist Jonathan Edwards's belief that the millennial reign of Christ would commence in America, Beecher, upon observing the new forms and patterns of religious liberty, had a change of heart: "When I first encountered this opinion [of a millennial American kingdom], I thought it chimerical; but all providential developments since, and all the existing signs of the times, lend corroboration to it."[41] Upon his epiphany related to disestablishment and these seemingly providential events, Beecher, aided by other ministers, systematized various volunteer societies throughout the existing nation into a "gigantic religious power," making him, according to Protestant historian Winthrop Hudson, "the real architect" behind this new reform movement within American religion and politics.[42] The abstract and even invisible nature of Christ's kingdom had undoubtedly led to its historiographical neglect, but as Niebuhr explained, these very real and visible expressions of faith not only created societies and transformed the nation, but "became a rallying point of ardent souls who had been kindled by the gospel of the kingdom of Christ."[43]

Like many of his ministerial colleagues, Beecher legitimated and linked this democratic conversion to the cause of Christ in ways that lent credence to it as this "new thing" that was to break forth in America that made possible Christ's coming kingdom and earthly reign. As such, though the American Revolution brought forth the contradiction between religious establishment and individual freedom, threats of separation created a Protestant backlash that instead linked religion to the state in ways more powerful than earlier imagined. Through Beecher and others, America produced a new and enthusiastic optimism that linked Christianity with American republicanism, causing Mark Hopkins, president of Williams College, to take heart and find in this "transforming influence of Christianity," an oncoming time in America when "wars, and intemperance, and licentiousness, and fraud, and slavery, and all oppression" was to end.[44] As it was argued, "the kingdom of Christ is to penetrate and transform like leaven, all the relations of individual and national life." For most political, religious, and legal theorists of post-Revolutionary America, "Christian faith was indispensable to the survival of the new nation," thereby inspiring a relationship between the two that was not separate but, as Schaff explained, instead "amicable." Indeed, the prevailing impression among politicians and historians was that it was the "religion of the Bible" alone that made Americans good citizens, thereby underlining "the foundations of our hopes as a people." American jurists in the 1830s, notes legal scholar Sarah Gordon, powerfully "recrafted links between democracy and 'general' Protestantism, reassuring themselves that their government was neither heathen nor sectarian."[45]

Disestablishment allowed powerful Protestants to wrestle the new challenges of a new nation in ways that allowed them to retain a powerful form of religious control and privilege within the country largely by rendering that influence invisible, and thus out of reach of legal restriction. This invisibility did not imply its secularization in the sense that it was less religious and apolitical, but instead that Protestant individuals took church business "out of doors," thereby keeping it under the radar of undue religious influence on the state. As noted by Tocqueville, Christianity in America following disestablishment remained "a fact so irresistibly established, that no one undertakes either to attack or to defend it," becoming, according to historian Mark Noll, thanks in part to these volunteer reform societies, the largest subculture and wielder of influence within the United States, second only to the federal government itself.[46] Any religion that thus proved inconsistent with Christianity was prohibited, while Christianity itself remained, under the guise of separation, "out of reach of Congressional interference."[47] In quoting Montesquieu, Baird made the point that having "no visible head" was "more agreeable to the independency of climate than that which has one."[48]

No longer relying on the actions of ministers to influence the state in the American nation, Protestants hearkened back to an old conception of "Love" as outlined in this earlier Puritan civil-theocratic covenant. In marking God as sovereign over society, Puritans brought themselves into this divine monarchal autonomy by way of this covenant, a concept that justified human efforts within an ideal that otherwise delegitimized human effort. Love represented no mere emotion but, as Niebuhr explained, was individual "action itself." As is clear at this point, American Protestantism was not a church in the traditional sense, but rather, as Niebuhr puts it, an imperfect *movement* of people, inspiring them throughout this century to "identify the visible with the invisible church, but it was determined that the visible should try to image the invisible."[49] Political action and community creation were informed by this invisible kingdom ideal and the importance Protestants felt in belonging to this higher kingdom and in seeking to replicate it in the real world. "Church," explained prominent nineteenth-century itinerant preacher Nancy Towle, was not limited to any particular tangible Christian organization but was, instead, "a body of believers."[50] Based on the voluntary principle, participation in this invisible kingdom of Christ was made visible by way of participation in mission fields, benevolent societies, and Sunday schools, as well as Bible and tract associations that organized, providing aid and religious instruction for America's ever-expanding unchurched and often illiterate population. The rural and isolated spaces of the frontier demanded the creation and recruitment of these organizations on a popular scale, providing a powerful conception of the kingdom and its potency within American society, and as long as these efforts "made the American," the kingdom and frontier worked hand in hand. Horace Bushnell posited that such volunteer patronage was "the first and sublimest Christian duty which the age lays upon us." Indeed, there "can be no other duty at all comparable to the duty of saving our country; none that God so manifestly imposes." In light of the visible barbaric forces of the frontier, volunteerism was the invisible yet "all-powerful influence" that could adapt itself, in the words of Baird, to this environment, acting "wherever the gospel is to be preached, wherever vice is to be attacked, and wherever suffering humanity has to be relieved."[51] Such efforts and structures restored life to this newly defined yet age-old American covenant, creating a community once again of the elect and chosen, making America, as outlined by Kenneth Wald and Allison Calhoun-Brown, "a gathering of those who received the promise of eternal salvation in exchange for accepting a mission to act as God's agents in this world."[52] American Calvinists refused to see themselves as earning this blessed chosen state as a reward for their voluntary efforts, but instead knew that without these works, their hopes were empty.

By the end of the nineteenth century, such cooperative efforts as engaged in by individuals had become an efficient arm of the state and a type of cultural "background" that Tocqueville acknowledged as existing, and required little by way of social or intellectual articulation.[53] As Tocqueville would further explain, Americans assumed without question or discussion "a great number of moral truths" that originated and were directly connected to popular forms of religion, governance, and religious expression. Described by one historian as a "religious establishment by proxy," the structures that emerged from these interdenominational efforts on the rural frontier produced a system that outside observers would perceive as "foremost of the political institutions of that country."[54] This democratic-styled theocracy or kingdom ideal, in the words of Baird, made Americans "co-workers for God," allowing, as Justice George Shea at the end of the nineteenth century attested, unchecked religious mobility and influence within all levels of American politics, be it legislative, judicial, and executive.[55]

The frontier allowed for the working out of these important religio-political developments as demanded as part of the invisible kingdom, inspiring volunteer efforts that both united and motivated many Americans, making visible, in the words of one historian, the "concealed quasi-theocratic ambitions" of American clergymen.[56] No longer the realm of a single, visible church entity, the responsibilities of the kingdom had fallen upon each individual in a type of invisible nation-wide and interdenominational network of voluntary Christian action or love. As learned from the unprecedented success of these volunteer efforts, all denominations, be they Presbyterian, Congregationalist, or Baptist, wrote theologian Charles C. Starbuck in the *New Englander and Yale Review*, share in the same grand effort to advance the political rule or "reign of Christ" in America. Concerning efforts later in the century "towards the reconciliation of our ecclesiastical with our civil Christi-anity," Starbuck reminded fellow Christians that one's duty toward civil ethics and public morality were just as important in being Christian as was church attendance and individual piety.[57] As such, the church may be separate from the state and its secular offices, but individual Chris-tians in their daily lives served just as much purpose in the edification of Christ's kingdom in America as the preacher's Sunday morning sermon. Starbuck explained that "the American State expresses more perfectly the highest conception of the gospel than the American Church," and as such, the state stood within this cosmic realm and was thus to stand as an example for the direction and makeup of the invisible church and kingdom itself. The roles of the American preacher and politician were thus deeply entwined with the obligations of the invisible kingdom. Indeed, in America, following disestablishment, individual American Protestants reconciled religion with the state, only after they turned the state itself into a church. "The churches, then, must adopt country as their highest symbol of God, or they become disloyal to the nation," and if "they are to endure," the "political convictions of our people" were to emerge out of and rest "upon a religious ground." American faith in Christian republicanism as expressed by Starbuck, together with its correlation to the invisible kingdom of Christ (or "American Church") was unmistakable.

In light of this moral establishment and the correlated principle of volunteerism as enacted on the American frontier, Americans were converted into "co-regents" of the "Incarnate King, who, accepting His people and His subjects," transforms individual Christians and "converts absolute authority, without any transmutation of its nature, into the eternal principle of spontaneous self-direction." Or put more simply: "God, the one God, is both our country and our king."[58] This "spontaneous self-direction" of volunteerism was what gave spring to

Lyman Beecher's unbounded jubilation over disestablishment and what provided such a cause for celebration over the principle of volunteerism for Robert Baird, Philip Schaff, Stephen Colwell, and other Protestant thinkers concerning the coming and realization of the kingdom of God in America. Disestablishment had not killed religious influence within American society and its experimentation with religious freedom, nor had it initiated Jefferson's vision of separation, but instead it had marked a new creative and innovative path in which this "Incarnate King" and "His co-regents" could transform American society into an actual realm of unchecked Calvinist-Protestant moral civil power. As this power and influence expanded on the frontier, it was not merely economic opportunism that governed American advance, but Manifest Destiny. Like a type of prewritten providential script, the Western wilderness had become a central place for these invisible forces to work themselves out and to prepare America for the divine kingdom that was seen to be fast approaching.

## The Protestant Kingdom and the Frontier

Despite Protestant visions of a religiously united nation, the United States was religiously diverse—inspired in part by the vastness and openness of the frontier. The frontier, both its physical and abstract quality, continued to engender ideals of new beginnings, progress, and even a sense of higher unity as seen with the invisible kingdom that promised to absolve such division. However, these ideals, played out within the actual rural spaces of America, led to creative and innovative paths which produced not just optimism and hope, but deep concern, doubt, anxiety, prejudice, and even war.

America was not, as prominent Presbyterian theologian Charles Hodge suggested, "essentially one religion," but was rather, as described by historian Jon Butler, "awash in a sea of faith." Indeed, America was and had always been much more diverse than the standard narratives suggest, and Hodge's definition, so dependent upon exclusionary racial and sectarian frameworks, imagined a world that related only to some. William Hutchison, for example, claims that "radical diversification" came "crashing in upon the young nation almost at the moment of its birth," however much one particular class of white, English-speaking Protestants pushed forward an American culture "to their own speci-fication," thus explaining the negative reaction against the explosion of diversification post-1820.[59] Jon Butler insists we allow for an expanded understanding of American religion that includes not just Christianity and Judaism, but also folk religion, including magic, astrology, and the occult, as subtle, complex, and sophisticated systems of religious prac-tice. Religious pluralism in America "guaranteed that to be religious in America was not only to make choices, but to choose among aston-ishing varieties of religion created in America and duplicated nowhere else."[60] As part of this post-1820 diversification, however, Mormons and Protestants similarly reflected important themes that mixed Ameri-can-style politics and traditional faith with American folk beliefs and practices in imagining and pushing forth this kingdom ideal. As a part of this unique syncretism, where even Mormonism and black Baptists and Methodists found insight and inspiration in folk religion and the occult, intensive religious revivalism on the American frontiers during the formative years of the nation further expanded upon these differ-ences in American religion—while simultaneously helping to initiate and expand religious creativity and innovation. Such innovation on the local level eventually influenced national and state policy, thereby moving to harness and control this diversity and innovation by way of Beecher's and Hodge's vision of the kingdom by means of national and state power.

As exciting and inspiring as religious change was in the develop-ing country of the United States, it was also a "storm-and-pressure period"—as described by Philip Schaff, thereby making "each Christian a priest and a king in the service of the universal High Priest and King of Kings." America's growing diversity on the frontier had to be quickly minimized in the realizing of the Protestant kingdom, in which the "fate of the Reformation was to be decided," and from where the "city on the hill" was to shine forth to the entire world. In Schaff's words, Amer-ica's "remarkable" ability to assimilate "all foreign elements, excepting only the African and the Chinese," was part of its "digestive power." In this narrowly defined assimilationist ideal, the American-oriented landscape was regarded as a "Phenix [sic] grave" that promised new life to "all European nationalities" and "all European churches and sects," and was part of "the last decisive conflict between faith and infidelity, between Christ and Antichrist" in anticipation of the "final reconciliation" following this Christian and national rebirth.[61] Visible religious difference then was translated into invisible cosmic terms of good and evil, engaging America's Protestants in a holy crusade against this growing American religious diversity. The process of closing the frontier and eradicating its diversity was viewed as a direction of progress, as well as a final stage in this ultimate reconciliation or unification of American religion. Seen as a place beyond mere geography, the frontier was where true religion came into contact with the forces of irreligion and chaos, a space that anticipated an overrunning of the one at the expense of the other.[62] This process to close the frontier offered great promise, while also holding the attendant potential of dire consequences—helping to create a narrative of immediacy that justified appropriate actions.

In nineteenth-century America, the frontier stood as a type of revelation of God's coming kingdom, allowing for only a narrow gap between piety and patriotism—concepts which most Americans in the new nation did little to segregate. Theologians such as Lyman Beecher and Horace Bushnell were convinced that whoever ruled the West directed the size and the shape of the entire nation and, as such, its destiny and global influence. By midcentury, it had become an intuitive and assumed truth that the frontier held deep religious significance, requiring deep investment by those in the East. The West had an important role to play in making visible not only the development of the kingdom of God in America, but ultimately the expansion of the kingdom throughout the world. In his *Plea for the West*, Beecher's words were both a celebration and a warning about the frontier, for it was obvious that "the religious and political destiny of our nation is to be decided in the West." With the huge influx of immigrants in the West, a "nation is being 'born in a day.'" Further, Beecher declared, "Let no man at the East quiet himself and dream of liberty, whatever may become of the West. . . . Her destiny is our destiny."[63] In fact, to ignore this destiny amidst these new concerns over non-Protestant immigration to the West stood as a type of "treason" and "infatuation with folly" that threatened the loss of the American covenant and birthright that underlined this kingdom anxiety.[64] It was this climate of sacralization of American independence and its associated social and political obligations that led American minis-

ters to engage in civil public policy with such feelings of public stewardship, particularly in regard to the West.

In line with traditional Protestant beliefs in America, these growing
visions of the West and its glories and perils were seen and expressed
in terms of ancient Hebrew scripture. "When an emigrant from those
States removes to the 'Far West,'" noted Baird, "he takes with him his
waggons [sic], his cattle, his little ones, and a troop of slaves, so as to
resemble Abraham when he moved from place to place in Canaan."[65]
The Bible was not an ancient historical account of God's dealings with
ancient humanity, but a living document that outlined and provided
a way of understanding current events and trends as they took shape
in nineteenth-century America. In linking themselves with the "pure,
virgin character of a great and primitive manhood" as epitomized in
the ancient biblical patriarch Abraham, Americans heightened the significance of the frontier by contrasting such frontier characteristics as
independence, determination, and individuality to that of the wicked
and barbaric Ammonites.[66] In line with Paul Reeve's "transtemporal
functions" of the frontier, this tendency of Americans to conflate their
experiences and attributes with those of ancient Biblical figures represented a ritual performance that granted a sacred status to this frontier
geographic space, establishing both a worldview and real response.[67]
While Beecher's "Plea for the West" drew alarm over the visible growth
of Catholicism in the western regions of the country, Bushnell even
more readily appropriated Old Testament scripture, labeling the vague
concept of barbarism itself as an even greater threat than Roman
Catholicism. Seeing the frontier as an invisible abstract yet real force
that defeated human civility and left barbarism in its wake, Bushnell
taught that only "extraordinary efforts in behalf of education and religion, will suffice to prevent a fatal lapse of social order." Despite this
anxiety over the frontier, popular volunteer responses to the Western
wilderness stood as the invisible principle behind American exceptionalism—the necessary heroic force by individual women and men that
arrested crisis and planted "Christian culture and virtue."[68] This expansionism, however, had its significant perils, as the "new West," declared
Bushnell, enlarged the "ground of barbarism," extended to it "room to
run wild," and multiplied "the chance of final anarchy and confusion."[69]
Not just Catholicism, but drunkenness, violence, superstition, and igno-

rance were just a few of the assumed degrading influences and natural consequences of frontier life which required check.[70]

Under such threats against the ruinous forces of the frontier, collective Christian action by way of patient persuasion as extended to the West was no longer a luxury, now demanding an uncompromising coercion when it came to matters of religious and civil control. The same year Mormons entered the Salt Lake Valley, and only months away from the United States acquiring millions of acres from Mexico that would include this region, Bushnell spoke of America as being in its "emigrant age of Israel," marking it as America's own "times of the Judges"—outlined in the Old Testament as a necessary response to a "decline towards barbarism." The "great problem of American society is not solved," he believed, however "socially complete" the people of New England were. Americans, and the nation at large, Bushnell predicted, would continue to be at risk on the frontiers until the kingdom was fully established, its frontier fully closed, and its wayward inhabitants controlled. Indeed, the West threatened the entire nation. Until this frontier was closed (that is, Christianized), American society must "bring back the times of the Judges," endowed with individual strength and determination (through volunteerism) to win the wilderness for this future American messianic king.[71] Prior to Israel having a centralized kingdom, these judges served as both warrior and public leader, arising only when the loosely confederated tribes of Israel fell under particular external threats from outside forces that required action. Indeed, perceiving the perils of the American West within this violent, anticentralized government, Old Testament lens, Bushnell conceived control by means of the "nail that was driven by Jael's hammer—not the ointment ministered by the graceful hand of Mary." In this biblical story, Jael took a hammer and a tent peg, went quietly into the tent of the Canaanite commander as he slept, and drove the peg through his head (Judges 4:1–23).

Despite this violent rhetoric, Bushnell, like other Americans, did not hope to save the country by "raising a crusade" or "filling the air with outcries of any sort," but rather by employing the benevolent Christian doctrine of the kingdom—love and liberty. Indeed, love and liberty were code words of the implied revolution of the kingdom, and "crusade" had reference to popes and ministers, not Christian individuals guided by Christ's love and liberty. Christian love, serving as a basis of an anticipated American covenant with God, and its attendant volunteer principle, was the real power behind cultivating the American frontier and uniting Christ with the nation. Such violence may not be the most respectable, but it was yet an act of love, as the unruly wilderness sometimes required an unruly hand. As it was popularly understood, ideals of liberty were thus contextualized by a rough environment that required such hands-on cultivating and uprooting, grafting and burning. This cry for violence against America's barbaric influences, however severe, served to break up "the age of frost, and brought in a new era of power."[72] As Bushnell would state in a commencement speech at Yale following the terrible loss of life as a consequence of the American Civil War, the "true economy of the world" was that "many of its grandest and most noble benefits have and are to have a tragic origin, and to come as outgrowths only of blood."[73] Love of neighbor remained the sovereign law of Christian scripture, but the frontier and its promise of liberty belonged to Christ, and violent Old Testament imagery, however extreme, forged the methodology of this expression of love.

However, this national vision was both embodied by and challenged by the nascent Mormon Church in Utah. This newly forged religious, economic, political, and social movement not only shared this national history of religion and founding, it also shared the nation's narrative of faith of both the kingdom and the frontier. This narrative included a cosmic battle appropriated by Mormons into their own story of religious persecution, blended with American republicanism and a powerfully innovative Biblical theocratic impulse.[74] Even on the point of Jael's hammer, Brigham Young similarly upheld the importance of extralegal violence within his own conception of God's kingdom on the frontier, something he understood within the category of Christian love, or as part of the authority and morality of Christ's kingdom on earth.[75] When Mormons parted from Protestantism, they effectively adopted and re-envisioned this shared frontier ideal, and forcefully reinvented this millennial vision by boldly striking out into the deeper reaches of the American frontier, increasingly emphasizing the importance of ecclesiastical ("priesthood") authority in this literal priestly kingdom.[76] For both Mormons and Protestants, the West was an uncultivated and vast wilderness that necessitated a link between Providence and spiritual human development, and both felt duty-bound to prepare this West, and by way of causation, themselves as the chosen leaders who would bring forth Christ's imminent "latter-day" reign of glory. The Mormons' attempt to unify themselves against challenges and criticisms as they established themselves within the virtual and abstract frontier powerfully configured their thinking, ideals, and programs—though they were popularly perceived to run counter to similar Protestant ideals.

## THE MORMON KINGDOM AND THE FRONTIER

In similar yet contrasting ways from the generally accepted notion of the frontier, the Mormons viewed the frontier as a place of withdrawal and a haven from persecution from the developed cities of "wicked Babylon." More profoundly, Mormons also saw the frontier wilderness as a space in which God's kingdom was given another chance, and where true republicanism and liberty could work themselves out, and where the millennial reign of Jesus would be ignited. For Christians more broadly, millennialism represents the idea that Jesus will rule on earth, either literally or spiritually, for one thousand years. While those who anticipated this spiritual rule to be through the church (or "body of believers"), a view widely held among nineteenth-century Protestants, Mormons anticipated it as literal and imminent. Part of this literal vision was that upon his return to earth, Jesus would violently destroy the wicked, gather his chosen, and reign as king in their midst for a millennium. For nationally stigmatized groups like Mormons who found their ability to transform society limited and overwhelmingly challenged, this gravitation toward the destruction of the world in order to fix it coincides with larger millennial patterns. For Protestants wielding national power, this reliance on bettering society through their combined volunteer and political efforts, the promises of the kingdom appeared possible without such global destruction. Indeed, Christ's kingdom on earth had already come in a spiritual way that assured Protestants of this forward march of social progress, as well as the necessity and morality of their efforts. However the millennium was approached, be it through Christ's literal and destructive return or before or after these thousand years, all believed the initiation of the kingdom as happening in real time, and as such, there was much to do to prepare, and much at stake in national and regional events.

As had Protestants at the time, Mormons saw themselves as God's chosen Israel in a new, even divinely preserved and chosen wilderness. According to explorer and military captain John W. Gunnison, Mormons saw themselves as "the Israelites of old under Moses," ready to enter their own promised land.[77] With the devastating failure of settling what Mormons believed to be the literal site of the Garden of Eden in Missouri in the 1830s, the Salt Lake Valley in the Rockies provided a new, visible sacred space for this new American Zion, offering an open canvas for their vision of the kingdom of God in America and space to cultivate the proper characteristics of a modern-day holy society and city, which Mormons called Zion. Mormon apostle Orson Pratt, holding one of the highest ecclesiastical positions in the church, just under the First Presidency, viewed the settled East as full of "bloodthirsty Christians" and "bandits," and conversely viewed "the dens and caves of the Rocky Mountains" as a place where "we shall die where freedom reigns triumphantly. Liberty in a solitary place, and in a desert, is far preferable than martyrdom in these pious states."[78] In 1852, in a small book titled *The Government of God*, fellow Mormon apostle John Taylor seemed to view the frontier as a place of escape from not just the United States, but the "Christian nations as a whole," which had not only failed in its incompetence and hypocrisy to bring in the kingdom of God and its "Millennial reign of peace," but rather presented a "picture that is truly lamentable; a miserable portrait of poor, degenerated, fallen humanity." Taylor was not denying the Protestant vision of the kingdom, but rather that Protestants were no longer worthy to carry it forth into fulfillment. In critiquing this popular sense of Christian triumphalism in the United States, Taylor reminded his readers that although "Protestantism bears rule unchecked" in the nation, they were "usurpers" of the kingdom whom Christ would "dispossess" once he comes to claim his true kingdom, and for Mormons, such expectations were imminent.[79] Brigham Young claimed that not only had Joseph Smith organized the actual kingdom of God in 1844, but that in 1845, the millennium itself had begun.[80] Mormons defined themselves by modified American ideals of the kingdom and its attendant millennial hopes—a perspective created and strengthened by their dwelling in and beyond the frontier amidst the Rocky Mountains, as made more real in their looking back on the "corrupt" settled cities in the East.

This imagined frontier and its garden mythology assisted Mormon leaders and their people in creative reconfigurations of American practices and beliefs. As has been seen, Mormons did not reject the American vision of the kingdom and its quest for national unity and political involvement as outlined by Beecher, Baird, Starbuck, and Schaff, but rather adopted it and refashioned it to meet their own civil and religious needs as presented on the frontier. While Americans defined their brand of republicanism as *vox populi vox dei*, where God's voice is revealed through "the people," Mormon leaders claimed that they alone, in the capacity of prophets, seers, and revelators, heard this voice. "If it is not revealed from heaven," wrote Taylor, then "it cannot be the *kingdom of heaven*," and to no others would God reveal Himself but through His chosen prophets and apostles. Through this medium of revelation to a specific body of ecclesiastical leaders, heavenly laws were to be enforced on earth, and once Christ came and further set up his law, absolute and universal obedience would be required. Contradicting democratic revivalist trends, Mormon leaders restored the Puritan notion of God's sovereignty and the kingdom as already on earth, and that through the principles of covenant and ecclesiastical obedience, the will of heaven would descend to earth. Though Mormons embraced the enthusiasm of individual volunteer efforts in building the kingdom, such efforts were understood from within the prophetic edicts already pronounced by the visible head of the church. Upon Christ's return, whoever would not obey this rule by the church would be destroyed, and Christ would then hand this purified global kingdom over "to the Saints," where "a King shall rule in righteousness and Princes shall decree judgment."[81]

In looking at the Mormon example in the West and their highly centralized hierarchy as framed upon rules of tight obedience, it is clear that Frederick Jackson Turner was wrong in his belief that the frontier produced a unique democratic spirit of individualism and freedom, but rather, as expressed by historian Donald Worster, the frontier required significant power and strict obedience to be given to a sole adjudicator. More often than not, the West was not that of unbridled freedom for the individual, but rather "a land of authority and restraint."[82] Based upon utopian American idealism, the Mormon kingdom took its unique shape on the American frontier, calling upon volunteer cooperative efforts in ways that veered from those of Beecher and other Protestants' emphasis on individualism and volunteerism. Church heads Joseph Smith and later Brigham Young and John Taylor imagined their national success and spiritual unity, not through the volunteerism of a popular bottom-up movement of individual believers, but instead through the popular volunteer obedience to a single top-down leader. Indeed, while Protestants celebrated denominational individuality as proof of their unparalleled vitality, however concerned they remained over increasing sectarianism, Mormon leaders condemned individuality as parallel to covetousness and selfishness, and even apostasy and a threat to the kingdom.[83]

As did many other Americans, Mormons looked upon the founding of the nation as an inspired and divine event. At the same time, these same leaders condemned and predicted the demise of the entire system of American civil republican governance, expressing the view that whatever good American civil society held, it would soon succumb to a superior kingdom that was both political and spiritual.[84] In anticipation of this imminent destruction due to America's lost birthright and thus tenuous existence, Joseph Smith's biographer, Richard Bushman, noted that Joseph Smith utilized this kingdom ideal to fill the anticipated oncoming vacuum.[85] Smith's vision was not that of national harmony through assimilation and intimidation, but rather a divine destruction of America's vast religious diversity; and the more Smith envisioned a fallen and apostate society, the more centralized his own authority and that of the church became, a theme powerfully continued and deepened by Brigham Young and others in Utah and throughout the Mormon colonies. It was not that Mormons claimed themselves to be popes in the same way Jonathan Edwards and other Protestants had that inspired so much opposition by other Americans, but rather that they had a single "American pope" that "out-popes" the Roman pope. In an evolving republican society, which Protestants believed to uphold the "people as preacher," Mormons were criticized as holding up one man as "prophet, priest and pope, all in one—a pope, too, who is not one whit less infallible than he who wears the tiara."[86] The attempt then by Smith was not to organize a simple denominational church comparable to the Methodists or the Baptists as Smith's revelations envisioned until 1829, but rather to singlehandedly accomplish what other denominations were attempting to accomplish collectively—that is, to unite American governance with Christ's kingdom via economic, judicial, cultural, political, and military structuring.

In observing Mormonism's nineteenth-century theocratic impulse and exceptionalist claims, together with repeated condemnations of the country's religious and political systems, it is easy to forget just how in-line with American republicanism and democratic values Mormons understood themselves as upholding. While Joseph Smith had criticized republican governance as futile in his push for theocratic rule, Brigham Young defined theocracy as synonymous with republicanism. In taking inspiration from individual state constitutions like Massachusetts and Connecticut, Orson Pratt argued in 1855 that "every intelligent man" knew that it was lawful "for another government to be organized within the United States, of a theocratic nature," as the Constitution guaranteed "to all religious societies the right of forming any ecclesiastical government they like."[87] In a July 4, 1854, speech in the Salt Lake City Tabernacle, Young argued that it was only here in Utah that a truly republican form of government was to be found. Young similarly acknowledged the divine inspiration behind the U.S. Constitution as had Pratt, but also noted that the fallen nature of humanity required a "president," or "dictator" and "lawgiver" who could serve in that capacity throughout the rest of his life, rather than the four-year constitutional term limit, thus presiding as sovereign and supreme leader over a national system that could then be designed to lead to "the perfection of mankind in righteousness."[88] John Taylor argued that no one, except those appointed by God himself, held legitimate rule on earth or wielded sufficient wisdom to keep society from degeneration, since they were outside the sound of God's voice and spirit. Pointing to the examples of Israelite kings Saul and David, authorized earthly kings were not to be just political and military rulers, but also priests who sought and received the mind and will of the Lord for those of their people.[89] It was as part of this anticipation of the dissolution of American civil governance and its replacement by Mormon power that Joseph Smith, Brigham Young, and John Taylor were set apart and anointed as kings and priests, not just over the church, but over the country and the entire world, and where the idea of obedience to them was consequently heightened in importance.[90] In this self-styled "theo-democracy," Mormonism's priesthood, as divided between the temporal Aaronic and the ecclesiastical Melchizedek, governed all sections of Mormon society as a single concern. As Leonard Arrington put it, "So far as the Latter-day Saints were concerned, their president was supreme in religious, political, and economic fields. His were the words of the Lord."[91] Joseph Smith expounded that a theocratic form of government on earth was the "only thing that can bring about the 'restitution of all things, spoken of by all the holy prophets since the world was'—'the dispensation of the fullness of times, when GOD shall gather together all things in one.'" In this "true spirit of republicanism" as described by Young, devoid of a two-party political system, Brigham and other leaders no longer prayed "thy kingdom come," for as they were now rejoicing, "it is among us, it is here, and we say let thy Kingdom roll forth and accomplish that which it is designed [to do]."[92]

Characteristically, in reconfiguring these structures to their own experiences on the "new frontier" in the deep American West, Mormons mimicked Old Testament paradigms as closely as possible. Polygamy itself, however problematic or beneficial for Nauvoo or Utah saints, was primarily justified as "Abraham-like," with a revelation given on polygamy to Joseph Smith to "go ye, therefore, and do the works of Abraham."[93] "In the same manner that Abraham took Hagar," Joseph Smith charged early missionaries to marry as plural wives "Lamanite" (Native American) women, as a way of lifting the presumed racial curse and fulfilling Book of Mormon prophecy. Smith sought to "restore" Abraham and his practices to the American context, restoring not just the principles of patriarchy, polygamy, and theocracy, but also, once the "sons of Levi be purified" and the "Temple of the Lord" built, then the performance of animal sacrifice as it was in the days of Abraham. When the Melchizedek priesthood was "sufficiently manifest," noted John Taylor, animal blood sacrifices would once again become necessary, "else how can the restitution of all things spoken of by all the holy Prophets be brought to pass?"[94] In line with this, Utah's military, recognized Western historian Will Bagley, was "patterned after Israel's armies of old," with its brigade of one thousand, broken into two regiments of five hundred, broken into five battalions of one hundred, then each into ten companies of fifty and fifty companies of ten.[95] Prior to his church's exile from the United States, Joseph Smith organized the "Council of Fifty," also called the "Kingdom of God," which included the likes of Joseph

Smith himself, as well as John Taylor, Brigham Young, Orson Pratt, and Wilford Woodruff. This secret council, explains historian Klaus Hansen, met regularly in Nauvoo under Smith's leadership to discuss principles of government and political theory. According to a revelation to Joseph Smith, the Fifty actually represented "the Kingdom of God, that my servants have heretofore prophesied of and that I taught my disciples to pray for, saying 'Thy Kingdom come, thy will be done on earth as it is in heaven,' for the establishment of my rule, for the introduction of my law, for the protection of my Church, and for the maintenance, promulgation and protection of civil and religious liberty in this nation and throughout the world." The Fifty assisted Smith in his run for president, and later governed Nauvoo after his death, and assisted Brigham Young in directing the exodus out west. In the new territory of "Deseret" (later named Utah), subordinated under the authority of Young and the Twelve, the council formed the state legislature and took the reins of government.[96] Largely, though not entirely, made up of church membership, since God's kingdom was to expand beyond that of the church, all of the Fifty were considered "princes" whose designated authority and priesthood directive was "to build up the Kingdom of God on earth." Forming a "nucleus of a popular government" that would become global and endure throughout the millennium, the kingdom of God stood distinctly separate from the church itself, forming instead, as explained by Fifty Benjamin F. Johnson, an "outer wall or government around the inner temple of the priesthood, until all are come to the knowledge of God."[97]

In such a sacralized space as the American West, Young discouraged the expansion of local parishes or churches outside Utah, instead insisting that Mormons from afar were to "come home" to the political and economic boundaries of Zion. In this larger, more invisible cosmic fight between angels and Satan, order and disorder, Mormon leaders stressed the supreme importance of building Zion on the American frontier, and called for all those "who have a wheelbarrow, and faith enough to roll it over the mountains," to come to the desert kingdom. The physical act of gathering was an essential part of this sacred framework of salvation. Brigham Young declared, "It is as much the duty of the Saints to gather, as it is for sinners to repent and be baptized for the remission of their sins, and every Saint who does not come home, when he has an opportunity will be afflicted by the Devil." The commonwealth of Utah was a place where spiritual and temporal unity was to prevail, "where the Holy One of Israel presides in the midst of his people, and where the power of Satan is destroyed, broken, or brought in subjection."[98]

The topography of the West, and the ideal of the frontier, became the central hub of God's expanding kingdom in its last days, in preparation of His imminent return. The West represented a place of safety and a means of escape from the wicked world; it became the fulfillment (or "restoration") of all earlier Christian hopes. Indeed, the altitude of the Rocky Mountains that imposed itself on the Great Basin kingdom placed Mormons literally, as they conceived it, closer to God. "We have the pleasing consolation," Young and his counselors wrote in a letter to the general membership of the church in 1850, "that we are nearer 'the tops of the everlasting hills,' and higher upon mountains than most other people," and "those regions of light and glory," from which inspiration and "blessings flow."[99] Similar to Bushnell's sentiment concerning America's utopic destiny that held no need for police or soldiers, Young envisioned in his mountaintop community, a society so perfected that there would be no need for such worldly occupations as doctors and lawyers, nor civil necessities such as courts with judges.[100] Young's early hopes in this regard demonstrate not just his distrust and anger when outsiders did come, but also the level of utopian naiveté exhibited during the first decade of this Mormon frontier settlement. This optimism paralleled that of Bushnell and other Protestant utopianists, thus informing Mormonism's vast colonization efforts in ways not unlike Protestant volunteer efforts in the West. In important ways, Mormonism's departure from their quasi-theocratic Protestant counterpart, was not so much a radical reconfiguration of how the ideals of government and religion were conceived, but rather an attempt to accomplish right now, through a visible head, what others were only anticipating with the impending millennialism and its attendant return of Christ.

However familiar Mormonism's own sense of divine mandate was in their westward expansion, they were viewed by the rest of the country as fanatics and heretics—dangerous not only to Christianity but to "the American way of faith." So entwined was religion with general social culture and the government, that Mormonism's questions of—and answers to—how religion was to be conceived and practiced in America emerged as no mere social and religious critique. Rather, as it was held, Mormonism assumed the proportions of an un-American force that was both an offense and a threat to America's conceptions of being a righteous and redeemer nation, representing instead a satanic and distorted copy of Christ's true kingdom. Protestantism was the steward of American law and order, essential to human progress, carefully preserved and protected by a proper form of republican government and Christian religion. Challengers to the established order were not merely un-American, but enemies of the new Israel—and God.[101] As argued by the *Southern Quarterly Review*, the "imperial Anglo-Saxon race" had a "mission on earth" akin to "the Jews in Canaan," to "subdue the land and possess it."[102] Mormonism questioned this American mission by proclaiming it their own. As a consequence of their dissent and growing numbers, the Mormons in Utah were considered a national threat—a threat compared to Native Americans and the Roman Catholic population, whose presence and practices also stood as a challenge to the prevailing notions of America as a unified redeemer nation. This Mormon challenge, as also seen with the presence of Roman Catholicism, came as a religio-political challenge from the frontier, long the hub of America's own Manifest Destiny. Many Protestants held this hub as an essential creative force and great import, from which not just the American character, but also the kingdom of God, had been coming forth and would culminate.

As a site of social, political, and environmental conflict, the frontier was a place of both destiny and peril, of awe and terror, both of which Mormonism adopted and exposed. Mormon descriptions of American politics and domestic policy as evidence of an emergent "priest-ridden generation" merely upheld Conrad Cherry's sense that America's destiny was that of an exclusively "Protestant destiny," a destiny that demanded the infusion of "the Protestant religion" into the fibers of the American political and social institutions.[103] Mormons represented the failure of this Protestant destiny in the West and the risks for such failure. For Bushnell, the "Mormon city and temple rise as proof visible before me" that "all fantastic errors and absurdities will assuredly congregate there [in the West]." Already "thousands of disciples" gather to this "wretched and silly delusion," thereby justifying Jael's hammer as an appropriate response to the West's "wild hunters and robber clans of the western hemisphere—American Moabites, Arabs and Edomites!"[104] As much as nineteenth-century Americans romanticized the rural-agricultural West and its isolation from the perhaps overly civilized cities of the East, American journalists, travelers, and writers cautioned against the barbaric forces of the frontier, which were depicted as both creating and attracting America's own breed of "Arab Bedouins" and "Asiatic Tartars." The dangers were that such shiftless and barbaric populations directly threatened the proper development of the West, and rather than making America, could break it.[105] "Thoughtful men see perils on our horizons," wrote Josiah Strong, Lyman Beecher's gifted student from Lane Theological Seminary in Cincinnati. "Our argument is concerned not with all of them, but *only with those which peculiarly threaten the West.*"[106] As Strong explained that the West held the "key to the nation's future," the *Louisville Journal,* in 1857, chastised the "Administration in Washington" for not acting against Utah, a land where "everyday all law, all order, all morality, all religion, and all human rights, were trampled." The conflation of religion, morality, liberty, law, and order carefully crafted a picture of barbarism in the West as fundamentally at odds with true civilization (a.k.a. Protestantism), thereby highlighting the hopeless nature of its reform capabilities, and the need for strong political and even military action. To deliver the country from such disgrace and danger, as rooted in false religion, the *Journal* called for the "moral nerve" and "the physical force by the General government" to perform such a delivery.[107] *The Ladies Repository* also added its voice: "It is for our statesmen to determine whether our Christian nation is to be charged with intolerance and arbitrary quarrelsomeness in suppressing a fanatical vice or evil corporation, such as Mormonism is."[108] When it was judged that "religious sects were inadequate or derelict," recognized historian Sidney Mead, Protestants felt that they had both the right and the obligation to defend themselves as a nation by enforcing "necessary beliefs."[109]

In addresses to foreign audiences, who viewed America and the church from a distance, Schaff turned the differences between Protestants and Mormons into the struggle between Christianity and "Mohammedanism" (Christianity's "inveterate foe"), while terming Mormonism an "irregular growth" and "abnormal" exception to the otherwise "gradual triumph" of Christian power in the United States. As he did with Islam or the "Arab Bedouin," Schaff assured foreign observers that Mormons "do not fit" in the Christian nation of America, and by natural law, are met with a "deadly hatred," as is Islam in Europe. Impressively, Mormonism represented an uncanny resemblance to Islam more broadly, for "almost like a second edition of Mohammedanism, has [Mormonism] risen in the extreme West, to the astonishment of the world; and just at the time, too, when the old Mohammedanism in the East is decaying and lying as a carcass."[110] Islam, and now Mormonism, were almost like predictable principles that opposed the advance of God's work throughout the ages and wherever it arose. In a similar comparison, Robert Baird optimistically predicted Mormonism's "speedy annihilation" in its attempt "to found a kind of Empire in the West." Furthermore, the leaders of this American Mohammedan sect "were to understand that America

FIGURE 1.2. "Coney Island and the Crowned Heads," by Friedrich Graetz. *Puck,* July 19, 1882. Nineteenth-century portrayals of Mormonism as a foreign Islamic entity were not uncommon, as seen here with the man wearing a fez leaning on his crutches, with a belt that reads "Mormonism" and adorned by a crescent moon, a recognized symbol of Islam. In this drawing, various heads of state (Pan-Slavism, Nihilism, Socialism, Pauperism, Communism, Feminism, and Mormonism) emerge from their respective bathhouses labeled Austria, Russia, Germany, Italy, France, and England. Welcoming them all for a swim at Coney Island in the menacing "republican waters" provides strong commentary concerning the perceived incompatibility of these foreign ideologies, especially Mormonism, with American republicanism. Courtesy of the Library of Congress.

is not another Arabia, nor he ['Joe Smith'] another Mahomet." Whatever hopes the Mormons held of "founding a vast empire in the western hemisphere must soon vanish."[111]

American authors and ministers likewise called for a Christian reawakening toward the American West—in the form of federal troops, Christian missionaries, and religious educational facilities, so as to ensure Mormonism's demise. Mormonism's hierarchal kingdom of ecclesiastical obedience ensured the dire need of Protestantism's more democratic kingdom of Christ that idealized a higher unity under a more catholic "universal" church. Overall then, Americans, when considering Mormonism, did not see a faith being practiced but the imposition of a foreign and degenerate people whose claim to religion mocked true Christian nationalism and the appropriate approach to religion and civil government in the United States—and continued to feel so despite Mormon attempts to wave their American flags. However, their inability to realize that the Mormons adapted and practiced the same Protestant kingdom idealism, however explicit and intense, was somewhat matched by Brigham Young's similar inability to move beyond these Old Testament cultural trends already used against them. For example, when the U.S. military arrived in Utah in 1857, Young referred to them as Midianites—oppressors of a latter-day Israel.[112] Simply, both Mormonism and Protestantism had simultaneously adopted and defied the American vision and destiny of the kingdom of God as they understood it, with both fusing themselves with their own grasp of republicanism that privileged the religious power of each, thereby making any form of reconciliation and mitigation between them impossible.

In 1850, Herman Melville, in his politically influential novel *White-Jacket*, explained that Americans (the "peculiar, chosen people—the Israel of our times") perceived themselves as living in a new dispensation that compelled them to carry "the arc of liberties of the world." God not only predestined, but "mankind expects, great things from our race; and great things we feel in our souls." This sense of American exceptionalism, experienced not only by the Puritans but by Protestants and Mormons in antebellum America, was not just part of the intellectual worldview of the times, but powerfully resided on the level of feeling and sentiment. Such sentiment often came out in explicit and unmistakable ways, but equally so, often remained either silently hidden or silently assumed behind commonly celebrated and accept-

FIGURE 1.3. *View from Mount Holyoke, Northampton, Massachusetts, After a Thunderstorm—The Oxbow*, by Thomas Cole, 1836. Though it is not explicit, this art suggests a popular view or allegory of how Protestants observed their environment throughout the 1800s—the juxtaposition of the dark wilderness with that of the expanding, lighted pastoral settlement, thus marking the struggle between savagery and civilization; that of cultivated Christian fields and farms (right) in contrast to the heavy elements of nature and the savage and uncultivated wilderness (left). However abstract, the contrast portrayed in this work presents a powerful "background" narrative that was well understood by those of the time, needing neither explanation nor defense. Courtesy of the Metropolitan Museum of Art.

able terms, such as "republicanism" and "liberty," revealing a deeper level of religious commitment and vision that can easily be lost in a modern secular mindset. Having been "sent on through a wilderness of untried things," Americans no longer saw themselves as an expression and contention of the "true English reformation," but rather, thanks to their wilderness wanderings and struggles, felt "something new"—that is, something entirely American that implied a new leading role in Christ's coming kingdom.[113] Such feelings of divine chosenness and the highly anticipated coming kingdom directly affected American sensibilities toward the West and its populations; not only this, but the white inhabitants of the West themselves adopted this popular mythology to reimagine both themselves and the destiny that awaited them. Though George Marsden had in mind only Protestants in his explanation that "Old Testament Israel, a nation committed to God's law," provided a powerful "model for political institutions," it could equally be said of the Mormons.[114] This sense of religious and social newness and anticipation, combined with new and innovative reading and interpretation of scripture, and highlighted by popular millennial zeal and fervor, was promoted by and partially acted out in the idealism and anxieties over the Western frontier—into which the Mormons carried themselves, both embodying and defying American religious and cultural beliefs. The kingdom ideal that had fashioned the significance of the frontier in the first place was now powerfully recreated and threatened by it.

In 1857, two powers and two religions were set to square off in a war—during a period of national tumult provoked by U.S. expansionism, religious excitement, slavery and sectional division, and divergent Christian nationalism. Both powers viewed themselves in similar religious terms in relation to Christ's kingdom, while both upheld a strong sense of chosen placement in America and its frontier. The Utah War, 1857–1858, apart from both sides seeking to establish sovereignty over the region, became a way to further create a sense of self and assert claims of civilization for both Mormons and Protestants. This political self directly related to particular notions of proper religion and morality, which both understood as the role of the state to uphold. This war, and its aftermath of further religious wrangling between Mormonism and Protestantism for the duration of the century, would, in some ways, quietly culminate at the World Parliament of Religions in Chicago in 1893.

# CHAPTER 2

## Frontier Expansion and the Utah War, 1857–1858

In the past is seen the stain of blood; in the future the stain presents the appearance of a vast fountain. Bloody India—slaughtered China—convulsed Mexico, bleeding Kansas and conquered Utah, are among the gloomy spots upon the moving canvass which attract universal attention and alarm. We turn our attention now to an equally vivid picture—to the moving light of pure and unalloyed religion, which has been and still is arousing the attention of thousands upon thousands in the year 1858. The historian who chronicles truthfully the eventful year's history, will point plainly to the two great pictures of light and shade—to gloom, crime and bloodshed, on the one hand, and the spread of everlasting gospel upon the other.

—*Weekly Vincennes Gazette*, June 23, 1858

Mr. Duncan [of Indiana] at once took the [House] floor, and, in a few brief, but severe remarks, opposed any and every appropriation to Utah, so long as the people were living in open and avowed hostility to the usages of morality and religion, as well as in actual violation of the laws of the United States.

—U.S. House Minutes, March 4, 1857

The Utah War (1857–1858) represents an anticlimactic attempt by the US government to control and increase its influence over its expanding frontier. In upholding their country's "messiah role," K. Jack Bauer posited that many Americans believed it to be their divine mission to not just "overspread the continent from the Atlantic to the Pacific," but to also save mankind through exporting Christianity and the "American Way." During the 1840s and 1850s, this political and religious doctrine made its way to the western frontiers of North America, as well as the international regions of Cuba and Mesoamerica, generating a period of extreme volatility and change.[1] This symbiotic volatility and change occurred as the United States expanded, while perhaps simultaneously defining the extension of religious and political supremacy over an unruly, savage, and now fanatical frontier. The Utah War stood as a part of this larger messiah complex and national vision of Manifest Destiny over the frontier, with Mormonism embodying its anticipated obstructions and barbaric tendencies which sat in the way of this divinely decreed national progress and white Christian rule.

Former associate justice of the Utah Territorial Supreme Court William W. Drummond, whom we will encounter again in this chapter, gave voice and shape to indistinct national fears by portraying the Mormons as an aberration that posed a threat to the well-being and survival of the entire Christian republic. By 1857, the republic of the United States and Utah went to war. At a moment in history highlighted by new waves of revivalism and religious enthusiasm, together with economic depression, expansionist expectations, and polarized politics, religion and politics were not easily separated; and while Mormons justified their resistance as a religious imperative within a larger persecution narrative, other Americans drew upon religion-infused political ideals and rhetoric that reached back to the Puritan era. These religio-political ideals fostered an understanding of society that necessitated a larger clash between faith and infidelity, in which Mormonism and the frontier played a key role. The Utah War of 1857–1858, rather than being merely fueled by fears of Mormon violence and fanaticism—as evidenced by the Mountain Meadows Massacre and the Springville murders—was a culmination of sorts as two powers which viewed themselves as carrying forth the true vision of Christ's kingdom to the frontier, came to grips with each other and eventually with their beliefs.

Attempting to transcend these similarly held faith narratives in this chapter, the Utah War is to be placed within a larger context of the international frontier the United States had become engaged with in the 1850s; which despite the nation's seemingly secular objectives of social order and expansion, were informed by religious themes and beliefs which have been overlooked, denied, or underinvestigated by historians. By seeing the Utah War as part of a much larger narrative of American expansion and attempts at self-definition, both politically and religiously, we can find an attempt by the U.S. government to rein in and narrow what American-ism meant. A narrower and more manageable definition could solidify its particular form of moral republican governance that the federal gov-ernment had developed by mid-century, and justify the social and reli-gious implications rising therefrom, which included "Bleeding Kansas," the Utah War, and the events that precipitated the Civil War. Obviously, these were no idle endeavors of a still-forming nation and struck at the heart of those who anticipated the millennial designs of the kingdom of God in America. In understanding this era's millennial beliefs as they affect the state, important points of focus would include Kansas, the Utah War, and William Walker's filibustering in Central America.

Historiographical difficulties with the Utah War do not arise from a lack of research or interest in the topic, but rather from the parochialism of Mormon historiography that has made it difficult to link it to these larger national religious contexts. Recent efforts by William MacKin-non, Will Bagley, and David Bigler have rightfully emphasized the reli-gious fanaticism and its resultant violence on the part of the Mormons, but overstated that emphasis by contrasting this scenario with that of a secular and reasonable democratic republic. For MacKinnon, the con-flict in Utah was reduced to differing philosophies of governance: "one secular, conventional, and republican, while the other was authoritar-ian, millennial and theocratic."[2] Historians of Mormonism have recog-nized the significance of religion with the Mormon kingdom in Utah, but there has been a deep disconnect with the significance of religion in antebellum America more broadly.

Another trend within Mormon historiography has been to downplay religion from both sides. Pioneering a new critical lens for the study of Mormonism, Juanita Brooks's watershed *Mountain Meadows Massacre* (1950) focused more on local fears of an oncoming federal army than on religious motivation in the infamous Mormon massacre, while Richard Turley's heavily footnoted study *Massacre at Mountain Meadows* (2008) employed a psychological narrative that served to humanize the event and its participants, thereby minimizing the role of religion from either side of the conflict.[3] The Utah War was a kind of "clash of civilizations" that, as noted by Sarah Gordon and Jan Shipps in their recent corrective to this historiographical neglect, included not just themes of violence, patriarchy, westward expansion, and slavery, but just as importantly religion. Though focusing more on Methodist and Mormon individuals who clashed in rural southern Utah, Gordon and Shipps articulate the importance of recognizing "religion as a central theme" in order to situate "Mountain Meadows more firmly in American history."[4] In important ways, religion represents a type of community resource that fashions and protects a particular group's identity and justifies their geographic claims, and the Utah War and the massacre at Mountain Meadows demonstrate a specific moment when those resources came into conflict and contestation with those of another group. Expanding beyond Gordon and Shipps's highlighting of religion on the individual and local level as it tragically intersected in southern Utah, this chapter looks at the major differences between the meaning of republican government and its implications for frontier settlement as an aspect of this kingdom of God narrative. Due to these "unseen" elements that Americans sought to orient themselves to in their quest to subjugate the frontier and cause it to "blossom as a rose," as well as the secular mediums employed, such as politics and economic policy, historians since Turner have had a difficult time discerning the role of religion in the history of the American West.

This neglect of religion is a much larger problem in American historiography and is not just a challenge for Mormon historians. Western historians Todd Kerstetter and Ferenc Szasz observe that "the religious dimension of the American West has been slighted" and that a "purely secular version of western history is a 'lie about the West.'"[5] As argued by Kevin Schultz and Paul Harvey, American historians have left this particular chapter of national history "to those who identify explicitly as religious historians," and in so doing they have failed to fully account for "what motivated leaders to push for social change" and thus miss "vital parts of what has created and sustained coalitions" that deeply influenced America's journey into the modern world.[6] By considering expansion attempts in Latin America, domestic crisis in Kansas, and overlooked aspects of the Utah War, religion illuminates an essential component of American ideology and engagements during this nation-building period. Better understanding of the nation's complicated relations with religious liberty (and the lack of such) contextualizes the Utah War as the nation's playing out of its Manifest Destiny and religion's role in its winning of the international frontier. Without claiming to exhaust the motives and factors of the Utah War or any of these events and their larger international, theological, and frontier contexts, we can rethink the traditional narratives that largely juxtapose theocratic Mormonism with a secular Jeffersonian republic. It is necessary to consider and reconsider the role of religion within general American society and its dynamic interactions with the functions of the state and its citizens in the decade of the 1850s.

In the year 1857, Protestant America and Utah were preparing to go to war, a war that grew out of and was encouraged by American expansionism fueled by religious anticipation, together with its symbolic and mythological visions of the frontier. Combined, these forces created a powerful, enormous political and theological narrative that made the frontier into a literal and symbolic border at which barbarism and Christian civilization came into conflict, revealing the invisible forces behind the visible conflict. The West thus became a sacred realm and resource that was a staging ground for this invisible cosmic battle, heightening the idea that the frontier must be visibly won and protected for Christ. Protestants fought this invisible cosmic battle that transcended ordinary time on a variety of visible levels, including the building of an overland railway and sending an army to Utah. The goal, then, of the historian is not just to include religion as one would economics or politics, but rather to recognize the religious themes within the contestations of both economic policy and political agitation. These national struggles, which seemed economic and political, can also be seen in terms of the religious struggle and transition in America, a transition which, just prior to the Civil War, brought forth a public and militant expression of national Christian faith—which, unfortunately, shaded into a particular religious approach to American power that made conflict and division in the 1850s and 1860s inevitable.

## MANIFEST DESTINY AND THE EXPANDING FRONTIER

To understand the national religious and cultural limitations that reactions to Mormonism both provoked and exposed, it is important to contextualize these boundaries within the larger national vision of what it meant to be American—in other words, presumptions of Christian morality, racial supremacy, and national progress as it pertained to new religious ideas. National progress and the need for geographic expansion were evident and deeply entwined with the popularization of the emergence of millenarian thought. Also entwined with this is the importance of the American kingdom of God as it related to Americans' idealized yet unofficial unity that worked to bring together various denominations for this shared higher purpose. Standing in the center of this millenarian drive, the shifting role of conventional religion and its presumptions toward social morality were more than ever anticipated to lead to and secure an international struggle at which this Anglo-Protestant kingdom of God would be extended and reborn.

Being anything but a static theological term, millenarianism had broad reference to the belief in a millennium, or thousand-year reign of Christ on earth with his saints. So influential had this new school of thought become in America by the mid-nineteenth century, that the Bible was now said to "wear a new visage and speak with a new tongue—a tongue not very intelligible, in many of its utterances, to the uninitiated." At this time for many Protestant Americans, nearly every domestic—and international—issue became part of the majority white Protestant vision of itself; a vision that upheld feelings of divine election, stewardship, and chosenness to serve and usher in God's reign on Earth. Indeed, the 1850s stood as a period in American history when millenarian doctrines created "very high pretensions" and "no small stir" among Protestant Americans, inspiring a new reading of religion and its relationship to society. In 1853, the *Princeton Review* charted the more popular version of millenarian thought that Christ's reign was "already here," and that the millennium was not to be some otherworldly event, but was instead "nothing more and nothing else than the increased expansion and power of our present Christianity," and nothing was to distinguish it from the present period "except the greater prevalence of true religion, and the various changes and blessings that are its natural accompaniments and consequents." According to this school of thought, Christ's actual return to earth was to follow this thousand-year period that the *Review* described as "Christ's great harvest period," where redemption and conversion were to envelope the entire world, thus readying it for the actual moment of his return, which these human efforts either hastened or slowed. Christ's kingdom, then, was separate from the millennium, as it was the medium by which Christ reigned on earth through his Holy Spirit, transforming the hearts of individuals and thus transforming through this kingdom popular expressions and expectations of America's political and social landscape.[7] In the same way that the school house stood as an adjunct of the Christian church in early America, the political realm now took upon itself heightened importance in expanding the Christian cause.

Christ's kingdom on earth was a voluntary engagement, and, as articulated by the *Princeton Review*, the millennium "has already commenced on earth in the hearts of his people" and is to be "perfected and perpetuated through everlasting ages in the world to come." Furthermore, the primary means of introducing the kingdom to the world resided in the "present agencies for spreading the gospel," in the "silent energy of the Holy Ghost."[8] Though representing an unseen order of God's sovereignty on earth, the expressions of this order were public and visible, and Americans began to imagine their implications. Anticipating the ultimate conversion of the entire world and its political ramifications, the *Review* outlined this philosophy as grounded in Nebuchadnezzar's visions as interpreted by the Old Testament prophet Daniel: "The God of Heaven shall set up a kingdom that shall break in pieces and consume all these kingdoms, and it shall stand for ever. The kingdom, too, all admit, is that stone cut out of the mountain without hands." Though this kingdom as a movement in America began small on the frontier of the British Empire, expectations of "its growth and powerful sway" were claims of global political inevitability. One did not need "peculiar laws of literal interpretation" in order to get this from the Bible, but rather those who had "a new heart who can understand the spelling-book, and can read intelligently the history of this country, can understand the greater and most essential portion of the word of God."[9]

As a testament to these new and great developments within Christianity, the converted believed themselves uniquely capable of discerning these invisible workings in ways that illuminated the true religious meaning behind national and even world events. As significant events like America's continued westward expansion came into such periphery of one Dr. Brainerd and others who read the "spelling book" of the times, they were able to discern from the newspapers "how God is governing his world." With such a framework, many Americans connected the vision of Daniel and the kingdom with the chaos and violence of the era including that of the expanding frontier, allowing for progressive interpretations of such destructive events as the natural progression, as this new kingdom was to be built upon the ruins of the kingdoms of the world.[10] During this new millennial dispensation, the Bible itself would become "out of date" and Christians would look for a "new revelation from God, to supersede, partly, if not wholly, the present revelation." It was thus "God's method, in setting up a new dispensation of religion, to make a new revelation, adapted to the nature of the dispensation."[11] Political scientist J. C. Welling stated, in 1855, "It is because God is in nature that nature has its necessary laws; and it is because Providence is in humanity and in history, that humanity and history have their necessary laws." "History" then, was but a "manifestation of God's supervision of humanity."[12] Similarly, political scientist Patrick Dove declared in 1856 that history is slowly but surely working prophecy into fact, bringing forth the millennium by natural law even if the Holy Writ had not declared it.[13] Natural theology was not to be a substitute for the written Word, but significantly "true natural theology may be the great preparative for the universal acceptance of the written Word."[14] According to Welling's and Dove's thinking, the sacred was within history and was history, thereby heightening the influence and importance of religion and its role within American governance and its extension and direction of power in the American territories.

Americans saw themselves, notes historian Ernest Tuveson, as soldiers in the last and final battle between the unseen forces of God and the forces of Satan, of eternal order pitted against ravaging chaos.[15] With these themes dominating nineteenth-century American Protestantism, politicians and religious leaders mapped out the destiny of the chosen land via frontier expansionism, exemplified by not only presidents and secretaries of war, but adventurers and social activists—and these destinies were played out on the foreign shores of Nicaragua, as well as in Kansas and Utah. Secretary of State and future United States president James Buchanan Jr. fully backed these expansionist visions, encouraging President James K. Polk to annex all of Mexico in 1848. Embodying the new policy of expansionism of the Democratic Party, Polk pushed for aggressive expansionism against the British in the Northwest and Mexico in the Southwest. With his electoral victory in 1844 based upon this principle of expansion, Polk and other Democrats believed it their divine mandate to acquire land through vigorous federal action.[16] In 1854, Buchanan's ambitions were further defined and extended by the Ostend Manifesto under Northern Democrat president Franklin Pierce, which Buchanan (then Minister to Great Britain) helped draft, threatening war if Spain did not surrender Cuba. Though obviously a descendant of Manifest Destiny, and directed by political balance and the desire to extend slavery, the Ostend Manifesto was also outlined by Southern Democrats as "divine law"; indeed, the *US Review* wrote in 1853 that such expansion was the decree of God and the salvation of inferior races and religions.[17] "Expansion is in the future the policy of our country," marked Buchanan, "and only cowards fear and oppose it."[18] Due to the fact that "Cuba is almost within sight of our shores," together with Spain's immoral engagement with the slave market, Buchanan argued that it was impossible "that the light of civilization and religion can ever penetrate these dark abodes," and annexation into the United States was not just necessary, but a divine mandate.[19]

American expansionism was perceived by many as a form of Christian philanthropy to a benighted and blunted world, with Buchanan's sights not just on Cuba, but on Mexico and Paraguay. Regarding hopes to annex Cuba, Reverend Henry F. Bond explained in 1854 that "the cruelty of native Cubans was a 'natural characteristic,'" and that crime, smoking, miscegenation, and mental and physical deterioration were rampant among this degraded population. As the colonial rulers of Cuba were Spanish Catholics, whose policy it was "to retain the masses in ignorance," it was believed that their conditions could not improve without military aid from the United States. "Cuba needed North America to annex it and bring it true Christian civilization," which, argued Reverend Bond, it had "an office of philanthropy to receive her."[20] Such beliefs also fostered calls for similar American extension into the Philippines, furthering the heroics of the American Christian in light of the heathen barbarians of the frontier.[21] Describing the inhabitants as "Oriental Negroes," the Filipinos were "a dwarf variety of the African race," whose women climbed trees like monkeys and were as "ugly as baboons." Winthrop Sargent evoked familiar rhetoric as he noted that these islanders possessed "no religion whatsoever," finding it difficult to imagine a people so "sunk in barbarism."[22] Such religiously defined imperialist frameworks reflected the United States' growing militant-expansionist view of liberty and "pure republicanism" which grew out of these religio-cultural assumptions of America's global Manifest Destiny. The authority of American power was thus vested in "the people," who were being defined in very narrow religious and racially monolithic terms.

Such civil and religious beliefs are well exemplified in the figure and exploits of William Walker. A filibuster and newspaper editor in New Orleans and in California, Walker was a Southerner and was scorned by those in the North for his attempts to expand the institutional enslavement of African Americans in the South, however familiar his views of white supremacy and the expansion of American religious rule. Unsuccessful in his attempt to subjugate Mexico's province of Sonora to white Protestant leadership, Walker went on in his convictions of Manifest Destiny that he was "driven forward by the force of events" to conquer and set himself up as ruler of Nicaragua (1856–1857).[23] This was no act of a singular fanatic; indeed, Frank Leslie's *Illustrated* wrote of Walker in the April 12, 1856, issue: "It is certainly a grand destiny to which this man seems to have been called, for it certainly seems to including nothing short of the regeneration of up building of this republic." Nicaragua would surely benefit as well, for it would be introduced "into the family of enlightened and civilized nations."[24] Seen as "rootless adventurers," these filibusters and their supporters expressed their religious convictions of Manifest Destiny beyond the political boundaries of the United States, pushing these visions of expansionism to the political and religious extreme.[25]

Walker proceeded to set himself up in Nicaragua via military rule as its national president, soon demonstrating there was no room for "half-breed" inhabitants, especially if they were non-Anglo Catholics. Deeds and land ownership were limited to white English speakers, slavery was established, and the Spanish residents who had interracially mixed with Native people and with those of African descent were ridiculed as defiling and connecting themselves with people incapable of self-rule.[26] It was therefore necessary that this new frontier be governed under the hands of white American citizens by way of a military dictatorship, rather than something more akin to the cherished models of American republicanism. Walker's supporters believed that such "vaunted institutions are not suitable to every clime and race," and that when presented with this lack of political voice, native inhabitants accepted this arrangement with satisfaction and gratitude. As Walker and other filibusters looked to Middle and South America, they saw massive resources being neglected, which they hoped to exploit and develop, create markets and transit routes, and ultimately open networks of trade with the United States.[27] In his military enforcement of this white-Christian military rule, Walker was hailed by U.S. Southerners as an exponent of Southern white civilization and its potential economic and political power and destiny, with racial and religious supremacy being an important biblical reference point.[28] Indeed, "enemies of slavery" were "the enemies of American civilization," and thus the enemies of God's natural flow of human events.[29]

Despite Walker's popularity in carrying these actions out in foreign lands, critics at home found parallels between Walker's murderous ventures[30] in Nicaragua and those of Buchanan and his attempts, according to Honorable Frank P. Blair Jr. of Missouri, to populate, civilize, and bring peace to Central America. Blair noted that Buchanan's hypocritical attempts to civilize the Bay Islands by denying them "the guarantee of the American bill of rights" to be "a scandal to the age."[31] Though critics celebrated Walker's first failed efforts to hold power in Nicaragua, supporters in New Orleans (itself a bastion of American slavery) hailed him upon his return on May 27, 1857, with a grand reception and declarations that Walker was "one of the greatest captains and statesmen of the age" and an honor to "our institutions of liberty, intelligence and religion."[32] For those who upheld such expansionist efforts, white-Protestant religion and liberty were inseparable, and were interwoven with providential expectations. With Walker becoming a symbol of this narrow view of liberty, a Colonel Fadens declared that the "cause of Nicaraguan independence is not dead. . . . It lives this very day in the hearts of millions of freemen!" His initial failure, admitted Fadens, was an unfortunate turn of events, but under the expectation of divine providence and the natural flow of frontier expansion, "triumph is certain, just as certain as tomorrow's sun will rise"—and went on to predict that within ninety days, Nicaraguans would call for Walker to redeem them.[33] Despite the naïve confidence and optimism, many Southerners were devastated as Walker, on his second expedition to Nicaragua, was handed over to the Hondurans by the British, who executed him.[34] In some ways, for supporters of Walker, the divine "script" of frontier progress, both international and domestic, had been written, based on "notes" furthered by President Polk and the Ostend Manifesto, both domestic and foreign.

While those in the North rejected Walker's filibustering expeditions to Central America due to their exploitations and extensions of slavery, they shared many assumptions about the divine frameworks of American frontier expansionism and its link between religion and politics. In 1861, at the start of the Civil War and with direct reference to the South, Francis Vinton publicly framed such religio-political assumptions in New York's Trinity Church: that the United States was "divinely established" and that "disloyalty to the Constitution is therefore impiety toward God."[35] His convictions that federal rule equated with divine rule not only evoked beliefs that took flight in the 1840s and 1850s, but previewed how, during the oncoming Civil War, the Northern churches preached this concept more than anything else. The biblical justification of a divine right to rule for American political leaders in the North was firmly established in the 1850s and thus wielded power to compel state obedience as a Christian imperative.[36] In light of this form of political piety with the onset of the Utah War, U.S. Captain Stewart Van Vliet reminded Brigham Young in Utah of his "duty to God, as well as to man" to "submit freely & willingly to the authority of the U.S."[37] Our specific interest, however, lies in how Vinton's statement looks back and reinforces thinking during a decade in which there was politically based violence in Kansas and the United States declaration of war on Utah. Both conflicts grew out of the concept of popular sovereignty and the question of its limitations as based on religious thought. Although the official beginning of the Civil War was in April 1861, the Kansas-Nebraska Act (1854), which overthrew both the Missouri Compromise of 1820 that had denied the expansion of slavery into new states and the 1846 Wilmot Proviso that denied slavery in annexed Mexican land, now made the extension of black slavery legal, thereby surviving to propel conflict in Kansas and Utah and further defining national attitudes toward them. With this 1854 act, popular sovereignty became the law of the territories and so opened sectarian and sectional conflict that would bleed Kansas and pave the way for the Utah and Civil Wars.[38]

Kansas had long been "the great overshadowing trouble" of Pierce's administration, and now Stephen A. Douglas (1813–1861) and other prominent Democrats hoped to resolve the crisis via local popular sovereignty rather than federal coercion.[39] Illinois senator and chairman of the Committee on Territories, Douglas designed the Kansas-Nebraska Act and had been the leading proponent of popular sovereignty as a basic American right within the territories. In a speech delivered in June 1857 in Springfield, Illinois, before President Buchanan and others, Douglas argued in light of calls for military intervention in Kansas that this principle of "self-government which recognizes the right of the people of each State and Territory to form and regulate their own domestic institutions" should be given fair play.[40] At the same time, however, such a basic American right was limited to those of Anglo-Saxon heritage, thus complicating the Calhoun doctrine of nonintervention: it is the "rule of civilization and of Christianity the world over, that whenever any one man, or set of men, were incapable of taking care of themselves, they should consent to be governed by those more capable of managing their affairs for them." Echoing contemporary justifications for American expansionism, Douglas's belief was at least in part racially and religiously motivated as he explained that blacks, Indians, and Mormons (whom he also referred to as "freaks") were a few examples of those who were to share the dugout with the "idiot, the lunatic, the insane, blind, dumb, the unfortunate," while the wise and competent white Protestants took the playing field.[41] Such teachings were not technically scriptural, but rather came from what many at the time believed to be natural and divine law regarding religion and civil society, often needing no comment. As noted by the *Philadelphia Ledger* that same year, Christianity was the "perfect expression of that religion which is the fundamental law of our natures," being inseparable from America's divine road toward progress and liberty—a sentiment negatively applied to various marginal groups, including Mormons and Roman Catholics.[42]

Liberty itself was not seen as a cultural construct, but rather, notes Samuel Eliot in his two-volume *History of Liberty* (1854), came directly from the "world Emancipator [Jesus Christ]" from Galilee, in contrast to pagan and "mahometan" lands and governments, where, by divine design, there is "avowed and irresponsible despotism."[43] With more than a little guile, Mormons were conflated in the national press with the "followers of MAHOMET."[44] In the same way that Americans looked at Muslims, race and religion were inseparably linked, thereby implicitly linking Mormons as deserving of the same federal subjugation as given to other lower races.[45] As Douglas, a strong supporter of the Supreme Court's Dred Scott denigration of blacks as fully human, would argue in his debates with Abraham Lincoln, our government was "founded on the white basis," and the framers of the country had "no reference either to the negro, the savage Indian, the Fejee, the Malay, or any other inferior and degraded race, when they spoke of the equality of men."[46] Thus, popular sovereignty, as framed by Douglas and other Democrats, rested on the assumption that only Anglo-Saxon Protestants were capable of self-rule and, by implication, alone capable of revealing God's voice in American governance. As Presbyterian historian Robert Baird put it, only "the Anglo-Saxon race possesses qualities peculiarly adapted for successful colonization," while other races and nationalities—and by extension their non-Protestant faith—were by nature inferior and incapable.[47] Echoing these racial supremacy ideals, Buchanan spoke of Texas's independence from Mexico and annexation into the United States in similarly degrading rhetorical tones, explaining that "Anglo-Saxon blood could never be subdued by anything that claimed Mexican origin."[48]

The civil war in Kansas revealed just how difficult and complicated popular sovereignty could be—particularly since both sides that added to the violence in Kansas could claim Anglo-Saxon and Protestant roots. The Kansas-Nebraska Act brought immigrants into Kansas in droves, transforming a population of 800 into 8,000 within nine months.[49] Though not a majority, the Kansas territorial government quickly resembled, via dubious and illegal tactics, a strong pro-slavery governing body.[50] Free-Soilers who protested the new and unfair territorial government and its slave establishments created their own Free-Soil government in Topeka, selecting their own governor and congressional delegate.[51] With significant support from Congress, Free-Soilers boycotted national elections, wrote their own constitution, and pled for statehood. Most Democrats, however, as led by Presidents Pierce and Buchanan, declared the Topeka constitution and the Free-Soil cause treason and a case of significant territorial rebellion. In an address to Congress, Buchanan blamed the entire Kansas fiasco on the "organized rebellion" of the Free-Soil movement, whose boycott of elections disallowed the principle of popular sovereignty to work itself out. Had the Free-Soilers acted as obedient and patriotic Americans, peace could have prevailed, the economy would have been strong, and "popular sovereignty would thus have been vindicated in a constitutional manner," and Kansas would have been "perfectly free to form and regulate their domestic institutions in their own way."[52]

Religion entered into this political turmoil as both a corollary and a natural element. As an unrivaled supporter of abolitionism and a slave-free Kansas, New England minister Henry Ward Beecher, whose popularity granted him the status of almost a national saint, raised much support and awareness to the Free-Soil cause of Kansas.[53] Revenge and hatred may be scripturally unjustified toward one's enemy, argued Beecher to his congregation, but such was a "state of mind" and did not touch "at all the question of what kind of instruments men may employ" on one's enemy. "We know that there are those who will scoff at the idea of holding a sword or a rifle in a Christian state of mind. I think it is just as easy to hold an argument in a Christian state of mind." Frankly, he explained, "there was more moral power in one of those instruments [Sharp rifles: a.k.a. "Beecher's Bibles"], so far as the slaveholders of Kansas were concerned, than in a hundred Bibles." Beecher went on to raise and send substantial support to the rebellious Kansas government, marking his Plymouth Church the "Church of the Holy Rifles," and helping to establish as precedent the pulpit as the "golden reed" in measuring the makeup of American civil society.[54] In the case of Kansas, Beecher clearly believed that Jael's hammer, in the form of religious violence and civil rebellion, were justified and demanded to break up unrighteous structures on the Western frontier and to bring in, in Bushnell's words, "a new era of power"—an era that was needed as delusional fanaticism and false religion (on the side of slavery or polygamy) caused the forfeiture of popular sovereignty. Such welding together of politics and religious certitude assisted in setting the stage for the nation's destiny and stewardship in the West.

Standing in the hub of American religious thought and experience in Boston at Park Street Church (a.k.a. "Brimstone Corner"),[55] Henry Beecher's father, Lyman Beecher, had argued two decades earlier that if we failed to establish an American religious purity in the West, "our destruction will be as signal as the birth-right abandoned, the mercies abused and the provocation offered to beneficent Heaven."[56] It was also from this capital of the Puritan commonweal that famed revivalist Charles G. Finney in December 1856 sparked new revivals and great millennial interest, causing "a general interest on the subject of religion" that was "felt throughout the city, among all denominations of Christians." As argued by Kathryn Long, these revivals increasingly turned an earlier disinterested benevolence to that of "the political arena as a more effective means to advance" religious concerns.[57] Politics could be deeply theological, and Northern ministers and newspapers criticized the idea that God's law was merely a Sunday affair: "Religion belongs to everyday; to the place of business as much as to the church."[58] Such revivals produced "extraordinary religious excitement," witnessing unprecedented growth of Protestant denominations and religious political interest.[59] "The Christian church," marked Finney, "was designed to make aggressive movements in every direction—to lift up her voice and put forth her energies against iniquity in high and low places—to reform individuals, communities, and government, and never rest until the kingdom . . . shall be given to the people . . .—until every form of iniquity shall be driven from the earth." In his *Systematic Theology*, Finney articulated that Christians were "bound to exert their influence to secure a legislation that is in accordance with the law of God."

In their attempts to sacralize the mundane, many revivalists in the 1850s found themselves making their religious mark in their daily profession—namely as editors, politicians, bankers, military leaders, soldiers, businessmen and educators.[60] The revivals of 1856–1859 powerfully affected urban classes, rather than just those of the rural American pastures. Even James Buchanan, near his summer house in Bedford Springs, Pennsylvania, was reported by revivalists as having "attended daily upon the prayer-meetings with most exemplary and respectful attention."[61] Though these revivals were not themselves political, those involved often translated their efforts in very political ways, as historian Leonard Sweet summarized: "Political change was to emerge out of a non political revival."[62] Henry W. Beecher, a leading figure in these urban "businessman" revivals, led the way in his political activism in Kansas and his active campaigning for Republican John C. Frémont in 1856, as had other Protestants in their organized political support of his opponent, James Buchanan.[63]

As seen with Henry Beecher, when revivalists like Finney spoke of prayer, he did not speak of otherworldly interests alone, but powerfully brought to mind the importance of immediate social reform and volunteer human action—including political reform and even war. It was not until the 1870s that more individualistic and pietistic expressions of Christianity took popular hold in American society, leaving the kingdom of visible laws as entrenched in this Old Testament Calvinist covenant definitive of the 1850s. While politicians at times appeared lax in mingling their religious influence with public matters of the state, Bostonians saw themselves as leading the country in the conflation of the two, sparking revivals throughout Massachusetts in 1856, and from there, the nation.[64] Beecher's Bostonian sentiments both framed and joined in a chorus of other voices concerning the American West as the place and pinnacle of America's religious and political identity and destiny, heightening his efforts in Kansas. These attitudes, canvassed in chapter 1, combined with the general sentiment that Mormon theocracy and polygamy were offenses to Christian morality and Protestant-style republicanism, however familiar they were to this Calvinist-Puritan kingdom of Old Testament law. Mormonism was seen as a perilous alternative to the traditional American kingdom and its normalized morality, representing a serious threat to America's prevalent millennial vision of the kingdom, thus sparking the fear which gave rise to the national political response. Indeed, the existence of Mormonism in the West made Christ's advent less imminent and, as argued by U.S. Col. Patrick Connor, a Mormon extermination would help quell God's wrath on the nation.[65] Stephen Douglas, who sought an "Empire of liberty," called for Congress to "apply the knife and cut out this loathsome, disgusting ulcer."[66] As it was being argued since 1852 within the highest realms of government that Utah was the one spot in the entire Christian civilized world where morality and civilization were not, it could hardly be expected that it would be ignored or that religion played no part.[67]

## THE UTAH WAR

When Buchanan sent troops to Utah in the late summer of 1857, the national press described Mormons as "a set of intolerable idolaters who have erected the odious Dagon of their worship on a portion of American soil." As a "Christian and civilized people," wrote the *New York Times*, Americans could not afford to tolerate such "absurdities, usurpations, indecencies and villainies of the worst form of Paganism."[68] In contrasting this blasphemy of Mormonism and its settlement upon "Christian soil," the *Times* assured its readers that its calls for "scenes of blood" were not a "crusade against religious faith" but a "war against treason, murder, arson and rapine."[69] As it was being felt by many, Mormonism ran "counter, as their tenets and practices do, to the cherished truths of Christian morality," thereby demanding federal attention.[70] That same year, U.S. secretary of war James B. Floyd and President James Buchanan made assurances regarding sending troops to Utah. Though not a "religious crusade," it was argued that the military had the benevolent and moral duty to bring Mormons to "their senses, to convert them into good citizens and to spare the effusion of human blood."[71] While his close friend and political ally Robert Tyler (son of former president John Tyler) admonished Buchanan to tap into "the almost universal excitements of an Anti-Mormon Crusade," Buchanan couched his actions against Utah as a populist and moral one: "This movement upon that Territory was demanded by the moral sentiment of the country."[72]

Having cast this religious anxiety into more secular terms, Buchanan and the *Times* retained a proscription against this aberrant religion, while maintaining intact the American idea of religious freedom—for to them, Mormonism was not a religion, but a threat to itself, true religion, and republican institutions.[73] Looking back on events in late 1858, Buchanan attributed his sending of troops to Utah as an "act of mercy and humanity to those deluded people, for it prevented the effusion of blood."[74] U.S. Capt. John Phelps spoke to this larger American ethos as he explained, on his march to Utah in the summer of 1857, that there was "evidently no place in Christendom for such extravagance as Mormonism"; and as Henry W. Beecher and Knox College president Jonathan Blanchard would attest, false religion and its associated sexual vices directly hindered the progress of Christ's kingdom in America.[75] Prominent historian Philip Schaff acknowledged that in the United States moral progress and Christian civilization via the voluntary principle toward political involvement had "triumphed in the whole country, except in the abnormal territory of the Mormons."[76] Only a few years before the Utah War, Schaff begged his foreign audience to "not judge America in any way by this irregular growth," demonstrating that Mormon barbarism in the American West was so out of place with American Christianity and progress, that "Americans cannot be particularly blamed for wishing to be rid of such a pest." Based upon these irreconcilable religious principles, Schaff predicted that an "armed interference" between Utah and the nation was therefore inevitable and imminent. "Separation of church and state by no means involves a separation of the nation from Christianity and Christian morality," and Mormonism demonstrated the limits of this American tolerance.[77]

With popular sovereignty defined within these widely held, yet narrow racial and religious boundaries, together with the massive influx of Irish Catholics in the mid- to late 1840s, immigration became a widespread concern in the 1850s. From an epicenter of the 1857–1858 urban religious revivals, James W. Alexander warned, from a New York City pulpit, that immigration to the western states and territories was more dangerous to the American vision of Christ's kingdom than slavery. "Unless the means of grace can be made in some degree to keep pace with the growth of our population, our rising States must be abandoned to error, infidelity, and disorder."[78] Massive Mormon convert-migrations made these fears all the more worrisome, causing Douglas to recognize Utah as full of "alien outlaws," and thus unworthy participants in popular sovereignty. Buchanan's motives against Utah, however, were many and complex, allowing for a broader view of how religion and politics had come to intersect.

There were clear economic and strategic benefits in subjugating Utah to federal power. Breaking up Mormonism's monopoly over freight and mail upheld the desires of speculators and contractors, something important to Democrats. For example, Magraw and Hockaday, close friends of Buchanan who had been outbid in 1856 over the Utah mail contracts, would have been particularly delighted. Sending troops to Utah also promised renewed army supply contracts as the Indian difficulties in Florida were coming to an end, inspiring some to call the expedition a "contractor's job." The "lucky individuals" who secured the "exorbitant contracts" to transport the thousands of cattle and immense supply trains across the plains in advance, wrote William "Buffalo Bill" Cody, were made "very wealthy."[79]

Geographically, Utah was an important location for the transcontinental railroad, essential for economic growth, safe travel, trade, military transport, and land speculation. Furthered by the discovery of gold at Sutter's Mill in 1848, Utah had become a necessary "middle route" to California and thus important for national speculation and trade profits, such as the Cattle Boom of 1857.[80] In opposing a bill that would open the possibility for slavery in the new Western Territories, Senator Edward Everett of Massachusetts argued in 1854 that the West beyond the Missouri held great strategic importance for the future of American power, not unlike Persia, Media, and Assyria did for Asia. "The commerce of the world, eastward from Asia, and westward from Europe, is destined to pass through the gates of the Rocky Mountains over the iron pathways which we are even now about to lay down through those Territories [meaning Kansas and Nebraska]. Cities of unsurpassed magnitude and importance are destined to crown the banks of their noble rivers." The internal development of the West could not be hindered by either black or white slavery (meaning polygamy), two themes commonly conflated at the time.[81]

In both his inaugural and his annual address, Buchanan set the transcontinental railroad as one of his top priorities, as it would secure uninterrupted access to the Pacific, aiding national security and Mormon control, together with economic expansion through land speculation and opening U.S. trade to international markets.[82] There was also great uneasiness if not fear in the East concerning Mormonism's highly efficient cooperative irrigation networks and expansionist colonial endeavors, which left individual Protestant ranchers and farmers unable to compete.[83] Though secular, many saw such needs as central to civilizing and bringing Christian morality to the frontier. Ten years earlier, for example, Horace Bushnell argued the "sooner we have railroads and telegraphs spinning into the wilderness, . . . the more certain it is that light, good manners and Christian refinement, will become universally diffused."[84] Not only would the rail effectively destroy the idea of the isolated frontier, ensuring sustained industrial growth and international trade, as well as bringing communication, people and goods, but it was only after the completion of the Union Pacific Rail that Utah's non-Mormon population became a significant minority.[85]

Buchanan had political concerns to be addressed, and the Utah War provided opportunities. For one, sending troops to Utah became a necessary distraction from Kansas, already an epicenter of the sectional crisis.[86] With a divided party and nation to consider, sending troops to Utah promised unifying factors for Buchanan, not unlike Secretary of State William Seward's 1861 suggestion to President Abraham Lincoln to quickly start a foreign war to unify the broken nation at the time of the Civil War.[87] Buchanan's friend Robert Tyler admonished him to "put down and utterly extirpate" Mormonism. Being an issue that concerned "all the religious bodies" and reached "every man's fireside," Tyler called on Buchanan to raise a "strong fearless and resolute hand." If only he would, Tyler assured his friend that "the country I am sure will rally to you" with such great enthusiasm that the "pipings of Abolitionism will hardly be heard amidst the thunders of the storm we shall raise."[88] Having promised not to intervene in the South, sending troops to Kansas would have destroyed Buchanan's support of the slave-holding South, but a military expedition to Utah presented a political and religious issue in which all could potentially unite, be they the xenophobic Know-Nothing Party (then at the height of its power), the proslavery Democrats in the South who desired attention be diverted from Kansas as well as new opportunities for corporate expansion in the West, or the antipolygamy Republicans of the North.[89] There were also concerns independently religious. According to family members and associates, Buchanan was a "very pious Presbyterian" who believed strongly in the moral law as then preached in America and its ideals of Manifest Destiny and expansion, much of which has already been explained. At the same time, as a proslavery Democrat, Buchanan denied the role of the federal government to attack sin (such as slavery) and appeared to take seriously Jefferson's ideal of the separation of church and state, at least as it was then being defined in the South against Northern abolitionist ministers.[90]

Though the tide of public opinion swung against the Mormons, Buchanan, and the Congress that committed to the war, the American public had been effectively influenced by the narrative that Utah posed a threat to the United States over religious and political differences to an Anglo-Protestant hegemony. In the early 1850s, Judge William W. Drummond, though of an excessively short and controversial tenure in Utah, promoted such a narrative in his prolific writings about Mormon-

ism and Utah to Buchanan and the eastern press.[91] Drummond cited
his failure as a federal official in Utah as evidence of innate Mormon
disloyalty and hostility toward the US government.[92] Not only were
Mormons naturalizing alien enemies, Drummond claimed, they were
inducting them into secret blood oaths against the nation. These new
secretive covenants that Mormons engaged in directly contrasted with
the public American covenant that had begun with John Winthrop,
expressing the incompatibility of Utah's claims of popular sovereignty
and statehood. Drummond went on to report that Utah had on hand
one hundred thousand Mormons who had covenanted to avenge their
slain prophets; they had sent over two hundred thousand "spies and
agents" throughout the continent; and were allied with three hundred
thousand Indians "upon our western borders."[93] Although official Mormon rhetoric throughout the nineteenth century spoke of taking over
the country, it was understood from within the shared visions of Daniel
which anticipated a divine (rather than human led) destruction of all
wicked societies and kingdoms, leaving only the righteous behind to
build God's Zion.[94]

Drummond declared that no one in the country was safe from the
grand Mormon conspiracy. Beyond threats of Mormon plots to attack
the United States, Drummond advanced ideas that Mormon missionaries were recruiting unsuspecting female converts throughout the
country, luring them in their naiveté away to Utah. Once there, such
converts did not find their promised eternal happiness, but rather
treachery and death. Though sensationalized, it is accurate that the
policy had been enacted by Brigham Young in Mormon missions at
the time Drummond was in Utah to not speak of polygamy or other
such peculiarities to Mormon converts. Instead, if converts wanted
to learn of "the mysteries," missionaries were instructed by Brigham
Young to "send them home" to Zion where such things could more
easily and carefully be understood.[95] Though many likely found what
they had anticipated and rejoiced, there can be little doubt that some
of these converts arrived in Utah shocked and confused at what they
found. Many, however, had little option of returning to their abandoned homelands with their newly strained community and family
relations back home, since most converts came from poorer economic
classes who largely looked with suspicion on these foreign missionar-

ies, and were, once in Utah, financially indebted to the church for their travels and settlement.

Hinting about the Danites, a secret vigilante movement, and the Mormon doctrine of Blood Atonement, Drummond took it even further by insisting that as such disenchanted converts attempted to leave Utah, a secret band under Brigham Young cut the throats of young men and made mistresses of the women. Feeding into the public taste for captivity narratives then popular within anti-Catholic literature, as well as popular accusations of "white slavery" as connected to Mormon polygamy, Drummond contrasted the light and beauties of the Anglo-Protestant civilization, to those of blighted and despondent Mormon Utah. In parallel with David Pletcher's argument regarding President Polk and the role of propaganda in the 1840s in justifying the Mexican War and its annexation of 602 million acres of Mexico, Drummond reignited this "artificial fury" of the press against Utah, reminding Buchanan and the American public of their "divine favoritism" in the annexation and possession of western lands, particularly Utah.[96] In his heavy utilization of religious imagery and obligation, Drummond found powerful national support by demonstrating how Mormonism brought forth the devolution of God's great millennial plan for America and the need to control Utah, being in direct contrast to the "pure and holy principles of the religion of the cross." While drawing on the triumphs of Protestant civilization over the frontier, Drummond pointed to a religiously bankrupt and morally broken Mormon Utah that now rolled "back the tide of time" to an age when "an almost Cimmerian darkness covered the earth."[97]

In ways similar to other former territorial officials, Drummond claimed that the "whole community" in Utah was swept away in "fanatic intolerance" and wholesale Mormon violence. Mormon fanaticism was accentuated by Drummond and the popular press by pointing to Mormonism's heavy emphasis on obedience to church leaders and their expounding of the "blood atonement" doctrine, one of the more infamous teachings of Joseph Smith, but made explicit during the heightened enthusiasm of the Mormon Reformation (1856–1857) as led by Brigham Young and other leaders. These sources also relied on Young's encouragement and support of vigilante justice and violence, against both Mormons and non-Mormons.[98] Not only was this propaganda alarming, but it posed a stark contradiction to the myth of the frontier that was said to instill individualism, religious conviction, and democratic liberty, bringing out fears that God's grand American designs were being mocked. In juxtaposition to America's great religious obligation over the West, Drummond called Mormonism under Brigham Young a "strange system of terrorism," a claim exacerbated by the Mountain Meadows Massacre in September 1857, in which nearly 140 emigrant men, women, children, and infants were either killed or kidnapped by Mormons under the direction of priesthood leadership.[99]

Debates within Congress and in the public sphere, as publicized by newspapers, not only reveal these religiously fueled beliefs, but demonstrate that questions of morality were becoming a matter of interest for a federal government centralizing its power, rather than just a matter for individual states and territories. For one, the newspapers, both Northern and Southern, while not ignoring the political aspects of Utah's issues, including controversies surrounding territorial officials, often touched on religious issues. The *Union*, a Southern-based periodical, described Mormon polygamy as "a frightful social evil," agreeing with the Northern pulpit speeches that Mormonism had no place in a "civilized and Christian country." However, heavy military and legal action against the sin of polygamy came too close to legitimating action against the sin of slavery, and thus Southerners sought to redirect religious energy to that of the local citizens via voluntary efforts. The *Union* spoke against using federal force "to improve the moral condition of a distant people like the Mormons" as "unadvisable and unnecessary," as the military was not "advanced far enough into the intensity of civilization to enter upon the work of religious crusades."

The energy and moral force of the American people, however, could afford such appropriate remedies. "The whole system of Mormon religion belongs exclusively to the people of Utah. If we may not look to them for the needful correction, we may surely rely upon the energy and moral force of the American people to apply the appropriate remedies."[100] The abolitionist periodical *The National Era* lambasted the *Union*'s light stance on Utah, and upheld the Democratic administration's use of military force to compel Mormon obedience to righteous Christian law.[101] In an article that positioned proslavery Fire-Eaters in Congress as supportive of Utah polygamy, the *National Era* reprinted a letter to the editor of the *Richmond South*. The letter declared that the Mormons were right in chasing out mean-spirited and slanderous territorial officials who were "strangers" to the territory: "My sympathies as a State Rights man are with the Mormons." The position was that if we "let the Mormons be crushed for their religion—for that is the real difficulty," then slavery itself would be crushed. "The same measure that is dealt out to them for our slaveholding, by the same people, if they had the power; and God only knows (if things go on as they are tending) how long that power will be wanting."[102]

On their side, in ways that parallel later ex-Confederate complaints against federal officers during Reconstruction in the South, Mormons insisted their defiance was not against the federal government, but rather against unworthy officials employed by the U.S. government who unnecessarily provoked the Mormon people. Though Mormons did their fair share of provocations, historian Norman Furniss gives credence to such claims, as Washington found filling territorial positions in the West difficult, and thus sent "inept, or, on occasion, morally reprehensible men to fill the positions." Drummond was no exception, and Brigham Young was quick to point out Drummond's personal immoralities and dishonesty in an effort to further Mormon self-rule and their attempt to obey God's higher law, which a strong federal government now threatened.[103] Despite defaming Washington-sent officials and retaining his seat as Utah's territorial governor, Young's belligerent tone toward Buchanan, together with the larger cultural-religious background that had in part defined itself against Young, provided strong sympathy for Drummond's testimony.[104]

Such reports of religious violence and injustice in Utah, some accurate and some not, played a key role in moving Buchanan to take up his duties toward Utah—duties which echoed his own sentiments of extension of American power and the primacy of the Anglo-Saxon peoples. Convinced of the developments in Utah as outlined by Drummond and others, Buchanan cancelled Utah's mail contracts and assembled a military expedition. When Utah's territorial representative, John M. Bernhisel, pled for a congressional investigation committee, the House instead resolved on December 23, 1857, to send into committee "the expediency of immediately excluding Mr. Bernhisel from his seat."[105] The national press weighed in on the issue: the *Cincinnati Enquirer* reported on Drummond's effectiveness in stirring national attention and building popular pressures that insisted on the stronger hand of federal intervention in Utah in hopes of its annexation to the "adjoining Christian communities." As it continued, "public attention has been turned so prominently by the statements of Judge Drummond, to the condition of things in Utah, that the Federal government can no longer omit the duty of prompt and energetic action in the premises."[106]

However much Democrat politicians denied that military action against the Mormons was motivated by religious concerns, the U.S. government nonetheless felt increasingly endowed with the correct religion and proper morality to respond to the sins of some of its citizens and leaders, even as individuals rallied through volunteer efforts. In October 1857, Brigham Young's counselor George Q. Cannon expressed his concerns that the state "would boil over with volunteers to go and clean out the 'Mormons,' if the Government would ever call on them."[107] In 1858 the House sent through a bill that called for regiments of citizen volunteers that could go to Utah under executive order. Though demonstrating its popularity, there was backlash. Opposing this bill, Representative Charles J. Faulkner of Virginia (Dem) and chairman of the committee on Military Affairs, called this good political posturing due to its massive popularity, but bad military policy, which would end in religiously fueled mob violence against America's unloved minorities. He contended that such "volunteers would be appealing to the passions of the community, and setting a precedent for carrying desolation to our own citizens, which might become, in the future, prolific of the most disastrous consequences." In light of John Brown's recent populist volunteer religious use of violence against the sins of slavery in Kansas which many in the North found inspirational,[108] and the heightened religious passions surrounding slavery and abolition, it was hard to miss the religious and military implications of this bill targeting polygamy, which might lead to and justify further violence. Faulkner understood that the "war in Utah was a war against the people on account of their religion. Whoever engaged in such a war, whether volunteers or regulars, would be guilty of murder."[109] Nevertheless, the North began to solidify around the idea that religion and related aspects of morality were an essential function of republicanism and the federal government, and both Kansas and Utah became the public anvil upon which to shape these political ideals.

Finally, President James Buchanan's experiences and pronouncements revealed how unavoidably politics and religion were entwined, and just how heated contestations between them were. Still, he claimed, sending troops to Utah was no religious crusade and had long resisted the idea. "From my soul," he retorted against presidential candidate General Winfield Scott in 1852, "I abhor the practice of mingling up religion with politics."[110] However, national events over the question of slavery and its religious implications overshadowed Buchanan's public statements on separation, placing them within a very particular context that was governed through the pulpit and press throughout the 1850s, and then widely printed in various popular magazines and journals.[111] Buchanan worried that mingling abolitionist pulpits with national politics created a treasonous gospel of antislavery, thereby challenging him and his party. After the 1857 Dred Scott Supreme Court decision, Buchanan's own Presbyterian Church, together with Methodists, Baptists, and other Protestant denominations, was more deeply divided than ever over the meaning and role of American religion and American governance. As proslavery Southern Presbyterian synods who supported the decision of the Court split from the New School General Assembly that year, the antislavery northern synods reported "satisfaction and delight."[112]

For Protestants in the North, the pulpit served the role of preaching the "pure word of God" as it pertained to civil life and government, while Southern Protestants argued for their distinction when it came to the institution of slavery. During the Fugitive Slave law debates of 1850, William Hosmer explained that the pulpit "is necessarily subversive of every form of human wickedness," and according to the "higher law," true "patriotism does the same." The Fugitive Slave Act required officers to return "runaway slaves" to their "masters" with little more proof than an affidavit, even if the fugitive slave was recovered in free states. Beyond this, the new law punished anyone giving aid to those who escaped slavery, and since they had no rights to trial or testimony, many free blacks were kidnapped into enslavement. In light of this higher law against such injustice, patriotism demanded moral/religious supremacy over civil law, and when moral and religious contradictions came, Northern ministers argued that "patriotism absolutely demands resistance to bad laws."[113] As many clergymen prayed "thy kingdom come" each Sunday, they were not to sit on the sides of politics, but rather join them together in the performance of His will on earth as it was in heaven, despite constitutional limitations on religion. It was their job, then, as members in this invisible kingdom of Christ, to transform earthly politics into God's will on earth. In this light, Northern ministers through the Fugitive Slave law debates, tightly linked together religious piety and political action, making themselves self-styled "heralds of the kingdom of God" and proclaimers of this "higher law."[114]

In 1857, the impossibility of separating religion from the federal government was further demonstrated when Buchanan's U.S. Army general Winfield Scott ordered Brig. Gen. William S. Harney to lead a military mission to Salt Lake City, which Harney interpreted as a religious mission that was in continuation with the ancient biblical wars of Jethro, Moses, Joshua, and David, Old Testament tropes that were familiar to many nineteenth-century Americans.[115] Indeed, in his letter informing him of his military mission to Utah, Harney was advised by Lt. Col. George W. Lay to bring with his soldiers volunteer Christian missionaries who "might do great good," further exemplifying the twinned political aims of the United States and those of Christian evangelism, which might be best indicated by Lyman Beecher's drive toward purifying the nation of non-Christians.[116] Even government surveyor and explorer Capt. John W. Gunnison exposed a popular hope of religious evangelism for Utah in his more sympathetic Utah travel account published in 1857: "For its virtuous industry we praise, for its brotherly unity we admire— and for its induction into the one Catholic Church we offer our sincere prayers."[117] Not all, however, had such sympathies, nor were attempts to convert Mormons into good citizens limited to the sending of Harney's army and accompanying missionaries. According to Harney's biographer, he had "fully determined, on arriving at Salt Lake City, to capture Brigham Young and the twelve apostles, and execute them in a summary fashion, and winter in the Temple of the Latter-day Saints."[118] In citing the nations "higher civilization" and associated "purer religion," the *New York Times* suggested that this "vulgar Islam" in the American West had to be struck down "with a firm hand" so as to break such pretensions of an *imperium in imperio*.[119]

Thus, in 1857, the Anglo-Protestant nation was poised for war against the Mormons on the receding frontier. As part of its official opening platform, the Republican Party in 1856 targeted the "twin relics of barbarism," slavery and polygamy, as within their political crosshairs. Prominent abolitionist senator Charles Sumner declared that Mormonism was an affront to the moral and religious sense of all Christendom. Senator Iverson demanded it be crushed, even "if it shall be necessary to sacrifice every individual in that country." Importantly, Buchanan himself ironically declared Utah, despite his earlier rhetoric on Kansas, to be the site of the "first rebellion, which has existed in our Territories," which should be "put down in a manner that it shall be the last."[120] Briefly stated, the Utah War, which sent 2,500 U.S. troops (nearly one-third of the U.S. Army) to Utah to replace Brigham Young as governor in the summer of 1857, came after several years of smaller federal-Mormon conflicts and growing rumors of Mormon murder (including that of Capt. John W. Gunnison), conspiracy, and treachery. Buchanan's lack of management and military background and Floyd's inexperience and inattention, together with such late directives for the westward-bound military expedition, left the military vulnerable to Mormon resistance, leading to a disintegration of the army troops who were forced to wait out the winter with few supplies in burned-out Fort Bridger, forty miles from Salt Lake City, in snow and temperatures that got to forty below zero.[121]

Though technically a success in replacing Brigham Young as governor, the Utah Expedition proved costly for the U.S. Treasury and President Buchanan's and the Democrats' political merit. The Utah Expedition was ultimately abandoned in April 1858 when Buchanan offered amnesty to Utah and the Mormon Church, following the diplomacy of Col. Thomas Kane, a friend to the Mormons and a philanthropist driven by his religious convictions.[122] Having recently converted to Christianity through the urban revivals in 1857, Kane directly framed his political actions as guided by God, a sentiment those who supported him appeared to share.[123] The irony in Kane's success via diplomacy was that such suasion was the very thing that Buchanan and others presumed the Mormons to be most incapable of due to their deluded religion in light of Christian civilization, leading Buchanan to believe that he had no other option but military force. However, such were the presumptions growing from the religious roots of the country, the beholding of the frontier as a sacred place of millennial expectations and Manifest Destiny, and the heightened and near-militarized quality of religious faith at midcentury.

Despite Buchanan's claims that the Mormon rebellion had been suppressed, that the American Constitution had been upheld, and that peace now "prevails throughout the Territory," Buchanan's policies toward Utah were in many ways unsuccessful, and to a degree backfired, as had Stephen Douglas's over Free-Soilers in Kansas and William Walker's actions in Central America.[124] Buchanan's secretary of war, James B. Floyd, criticized Buchanan in his official 1860 report that he should have seized this golden opportunity against Utah. Brigham Young's power continued to grow unchecked as he sat in his palace, warned Floyd, with his "destroying angels" standing nearby "to execute his orders, whatever they may be." "And yet," he angrily laments, "the army must be withdrawn, when it is known to the Government that this state of things exists."[125] However, as historian Norman Furniss observed, by 1858 the consensus in Washington, despite much bitterness among the military and civilian personnel at Camp Floyd,[126] "was veering away from the view that extermination or at least forceful punishment of the Mormons was wise."[127] Nevertheless, there continued to fester a politically aggressive and militant form of American Protestantism as it pertained to the kingdom ideal that drove these theological stakes, which proved to be violent anchor points during the Civil War just a few years later.[128]

By the end of the 1850s, the role of religion within American society and its dynamic interactions with the functions of the state reached somewhat of a high point, but with the Civil War and thereafter began its decline.[129] Through this critical decade—which saw several internal rebellions and the final steps toward the secession of the entire South—such dynamic interactions and their connections with the American vision of the kingdom of God and the optimistic anticipations toward the millennium exacerbated the physical and virtual qualities of the frontier. Importantly, however, as George Marsden explains, American Protestants continued to uphold the idea of a "here and now" millennial reign of Christ, together with "the Christian ideal" that was "to introduce God's kingdom—a New Israel—not only in the lives of the regenerate elect, but also by means of civil laws that would both restrain evil and comprehensively transform culture according to God's will."[130] As the North and its new southern frontier following the war sought reunion, and as these ideals of the kingdom began to strain under the weight of national urban and scientific developments, federal responses against Utah forged a new era of national crusades against the Mormon kingdom in the 1870s and 1880s, which sought to restore the importance and efficacy of this kingdom that was then waning. By the time Mormons declared an end to crucial components of their kingdom such as plural marriage in 1890, the country fittingly declared the frontier closed; more importantly, however, new secular transitions in religion and government began to be seen that challenged how both understood the Christian nation-state and its religiously styled ideas of republican governance.

# CHAPTER 3

## Antipolygamy and the Closing of the Frontier, 1870s–1890

The Church is now passing through a period of transition, or evolution, as some might be pleased to term it. Such periods appear to be necessary in the progress and perfecting of all created things, as much so in the history of peoples and communities as of individuals. These periods of transition have most generally their pains, perplexities and sufferings. The present is no exception to the rule.

—Mormon First Presidency, April 8, 1887

I left Great Salt Lake a good deal confused as to what state of things existed there—and sometimes even questioning in my own mind whether a state of things existed there at all or not.

—Mark Twain, *Roughing It*

President James Buchanan's boast before Congress in December 1857 that his military efforts had "subjugated" the "phrensied fanaticism" of Mormonism to the authority of the federal government was exaggerated, and, with the idea of the frontier as that of closure, relations between the United States and the Church of Jesus Christ of Latter-day Saints remained tense.[1] While warfare was avoided, it was replaced by federal legislation, congressional debate, and court cases. Though directed against Mormon power itself, polygamy was singled out as being particularly dangerous to the nation and became subject to legislation and enforcement. This legislation and other federal acts against Mormonism, as well as the church's responses, bring into focus the United States' vision of itself as a religious redeemer nation—which conflicted with the church's vision of itself as redeemer of the nation. Visions among both Protestants and Mormons would undergo a variety of changes by 1890, the year of the declared closing of the frontier and the church's agreement to end polygamy. Well revealed in this period of time is that the United States' "fair experiment" of religious liberty was not entirely enlightened and rational, but was characterized by historical moments of disarray, confusion, coercion, and desperate contestation over how theology had become entangled with civil governance. This entanglement created what legal scholar and historian Sarah Gordon has called a "language of faith," the language in which the religious and national narrative of the United States was told, and by which its laws were created. Religious freedom in the United States was not really established when the First Amendment was enunciated, nor was religious pluralism encouraged, but were rather the heart of the American religious experience that was, throughout the nineteenth century, in the "process of being made."[2]

Though open warfare had been avoided, a history of problems between the United States government and the Mormon Church led American Protestants to see Utah and its Mormon population as obstructions to an American character, and its closely connected religious identity as anathema to national progress. Fittingly, it was at the height of this conflict that historian Daniel Dorchester identified Mormonism as a particularly loathsome "divergent current" within America's otherwise progressive narrative, together with Jews, Shakers, Universalists, and "Free Religion," among others.[3] This conflict, however, reveals how the ideals of progress and the meaning of Americanism were neither obvious nor inevitable and how they were tied to hegemonic Protestant definitions of religion and its presumed roles within American society. Whether the American hope was to politically secure national unity on the grounds of sexuality and religion or to religiously prepare for the imminent event of Christ's coming, Protestants saw themselves as uniquely qualified to interpret what was correct and right. Fears of the frontier savage— which came to encompass the Chinese, Catholics, African Americans, and Native Americans—defined the boundary between the civilized and the noncivilized, thereby creating relations of power in support of the dominant narrative and its relation to the West. As fear of the savage was directed toward Mormons, together with assumptions of their noncivilized nature, the contrast with civilized America would prove important for the United States in formulating ideas of a national character and its attendant religious liberty as well as its connections to an appropriate sexual morality, gender, and family relationship.

In looking at this dynamic encounter between Mormonism and the nation in the 1870s and 1880s, partly in the conflict over the issue of polygamy, there are new insights to be had concerning the development of America's central narrative. Historian David Brion Davis has recognized that it was in these "glorious crusades" against Mormons as well as Catholics and others that Americans unexpectedly reveal, by way of an inverted image, the shapes and boundaries of Jacksonian democracy, and by way of extension, religious liberty, gender, and the meaning of America. In framing these structures, Americans sought to encode a particular form of national unity, to restore continuity of a progressive future with a covenantal Puritan past, and to provide a sense of high moral sanction and righteousness. As Davis explains, national propaganda in the form of exposé novels, travel accounts, and news weeklies informed the American mind concerning minority populations and thus guaranteed "a sense of self-identity and personal direction in an otherwise rootless and shifting environment."[4] Therefore, Mormonism became a type of ideological construct, or fictional narrative, that allowed the national narrative to be rendered safe, understandable, predictable, stable, and progressive toward the fulfilling of Christ's kingdom, a narrative in which the white-Protestant influence appeared unchallenged, natural, and providential.[5]

As already observed with the Utah War, Protestant Americans identified civilization with Protestantism, and human progress with the expansion of white Protestantism. As it was held, republican government was necessary to promote civilization and also as something good in itself that resulted from and required civilization. Further seen with the anti-polygamy crusades, Mormonism, in the minds of other Americans, threatened all three: republican government (with its endorsement of local theocracy), Protestantism (with its endorsement of polygamy), and therefore civilization itself (with its "Asiatic barbarism"). Intolerance toward Mormons wasn't just religious intolerance based on a doctrinal difference about the permissibility of polygamy, but rather this triple threat that Mormonism was seen as embodying. Mormons, however, saw themselves as able and constitutionally protected Americans, just as others did, equally civilized and equally upholding their vision of what American could and should be, thereby placing Mormonism and its millennial vision of America in provocative competition with the dominant one.

## CREATING AMERICA

The time period under consideration commences in 1862 when the federal government actively intervened with Mormon marital practices through the Morrill Anti-Bigamy Act. The object of this law, though attacking polygamy, was also political and economic. As Senator Bayard of Delaware (its chief sponsor) said, it was to ensure that "theocratic institutions inconsistent with our form of government" were denied wealth and property. This bill disenfranchised the church, limiting the amount of real estate it could hold ($50,000).[6] Though President Abraham Lincoln signed this law into effect, he provided no means by which it could be enforced, leaving it instead a symbolic statement of American power over the territory of Utah at the time of the Civil War, and a reminder for Utah to stay out of the conflict.[7] Replacing former concerns over slavery, postwar America brought new attention to old problems in a once far-flung section of the United States, settled by people presenting issues over political, economic, and—most concerning—marital practices. With polygamy a growing national concern in the 1870s and 1880s, the Edmunds Act (1882) and the Edmunds-Tucker Act (1887) amended the Morrill Act, giving it power to finally destroy both polygamy and the economic and corporate church that espoused it. Once such laws were deemed constitutional by the Supreme Court in 1890, church leaders ultimately promised to abandon the practice.

On July 4, 1885, a particularly vivid incident enunciated Mormon protests against having their religious beliefs and practices not merely questioned, but legislated against. President George Q. Cannon, First

Counselor in the church's First Presidency, at that time in hiding for engaging in polygamy, expressed the contentious relationship between the church and the United States by ordering, on the Fourth of July, several flags at public, church, and business buildings throughout Salt Lake City to be flown at half-mast. Cannon proposed that several American flags in Salt Lake City should be thus flown as "a symbol of our sorrow for liberties departed."[8] The church's own *Deseret News* supported Cannon's proposal, stating, "The Mormon people have no reason for engaging in expressions of joy under the existing circumstances." Half-masting the flag was an "insignia of mourning" and an intentional protest against celebrations of American liberty in light of federal "tyranny" and its assassination of "fundamental principles upon which this great Government was built."[9]

Mormon denunciations of anti-polygamy legislation as tyranny openly and boldly confronted America's national narrative of itself as a redeemed and redeeming nation of millennial vision. Though this public vision of the kingdom as upheld on both sides would dramatically change by 1890, the church and the United States remained at loggerheads with each other until then, where the national anti-polygamy crusades of the 1880s stood as a salient feature of this larger national struggle for righteousness and moral stewardship that sought to make Mormons—and others on the margin—"more like us." And, as troublesome and worrisome as these unassimilated children were, their practices, by negative reflection, upheld proper and right practices that encoded and enshrined the hegemonic Protestant tendencies guiding the United States government and perception of who we are—which meant white and Protestant. These ideals of the Protestant hegemony spoke of Mormonism as an anomaly to the rest of the United States. Despite their Protestant origins, their language and general culture, their "industry and sense of economy," they were seen and openly declared to be non-Americans, and in need of salvation and cultivation—and thus placed alongside other problematic and subversive groups: Chinese immigrants, Jews, African Americans, Roman Catholics, and Native Americans.

Though the stories of each differ and are unique to their own, many parallels can be found between the Mormons and these named groups as the United States moved into the late nineteenth century; such were noted by the comic weeklies *Puck* and *The Wasp*: "Three Troublesome Children" (figure 3.1) and "Under False Colors" (figure 3.2). These images depict the popular rejection and dehumanization of minority groups deemed outside the accepted parameters of true religion and Americanism, all of whom held a strong presence in the frontier regions as defined in the late nineteenth century. In "Three Troublesome Children," Chinese immigrants, Native Americans, and Mormons, who had all failed to assimilate into white Protestantism, are portrayed as difficult and unruly children, mauling a distressed Columbia who passively and mistakenly attempts to mother them. With racially demeaning monkey-like characteristics, the Chinese child hangs from the mother's hair. Sitting on the floor, the sociopathic Native American child amuses himself by chopping U.S. soldiers in half with his hatchet. Tellingly, the sexually unbridled Mormon, who looks like the stereotyped Mormon elder, attempts to kiss (or spit on?) the overwhelmed mother Columbia. Ignoring this, father, or American law, reads the newspaper labeled "Politics" with dollar signs.

More meaning can be inferred to this image than mere insensitivity to America's racial groups and fatherly inattention. For example, moral suasion from volunteer efforts had failed, as had popular sovereignty, to control these troublesome children and provide an effective answer to the Mormon, Chinese, and Indian questions. Moral suasion of the 1830s and 1840s and its idealized weak federal governance (an early signifier of individual liberty), now in the 1870s and 1880s was reimagined through the lens of the Civil War and Reconstruction efforts in the South. This postwar context articulated the importance of force in formulating a stronger form of Christian moral government that functioned under parental-styled government instruction and coercion, both in reconstructing the southern as well as the western frontier; this growing sense of federal power is well exemplified by its legislation against polygamy.[10] With the male figure of law neglectfully sitting nearby, the out-of-control children mauling an ineffective woman suggest how discipline and obedience must be enforced by powerful, white Protestant men—who must temporarily look up from politics and money to rescue the country from these barbaric and wayward children by stopping their practices and whipping them into obedient citizens. This whipping would take several forms, from

THE THREE TROUBLESOME CHILDREN.

FIGURE 3.1. "The Three Troublesome Children," by George F. Keller. Cartoon, *The Wasp*, December 16, 1881. Courtesy of University of California–Berkeley, Bancroft Library.

exclusionary laws, to military campaigns, to increased legislation against marital practices outside conventional Christian norms—the latter reserved for Mormons.

In the case of the Chinese community and Native Americans, the racial attributes of these peoples, coupled with their refusal to assimilate with Protestant ideals, resulted in a unified Christian society calling for harsh responses. According to one minister before Congress, what was to be feared from Chinese immigrants was that "very few of these ever change in character, to become Americanized"; furthermore, it was observable that few of them "in the last twenty-five years have renounced their native heathenism to profess Christianity."[11] Their lack of Christian identity, and their non-Protestant "heathen" ways were expected to become even worse on the American frontier. This fear encouraged widespread acts of violence against Asians in the West, including massacres, riots, lynchings, and round-ups in hundreds of Chinese communities.[12] In 1882 and 1892 Congress reinforced this violence with severe anti-Chinese laws that left Chinese immigrants vulnerable to arrest without trial, as well as unfair and unusual punishment, since it had been decided that the U.S. Constitution had "no application" to them.[13] These acts were upheld by the Supreme Court in 1893. In 1892, Justice David J. Brewer, himself a former missionary and the son of a Congregationalist minister, offered an uncontested opinion of the Protestant-only Court: America still stood as a "Christian nation."[14] Supporters of such responses against Chinese immigrants and Chinese-American workers denied charges of religious or racial bigotry, attributing such actions instead to an overwhelming patriotic moral response due to concerns associated with the Chinese false religion and presumed un-American characteristics.[15]

Native Americans were also victims of legal interpretations and Christian violence. Christian missions, volunteer societies, national policy, and even educational programs and colleges were designed to destroy cultural rituals and beliefs, and to break up tribes, thereby converting them to the American Protestant ideal, both in appearance and cultural assimilation. Native resistance to these efforts and other Americanization and Christianization efforts inspired national concern and cries for their removal, and ultimately tribal decimation and eradication, which led to several decades of military massacres, casual murders, and retaliatory killings.[16] Seen as obstructions to white Christian progress, white children were taught to hate Indians as those in the West were taught to hate the Chinese, and newspapers and politicians spoke of violence against them as glorious and heroic.[17] In 1890, this protracted struggle reached an apex with the Wounded Knee massacre, in which federal troops killed native leaders, rounded up nearly three hundred Lakota Sioux, inclusive of men, women, and children, disarmed and killed them, thereby devastating the resistance.[18] Not seeing the part they played, white Protestants had long attributed the plight of America's "red aborigines of the country" to the consequence of racial inferiority, drunkenness, and heathenism, establishing in their minds the true reason for their self-destruction and their own failed attempts to "Christianize and civilize them," thereby labeling Native Americans as incapable of receiving such benevolent attempts of Christian philanthropy.[19] Scholars influenced by Turner interpreted such themes as part of the inevitable decline of the "noble savage," in light of the progressive march forward of white American civilization—thereby enshrining the sense of Native decline and its attached memory of the unchanging frontier "Indian."[20]

FIGURE 3.2. "Under False Colors," by Joseph F. Keppler. *Puck*, March 22, 1882. Print shows James Russell Lowell, minister to England, responding to the pleas of an Irishman dressed up in Uncle Sam clothes under custody of the British military for anarchistic activities. In his pocket is dynamite. The lower caption reads: "Minister Lowell: 'No, sir, you are not the kind of American Citizen I am sent here to protect!'" Courtesy of the Library of Congress.

Another serious threat to Protestant idealism pertained to America's now-free black population; nearly four million former enslaved Americans needed assimilation. During the Radical Reconstruction period (1865–1877), Northern-imposed laws on the South displaced white power, inspiring, noted historian John Franklin, "a kind of guerilla warfare" and "holy crusade" against blacks and their white sympathizers. Secret patriotic and religious societies formed; the well-known Ku Klux Klan was joined by other Christian terrorist societies such as the Constitutional Union Guards, the '76 Association, and the White Brothers. Such societies declared themselves responsible for preserving a sense of white Christian nationalism and the American Revolution, often harkening back and conflating these images with the life and ideals practiced in the original American covenant of Massachusetts Bay, however now distorted for regional interest.[21] Various kinds of intimidation, black codes, grandfather clauses, local violence, and Supreme Court decisions were important methods for restoring white Southern honor and its associated Christian rule on the new "southern frontier."[22] Over 2,500 lynchings in the last sixteen years of the century, mainly of African Americans, attest to the strength of white Protestant idealism.[23]

Another "troublesome child" not featured among the trio was Catholics. Their perceived lack of assimilation is addressed in figure 3.2, "Under False Colors," by *Puck*'s founder, Joseph Keppler. By the 1880s Americans had become increasingly alarmed at the growth of incivility in American cities, and, in an 1884 essay, American minister to England James Russell Lowell argued against universal suffrage in this time of increased immigration and urbanization, arguing that there were too many "untrained" immigrants. Government was under threat of being utilized by "the most ignorant and vicious of a population which has come to us from abroad, wholly unpracticed in self-government and incapable of assimilation by American habits and methods."[24] The anti-Irish drawing in *Puck*, "Under False Colors," provides representation of this national struggle over what defined an acceptable American and the limits of America's "fair experiment" with religious liberty. Here a stereotyped Irish American, presumably Catholic, pathetically dressed in an Uncle Sam costume, attempts to pass himself off as an authentic American, deserving of U.S. protection overseas. As this false American begs Minister Lowell for protection, the Irish American is waved off with clear annoyance: "No, sir, you are not the kind of American Citizen I am here to protect." Lowell's other hand holds a strong warning to all Irish immigrants hoping for American citizenship "to understand distinctly that they cannot be Irishmen [i.e., Catholics] and Americans at the same time." Graphically conveyed was the message to all, and particularly to the Irish and Irish Americans, that as long as there remained any sense of Irish heritage, which included the Catholic faith, such could not be accepted as Americans overseas or at home. With the coming of Bishop Satolli, the apostolic delegate to the United States, Keppler commented: "It is just a little more impossible than ever for a man to be a good Catholic and a good American."[25]

With immigration and the attendant fears over unassimilated groups, Protestant America increasingly sharpened its sense of civilization and then worked to actualize it in accordance with its own unique and peculiar notions of Christian civilization. The United States government, argued historian Erika Lee, nearly stopped at nothing to impose and maintain a specifically Protestant ideal of civilization, helping establish a predetermined national character based upon particular theological precepts.[26] Religious liberty was salient to this national mythology and upheld popular presumptions of transcendent religious ideals that helped enforce, emphasizes David Sehat, a specific Protestant "moral establishment" that "led to the illiberal legal and political policies that characterized much of the American past."[27] American Protestants did not feel any sense or need to understand, tolerate, or protect vulnerable minority groups, but rather displayed a shared religious view and patriotic obligation to either treat them as troublesome children to be punished and/or taught, or rejected as imposters.

Though not to be equated with the same level of violence and dislocation that met America's black, Chinese, and Native American populations in the 1870s and 1880s, this combination of religious conventionalism and patriotic obligation clashed over the presence of Mormonism as well. Due to the sensationalism attached to the issue of polygamy, Mormonism was met with widespread attention and disdain. Mormons were deemed to be outsiders but stood as a special kind of American outsider: Mormons were largely Anglo-Saxon, spoke English, were of Northern European stock, and shared a strong work ethic, but held an alternative vision of America that was threatening in all sorts of ways, thus eliciting significant backlash. Exposing the categorized presumptions of qualities necessary for self-governance, polygamy was used to demonstrate this divergence from what it meant to be American—thereby painting Mormons and their peculiar marriage practices as outside American acceptability. In ways that represented a type of inversion of the Americanizing effects of the frontier, polygamy was articulated as having a degrading influence that characterized Mormons into an altogether new race—to which Assistant Surgeon Robert Bartholow of the U.S. Army attributed a "Mormon expression and style" that illuminated this negatively affected physiology as well as mentality.[28] *Harper's Magazine* in 1881 declared that the institution of Mormonism itself was "so absolutely un-American in all its requirements that it would die."[29] Also by way of contrast to the imagined democratizing influence of the frontier, the influential anti-Mormon *Hand-Book of Mormonism* declared in 1882 that Mormons were "so controlled by the Mormon leaders that until this power is broken by some means, there is no hope that Utah will ever be in harmony with the rest of the Union." The explanation of how this could happen on the American frontier, was that Mormons were largely adult foreigners, "generally ignorant and unlearned" rather than "intelligent citizens in a free government." Continuing in a more positive vein, the writers declared, "It is also true, as we believe, that under proper training they would in time become liberty-loving, patriotic citizens, as they are now industrious and economical."[30] However distrusted and looked down on, there was always hope for Mormons, even if there was no hope for Mormonism.

As benevolent as these last words are, they echoed Josiah Strong's racial positing that all races have their own specialization of gifts, and that only white Anglo-Saxons ("the English, the British colonists, and the people of the U.S.") possess the talent for liberty and for true religion. Because of the presumed nature of self-government itself, the Anglo-Saxon race was the sole exponent of "a pure *spiritual* Christianity." The civil and religious test for self-governance, as proposed by Strong, was simple and "without controversy": the more Anglo-Saxon you were, the more likely you were to exhibit both liberty and spirituality.[31] Religion was thus a central feature and function of race, which, Matthew Jacobson argues, was understood in the nineteenth century to be "entwined with ideas of citizenship."[32] In a way more relevant to

Mormons, as David Brion Davis notes, certain subversive groups were criticized because there was no outward stigma that set them apart from other Americans, unlike the Chinese, African Americans, Native Americans, and, to a lesser degree, Catholics. This stigma-less group could not easily be excused or ignored as racially deficient; rather, these apparently Anglo-Saxon types thus practiced a "system of delusion" which "insulated members . . . from the unifying and disciplining force of public opinion," and thus hindered the natural pressures of progress and reasonable religion.[33] Mormons, due to their frontier isolation, together with their peculiar system of religion and its practice of plural marriage, proved them to be incompatible with citizenship, and as presumed by Bartholow, had produced real physiological and mental effects. The Mormon people could become successfully Americanized only if the Mormon Church as a system were "at once effectively and permanently broken."[34] Though Mormons physically looked like other Americans, Mormonism was an institution that disallowed its members to think like, and in the minds of Americans, to actually look like them, and thus was not only un-American but impeded America's vision of itself. Also a central complaint long applied to Catholicism, the concern that institutional memberships stymied independent thinking was now applied to Mormonism. In short, there was no bridging the gap between Mormonism and Americanism, unless of course Mormons left their false religion—and only then could a Mormon become an American.

Mormonism's refusal to reflect Anglo-Saxon and Protestant conventions, together with the power of popular literature, combined the thriving geographic presence of Mormonism in the frontier regions, and its astonishing numerical success, compounded popular fears that the West was being overrun, threatening to push the frontier line eastward. No matter if the Mormons flew the American flag, engaged in business or welcomed the railroad, their religious practices defined them as outsiders to the white Protestant hegemony and therefore subject to the federal government's attention. In short, Mormon theocracy and polygamy contradicted this white Protestant civil and social structure in regard to the acceptable allowance of different races and different beliefs. The strength of the federal government's reply to, pressure on, and eventual winning of this contentious issue is negatively reflected in the government's relative ignoring of the marital (and sexual) practices of the other marginalized groups with whom Mormonism was placed aside. Native Americans regularly practiced multiple marriages; some Chinese women were pushed into prostitution and sold as sex slaves; African Americans were forced to adopt casual marriage practices, and even the Catholics were beheld with some suspicions as some members, particularly nuns and clergy, withdrew from marriage altogether and practiced celibacy. These practices were addressed in exclusionary laws, and surely reproved by missionaries and social groups, but never really becoming the crusading focus of an angry federal government. The polygamous church in Utah, however, became subject of deep concern, if not religious and political hysteria.

Drama against Mormons had its role in this growing feeling: paranoia not usually extended to other unassimilated groups' marital practices was surely created and promoted by highly charged popular literature that had mimicked Indian captivity and slave narratives. Accounts relating secret Mormon murders, human sacrifice, blood atonement, conspiracies, terrifying temple oaths, female and child slavery, and priesthood despotism were fascinating and enraging. Works such as *Wife No. 19*, written by Brigham Young's former wife, Ann Eliza Young, and *Tell it All* by disaffected Mormon polygamist Fanny Stenhouse helped to fill the public mind with Mormonism throughout the century. In both narratives there are heartbreaking repetitions of familial neglect, secrecy and abuse in Mormon homes, the personal and social degradations of polygamous unions on individuals and society, unnatural expectations of unquestioning obedience, terrorizing violence against apostates, dishonest missionary tactics, and the despair, hopelessness and betrayal Mormon women commonly felt as they learned about polygamy and their inability to resist or dissent. With negative implications that followed Mormonism throughout the nineteenth century and into the twentieth and twenty-first, Stenhouse described the sacred Temple ceremonies in great detail, outlining strict covenants of obedience to Mormon men, but also the explicit threats of hell to all offenders, detailed by slit throats and disemboweling.[35] For Ann Eliza Young, America was not "Babylon" as Mormons were apt to call it, but a "Christian realm," even "THE PROMISED LAND!" Young provided strong contrasts throughout her narrative between Jesus and Satan, or between "the light of Christian faith" and "the dark bondage of fanaticism and bigotry."[36] Polygamy broke down American chivalry and morality and made men brutes to their wives and children. By way of contrast, Christian monogamy instilled courtesy and familial love.[37]

Reflecting on his visit to Utah, Mark Twain recounted scenes of sexual absurdity and violence as accumulated at a "Gentile den," full of smoking pipes and fantastic story-telling (which were admittedly, as he put it, "unreliable"). Still, Twain's accounts provided a convincing core of truth that upheld popular disdain for Mormons and Mormonism that church leaders found difficult to diffuse.[38] Such narratives not only entertained the rest of the country and brought assurance of the nation's own sense of righteousness, but, as in the case of Stenhouse, were first-hand accounts endorsed by some of the nation's most pronounced and public heroes, such as abolitionist Harriet Beecher Stowe (of the famed Beecher family), and provided a platform for popular fears that supported federal legislation. At the same time, Twain's account implied that the dangers posed by Mormons were largely exaggerations of the drunken taverns, and that beyond their physical ugliness and religious silliness, they posed little threat. Nonetheless, anti-Mormon texts and exposé novels sold well nationally, creating an efficient forum that spoke to the psychological needs of Americans and provided important moral teachings of what it meant to be American.[39]

## IN CONGRESS: PUNISHING POLYGAMY

Perhaps not surprisingly, the Mormons were also recipients of Christian missionizing and Americanization efforts: secretary for the Bureau for Mormons, Angie F. Newman of Nebraska, petitioned Congress on June 5, 1886, on behalf of the Women's Home Missionary Society of Utah Territory. Formed at the suggestion of the supervising Methodist bishop Wiley in 1881, the bureau intended to offer escape to "great numbers of persons now entangled and fettered in the structure of Mormon society" now in Utah.[40] Newman's more compassionate but no less determined approach to break up Mormon society and homes was to create, as an auxiliary of the Women's Home, a Christian Industrial School that could "provide support for the innocent victims" of the Mormon peril, which she painted as an unparalleled anomaly in the progress of American history; a hostile, defiant and theocratic empire whose aim was to take over the country. Steeped in theological perverseness and social, physical, and mental degradations, Mormon atrocities such as kidnappings, forced marriages, suicides, priesthood treachery, and conspiracy demanded immediate action. Sharing her concern with this "high carnival of hell," Congress upheld Newman's request to restore Christian sanity to the American West.[41] Describing herself as a child of "Pilgrim Fathers," Newman's religious concerns inevitably entwined with patriotism, as depicted by the "immense national flag" flying above the Salt Lake Seminary. "Let it wave in wind or storm, by daylight or darkness, so that every weary eye which looks upon it shall be assured that the women of the nation are thinking of them, and that in those crimson folds there is refuge for all women."[42] If only the "national heart," lamented Newman, could have "knowledge of the wrongs which are perpetrated under the shadow of the flag." Such wrongs caused one child to look into his mother's face and say, "Mama, I wonder if there is any God."[43] Newman, despite benevolent motives, declared, "Mormonism had to go down before the civilization of Christianity," "just as the pale-faced Indian has had to go down before the civilization of the white man in the United States."[44]

Financial support for Newman's Industrial School served, according to R. G. Moniece of the Presbyterian Church, as part of their larger commitment toward the "great work of Americanizing this splendid Territory by rescuing it from the clutches of the Mormon priesthood."[45] Such Americanization efforts were repulsed by not only Mormon men, but vigorous women's voices. When Mormon women, particularly suffragist Emmeline B. Wells, responded against Newman's Christian attempt at public funding to save Mormon women, she wrote that Mormon women were free to come and go, marry and divorce: "No Mormon woman, old or young, is compelled to marry at all; still less to enter into polygamy." Furthermore, "Mormon girls have homes as happy, as pure, and as desirable as any of their Eastern sisters, and are far more independent." Other women denounced Newman's claims of temple oaths, ecclesiastical punishments, and female financial dependence, and that no Mormon woman or child would seek refuge from the hands that served to bring "sorrow and desolation into their once happy homes."[46] Phebe Woodruff, plural wife of prominent Mormon leader Wilford Woodruff, joined the fray: "Shall we as wives and mothers sit still and see our husbands, and sons," while following the "highest behest of heaven, suffer for their religion without exerting ourselves to the extent of our power for their deliverance? No! verily, no!"[47]

However strong and intelligent such responses were, they were accepted by Newman as proof of Mormon patriarchal control. Surely, it was argued, these words indicated the depth of Mormon duplicity and priestly power and responded once more in a religious vein: "These women, by their treasonable political attitude, and their avowed hostility to Christian marriage," responded Newman, "have cut the chords which bind them to the world's heart."[48] Thus, the religious stakes of both were set and the Senate committee upheld Newman's request—in a crusade that admittedly attempted to soften the cruelty of current "bayonet rule" legislation with Newman's more benevolent philosophy and logic. It was this type of "womanly sympathy," noted the satirical newspaper *The Wasp* that same year, that inspired "women's-rights-women" to get involved in this crusade and thus save Mormon children from their parents, thereby helping the nation "find a Christian solution to the [Mormon] problem."[49] Nevertheless, increasingly harsh anti-Mormon legislation went on, exemplifying how the federal government was bringing its increased powers to legislate marital and family matters. Under the Edmunds Act (1882), Congress established civil disabilities on the Mormon people and their structures of power in Utah, by controlling juries, disenfranchising those suspected of polygamous relationships, and declaring vacant Utah's registration and electoral offices, while the Edmunds-Tucker Act (1887) disincorporated the church, seized its property, and dissolved Utah's military, educational, and immigrant structures. Wives were required to testify against their husbands, polygamous children were denied inheritance, Mormon women were disenfranchised, and an antipolygamy oath was required for civic participation, thereby disenfranchising all Mormons.[50]

Despite these vivid clashes between the two sides, such as half-masting the flag to resist what Mormon officials considered a breach of their constitutional rights, and Wells's and Woodruff's spirited responses to Newman's charges, the clashes arose from shared values. For both Mormons and Protestants, republicanism was a religious concept that was deeply connected to their self-understanding of whiteness and their claims to self-governance. Mormons, too, subscribed to Josiah Strong's position that only white Anglo-Saxons had the talent for liberty and true religion, which had indeed impelled their own faith and its notable departures from its shared Protestant roots. As Brigham Young explained it, Anglo-Saxon Mormons were "the sons of Ephraim," a race that was resolute and determined to conquer the wilderness and "overcome almost insurmountable difficulties," "bearing the spirit of rule and dictation, to go forth from conquering to conquer."[51] Religion was thus a central function of race and citizenship and what it meant to be American; indeed, Mormons believed the American government to be "instituted by God" and looked with nostalgia on their shared Puritan forefathers. By such beliefs, Mormons similarly marginalized within Utah and the church African Americans and Native Americans, whose cursed racial status before God was juxtaposed with their own racial privilege. Through their beliefs they created and defended polygamy as a legitimate institution, indeed Biblical and therefore not sinful—even protecting them from the sexual sins of wicked "Babylon."[52] Sharing a similar national origin story and disapproval of sexual deviance, Mormons upheld sexual propriety as "more highly esteemed than life itself," thereby responding violently against their own for breaches in chastity. Religious intimidation and violence were tactics commonly employed throughout America, not just against Mormons and polygamy, but among Mormons in Utah in their attempts to suppress sexual impropriety within their own territory.[53]

Overarching these shared beliefs and attitudes between Protestants and Mormons was the belief that Zion, or Christ's kingdom, situated on the American frontier, was to be a refuge for a dying world that was steeped in sexual sin and God's disfavor, with both laying claim to their own religious institutions and sexual practices as the favored one. As with the Utah War and their fight over polygamy, Mormons regarded their dissent from American law as an authentic demonstration of their patriotism and an expression of their own divine right of self-governance. In attacking the church and its nontraditional marital practices, Protestants similarly relied on a strong sense of patriotism and Christian exceptionalism that at times trumped American law. America, and specifically the western frontier, had an important role to play in the developing scene preceding Christ's millennial earthly reign. Central to this kingdom mythology, Protestants optimistically anticipated steady societal improvement via the enforcement of religious moral behavior that eradicated national sin and impurity. Christ was not to come to a destroyed and immoral world, but rather one purified and made ready for him by way of Christian unity and morality. As Josiah Strong noted, Christians held the power "to hasten or retard the coming of Christ's kingdom in the world by hundreds, and perhaps thousands, of years."[54] Brigham Young similarly taught that Zion and the kingdom of God could not be built up in a day, but rather as quickly as "the inhabitants of this city" possess holiness and the Spirit of God, "here is the Millennium. Let the whole people of the United States be possessed of that spirit and here is the Millennium, and so it will spread over all the world."[55] As such, this optimism implied the opposite was also true—that humans could impact society negatively, and thus delay this coming kingdom. The moral reform volunteer movements such as Angie Newman's came from this alarmed millennial anxiety, implying the need for serious social, religious, and political improvement and involvement, where home and family proved central. This inverted image of American morality thus makes visible the otherwise invisible contours of this kingdom, for both Mormons and Protestants.

Representing the darker side of the nation's attempts to establish white-Christian rule in the United States, these advancements were in large part viewed as the final chapter of the closing of the American western frontier.[56] Creating an important mythology of the West, westward expansionism and development helped fashion a particular unified national identity via demonization of the barbaric and uncivilized frontier—becoming an actual descriptive category of Americanism, however inverted. Indeed, the constructed fears of Chinese, Native Americans, and Catholics made real the anticipations and hopes of the self-professed civilized.[57] The argument that identity discourse is a symptom of one's anxiety about others is thus applicable, not just in the creation of the developing nation-state, but in the very frameworks in which minorities were to be understood and engaged. As it was, definitions of the savage defined the boundaries of the civilized, thus re-creating (or inventing) the meaning and significance of both, and by extension, creating power relations and structures of normality in which competition would be legitimated and progress defined.

While standing as the inverted image of what it meant to be truly

American, Mormons met broad and heavy resistance by both the government and the country as they proclaimed their rights as American citizens. As previously reviewed, the Morrill Anti-Bigamy Act (1862) was passed by Congress and then not enforced. Enforcement of this law and more severe amendments to it were routinely demanded and justified during the 1870s. Resulting from a mass meeting of the Ladies of Salt Lake City on November 7, 1878, a petition and address to Lucy Webb, wife of then President Rutherford B. Hayes, was sent to every relevant clergyman throughout the United States and was asked to be read in each congregation so as to arouse public sentiment, and then to each congressman in that district. Nearly seven hundred women from throughout the United States and across denominational lines signed the petition, including those of the Restored Church of Jesus Christ of Latter Day Saints, then led by Joseph Smith III, oldest son of the founder of Mormonism and an avowed antipolygamist. President Hayes forwarded the petition to the Department of the Interior, which then presented it to Congress for action. In the address prefacing the petitions, Christian women were called to unite against this "great sin" and "evil" in urging Congress to enforce the Morrill Act and to abolish polygamy, for not only was Mormonism "rapidly extending" throughout the frontier West, but never had polygamy "taken such a degrading and debasing form in any nation or among any people above the conditions of savages, as in Utah." Beyond this, the fact that polygamist apostle and member of the First Presidency George Q. Cannon could sit as territorial delegate in Congress made the situation all the more "revolting to our common Christian principles."[58]

The Supreme Court *Reynolds* decision on January 6, 1879, had been devastating not just for Reynolds himself, who now faced prison, hard labor, and fines, but for Cannon who had orchestrated the affair and whom this petition considered a revolting influence within American governance. Amending the Morrill Act on the wave of anti-Mormon hysteria, the Edmunds Act was signed into law on March 23, 1882, and Cannon's congressional seat was declared vacant. The Edmunds Law closed gaps left open from the Morrill Act that made prosecution difficult and imposed heavy punishments for polygamists and those who upheld polygamy as a divine institution. Politicians behind these efforts recognized these laws as harsh but, as recognized by Edwin Firmage and

Richard Mangrum, they were acceptable because they "helped destroy the polygamous marital system that produced them."[59] By 1885, national excitement and resolve over Utah reached an important height within American politics, empowering Utah's territorial marshals and judges to enact anti-Mormon legislation with as much strength as they felt necessary—and prompted George Q. Cannon's request that the flag be half-masted on the Fourth of July.[60] In 1886, Senator John R. Tucker of Virginia (Dem) declared that the Edmunds Act had not accomplished enough and that legislation against "Asiatic" polygamy "should be radical"—and because it needed to harmonize with the constitutional principles of government, would "require a change in the Constitution of the United States."[61]

Though polygamy was the most discussed target, Mormonism had become a powerful economic and political force in Utah, and the Edmunds Law explicitly went against both, thus making the Mormon kingdom a direct target of American law.[62] Beyond its influence in the pro-Mormon People's Party, the church involved itself in various economic enterprises, inclusive of railroads, street railroads, a gas company, and telegraph lines. Mormon cooperative enterprises also boomed, including iron works, banks, textile and cotton factories, and woolen mills. Such progress, particularly as it often came at the expense of non-Mormons in Utah (sometimes disparagingly called "merchants of Babylon"), provoked jealousies and bitter rivalry—only swelling the allies of the anti-Mormon movement. Though successful, Mormonism's communitarian policies appeared insular, backward, and resistant to a new era of private enterprise and uncontrolled laissez-faire capitalism.[63] Indeed, as an essential component of Christ's kingdom which idealized in Abrahamic terms a kind of "family-type" economic order, Mormon economy translated religious piety into specific church programs, heavily condemning as wicked any independent involvement in mercantile pursuits.[64] Though efforts took shape in the 1870s to impede these Mormon economic efforts, it was in the 1880s that a new level of prosecution emerged that forced Mormon leaders to rethink their economic, political, and familial policies.[65]

Extinguishing the immense political and economic power of the Mormon people, it was thought, was an act of love, for it would destroy the ecclesiastical institution that oppressed them. Senator Thomas F.

Bayard of Delaware, a supporter of the Edmunds Bill, explained that even though its provisions were "an unrepublican theory of proceeding in regard to elections," they were necessary in breaking an even worse unrepublican theocracy in Utah. These laws, though severe, were deemed necessary. "They have been said to be rough provisions," explained Senator George F. Edmunds of Vermont, whose name the Edmunds and Edmunds-Tucker Acts bear; "they were intended to be rough. Desperate cases need desperate remedies."[66] Ironically, Senator Tucker, a Southern Democrat, devout Presbyterian, and long-time supporter of states' rights, who later joined his name to an even more severe antipolygamy legislation known by the name of Edmunds-Tucker (1887), saw this as an issue over fair representation and biblical order concerning the "monopoly of power" held by Mormons in Utah. Tucker's united efforts with republicans represents a significant shift within Southern politics and its willingness, despite the memory of Reconstruction, to enlarge the federal government in the support of Christian morality. As Gaines Foster observed, race oppression as then enacted in the South comfortably fit with the politics of morality, allowing anti-Mormon legislation to achieve significant Southern support.[67] This legislation was rooted in his conviction that Mormon leadership oppressed its members and dictated elections, and that in this case of morality, the federal government trumped local autonomy. Thus, an oath, which judged citizens on grounds of religious belief, was necessary to "protect the local minority and the whole of the people of the United States."[68]

While taking shape within the secular sphere of law, neither side saw the issue as purely that. In ways similar to General Harney and the Utah War, the new wave of anti-Mormon hostility that inspired this law was evident in the words of President Grant's appointee, Chief Justice James B. McKean of the Superior Court in Utah, who set it as his patriotic and sacred mission in the 1870s to destroy Brigham Young's "polygamic theocracy":

> The mission which God had called upon me to perform in Utah, is as much above the duties of other courts and judges as the heavens are above the earth, and whenever or wherever I may find the Local or Federal laws obstructing or interfering therewith, by God's blessing I shall trample them under my feet.[69]

Though steeped in their own conflation of religion and politics, Cannon accused Congress, with reference to the Edmunds Act (1882), of legislating from the "pulpit of our nation, the orthodox pulpit," enforcing both religious and cultural "orthodoxy" in the United States. As it was, Mormons began to feel the weight of their opposition. Powerful Mormon ally Judge Jeremiah S. Black wrote to the secretary of the interior, warning of the renewed hostilities then facing Utah. He explained that Congress felt its current fines against the church and imprisonments of Mormon leaders as "altogether too merciful," and that Mormon complaints of cruelty were in vain. Consequently they "super-added the penalty," effectively removing all rights Mormons claimed as American citizens, effectively implying "civil death and infamy besides."[70] Senator Edmunds was determined to close any gaps left open from the Morrill Act, moving strongly against Utah's delegate in Congress, George Q. Cannon, whose "adroitness and ability" had been effective in "averting adverse legislation," but now would "get no advantage of me." "All hell," wrote Cannon, "seems to be boiling over."[71]

Now a former delegate in Congress, Cannon did more than order the half-masting of flags. Even though in hiding against increasing raids, Cannon appointed a committee to construct a document known as the "Declaration of Grievances and Protest." Sent to and read to members of the church throughout the Mormon territories, this document complained that the Edmunds law had been enacted unjustly, and those willing to "fall in line" with the law, including Mormon president John Taylor and other prominent Mormons who agreed to surrender polygamy, continued to be "harassed and prosecuted."[72] President Grover Cleveland, upon receiving a copy of this document outlining Mormon grievances, promised to see that the law was administered impartially, but then remarked, tellingly, "I wish you out there could be like the rest of us."[73]

Cleveland's assimilationist remark unsurprisingly drew the ire of Mormon leaders. In an epistle read *in absentia* to the April General Conference of the church while in hiding, the First Presidency declared, "We are inconsiderately asked to rend our family relations and throw away our ideas of human freedom, political equality and the rights of man, and 'to become like them.'" The epistle then challenged, "Be like them for what?" In answer, the epistle declared, unsettlingly,

It means that *E pluribus unum* is a fiction; it means that we tamper with and violate the grand palladium of human liberty, the Constitution of the United States and substitute expediency, anarchy, fanaticism, intolerance and religious bigotry for those glorious fundamental principles of liberty, equality, brotherhood, human freedom and the rights of man.

The church emphatically went on to declare, "We cannot do it. . . . We cannot and will not lay aside our fealty to the nation at the bidding of political demagogues, religious fanatics or intolerant despots."[74] Mormon leaders indeed acknowledged the difficulty in accepting polygamy, as "the idea of marrying more wives than one was as naturally abhorrent to the leading men and women of the Church . . . as it could be to any people," but averred it was unconstitutional and contrary to the American promise of freedom to legislate against it just because it was abhorrent and offensive to America's priestly structures of power.[75] In a parallel denial of popular sovereignty in 1857, Mormons were once again being reminded that religious liberty remains within the boundaries of popular notions of Christian morality.

The half-masting incident had severe repercussions, due in part to the symbolic irony of the day on which it was held. The Fourth of July, which celebrated America's victory over tyranny, had become a type of official American Passover that reinforced not just the ideal of liberty, but that of a particular understanding of the divine covenant as well.[76] These feelings of social and political exclusion were most powerfully displayed in juxtaposing it with the irony of July Fourth, where we see others do so not just on the grounds of religion, but race and gender, demonstrating just how interconnected all three were to this American identity. In Rochester, New York, on July 4, 1852, Frederick Douglass did not join in the celebrations, but instead spoke of the "inhuman mockery and sacrilegious irony" of the sacred day while humans were enslaved. His speech was tellingly titled, "What to the Slave Is the Fourth of July?"[77] In 1876 on Independence Day, the National Woman Suffrage Association similarly brought attention to national hypocrisy while half the population could not vote.[78]

Similarly steeped in this American culture of exclusionary binaries, the Independence Day protest by Mormons transformed America into an oppressive Egypt or Babylon and themselves into oppressed Hebrews who were God's chosen people. Americans responded by reminding Mormons that they were not God's people but were instead immoral Canaanites still in need of subjugation or even eradication. Newspapers, both local and national, called for immediate and severe action. A similar sentiment was enunciated in the Cincinnati periodical, *Sam the Scaramouch*, where Uncle Sam was "to rise upon [his] dignity with a club." Speaking in a possessive tone, Sam rejects this half-mast protest as illegitimate. In this illustration (figure 3.3), Uncle Sam's initial shock and recoiling hints at the stunning severity of the offense; the necessity of heavy government action to deal with the offense is suggested by the military general, waiting for Sam's instruction. Comparing the incident to the firing on Fort Sumter, the averted violence of 1857 seemed imminent again as *Sam the Scaramouch* called upon "Mormon Elders" to account for their treason

FIGURE 3.3. "Uncle Sam in Mormondom." Cartoon. Cover from *Sam the Scaramouch*, July 18, 1885, by Porter. Reproduced in Gary L. Bunker and Davis Bitton, *The Mormon Graphic Image, 1834–1914: Cartoons, Caricatures, and Illustrations* (Salt Lake City: University of Utah Press, 1983), 49.

by being "moved out of the country, house, foot, dragoons, wives, twins and triplets."[79] This long-held religious-cultural binary that reduced the nation's relationship and understanding of Mormonism to that of conflict had once again arisen, nearly fulfilling its necessary demands to expel or erase Mormonism as an unfitting contamination that threatened a type of innocent and purified national sense of behavior, belonging, and identity.

The local and national press reported on a Utah rebellion. The *Salt Lake Tribune* spoke on July 10 of the mass "indignation meeting" that was to be held in Salt Lake City on the twenty-fourth, the day Mormons commemorated the entrance of Mormon pioneers to the Salt Lake Valley, and the day of an anticipated repeat half-masting. The *Salt Lake Tribune* advertised this meeting, noting that railroads were offering half-fare rates and that hotels agreed to provide "reasonable rates," thereby heightening attendance. With direct reference to "ex-confederate soldiers" that were to form a significant portion of this "indignation meeting," the *Tribune* wrote, "That would be a good day for the presence in this city of two or three thousand old soldiers, federal and confederate. It would probably result in a speedy and effectual settlement of the whole Mormon business, for with such men here in force the nation's flag would not be insulted with impunity."[80]

As rumors of riots and impending violence continued to mount, the local event easily and quickly achieved national attention and significance. The *Texas Siftings* reported, "The Gentiles have been exasperated to a point where they may be led into violence at almost any time."[81] An editorial in Chicago's *Western Rural and American Stockman* lashed out, saying that it was "certainly time that an end was put to this sort of treasonable nonsense. . . . The unwritten law of this nation is, 'if any man pull down the American flag, shoot him on the spot,' and there is a first rate opportunity to put the law into execution in Salt Lake City." Though a delegation of former soldiers was sent for during the initial point of treason, lamented the editorial, their numbers were insufficient to significantly aright the offense. Similar to Cincinnati's *Sam the Scaramouch* that called for a show of backbone to "put the Mormons out!," the *Western Rural* asked for President Cleveland, who had already demonstrated "considerable animosity" toward the Mormon Church, to send federal and confederate soldiers "to bring this crowd of traitors to their senses; and if volunteers are wanted they can be had by the thousands in every section of the country." The half-mast insult threatened the legitimacy of the American nation itself: "Either we are a nation or we are not," and as long as such insults were tolerated, they were an affront to the lesson of the Civil War—that America was a real nation. It was time that Utah learned this lesson of American nationalism, and that such disloyalty was not to be tolerated.[82] On Friday, July 17, as public sentiment and national anger continued to intensify, Cleveland ordered the military to "keep all posts . . . in full strength," as to be "prepared for any emergency that might rise in Utah in the near future."[83] On Saturday, the *Lincoln Post* of Butte, Montana, reported that there were two companies of soldiers, eighty strong, "armed, uniformed and equipped," and "ever man of them a veteran."[84]

Governor Eli H. Murray telephoned General A. McDowell McCook at Fort Douglas to send in the military but was dismissed as unwarranted.[85] On Saturday evening, the Federal Courthouse housed an "indignation meeting" that was so packed it adjourned to the open street. Showing little effort at appeasement, the *Deseret News* mocked the attendees as "rabble-loafers and saloon bummers—the lowest order of society with which our community is afflicted." With frequent reference to the Civil War, various speakers lashed out against the open treason of the LDS Church, together with the *Deseret News*'s earlier apology, which many felt was worse than the original July 4 half-masting. In his fiery speech, lawyer Colonel Kaighn lamented McCook's refusal to send in troops, saying that if Col. Patrick Connor were here, things would be different, as he "would have poured hot shot into the streets of Salt Lake City." Colonel Kaighn then spoke of his own old uniform and rusty sword, noting his willingness to put them back into use.[86]

The evoking of past military heroism and possible present sacrifice heightened the symbolism of the event, and further conflated Mormon polygamy with the Civil War and the abolition of Southern slavery, and the need for a strong federal presence to help close the frontier. As was reiterated by the General Assembly of the Presbyterian Church to Congress, the "extermination of the one (slavery), should sound timely warning as to the latent perils of the other (polygamy)."[87] Prominent Presbyterian theologian Albert Barnes had explicitly linked the two as he argued in his tract, *The Church and Slavery*: that apologetics of either polygamy or slavery threatened the biblical faith of honorable

Christians.[88] The *Salt Lake Tribune* promised violence if the Mormons repeated the half-masting on their annual July 24 Pioneer Day celebration.[89] Fortunately, the crisis quickly passed as the entire nation was asked to half-mast its flags on July 24, due to executive order: Ulysses Simpson Grant, former commander of the federal armies and president of the United States, had passed.[90] Another civil war between Utah and the United States may have been averted by the coincidence of Grant's death, but anti-Mormon feelings did not abate. Rumors of violence and threats of military action continued off and on throughout the remainder of the decade.

Mormon leadership explained its remarkable action as a kind of patriotic dissent, and though being waged on Independence Day, it was to be "distinctly understood" that the church was not against the "Republic as a nation," but rather in opposition to those "sitting in high places and administering the laws," who were "guilty of outrageous acts of oppression towards their fellow-citizens."[91] Indeed, the Mormons viewed their half-masting as an effort to fight "for our rights, inch by inch," through patriotism, and in support of the Constitution—and against those who mistakenly or corruptly interpreted it and administered it.[92] The earlier words of prolific author and pastor of several Congregational and Presbyterian churches in New England, Leonard W. Bacon, from the *Princeton Review* prove relevant, "The disgusting defenders of Mormonism will do well to count the cost before attempting any such attack upon the Christian civilization of New England." It was the enforcement of Christian civilization that was at stake, as it was for the Civil War, and however unenforced earlier legislation had once been, no allowances were now being entertained and no law unenforced for the "brazen advocates of the base systems of Mormonism."[93] As George Q. Cannon lamented, "There are those who would have no sentiment of pity for us [even] if they knew we were innocent of the charges made against us."[94] In response, fellow apostle Moses Thatcher added, we have always been treated like "an unloved child," and "who ever knew a father to be just to an unloved child?"[95]

However, Mormonism both retreated and throve in such an atmosphere—victimhood offered them evidence of their birthright and chosen status, further legitimating their global destiny despite their current Egyptian captivity, while bringing the future into focus—in the courts of the land, defending their rights under the principles of the First Amendment. Several months before these events in 1885, Cannon spoke before the general membership of the church of the era as "an important epoch" for the church. "Events are taking place now that are worthy of our remembrance and we are being put in a position to be tested thoroughly."[96] In 1887, the First Presidency wrote, in an epistle to the general membership, an admission that the church was "passing through a period of transition, or evolution, as some might be pleased to term it." Mormon leaders adapted this belief, and spoke of how this short period of pain and persecution was in reality a time of God-ordained opportunity to prove their patriotism, to learn justice and mercy, to purge the church, to expose the wickedness of the persecutors, to express their loyalty amidst corruption, to practice tolerance, to learn to deal with pain, to unite, to reconcile sinners, to stir up complacent members to a remembrance of their religious duties, to prove themselves saints, to demonstrate that polygamy was not inspired by lust, and, in short, to quote Mormon scripture, to bring about "righteousness."[97]

Following these failed protests and in the midst of court cases that threatened rights of citizenship to Mormon immigrants, thereby making real the possibility of losing church political power in Salt Lake City in upcoming elections, church president Wilford Woodruff framed current events within apocalyptic terms. In a revelation on November 24, 1889, leaders were cautioned not to "deny my word or my law," inclusive of polygamy, and were reminded that all that had been promised to that generation of Mormons, including Christ's imminent return and the downfall of the nation, followed by their global rule, would be fulfilled. Though Mormons resisted the idea that Jesus would return before 1889, the idea was widespread among prophets, apostles, patriarchs, and laity, that just after this date, he would return, creating a type of prophetic count-down among fellow saints. Woodruff's revelation emphasized the idea that divine judgment against the nation (a.k.a. "great Babylon") was assured, and the kingdom and their deliverance as a people was at hand, and the "dominion of the wicked" was to be overthrown by one who was to "come quickly," and whose "judgments are at the door." As a direct response to heightened fears over treasonous Mormon endowment oaths, as given in the Endowment House, Mormons denied throughout November before the courts any attempt or plans to supersede the U.S. government; rather, Mormons understood these prophecies in light of the anticipated divine judgment against the nation and its consequent disintegration. Nonetheless, it was ruled in Utah's 3rd District Court on November 30 that a Mormon immigrant was "not a fit person" to become an American citizen, thus marking Mormons as not American.[98] On New Year's Eve, following a decade filled with what John Taylor called "suicidal and traitorous enterprises," Woodruff wrote in his diary, "Thus Ends the year 1889 And the word of the Prophet Joseph Smith is begining to be fulfilled that the whole Nation would turn against Zion & make war upon the Saints. The Nation has never been filled so full of lies against the Saints as to Day. 1890 will be an important year with the Latter Day Saints & American Nation." In response to the early 1890 ruling that escheated church property, both real and personal, Woodruff declared the nation had at last turned "the Last [key] that will seal [its] Condemnation."[99]

While Mormons expected in the 1880s that God would soon intervene and transform the nation in its negative response to Mormonism, important internal dynamics, intensified by external pressures, were transforming the church. Though revelation was credited as the genius behind these changes, several unsuccessful cases brought before the Supreme Court in the 1880s led Mormons to reimagine the meaning of both their faith and its public role within the nation. In light of Woodruff's November 24 revelation of deliverance "from the dominion of the wicked," Woodruff and his counselors sent an epistle to church authorities for a churchwide general fast on Joseph Smith's birthday, December 23. Members of the church were not to pray for national condemnation as they long had, but instead for their own sins and for softened hearts and opened eyes, in the hopes that the country would be more "inclined to treat us with that kindness and consideration which are due to fellow citizens who are loyal and true in upholding the Constitution of our great country."[100] Ultimately, these considerations that pushed toward better relations with the country, were granted only once Mormons surrendered these more provocative exclamations of faith and certain religious practices, and redefined themselves from within a more individual, monogamous, and privatized understanding of faith.

As the nineteenth century was winding up, religion, and the role of religion in public life and its connections with and use by the government, were in unprecedented upheaval; or, as sociologist Max Weber put it, was undergoing a period of international disenchantment. Despite doubled efforts to renew millenarian thought and fervor as spearheaded by national and international conferences throughout the late 1870s and 1880s as a response to this disenchantment, the country was increasingly rethinking the role of religion as part of the public sphere.[101] Traditional religion and its influence on public events and figures were indeed still recognizable in 1890, remaining a significant factor in how the country continued to conceive itself and defend its belief. Protestant supporters of the millennium, however, grew ever more unsettled upon points of scriptural interpretation, embracing the increasingly popular understanding of Christ's coming and judgment as imminent, potentially occurring "at any moment." In contradicting earlier ideas of preparing the earth for Christ, Jesus was now thought to return to earth and destroy it and its wicked inhabitants by fire before the traditional utopian dreams were to be had, revealing a new and growing popular disinterest if not pessimism toward social progress. This new, gloomy outlook in the ability of Christians to prepare the country for Christ's advent, recognized George Marsden, inspired new levels of political and social noncooperation among many churches, allowing them to redefine their "separate and holy" status with that of the world itself.[102] Though the trends among these new premillenarians that one's Christian duty to the kingdom could be reduced to that of private prayer and "other-worldliness," there remained significant diversity of thought in the actual details of the doctrine and how they related to political involvement. What was beginning then, was not just a split in how Americans discerned the coming millennium and return of Christ, but a dramatic schism within American Protestantism between those who embraced political activism, social progress, and science, and those who defined themselves against these ideals and expectations.

These important shifts began as early as 1870, having dramatic implications that we will explore in later chapters. What is important here, however, is to recognize that this earlier idea of the kingdom and its relationship to politics was no longer assumed within American religion but contested from within and without. New social and intellectual trends compounded these divisions, bringing up not just scientific concerns with religion and the role of religion in politics, but the fundamental shape of the kingdom itself and how it was to be more efficiently engaged.

Marsden notes that this new "dispensation of the spirit" and emphasis on the New Testament came in contrast to the earlier "dispensation of law" as defined through earlier Calvinist Old Testament ideas and attitudes, as outlined in earlier chapters. American religion at the end of the nineteenth century was being inspired by new national visions that helped shape how many approached the new challenges of an increasingly urbanized and industrialized society. Part of these developments came in response to the rising popularity of holiness teachings during this era as well, providing a powerful literalist approach to religion as personal experience, over that of public politics. Charles Finney's earlier teachings of political involvement remained important throughout the last decades of the century, but they began to lose influence with this new emphasis on an individual pietistic form of Christianity. Divided by this conservative holiness movement, together with the increase of secular and progressive thought within American society and religion, the American kingdom ideal that once sought to bring forth Christ's advent through the eradication of sin was quickly losing power as we came to the end of the century.[103] But, as seen with the Supreme Court, the redefining of religion that led to a form of legal national privatization was not a secular attempt to destroy religion, but rather an effort by the Protestant court to encourage true religion and to protect America from its counterfeit.

## THE SUPREME COURT: DEFINING RELIGION, DEFINING THE AMERICAN

In unanticipated ways, the U.S. Supreme Court, via secular logic and reasoning, encouraged this particular form of privatized religion and distanced millennialism as a way of discounting the presence of undesirable religion within American society and an attempt to uphold the moral establishment of the Protestant status quo.[104] It seems that many Protestants, either those who now looked to the heavens for the coming kingdom, or even those who sought to establish it in this world, ironically shared in the attempt to minimize the role of religion (or at least particular kinds of religion) within American society. As pertaining to Christ's advancing kingdom and its association with national progress and the closing frontier, Mormons stood, marked J. W. Mendenhall of the *Ladies Repository*, as "a chief obstacle in the way of territorial development, and to the nation at large." Writing in 1875, Mendenhall lamented that statesmen had so far been ineffective against such national enemies, calling on Congress to fulfill its mandate and to "cast it out, Jezebel-like, to the dogs." Reigniting lessons learned from the Civil War and the final abolition of slavery, churches and reform societies were to once again work in tandem with the government for the "abolition of polygamy." With the kingdom and the state working as a unit, it was the job of the churches and their volunteer societies to first rally national attention against national sin, while "the government must put its strong hand on the giant" and "execute the plain law of necessity and right." As it was "in the slavery epic, so now, the church must discover to the people the solemn duty of the hour, while the Government must risk its own fate in performing it." This fight, which at times conflated coercion and exclusionism with republicanism, suppression with philanthropy, and church goals with politics, this fight "between Mormonism and civilization" was not new but was understood to be the continuation of that ageless fight in the wilderness against barbarism and civilization, Satan and the angels. Emphasizing faith in the cosmic and progressive forces of the frontier, Mendenhall reminded his readers that Brigham Young was growing old and "the Protestant element is infusing itself in Mormon society, and has an educational influence hard to overcome." Indeed, Americans in the 1870s and 1880s had the joint religious and patriotic responsibility to unite themselves, not just in opposition to Mormonism and the barbarism of the ever-receding frontier, but in anticipation of the "Anglo-American Union" and the progressive "march of modern civilization," being equated as two parts of the same entity.[105] The significance of this is not just Mendenhall's call for religious influence in matters of the state, but that such a crisis as he presented actually illuminated within the narrow formulation just a few years later in *Reynolds* what had long been taken for granted—the case that essentially established religion as a private affair.

Though change was in the air, Mormon differences were once again subsumed as part of the shaping narrative of the United States' vision of itself. An important development within this debate over the nature and role of religion as a defining quality of the republic took place in the Supreme Court, which not only ruled on the practice of polygamy but in the definition of religion. In this we can see, as was described at the beginning of this chapter, how Mormonism was conceived and particularly well used as an ideological construct, or fictional narrative, that allowed the sanctioned national narrative to be defined and rendered safe, understandable, predictable, stable, and progressive toward Christ's kingdom, however diverse American thought now took it up. With the aid of this construct, white Protestant influence was naturally appealed to as natural and providential, its conventions the standard by which all Americans should live.

To some degree, the specific debate began in 1874, when President George Q. Cannon requested his close friend and member of the church Seventy, George Reynolds, to protest against the constitutionality of the Morrill Anti-Bigamy Act (1862) and present a test case for religious liberty under the Free Exercise Clause of the First Amendment.[106] Such constitutional limits, however, had not yet been defined within American jurisprudence on the national level, and Reynolds went on to argue that the 1862 law was unconstitutional because it infringed upon the First Amendment; that is, Congress had abridged the freedom of religion of the church in its antibigamy legislation. In Reynolds's second trial, Judge Alexander White rebuffed the plea by explaining that there "must be some limits to this high constitutional privilege" of religious freedom.[107] Reynolds appealed to Utah's Territorial Supreme Court, which sustained the verdict on June 13, 1876. On November 14, 1878, the U.S. Supreme Court heard the case and eventually upheld lower court decisions against Reynolds on January 6, 1879. The Court's decision, and the definitions by which it based its decision, succeeded in making the Mormon's attempted practice of freedom of religion a breach of the hegemonic Protestant religion and its sectarian and exclusionary claims about religion.

Refusing to instruct the jury in its summary that Reynolds had married a second wife as a point of religious obligation, Judge Alexander White, the appointed territorial district attorney, reminded the jury of their moral obligations as Americans concerning this case. White defined Mormonism as delusion and a false religion with terrible consequences upon its innocent victims, particularly children. Furthermore, the jury was encouraged to think upon the "pure-minded women" and "innocent children—the innocent in a sense even beyond the degree of innocence of childhood itself." The court then went on to warn the jury that if they "fail to do their duty" against Reynolds, the "victims" of Mormonism would "multiply and spread themselves over the land."[108] Reynolds appealed to the Supreme Court that this was unfairly prejudicing the jury. However, marriage and the home, declared the Supreme Court, was the "most important feature of social life," stating that the founding fathers "never intended" for the concept of religious liberty and freedom to destroy innocent women and children of the republic. Citing Professor Francis Lieber, a pioneering political scientist and influential intellectual of the day, Chief Justice Waite followed old paradigms as he offered the contrast that "polygamy . . . fetters the people in stationary despotism," while monogamy frees people from it. It was therefore the opinion of the Court that Congress has power to enforce monogamy as the "law of social life under its dominion."[109] Quoting Thomas Jefferson, Waite explained "that it is time enough for the rightful purposes of civil government for its officers to interfere when principles break out into overt acts against peace and good order."[110] For Justices like Stephen J. Field, who largely concurred with the majority of the Court, "peace and good order" were understood within a framework of religion, as seen in Field's earlier support for California's Sabbath law which he understood as crucial in the well-being and preservation of civil society.[111] As such, relying on this form of religious logic, the U.S. Supreme Court upheld such instructions to the jury as appropriate, arguing that their purpose was "not to make them partial, but to keep them impartial."[112]

The case concluded on January 6, 1879, with the Court upholding the antipolygamy legislation of 1862 as constitutional. Not surprisingly, the Mormons declared the decision unfair, prejudiced, and in itself unconstitutional, and therefore not legitimate or binding. Indeed, the idea that religion could be reduced to the private sphere of "mere opinion" was absurd to Mormon leaders. "Wonderful doctrine!" Erastus Snow sarcastically reacted to this decision at a general conference of the church.[113] In this and continuing challenges against the Protestant moral establishment, Mormon leaders accused government officials and chief justices of corruption and religious bigotry. Nonetheless, the same leaders were careful to reemphasize their loyalty to the Constitution itself. "Whatever some may have thought of the mal-administration in our government and of the efforts of individuals and sometimes of large factions, to abridge the rights of the people," spoke Erastus Snow, "we must charge it always where it belongs—to the bigotry, the ignorance, the selfishness, ambition and blind zeal of ignorant and corrupt politicians, their aiders and abettors."[114] Snow then recalled that the "fathers who framed our Constitution were not such dunces" as he accused the chief justices of the Supreme Court of being in *Reynolds*.[115] The case served to reveal that the Mormons sought religious liberty as provided by the Constitution; it also served as a strong reminder that religious expression was limited to what did not offend the national norms of Protestant religion and its aligned sense of Christian morality.

Another court case, in 1889, provided public platform on which Mormonism once again sought to defend its right to religious liberty, and its rights were once again denied. Responding to an influx of Mormons, the territory of Idaho enacted a law that made it illegal to believe, or to have once believed, in Mormonism. The Idaho law stated that no man could vote or run for office without first taking an oath that denied affiliation with or belief in the church. Attempting to evade this law, some Idahoans renounced their membership in the church; election officials, however, disregarded such renunciations and continued to bar former Mormons from voting. Unsurprisingly, this legislation was challenged as unconstitutional, and was eventually brought before the U.S. Supreme Court by former Mormon Samuel D. Davis in 1889 in *Davis vs. Beason*.[116] In the resulting ruling, Justice Stephen Field once again ruled against the church, and upheld the Idaho "test oath," explaining that such a law "is not open to any valid legal objection to which our attention has been called."[117] The decision rested upon the simple assumptions that to be Mormon was to be against the law—and not just against any law, but against the very moral laws upon which the United States government was founded. The only concern, it seemed, of this Protestant Supreme Court was whether Idaho had the authority to enact such a law, and it found in the affirmative.

Mormonism was once more being denied the status of religion and the protection due religion by the highest court of the land. Justifying this overt breach of the principle of religious freedom, Justice Field wrote, "To call their advocacy a tenet of religion is to offend the common sense of mankind." As in *Reynolds*, the church's practice and condoning of polygamy was considered to be a crime "by the laws of all civilized and Christian countries," and thus undermined the church's claim to legal and constitutional protection. By natural consequence, polygamy tended "to destroy the purity of the marriage relation, to disturb the peace of families, to degrade woman and to debase man." In fact, he continued, "Few crimes are more pernicious to the best interests of society and receive more general or more deserved punishment. To extend exemption from punishment for such crimes would be to shock the moral judgment of the community."[118] In furthering the *Reynolds* definition of religion as residing in the realm of "the field of opinion," Field explained that "the term 'religion' has reference to one's views of his relations to his Creator, and to the obligations they impose of reverence for his being and character, and of obedience to his will." He continued: "It was never intended or supposed that the amendment could be invoked as a protection against legislation for the punishment of acts inimical to the peace, good order and morals of society." On "this point," Justice Field explained, "there can be no serious discussion or difference of opinion."[119] Having thus defined religion and reduced it to a particular theological understanding of God and a particular form of obedience to his will, Field indicated that Mormons could no longer be trusted with their own sense of morality, particularly since that morality was seen as abnormal to general society—if not criminal. If Mormonism would not subjugate itself to the Christian moralities of the state, then it could not be considered a religion and, as such, had no constitutional guarantee of state toleration and protection. Knowingly, or unknowingly, the Supreme Court had further shored itself up as the upholder of the national sense of ethics and social morality, thus setting a precedent for the true religion of the whole country, as well as exposing a certain coercive and visible nature of the invisible Protestant moral establishment.[120]

George Q. Cannon protested against this governmental presumption of authority to challenge an organized religion, let alone advance a normative definition of religion and thereby limit its freedom of expression. Just a few months following President Chester A. Arthur's signature on the Edmunds Act that made polygamy a felony, Cannon contested that men had the right to worship God according to their conscience, "despite the Supreme Court decisions, despite the action of Congress, despite the expressions of pulpit and press." Moreover, in an appeal to a type of "higher law," Cannon declared that the Constitution was above dictates of any court or group of men, and that as moral agents, all men were responsible to God, and God alone, regarding the legitimacy of those religious practices and expressions of what was "moral." Cannon spoke against those attempts to define and thus limit religion: "I would just as soon be dictated to by the Pope of Rome, by Mr. [Robert] Inger-soll[121] or by a 'Mormon' Bishop, as to be dictated to by popular preach-ers, as to what I must accept as religion." Furthermore, in a way that furthered their own sense of being a redeemer church, Mormon leaders expanded the scope of their protest to include the fight, of not just Mor-mons, but non-Mormon alike. As Cannon explained, "we are fighting the battles of religious liberty for the entire people; it might be said, for the entire world."[122]

At the heart of these protests was a popular idea among Mormons that the American experiment in religious liberty, as they perceived it, would revolutionize the world. Such attitudes and sentiments were put to the test during these and other court proceedings in the 1880s, only to be ruled time and time again in the disfavor of the church—thereby enlisting the courts, notes Gaines Foster, as an important player in the national moral reform crusades.[123] The question of existence within the face of overwhelming opposition by the federal courts finally led Mor-mon leaders to rethink their ideals and the role they were to play within the nation. The apparent final blow came when the Supreme Court once again ruled against the church in *Late Corporation of the Church of Jesus Christ of Latter-Day Saints vs. United States*. This case was a final attempt by the church to protest the unconstitutionality of anti-Mormon legis-lations. As with *Reynolds*, this case had its share of charged religious rhetoric and anti-Mormon hostility and it, too, reveals that the Court was unwilling to understand Mormonism and its practice of polygamy as a legitimate religious tenet of faith. Americans expected the Court to uphold popular Protestant morality surrounding the family and prac-tices of sexuality, and this case provided an excellent opportunity to do so. The Court did not disappoint as it pronounced Mormonism a "blot on our civilization," a "return to barbarism," and a "contumacious organization," and thus beyond the protection of the Constitution.[124] In effect, the Court again denied that Mormonism was a religion, and had no recourse to the First Amendment.

By 1890, the Latter-day Saints found they had few friends, and Christ's return appeared farther out than expected. Moreover, their allegiance to the Constitution and the First Amendment was not enough, nor their claims to moral authority. All the higher and lower courts, houses of congress, and executive authority, as well as what seemed the entire national populace and its clerical and literary forces, united in a common cause to destroy the immorality and immense power of Mormon irreligion. Christian marriage and the monogamous family were heralded as the central units of civilization—a white Protestant civilization—and thus the basis of how American society endured and throve. Mormonism was perceived and treated not as inconsistent with prevailing notions and standards of American Christian civilization, but as a hostile affront at the moment of growing public challenges that could not easily be ignored or tolerated without consequences.[125] As the Court affirmed, it was the function of the federal government to encode "our Anglo-Saxon system of laws" and thus encourage "religion, morality and knowledge" as shaped by an Anglo-Protestant majority.[126] A succession of court rulings declared Mormonism as outside the bounds of the proper definition of religion—and at odds with the Constitution. Mormonism as an institution had to either drop polygamy and adopt court-sanctioned definitions of religion (a.k.a. a privatized, nonpolygamist faith) or retain their irrelevance and stigma. After 1890, Mormons could no longer appeal to the courts or the Constitution as a religious tenet, and became open to prosecution.[127] Moreover, the frontier line was declared by the Surgeon General to have officially closed that year, and as a response, the church publicly renounced polygamy and to a degree "became like them."

As the Supreme Court indicated in its decisions, the exercise of religious freedom was a principle largely extended to those who did not challenge or deliberately annoy the dominant religious moral establishment in nineteenth-century America. The divisions then ravaging within Protestantism during these decades had little impact on this national crusade against Mormonism and, if anything, provided a sense of familiarity and continuity with an earlier Christian nationalist vision and political activism. Following the Civil War, the North achieved significant power to define America for both the southern and western frontier, thus bringing into fruition a powerful federal government that could ensure a united Christian nation-state.[128] The American experiment in religious freedom was thus defined at this time as a privilege only given to those "like us," rather than an assumed right granted to all equally. The American jurisdictions of courts and congress guided this process and refused to grant legality or understanding to the Mormons' particular practices of their religion. Indeed, the definition of religion in America was redefined, both within Protestant structures of power, as well as from without, and it was in part this specter of an overreaching and immoral Mormonism that helped provide its creative energy.

Religion, though now ruled a matter of private belief by the Supreme Court, was also subject to the law. Religion and religious liberty, then, were not already made, but rather, as put by scholar of American religion Ann Taves, were in the *process* of being made.[129] In looking at the "Mormon Question" of the 1870s and 1880s, Sarah Gordon observes that the link between religion and law was apparent and profound, creating and allowing for a united front by ministers, Christian social reformers, the judiciary, and Congress. Extending beyond sociologist Robert Bellah's more generic sense of "civil religion" that understands portrayals of public religion as little more than trite expression of faith by public officials, David Sehat demonstrates how this united front created a powerful network of Christian organizations in the 1870s and 1880s that infiltrated all levels of U.S. power, thereby subjugating all Americans to their own peculiar sense of Protestant freedom of religion.[130] By the 1880s and 1890s, according to Gaines Foster, an informal alliance of Christian reformers (largely led by women) and lobbyists pushed for a Christian government, and a broad agenda of moral legislation had clearly emerged. Despite religion being defined as private and individual, the crisis posed by Mormonism actualized these efforts and elevated national moral crusades that enabled the passing of coercive laws at the national level at the behest of the Christian pulpit, thus expanding "the moral powers of the federal government and establishing its religious authority."[131]

By 1890, the nation, whether its citizens were aware or not, had joined together religion and patriotism so strongly that it had little or no conception of how constitutional principles had been set aside for the purpose of conflating Protestant morality with the morality of national progress.

This conflation helped fashion a comprehensible national narrative, one that provided direction and an assurance of Christ's favor with the country in this transitional and contested era. The American experiment of religious liberty was thus further crafted within these perceived national threats against it, thereby imposing a particular brand of progress and morality that America's religious minorities were to assimilate, presenting not simply a narrative of freedom and fairness, but also that of disarray, coercion, and deep contestation between religion, theology, and governmental mandates.[132]

At the same time, this is not a story of unidirectional change over time, but rather one where things move in opposite directions simultaneously, a dynamic that became especially clear in 1893. On the one hand, we see a nation whose identity had strongly fused with religion; but on the other, we observe this very dynamic aid its own disempowerment in society through enforcing religious privatization. Privatization was a theme pushed not only by the Protestant courts, but also by secularists who feared religious influence on politics. Liberal Protestants upheld these privatization ideals through the old Madison-Jeffersonian notion of religious separation, while the growing conservative holiness revivalists took a more pessimistic approach to religion as incapable of solving society's ills, and thus removed their hands from the national steering wheel in anticipation of an epic crash that Christ himself promised to deliver them from. Either way, privatization was becoming a powerful force among multiple unlikely allies. In 1893, it would be these dynamics and their varied contradictions, ironies, and complexities, as worked out through a new era of social, economic, intellectual, and political anxieties, that Mormonism hesitantly traveled to the World's Fair, and to their surprise, found a changed America that not only rejected them as expected, but simultaneously embraced and celebrated them.

# PART II

## KINGDOMS IN TRANSITION

# CHAPTER 4

*Closing the "Frontier Line" and the Exclusion of Mormonism from the Parliament of Religions, 1893*

The Parliament of Religions simply recognizes the fact, which is indisputable, that there are on this planet a number of religions, among which Christianity numerically counts one. It tries to epitomize that fact in a single room. If the Christian ought not to recognize in a single room what he perforce recognizes in God's earth as a whole, then he must logically class all other religions under the category of things that have no right to be. . . . The religion, so big with its own authority that it cannot stoop to hear and understand and welcome the worth of other human strivings after God, seems but a sorry caricature of the Meek and Lowly One.

—Rev. R. Herbert Stead, 1892

The end of the nineteenth century saw significant cultural shifts which had introduced the United States to a new, much broader world of social, spiritual, intellectual, and economic inquiry and reorientation, which soon produced creative and diverse responses. In a period that has been described as an "ordeal by faith," the responses and discomforts arising from such intellectual and religious challenges mark the beginning of an era in which the Bible was no longer assumed to be the crucial element in discerning the meaning of American public life. In real ways, this ordeal shifted religion and religious opinion away from what it meant to be American, providing for a new cultural and intellectual framework that began to rethink them as separate from the state. Mormons found themselves once again disadvantaged by this evolving secular narrative, yet the church and its faithful also came to find that this revising narrative offered new opportunities for understanding previously denied them. In direct contrast to its more antireligious trends in Europe, the emergent scientific study of religion as adopted in Chicago instilled a deeper level of religious empathy, which informed the intellectual structures of the Parliament, allowing for once unpopular religions to be reimagined. Though Mormons were not to provide or contribute to this new intellectual framework of religious pluralism that Americans created in the late nineteenth century, these frameworks can be exemplified by the church's simultaneous inclusion—and exclusion—at the World's Columbian Exposition in Chicago in 1893. The church's experiences at the fair posed and pose new questions about the church's role in the changing American religious narrative as it evolved into something new and different—while not completely leaving behind principles of theology.

This remarkable era for the United States and the church can be understood by delving further into Frederick J. Turner's previously referenced Frontier Thesis, the forces that produced it, and the concerns it addressed, both secular and religious. Then the Mormon and the larger national experience at the World's Fair in Chicago and in the Parliament of Religions will be considered. All three—Turner's thesis, Utah Day at the fair, and the Parliament reveal a United States in the throes of social and religious change—which would benefit the church by allowing a new narrative for the once-perceived barbaric frontier faith and people. Turner's theory of the American character and the frontier provided a new secular romanticism of the receding West and its glorification of the pioneer spirit that American progressives were then highlighting—thereby providing new options for national inclusion for this frontier religion that had recently been humbled by the coercive power of American liberty. As part of the World's Fair celebration, civil service commissioner and progressive Theodore Roosevelt dedicated a frontier exhibit built by the Boone and Crockett Club, which he himself founded, whose dedication was not just to depict life on the American frontier as part of some bygone era, but instead to stand as a reminder of what made Chicago's White City uniquely progressive—the frontier and its pioneer heritage.[1] Mormons subtly emphasized the term "pioneer" as they sought to take advantage of the changing national environment and engage this new era of anticipated progress by redefining themselves as similarly progressive and a vital element of the American imperial frontier, as seen at the more secular components of the World's Fair, but even more so during the Reed Smoot hearings ten years later, in which Roosevelt took a central and active role.

## RELIGION AND THE FRONTIER

In the opening of this book, I defined the frontier as its own type of religion with its own level of faith and cosmic order. Looking at the frontier as a religion allows us to emphasize this "unseen order" that many relied on to define what it meant to be American throughout the nineteenth century, together with the central role the frontier played in this experience. Steeped in its own sacred language, cosmic time and space, mythical storytelling, and ritualistic actions, this order appeared to be just as real as the imagined barbarism it sought to define itself against. The belief in this frontier actually stood as the emotional dividing line between this imagined advancing force of civilization and barbarism, indeed the meeting place between the two. Fundamentally, then, the idea of the frontier was one defined by conflict and tension, and viewing it through its own religious lens allows us to make sense of peculiar cultural themes such as Manifest Destiny, together with the deeper cosmic meanings of expansionism, nationalism, liberty, and republicanism. Though not a "religion" in the typical sense in which we think of Christianity or Islam as being a religion, the frontier was instead an idea that functioned like a religion and accordingly transformed and informed how people thought and acted. The frontier was not primarily geographic, but instead a figurative and symbolic meeting place where Americans hashed out what they meant when they thought of themselves as "American." As posited at the beginning of chapter 1, the frontier was a religion, not just because it consisted of this belief in this "unseen order" that Americans sought to harmonize themselves with, but because it represented a "system of symbols" that established powerful moods and motivations that formulated strong conceptions of a "general order of existence" that felt real—creating an "American" existence that reveals how Americans discerned "ultimate order and meaning" in the course of their existence. With the emergent claims that this frontier had now closed, a new way of thinking about the American past and present, together with its shifting relationship with the sacred, became important.

Within these more abstract concepts, industrial progress, social change, and religious change—all marked in very specific ways the second half of the American nineteenth century. In noting these technological, economic, and social shifts, Josiah Strong observed a new landscape in which "steam and electricity are making the whole world a neighborhood and every man a neighbor." In his book, aptly titled *The New Era* (1893), America's technology boom revolutionized living standards as well as ways of thinking, refashioning in literal and abstract ways this new American landscape. The new landscape also created a host of new problems, ranging from monopolizing corporate industries, the unemployment of the skilled artisan, the loss of cheap and available land, growing discrepancies between the economic classes, the growth of cities, and the exploitation of unskilled as well as women and children laborers. After pointing out widespread social, religious, and economic uneasiness and discontent, Strong sought to assure his Protestant readers that these changes and challenges were not cause for despair, but were instead evidence of "a progressive civilization"—indeed, one leading to a higher kind of human evolution that promised to waken and redeem America, bringing in the "fuller coming of his [Christ's] kingdom."[2] Though recognizing current efforts to respond to society's problems as "sadly deficient," Strong offered an overly optimistic reading against Christianity's growing powerlessness and decline in the face of national affluence.[3]

Hopes of a united Christian front based upon an earlier higher Christian unity were devastated as the once invisible but politically powerful network of volunteer church communities began to give way to nonpolitical and visible church bureaucracies. Christians were more divided and parochial than ever, and those who resisted these new technological and intellectually progressive trends no longer felt themselves at home in the nationally prominent structures of power and were becoming marginalized. Even once-prominent Protestant church historians found themselves pushed aside to more parochial seminaries and divinity schools as the scientific study of history, at the universities, became professionalized and secularized. In what Charles Taylor deemed as "secularity," God's role in public spaces and affairs was diminished and the nation-state, rather than the church, had become the new reference point for economic and social prosperity—and identification with a larger community.[4]

This growing nationalism at the end of the century cannot be seen as a natural response to liberalism or an inevitable product of some modern-secular evolutionary awakening, but rather a type of created and even imagined political community that fashioned itself over and against that which came before. Based in a shared language and ideal toward progress, nationalism at the end of the nineteenth century in a sense did not abandon, but utilized religion as a framework for this newly imagined modern and progressive consciousness.[5] Rooted in this religious ideal of progressivism and the kingdom, American secularity confidently embraced a new myth of progress rooted in modernity and its corollaries, leaving millennial thought either behind or transformed as it sought to retain relevance and to adjust to the demands of these changes within American society.[6] As already suggested, some of this reimagining was optimistic, anticipating the perfection of the world prior to Jesus's return, while others were more pessimistic, instead preferring social rejectionism as they awaited the destruction of the unrepentant wicked world.[7] Though fairly at odds, events at the end of the century exposed these growing tensions, thus setting the stage for the oncoming conflicts between social gospelers, modernists, and fundamentalists, as well as the alliance of liberals and social reformers with various progressive movements.[8] These shifts toward the secular at the end of the century are not to be misunderstood as the disappearance of religion from American society, but rather, as Taylor explains, the allowance for an increase of options and imagination for what was allowable in American society.[9]

Religion was not being easily set aside in the face of industrialism and the growing power of science, but the latter was increasingly called upon to explain everything, including the United States itself. Conservative Protestants warned that this growing trend to separate religion from the secular was a "pernicious blunder," and indeed many Americans preferred to recognize Protestant Christianity as the leading driver and adjudicator of scientific and social progress, even as the scientific community began to define itself as separate from religious motive and insight.[10] In this climate, science, for a while, became of service to religion, assisted by prominent Protestant intellectuals—among them the pastor of Plymouth Congregational Church in Brooklyn, Henry Ward Beecher, who claimed that natural science would play an important role in bringing forth Christ's kingdom in America.[11] Josiah Strong also argued at the beginning of this era that science not only represented an extension of this Protestant kingdom, but was also a new revelation from God. Strong went so far as to explain that scientists could therefore be considered as akin to ancient prophets declaring "the kingdom of heaven is at hand."[12] Strong's words echoed the alliance between Protestant theology and modern science, which scholars have recognized to have predated late-nineteenth-century debates over Darwinism, which was now being increasingly seen as separate. Evolutionary theory was not necessarily antireligious, but had been incorporated into leading textbooks with a theistic twist that reflected prevailing scientific opinion.[13] However, Strong's warning in 1893 that "religion has been made an adjunct" of American public life appeared accurate as popular scientific awareness increasingly rejected the authenticity of traditional religious inquiry and faith, with many beginning to define it as an antithesis, rather than a synthesis.[14] Ironically, a degree of this awareness was the result of Protestant leaders' engagement with, and seeking to adapt itself to, new social, economic, and intellectual standards. This engagement, however, helped to expose the inadequacy and growing lack of cohesion between conservative religion and these new scientific modes of thought.

In 1850, belief in God was the bedrock of American society and the mythological center of Anglo-Saxon Protestant civilization, and so far had been strong enough to deal with and subsume growing scientific knowledge. However, by 1859, Charles Darwin's theories started cracking science's partnership with religion and by 1870 belief in God and its relation to the natural sciences had become to a degree gelatinous. In particular, Darwinian theories of evolution brought into question a more literal biblical account of the creation of the earth and the divine creation of humankind. In response, Charles Hodge, professor of sys-

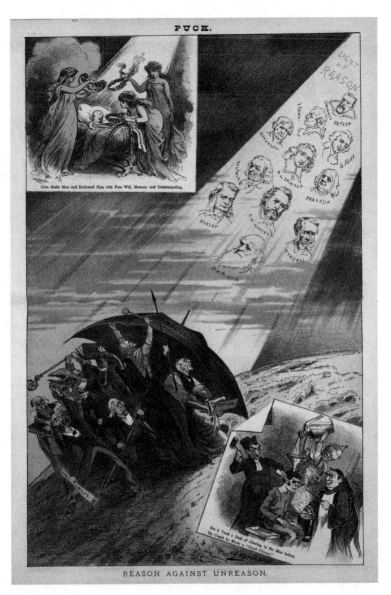

REASON AGAINST UNREASON.

**FIGURE 4.1.** "Reason Against Unreason," by Joseph F. Keppler. Cartoon. *Puck*, August 4, 1880. This illustration demonstrates an increasingly popular view of religion as an umbrella of ignorance, bigotry, and superstition. The umbrella of religious fanaticism shields itself from the "light of reason" as embodied by leading intellectuals like Darwin, Franklin, Huxley, and Tyndall. In the top left corner we see a baby endowed with "free will," "memory," and "understanding," whereas, by way of contrast on the bottom right, a Christian sits passively as he undergoes the ritual of having "superstition" poured into his head by the Catholic pope, while a bishop and monk pound a deafening cone into his ears and burn out his eyes with a glowing, searing iron, leaving him blind, deaf, and ignorant. Courtesy of the Library of Congress.

tematic theology at Princeton, agreed that Darwinism, as a symbol of atheistic empiricism, threatened to "dethrone God" in the quest for ultimate truth.[15] Together with these newly constructed controversies and challenges from evolutionary theory emerged greater challenges in the 1880s of German higher criticism which powerfully questioned the historicity of Christ's life, death, and resurrection, and the infallibility of the Bible. Finally, German moral relativism and atheistic philosophy questioned the very concept of civilization and morality itself and the viability of Christianity altogether.[16] By 1900 a new epistemology provided an intellectual foundation for new forms of belief and unbelief, which helped strip theology of its ancient sources of belief. With its strong emphasis on the emotional, Protestantism's sense of intellectual bankruptcy reinforced growing ideas of religion as being socially irrelevant.[17] In reaction, more traditional Protestants aligned themselves with a new type of emergent frontier, one that began to define religion against and at odds with an emergent scientific enterprise that they now defined as being their antithesis. With this division enunciated, lines were drawn, with many proponents of this new secular vision castigating religion as an ancient vestige of superstition, bigotry, and ignorance in a new era of reason and tolerance, while others sought to extend interest and cooperation between the two.[18] As is seen here however, both sides emerged together and mutually defined the other, leading to an artificial dichotomization that became the very process of secularization itself—a process that has been self-deceptive and misleading.[19]

Initiating the new scientific approach to religion based upon this newly constructed dichotomy, prominent international scholar Edward B. Tylor set forth the proposition that religion originated from "primitive" childish delusions. British linguist Max Muller and other international scholars further framed the study of religion from within Darwin's theory of organic evolution, thereby solidifying this new scientific method of studying religion, helping to transform the study of religion in the 1860s and 1870s from merely being a discipline of revealed religious truth to a developing organism that could be professionally studied scientifically in a lab. Religion, like language, had come to be understood, as articulated by sociologist Émile Durkheim, as a real and observable social fact, and as such demanded serious attention from social scientists, despite its fiction. By 1890, with the publication of Scottish anthro-

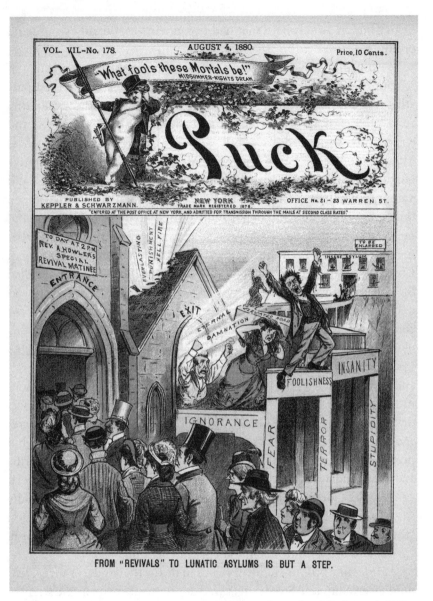

FIGURE 4.2. "From 'Revivals' to Lunatic Asylums Is but a Step," by James A. Wales. Cartoon. *Puck* cover, August 4, 1880. Personal collection.

pologist James Frazer's ambitious two-volume work *The Golden Bough: A Study in Comparative Religion* (later to expand to twelve volumes), the application of evolution to the study of religion was no longer just a theory but an atmosphere that had become internationally secure and prolific.[20]

Within this growing division between the science and practice of religion, believing scholars envisioned the scientific study of "comparative religion" as an exciting opportunity for learning and expanding certain ideas, notably that Christianity would only be enhanced and enriched by such academic work. Innovative British linguists such as Monier Monier-Williams and Max Muller argued that comparative religion actually highlighted through juxtaposition the uniqueness and authority of Christianity and the Bible, rather than diminished them, thus inspiring a new Christian motive in studying non-Western and non-Christian religious traditions. In his "dying speech" at the Parliament of Religions at the 1893 World's Fair, following a half-century of Christian apologetics and pleas for Christian unity, Philip Schaff called for a higher kind of Christianity. This higher form of Christianity was one in which all Christian denominations could participate, and viewed comparative religions not as a threat, but as a tool to bring about this old-kingdom ideal in its illumination of Christianity's unique glory. As with Strong, Schaff and other theological intellectuals embraced the scientific method of inquiry as an important development (even revelation) in the kingdom of Christ in America. Indeed, the "theory of historical development," as long practiced by church historians, not only corresponded to the new secular-scientific "theory of natural evolution," but preceded it and was "endorsed by Christ himself." Thus, the scientific study of comparative religion had not actually threatened the American kingdom ideal and its sense of Christian triumphalism, but actually would become the new means by which God would bring into fruition "the Kingdom of God, whose height and depth and length and breadth, variety and beauty, surpass human comprehension."[21]

At this time prominent universities in the Netherlands, France, Denmark, Germany, and Sweden featured department chairs in the study of comparative religions. Academic journals, encyclopedias, conferences, and international congresses emerged to address the issues and questions of scientific religious studies, most of which looked on religion as a human construct within the then popular theories of social evolution, and as such, saw religion as destined to disappear—European world fairs thus ignored religion as irrelevant to the forces of human progress.[22] Amidst this array of challenges, options, and new ways of imagining religion, the Chicago World's Fair Columbian Exposition defied European precedent by prominently including religion as a crucial element of human progress. Though claiming scientific methods, it was apparent that these more liberal Protestant doctrines of comparative scientific inquiry, expounded on by Schaff, Muller, and others, held the reins at the Parliament of Religions.

The role of religion and science at the World's Fair in Chicago was, in important ways, somewhat complicated, due to the newness of these larger intellectual and cultural shifts. Frederick J. Turner's Frontier Thesis was presented at the World's Fair in 1893 and became an important voice concerning the question of observable and comparable progress in America, opening up a new era of scientific inquiry. Popular perceptions of progress were powerfully informed by the changing context of the American landscape, as between 1870 and 1900 the United States went from being an agricultural nation of farmers, artisans, and merchants to what historians recognized as the "world's foremost industrial power," surpassing even Britain, France, and Germany. Immigration exploded into the tens of millions and manufacturing jobs doubled during these decades, with the nation's mining, construction, and transportation boom tied directly to the West's newly exploited mineral wealth.[23] Changes in American thought during these years were no less dramatic. American historiography, for example, shifted from Philip Schaff's spiritually guided search for the footsteps of Jesus in American history, to that of the iconoclastic and empirically based seminar of Herbert Baxter Adams at Johns Hopkins University, who more than any other helped fashion the link between history and science at the exclusion of the metaphysical. Mentored under Adams and the seminar, Turner signified the birth of a new era of historical scholarship, while Schaff's death just after his return from the Parliament signified the ending of another.[24] Turner's Frontier Thesis not only intellectualized and celebrated this imagined closing frontier, but also presented a new, dynamic script for American historians—a script that helped replace earlier speculative theological models for one based in scientific objectivity and empirical evidence.

The frontier had long been held as a point of conflict by historians, by either seen or unseen powers, and Turner's thesis now implied both the cessation and legitimization of that long-running struggle. Importantly, however, while replacing an older, overly simplistic theological script of American progress as embodied by Schaff, Turner's model similarly bordered imagination and fantasy, sharing an extremely loose relation with the empirical and objective. Turner's vision helped answer what it meant to be an American now that the frontier was considered subjugated, and as Schaff had no equivalent successor, church historiography became marginal. Though not claiming the kingdom of Christ as history's destination, Turner nonetheless provided for a new generation of secular historians a perspective that based itself in science, but framed it from within a sense of history that was still directed toward a "moral whole."[25] Thus, despite his more secular-scientific perception of American history, Turner's academic model yet retained and solidified an attitude of national progress that was no longer dependent upon Europe, one that many now believed to express what it meant to be truly American.

Another side of Turner's theoretical appeal rested in his ability to respond to, make sense of, and justify the past two decades of social and political chaos and violence, inclusive of the Indian Wars, antipolygamy crusades, Reconstruction, Jim Crow, and Chinese exclusionary laws. As argued by Wilbur Jacobs, Turner's thesis provided a ready-made patriotic self-image that assured both social Darwinists and middle-class white Americans that their new institutions of American power were moral.[26] The newly created scientific study of history and comparative religion was thereby central to this new world order as envisioned in the natural sciences, becoming a tool, not just in the attempt to justify the subjugation of the American frontier, but in the entire global colonial project itself, as confirmed by U.S. involvements in Cuba, Samoa, Hawaii, and the Philippines.[27] Though historians masked such bias as "the ways things really are" (a.k.a. objectivity), scholars had begun to recognize that this scientific discourse actually helped regulate and control troublesome groups on the margins of society, as well as those of their colonial possessions, illuminating expressions of power that were demonstrated in the very structures of the Chicago World's Fair itself.[28] Aptly given at the fair in Chicago, Turner's thesis of the frontier and its closure provided new enthusiasm and interest in this process of Americanization, having both national and international implications.

It was in this general atmosphere that Turner developed his thesis, in some ways dismissing a specific understanding of the past and projecting a particular future. Turner effectively dismissed the traditional colonial European reference point of progress, adopting instead the idea that the American environment itself, specifically that of the frontier, brought forth what Americans prized as a unique national character and polity. In place of an earlier sense of religious chosenness, Turner declared a new intellectual paradigm of American exceptionalism that was entirely American and, as many thought, scientific. As Henry Nash Smith observed, the humble servant-hero of the western frontier had become secularized, as nature now had its own independent meaning, devoid of divine Providence. The stigmatized cowboy of the Wild West was now replaced by the hero cowboys who stood in between barbarism and civilization, paving the way for American progress. By 1893 Americans held great anxiety over the frontier, as the biblical garden and its promised utopia were largely broken through corporate and private ownership, and as Smith argues, the unseen order of the frontier lived on in American minds in the form of "manly cultivation."[29] Within this new theoretical vision of American history and character, Turner, more than others, revolutionized the American story and its telling in his demand to unify an empirical scientific discipline to the craft of writing history, thus removing potent religious anxiety from popular nineteenth-century historiography.[30] Turner believed that in the closure of the frontier from its more primitive and savage past, he would open up a way to envision the present in accord with a new secular-scientific era that had dawned. This would bring forth new interpretive possibilities that would take into account regional politics, pioneering, and their economic contexts in the story of America, rather than a single religious goal and vision. This new approach, presented at the World's Fair, together with developments in the scientific study of religion, opened up new ways of envisioning the mythology of American characters and the national placement of religious minorities—which of course included the Mormons.

As described in previous chapters, national responses against Mormonism were not simply isolated campaigns of the United States government during times of otherwise consistent and steady tolerance and progress. Rather, such responses represented larger aims by American nativists to preserve and expand a narrow sense of Christian nationalism and Protestant orthopraxy at a time of increased religious pluralism. Although Turner's Frontier Thesis did not integrate this theological necessity held by many American Protestants in the nineteenth century, this new secular narrative reaffirmed and integrated a new script of the frontier environment and made it possible for the nation to see Mormons as allies of the new secularized progressive narrative, and Utah as an important commercial and mineral resource. Most powerfully, this transformation in thinking about the West as an agrarian Christian kingdom to one of industry and commercialism, Mormons were able to transition from being seen as simply barbarians to be conquered, to being recognized as conquerors themselves.[31] While American Protestantism had dismissed particular groups as hopelessly "other" due to theological and racial differences, Turner, in contrast, ignored or at least did not address this religious factor. Instead, Turner emphasized how certain groups effectively transformed the wilderness and themselves, "little by little," into a "new product that is American."[32] Manly character, not theology, became the new emphasis on what made America American.

The western frontier represented a type of factory where people could be transformed into Americans, and where society could be made both free and democratic. Turner himself had confidence in this constructed frontier spirit, allowing for the hopeful belief that even those of "the dull brains of the great masses" of immigrants from southern and eastern Europe could also become Americanized. The genius of this new product was that of its uniquely formed American mythology of progress and its uniquely American national identity that was independent of European institutions or religious forms. Americans were not being infected by these immigrants, but rather, the un-American ways of these immigrants were being rooted out by way of the unseen forces of the American frontier. Furthermore, according to Turner's vision, national attempts to subjugate the frontier (that is, to close it), however crude and unfortunately cruel the tactics, were a very American, and thus civilized and expected, response to America's vast and savage diversity. An important idea within these new formulations of the West were that the longer these encounters against frontier barbarianism endured, the less European and the "more and more American" its end was understood to be.[33] This is an uncomfortable reading of Turner, but Turner's secular and real-world vision did allow a significant dynamic: it allowed for non-traditional groups of the frontier—such as the Mormons—to become more American. Thanks to their amazing travels to and on the frontier, their building of cities, colonies, and irrigation systems, and tilling of the land, Mormons were members of this unique frontier and recipients of a frontier character, even though part of their earlier behavior was considered barbarian and indeed un-American—being another product of the frontier. Even the coercive and unrepublican tactics of the nation against this group could now be perceived as part of the larger script of American progress—a script that went on display in Chicago.

## ENVISIONING THE PARLIAMENT AND THE
## AMERICAN KINGDOM

The Columbian World's Fair of Chicago in 1893 was one of the most publicized events of the nineteenth century and an explicit celebration, argued the publishers of the *Religious Herald*, of "one of the greatest events in all history—the discovery of America by Christopher Columbus" in 1492.[34] Columbus stood as a type of ideal pioneer, initiating the fight against the grand American frontier, which now was being heralded, after four hundred years, as subjugated. Building off this history and growing international trends, the fair's intentions were to represent the beginnings of a new age, one characterized by progress, intellectual sophistication, cultural awareness, and technological advancement. Suitably, the fair had three physical stages: the White City, the Midway Plaisance, and the massive Congress Auxiliary. The White City celebrated the glories of secular government, commerce, and manufacture; the Midway portrayed—or exploited—cultural as well as racial differences so as to demonstrate the "evolutionary ladder" of humanity and its abilities toward self-governance and civilization.[35] The Congress Auxiliary was devoted to even more diverse interests, ranging from fine arts and social reform, to the latest developments in surgery, electricity, and medicine.[36] Notably, Frederick Jackson Turner delivered his Frontier Thesis at one of the sessions featured in the Congresses. Far better remembered than the Congress of Religions, Turner's thesis temporarily takes a back seat to an examination of this Parliament which was conceived in the spirit of intellectual progress, but led to questions and divisions, and revealed that the Parliament's organizers had, despite a liberal outlook, a belief that the Western Protestant hegemony yet held the reins.

Despite the seemingly secular emphasis of the fair, the Congress (or Department) of Religion, which culminated with the Parliament of Religions, attracted more media attention, applause, and controversy than any other department.[37] The significance of the Fair was set by S.C. Bartlett, former president of Dartmouth College, who said the Parliament was "the most important and noteworthy aspect of the most noteworthy gathering of our generation."[38] Ideas for this congress originated in 1889, and serious organizational efforts commenced in the summer of 1891, with proposals and tracts being published by the Auxiliary Committee and widely distributed. Widespread enthusiasm and excitement over the congress was documented. Notably, not all religious leaders and figures were interested. In particular, the Sultan of Turkey, the Archbishop of Canterbury, and China's premier flatly rejected the committee's invitation. At the same time, the committee, perhaps intentionally, marginalized and underrepresented Native Americans, African Muslims, and African Americans, among others. Quite notably, the Church of Jesus Christ of Latter-day Saints was left uninvited.[39]

Such exclusion can be glimpsed in the publicly stated objectives of the parliament itself, objectives that purposefully contrasted with earlier fairs of a more secularized Europe. John Henry Barrows, a prominent, indeed liberal, cleric of the First Presbyterian Church of Chicago was brought on by Charles Carroll Bonney, Swedenborgian and president of the World's Congresses, to be the parliament's chair. According to Barrows, this parliament was not just to exhibit religion, but to demonstrate the "supremacy of evangelical Christianity." As announced by the *New York Times*, the parliament was expected by many to bring forth the divine means by which "the Kingdom of Christ in America" was to be engaged.[40] "Who can tell," wrote Bishop Whitehead of Pittsburg, "that the great Head of the Church may, in his providence, make use of this immense gathering to usher in the triumph of his truth, when at the name of Jesus every knee shall bow?"[41] Notwithstanding claims to appropriate the findings and sentiments of the new discipline of comparative religions and the scientific study of religion, few participants and organizers doubted the role and hand of Divine Providence. Indeed, with its employment of scientific trends, the parliament demonstrated the modernization of American Christianity and its kingdom ideal, directly linking them to an imperialistic world. As part of American Protestantism's messianic heritage, during the same year of America's support for the overthrow of Hawaii's monarchy under the guise of extending the gift of American civilization, the parliament buttressed the hopes of a global Christian conquest.[42] In effect, in both challenging and appropriating the new scientific approach to humanity and religion that had by now powerfully questioned the legitimacy and relevance of religion in the modern world, American Protestants now used it as God's new methodology in the establishment of the American-styled kingdom of God throughout the Americas and the world. Such is indicated by the parliament's pronouncement that this impressive event stood as a "latter day Pentecost," even a "blueprint for the kingdom of God on earth."[43]

Despite shifts in thinking and scientific inquiry into the foundations of faith, the ideal of the kingdom was still alive, and, as was now being seen in Chicago, religion's role within this new era of science and secular progress had to be reclaimed and redefined. Indeed, Chairman Burrows and his associates saw the opening of the parliament as the beginning point of a new millennial epoch in the religious history of mankind. "Within a hundred years," predicted the chairman, "pilgrims from many lands would flock to the scenes of the World's First Parliament of Religions, in the unhistoric City of Chicago, almost as they have for centuries flocked to Westminster Abbey, St. Peter's Church, and the Holy Shrines of Jerusalem."[44] Hon. H. N. Higinbotham, president of the World's Columbian Exposition, regarded the parliament as "the proudest work of our exposition."[45] Josiah Strong, then secretary of the Evangelical Alliance and the nationally known advocate for the Congregational Home Missionary Society, echoed such sentiments of what the moment represented for the nation and its millennial destiny. He suggested that the nineteenth century and its frontier past, however great it had been, was merely a type of John the Baptist, previewing the next great century as it would be envisioned at the World's Fair.[46] Bonney, the originator of the parliament, explained that its purpose was to bring together into "brotherly sympathies any who are groping, however blindly, after God."[47] Such an aim was not so much to celebrate global diversity, but more importantly, to "unite all religion against all irreligion."[48] Nonetheless, however pluralistic and liberal his words, and however exalted the sentiments expressed, the parliament was designed to support and further a message of Christian triumphalism, though broadened and legitimated through a new and secular academic medium of the scientific study of comparative religion.

The parliament seemed destined to succeed, especially with the new breadth it provided in making sense of Christianity in a more global world. An important part of the parliament's agenda of comparative religion was its ecumenical and interfaith motto, taken from the biblical prophet Malachi: "Have we not all one Father? Hath not one God created us?" Divided into four parts, the presentation sessions of the parliament focused upon the "distinctive faith and achievements" of the "great Historic Religions of the world." It was within the great Columbus Hall that the heart of the parliament was felt—however, those without were considered mere appendages whose relevance was marginal. As put by historian Richard Seager, "If one was not among the speakers or the 3,000 observers in the Hall of Columbus in the Chicago Art Institute . . . one was not at the World's Parliament of Religions."[49] Columbus Hall, housed in the newly constructed Memorial Art Palace (now the Art Institute of Chicago), was the location that these presentations were to be given "to the world." They represented the real crescendo and pride of the entire Congress Auxiliary.[50] The other three divisions of the Congress of Religion were less significant and limited to more parochial and denominational concerns, such as missions, religious associations, suffrage, literature, Sunday rest, and ethics.[51]

A celebrated speaker for the parliament was Col. Thomas Wentworth Higginson, a Civil War veteran and influential Boston publisher, and vice president of the Free Religious Association. Looking into Higginson's beliefs and those of his cultural surrounding assist in understanding how comparative religion was understood, but also help reveal the cracks underlying the foundation of the Parliament of Religions. His influential essay "The Sympathy of Religions" argued that religious unity lay not in condescending to other religions, but rather in extending a form of sympathy toward all religions. The article's fame spread throughout New England and apparently the world to become an international sentiment. Framed within larger scientific structures,

Higginson's thesis became an important source of inspiration to the World's Fair, including Chairman Barrows. Barrows himself introduced Higginson to the parliament as an "American of Americans," and one whose "own heart has been a Parliament of Religions."[52] Following this generous introduction, Higginson assured his audience that although science had revolutionized the world of thought and had challenged traditional religion, science had not "dethroned religion forever," but, like John the Baptist, dethroned itself as to make room for its superior—"human aspiration, or in other words, man's creative imagination." In line with Julia Ward Howe's parliament speech and her definition of religion as a universal human "aspiration," or Max Muller's as a "natural spark," or even Philip Schaff's "higher unity," Higginson's "imaginative aspiration" reduced religion to its core universal essence, one that could then be compared and analyzed, in a setting such as the Parliament.[53]

Higginson's scientific model for understanding and even defining religion grew out of a basic Enlightenment presumption that furthered the privatization of religion, thereby making it into a new scientific and even religious innovation, as pushed by the parliament and Higginson's own Free Religious Association. On an international level, this particular rationality served as a universal yardstick in which all other religions were to be measured, becoming not just a model that aided in the observation of other religions, but rather one that formulated a structure that helped manufacture the very thing that was being observed.[54] In 1893, the term *religion* and its secular counterpart were still in creation and were continually overlapping and interweaving, and for many, Christianity remained above and separate from other religions, becoming even the paradigm for religion itself. Not only did the scientific study of comparative religion create a type of moral standard for other religions, but it demanded a new separation of religion from more secular and external expressions of status and power.[55] For American society at the end of the nineteenth century, this distinction between religion and the secular was altogether new, creating a new emphasis on this world when it came to imagining American belonging.[56] Thus, the study of comparative religion in America as articulated by Higginson and others at the parliament and its congresses, however supportive of Christian religious triumphalism, utilized and helped further this new divided understanding of the religious and the secular, allowing Christians at the parliament to look for common ground by way of focusing on the observable world of a shared essence, while still proclaiming their stewardship over it.

Furthermore, Higginson's "Sympathy of Religions" was more than mere sympathy for religious difference; his beliefs took shape with the cultural rationality that true religion was *not plural*. All religions, if they were considered worthy of the term, shared the same ultimate truth (or essence), the same human aspirations (different only in imagination and expression), and the same fundamental assumptions that such could be externalized and objectively studied and compared in a kind of scientific lab, such as the parliament. In the attempt to define and understand this term, Wilfred Cantwell Smith explains that the concept of "religion" in the West gradually became conceived of as an "objective systematic entity" or "thing," thus able to move away from cultural or even political action to that now being expressed as a privately held universal "human aspiration."[57] Sympathy for religions was thus a type of Western rationality that allowed for liberal Christians to dispossess themselves of that which divided and allowed for them to become "possessed of that which all faiths collectively seek." "If each could but make himself an island," spoke Julia Ward Howe at the parliament, "there would yet appear at last above these waves of despair or doubt a continent fairer than Columbus won."[58] Higginson's sympathy and the science of comparative religion represented a new Columbian quest of colonial discovery where science and religion were two separate and mutually exclusive *things* that aided human discovery, rather than unique cultural categories that emerged within particular regional transformations.[59]

Upon such a problematic premise, Sydney Ahlstrom explains that the parliament became a "kind of landmark or watershed" in the "epoch-marking role" of the study of comparative religions in "American social and cultural history."[60] Countering more caustic perceptions of religion from their European counterparts, parliament speakers and organizers reframed the scientific study of religion as a religious enterprise. In line with earlier visions of God's kingdom in America, arguments were being made that religion had not only not failed to transform the world, but that it would yet do so in a more efficient and global way, thanks to science. With the stated exceptions of "feticism and Mormonism," Rev. S. J. McPherson spoke at Chicago's Second Presbyterian

Church of his delight just before the opening of the parliament that papers were to be read from representatives from all "the existing historical faiths." This great event then stood as "the best single opportunity in the history of man for the study of comparative religion," as it was designed to demonstrate in one room "the grandest successes and the most pathetic failures in the highest place of human endeavor." As the parliament was declared by its organizers to be "Christ Exclusive," it had "nothing to fear from the light. If our faith has not the inherent power to conquer the world, we can't save it, for the power that made it great was not that of man."[61] Following this premise, the president's General Committee (made up almost exclusively of Christians) sent out an "invitation of Christianity, addressed to all the great historic faiths, to come and give an account of themselves." With eyes fixed on that kingdom which was "yet to cover the earth," the committee believed "that the best representation possible by the ethnic religions would tend to the exaltation of Christianity."[62] Paralleling the optimism that followed the great revivals of the early nineteenth century, liberal Protestants now anticipated, through the method of comparative religions, that "something new" would break forth in the world of religious knowledge as related to Christ's impending kingdom. For Schaff, such an event brought forth the hope that all "corresponding errors and defects" would break down, forming "not a *new* church, but the final perfect product of that of the present and the past."[63] For Barrows, one of the parliament's leading organizers, "the science of comparative religions . . . has shown the necessity of religions to man, and the supreme necessity of the highest of them all," which he understood to be white Protestantism.[64]

## CHALLENGES IN THE KINGDOM

Such ideals, beliefs, and agendas helped define the Parliament's lofty pursuits and its perception of itself as a world redeemer. Though the parliament has rightly been celebrated for its innovation and pioneering work in global ecumenical gatherings, these earlier expressed qualities would undermine the ecumenical rhetoric of the fair, while other issues, far less intellectually sanguine, brought into question the parliament's ultimate irrelevance in influencing American society. Sabbatarianism, or the question as to whether the fair should be open on Sunday, shook Protestant America and demonstrated a new level of cultural powerlessness. Lyman Beecher had long spoken of the Sabbath as a critical part of upholding national morality and unity, while Associate Justice Stephen J. Field of the Supreme Court, of antipolygamy fame, similarly upheld Sabbath laws as a necessary requirement in the promotion of character and "good morals."[65] Under threat of the fair being open on Sunday, local and international Sabbath associations combined their efforts. Congressman Henry Blair (R-New Hampshire) attempted to pass a comprehensive national Sabbath observance law, even as Josephine C. Bateham, head of the "Department of Effort to Prevent Sabbath Desecration," argued that if the Sabbath went down, so would God's wrath on the nation in the form of financial instability and ruin.[66] For Bateham, controlling this one issue held great significance, representing a "turning point" for Christian power "in our nation's career."[67] Though no one disagreed upon the importance of cultivating moral character for the collective benefit of American society, it was beginning to be questioned with the challenge to these Sabbath laws as to how important religion was in that equation.

Not surprisingly, then, as reported by the *Chicago Times*, the intensity of this cultural, religious, and legal fight had been "tortuous" and full of "agony." In response to the fair's failure to remain closed on the Sabbath, numerous denominations protested; the Baptists and the Christian Endeavor Society pulled out of the Congress, as did the Congress of Anglican Churches, which had come only after the most "earnest toil" of organizers to get them there in the first place.[68] Despite this issue returning to court seven times, it was finally declared on July 2, 1893, that the fair was to be "open every day." Fair organizers sought to soften the effect of the ruling by offering "music of a sacred nature" on Sunday, and there were hopes that Christian preaching would "be carried on" at the fairgrounds. Although many Protestants boycotted the fair on Sunday, the *Chicago Times* jubilantly wrote, "Since no Judge will close the Fair Sundays why not open it enthusiastically?"[69] For parliament organizers, including the avowed Sabbatarian Barrows, one of the original visions of the broader Congress Auxiliary was to counteract the fair's emphasis on "material achievements and mechanical progress" with that of the "intellectual and spiritual sources of civilization."[70] In the end, the fair stayed open on Sundays and a significant cultural battle had been lost at a time of significant cultural redefinition when the nation and its dominant religion stood on display for the entire world.[71] As part of these challenges, the parliament helped clarify this growing sense of separation between the emergent scientific community and that of religion more generally as it came to the regulation of American society. Indeed, at the very moment the American Protestant hegemony sought to demonstrate its resilience over new national and even international secular-scientific trends, it was quickly reminded of its own domestic impotence.[72]

More conservative-minded Protestants felt increasingly threatened and offended by the secular-atheistic approach of this international scientific community and its at-home Sabbath desecrations. In direct response to the secularism and religious liberalism as espoused at the fair and parliament, internationally famous evangelical preacher Dwight L. Moody placed himself and his Christian vision in strong contrast. Following Josiah Strong's warnings against the multiple perils of modernity and its trends toward materialism and secularism, Moody, a resident of Chicago, held his own six-month World's Fair Gospel Campaign in parallel with the World's Fair, drawing in hundreds of thousands of fairgoers. This campaign aimed to inspire visitors to think on religious things, including the importance of scripture, keeping the Sabbath, the dangers of worldliness, and the follies of infidelity and false religion. With daily all-day sermons being held in overflowing tents, packed theaters, and well-attended churches throughout the city, together with speaking arrangements at Central Music Hall, Moody and his associates fought to "neutralize the bad influences which beset of the World's Fair visitors." In light of the "beautiful Sabbath of the Lord" that had been "utterly wrecked in Chicago by the power of Philistia," Rev. John McNeil of Moody's Bible Institute called upon the long history of Christian volunteerism. Similar to Jael's hammer, McNeil inspired his listeners to rise up and be like Shammah, a mighty man of "individual valor" during the reign of the Israelite king David, who defended his territory and "wrought a great victory" for the Lord.[73]

Optimism for the kingdom over the effects of this crusade rivaled that of the parliament itself. The *Epworth Herald* wrote, "This Moody campaign will undoubtedly go into history as one of the most sagacious and influential religious movements of this century." The *Union Signal* compared "this great, victorious, peaceful campaign of faith for the redemption of the world," of which the "bloody campaigns of the Napoleons of earth pale into insignificance." For those who thus sorrowed over the proliferation of sin at the World's Fair, together with its court-ruled Sunday opening, Moody's conservative counter-fair campaign brought hope that it had accomplished "more effectively for the kingdom of God than all the combined forces of evil were able to accomplish against it."[74] For Moody and those who attended these alternative meetings, Moody's crusade daily criticized the materialism and liberal ecumenism of the fair and provided individual strength against these modern-day enemies of God's kingdom in America, positing his services as "a daily standing protest against the mammon worship of the busy mart, and an appeal to the unsatisfied cravings of the soul that cannot live by bread alone."[75] As part of these rather significant internal divisions within American Christianity, such a popular protest outside the fair implied a level of lost control among Protestants over American society and the acknowledgement of a feeling of stewardship that had once, yet no longer, existed.

One of the more profound concerns that arose among conservatives was the popular appropriation of the insights and intellectual developments associated with international responses to modernity and the new definition of religion, which indicated a new powerlessness of religion over the state. As part of this, while liberal Christians embraced new international and universalistic trends in theological inquiry, conservatives looked down on anything foreign, especially if the foreign element appeared linked to the natural sciences and their attacks on religion. Particularly rejected were scientific implications on biblical scholarship and the notion that non-Western religions could be studied on par with Christianity. According to Rev. E. J. Eitel of Hong Kong, the parliament was "coquetting with false religions" and even unconsciously planning "treason against Christ." The *Presbyterian Journal* labeled the parliament "a mongrel gathering"; the *Missionary Review* referred to the parliament as a "golden calf" that "all men are now called upon to worship."[76] In the parliament itself, Rev. William C. Wilkinson reminded attendees that Christ's attitude toward all non-Christian faiths was one "of frank and uncompromising hostility," and the attitude Christians were duty-bound

**FIGURE 4.3.** "Puck's Suggestion to the Congress of Religions," by Frederick Burr Opper. *Puck*, September 13, 1893. Centerfold. The iconic boy Puck is shown handing out placards that read: "Do unto others whatsoever thou wilt that others shall do unto thee." Puck then states: "Here's the best religion in existence, gentlemen,—don't waste time in useless discussions, but—call your meeting to order, endorse it, and adjourn. You'll have more time to see the Fair!" As shown here, the faces of the various representatives of religion appear annoyed and even angry at the simple suggestion, with one holding a book titled, "Outworn Creed," suggesting religion's backwardness at the opening of the modern era. Courtesy of the Library of Congress.

to uphold "towards religions other than itself is an attitude of universal, absolute, eternal, unappeasable hostility"[77]—a belief countered by the more liberal Julia Ward Howe who rebuked Wilkinson for his intolerance. Howe declared that Christianity was "an infinite and endless and joyous inclusion," one that offered a new level of religious discovery by way of comparative religion that was true to the legacy of Columbus of the modern age.[78] Conservatives and modernists had long sat in the same pews throughout the nineteenth century, but as seen with Wilkinson and Howe, together with Moody's outside crusade, divisions within Protestant Christianity concerning these diverging paradigms of the kingdom were becoming too wide to bridge, thus foreshadowing the Fundamentalist controversy of the 1910s and the national evolution debates of the 1920s.[79]

Yet, despite their broad divisions, both liberals and conservatives still held Christianity as triumphant, and as already expressed by McPherson, the parliament stood as the "best single opportunity" to study "all existing faiths" by way of comparing our best with their worst. For Barrows, the parliament would reveal the necessity of religion for humanity, which he understood to be Protestant Christianity. Such bland dismissal makes it

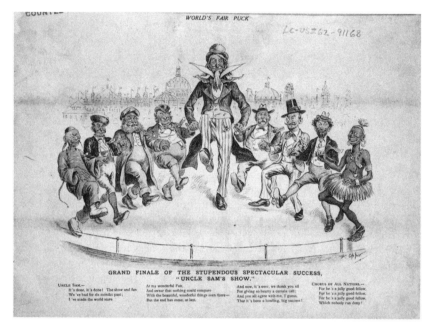

FIGURE 4.4. "Grand Finale of the Stupendous Spectacular Success, 'Uncle Sam's Show,'" by Frederick Burr Opper. *Puck*, October 30, 1893. A centered and towering Uncle Sam holds hands with Protestant Germany and Great Britain. The outward reach extends to France and Orthodox Russia, and then Roman Catholic Italy and Spain, which then includes negative stereotypes of pagan Africa and idolatrous Asia—representing the margins of civilized nations. In this essentialized comparative model that devolved outward, America's iconic Protestant white-male figure is cheered by all for his ability to bring together and lead an entertaining show of global diversity. By way of such uneven comparisons and stereotypes, Anglo-Saxon Protestant global leadership appeared "natural," and even scientific. The caption reads: "UNCLE SAM—It's done, it's done! The show and fun/ We've had for six months past;/ I've made the world stare/ At my wonderful Fair,/ And swear that nothing could compare/ With the beautiful, wonderful things seen there / But the end had come, at last./ And now, it's over, we thank you all/ For giving so hearty a curtain call;/ And you all agree with me, I guess,/ That it's been a howling, big success!/ CHORUS OF ALL NATIONS—For he's a jolly good fellow,/ For he's a jolly good fellow,/ For he's a jolly good fellow,' Which nobody can deny!" Courtesy of the Library of Congress.

FIGURE 4.5. "On with the Dance!: The American Woman Leads the World," by Joseph F. Keppler. Cartoon. *World's Fair Puck*, 1893. Such art demonstrates the American-centric view of the World's Fair. Others were invited and even allowed to participate, but, as this shows, the dance was not on the terms of unity through equality, but unity under American leadership and presumed supremacy. Courtesy of Chicago History Museum.

clear that despite new scientific thinking and methods, imperialism and religious supremacy had been rolled into social evolution and helped forge the Columbian myth of American civilization, and thus little criticism arose against the negative depictions of the Chinese, Native Americans, Africans, African Americans, Inuits, Gypsies, and other long-marginalized groups at the fair. Such negative portrayals did not merely support Anglo-Protestant supremacy at the fair, but also renewed a sense of divine leadership and missionary agenda, both at home and abroad.[80] Dismissing Asian and other religions as an abomination in an era of "steamboats and telegraphs," Dr. W. A. P. Martin, president of the Imperial Tungwen College in Peking, believed it "preeminently the duty of Americans to seek to impart" the blessings of Anglo-Protestant civilization to the world.[81] With such sentiments, combined with the racist legislation against Asian immigration to the United States (i.e., Geary Act, 1892), it comes as little surprise that China's premier, Li Hung Chong, was adamant that China "would have no exhibition at Chicago." Fair organizer Minister Denby expressed his regret at Chong's "*irrational* conclusion."[82] Clearly, the comparative study of religion, as noted by Jonathan Z. Smith, was "by no means an innocent endeavor." As colonial scholar David Chidester affirmed, this new "discipline of comparative religion emerged . . . not only out of the Enlightenment heritage but also out of a violent history of colonial conquest and domination."[83]

The new and exciting perspectives furnished by scientific modeling of the study of religion had expanded world knowledge, but it came with its own set of problematic structures, structures that may have showcased marginal religions but such showcases framed them in ways that certain observers refused to find appealing or fair. Nonetheless, this comparative model promised to breathe new life into old religious agendas and stimulate new Christian action in America and overseas. Despite the lofty ideals of the fair's liberal organizers, and new ways of regarding religions, Christianity would still be upheld as "the complement of all other religions, filling out what is imperfect in them, and correcting what is erroneous," as well as a "direct, miraculous revelation" that was to provide Christians with powerful new opportunities "to proclaim it as never before." Indeed, writes Rev. George Dana Boardman of the First Baptist Church in Philadelphia, there could not be "a better tribute" paid "to Christianity than to put it in fair comparison with other religions." After all, notes Dr. Ellinwood of the Presbyterian Board of Missions, it is through "a clear and accurate knowledge of their merits and demerits, and of their true relations to Christianity," that "false systems" are to gain their necessary disenchantment.[84] As seen with Lyman Beecher's enthusiasm with disestablishment and now with this new optimism for the Parliament, American Protestants were continually finding ways in which their preconceptions of Christ's kingdom in America would be brought into reality.

## THE EXCLUSION OF MORMONISM FROM
## THE PARLIAMENT OF RELIGIONS

McPherson, as stated above, made a point in his celebration of Christianity, of excluding both Mormonism and fetishism from the great World's

Parliament of Religions. To include them would have diminished the status and seriousness of the parliament itself, rendering a level of disconnect that many were unwilling to entertain. Despite the parliament's ecumenical claims, the Church of Jesus Christ of Latter-day Saints was left uninvited and thus deliberately excluded. This is not surprising, considering the parliament's sense of Christian triumphalism, together with Bonney and Barrow's own personal dislike of Mormonism,[85] all of which inspired the General Committee to dismiss it as an unworthy and "disturbing element."[86] Just how unworthy the church was in the mind of fair organizers is evident in the fact that one million circulars were sent out, drawing in nearly six thousand delegates from all over the world—and not one circular was mailed to the church in Utah, despite Barrows's claim that he personally saw to it that appropriate literature and official invitations were extended to all religions deemed worthy of the event.

Thus, although the Woodruff Manifesto against polygamy had been issued in 1890, many Americans continued to view Mormonism and its authorities with great suspicion, and the parliament committee held doubts over Mormonism's sincerity. In some fairness, the church was somewhat slow in recognizing the parliament as a significant event and thus delayed their inquiry, but in July 1893 conceded to the pressures of Brigham H. Roberts and the ecumenical rhetoric of the parliament and ultimately deemed it of great "value and importance."[87] The Mormon First Presidency (Wilford Woodruff, George Q. Cannon, and Joseph F. Smith) petitioned the parliament's president, Charles Bonney, for Mormon inclusion, noting that Mormonism would be of "special interest in such a religious parliament as that proposed"—they received no answer.[88] Ten days after the first letter was sent on July 10, the First Presidency sent thirty-six-year-old Roberts to Chicago. A member of the church's First Council of Seventy and long-time lobbyist for the church, Roberts inquired about the church's exclusion in person and learned that the parliament committee had given thought to inviting the church, but held "serious objections" toward extending an invitation. They considered it unwise to invite Mormon representatives, claiming that it was due to their association with the only recently settled controversy over polygamy.[89] Connected to these national doubts about Mormonism, the Mormons had held doubts about inclusion, but Roberts took up his task in Chicago.

After several interviews and "much correspondence on the subject," the increasingly annoyed parliament managers sent the unrelenting Roberts a letter on August 28 with an offer: the parliament was willing to host "a statement of [the church's] faith and achievements." The belated and reluctant invitation failed to say exactly when and where Roberts would be allowed to represent the Mormon religion, or even if he himself would be allowed to read a prepared speech. Perhaps this lack of clarity reveals the uncertainty within the committee; Roberts, however, felt sure his invitation implied a spot "in the full parliament before all the world, having full time (half an hour) allotted to her, as to other religions, in which to proclaim what to her were the great truths of her faith."[90]

In response to Roberts's anxious letter at the start of the parliament, Barrows assured Roberts in a letter a few days later that he would be able to read his own paper but could not give a date. Six days later Barrows, in a short letter, asked Roberts if he could read his paper on September 25, in Hall No. 3, a small committee room at the side of Washington Hall as part of the "Scientific Section," where participants discussed the relation of science and religion—a topic covered by Roberts in his prepared speech. Roberts quickly responded that he would be happy to read his speech in Hall No. 3 provided "that such presentation shall not bar me from presenting the paper also before the full Parliament of Religions in the Hall of Columbus."[91] On September 21, Roberts met Barrows in between sessions and handed him his reply. Without reading the note, the already overburdened chairman hastily explained to Roberts that no other hearing would be given him but in Hall No. 3. In Roberts's own account, this location represented a "very unworthy effort" by Barrows and Bonney to "side-track" his already prepared speech and thus further minimize the Mormon presence.[92] As Robert paraphrased Barrows, the parliament would hear of the "Mormon faith and church either not at all, or else only as in a corner and darkly."[93] The indignant Roberts rejected the proposal and response as an insult and left the parliament, deeply embittered. Roberts, in a letter to Barrows, contrasted his exclusion against the parliament's reputation for high-minded toleration. As he simply put it, the Utah-based church had "the distinction of being refused a hearing in the World's Parliament of Religions."[94]

The church's recent controversy over polygamy and its long-time defiance was sufficient for Barrows to exclude Mormonism, particularly in light of his own background as a Presbyterian minister long distrusting of Mormonism, together with that of Roberts who was then a practicing polygamist. In the parliament's vision toward eliciting a form of Christian triumphalism, Barrows took the opportunity with a speech on Islam to demonstrate this out-of-place character of Mormonism. Roberts's "paper was on the program all right enough, but he is a Mormon," explained the *Chicago Herald* in reference to a previous paper involving polygamy, delivered by Mohammed Alexander Russell Webb, an Anglo-American convert to Islam. As Mormonism and Islam were understood to be similarly dominated by tyrannical men who together imposed the wholesale subjugation of women and sexual aberrancy on their religious communities, it was common to conflate the two at the parliament, as had Cardinal James Gibbon as he spoke of the two as "usurping rivals" to Christendom.[95] Following the predictable outcry to Webb's speech, the congress committee dismissed Mormonism as too detracting.[96]

On Wednesday, September 20, the same day Roberts was scheduled to give his speech in Hall No. 3, Webb presented a paper before the main parliament entitled, "The Spirit of Islam," and was apparently requested by Barrows to make a brief statement on the practice of polygamy.[97] Webb did so directly and stirred up considerable controversy in his defense of polygamy as a social rather than religious practice, and defined the fear of polygamy as a widespread paranoia: "There are thousands and thousands of people who seem to be in mortal terror that the curse of polygamy is to be inflicted upon them at once." According to the official summary of the morning session during which Webb spoke, the outburst against Webb's defense of polygamy had been "sudden" and "unpremeditated," based not upon an issue of doctrine, but as "an attack on a fundamental principle of social morality."[98] In his official volume of speeches, Barrows omits Webb's explanation of polygamy with the brief assurance: "The few words omitted here opened a subject requiring more than a bald statement in five lines to be at all rightly understood."[99] The Mormon *Deseret News* reported that the outburst arose over Webb's presenting polygamy as a cultural rather than religious practice. Apparently, he startled the audience when he claimed, "Polygamy is no curse. A man can be a good, honest gentleman and yet be a polygamist. But I do not accept him as such if he be a sensualist." An unofficial account of the speech reports Webb as saying, "There are conditions under which it is beneficial. . . . I say that a pure-minded man can be a polygamist and be a perfect and true Christian, but he must not be a sensualist." Predictably, the audience erupted with hisses and cries of "Shame!" and "No, no; stop him."[100]

Webb responded that he was as equally American as the speakers who had preceded him, and found that unhinged animosity against polygamy was inspired not by a pure mind but by ignorance:

> When you understand what the Mussulman means by polygamy, what he means by taking two or three wives, any man who is honest and faithful and pure minded will say, "God speed him." . . . I carried with me for years the same errors that thousands of Americans carry with them to-day. Those errors have grown into history, false history has influenced your opinion of Islam. It influenced my opinion of Islam and when I began ten years ago, to study the Oriental religions, I threw Islam aside as altogether too corrupt for consideration.[101]

The controversy suggested that the scientific comparative model at the parliament had its limitations, as some things, like polygamy or Mormonism, were deemed unworthy of comparison or even sympathy. In the minds of most Americans, whether scientifically or theological oriented, polygamy, being practiced by either Muslims or Mormons, symbolized the antithesis of human progress and spiritual aspiration, and the epitome of digressive religion—which requires inquiry as it was now being considered scientifically and politically—rather than as a "mere" moral outrage.[102]

In the Progressive Era, for contemporary scientists and preachers alike, polygamy was viewed as tending toward the degeneration of the human race and would lead to the downfall of civilization. As parliament organizers were seeking to demonstrate to the world the continued importance of Christianity to human progress, polygamy could not be tolerated, especially as a religious principle. Phrenologist Thomas Laycock described polygamy as a barbaric characteristic of "gregarious mammals."[103] A few years after the fair, Barrows justified biblical polygamy with evolutionary insight, "that polygamy may suit a race in a certain stage of its development, and may in that stage, lead to a purer living and surer moral growth than its prohibition, may be granted. But, necessarily, a religion which incorporates in its code of morals any such allowances, stamps itself as something short of the final religion."[104] However, though condemned and stigmatized, at least it was no longer a simple sin against God, but now a point on the social evolutionary scale of human development—which was part of the built-in intellectual and organizational structures of the fair itself. At the same time, the parliament was seeking to demonstrate that true religion, being the highest evolution of humanity, furthered the highest forms of American morality and character. Mormonism and Islam together fell well below the "final religion," and thus ran counter to the larger assumptions of civilization and progress—and thus out of bounds with the vision of the parliament, whether an explanation of polygamy came from an Anglo-American Muslim or a Mormon. Whether it was hoped that Webb's comments on polygamy, due to his Anglo-American heritage and prior Presbyterianism, would lead him to denounce polygamy, or that he wished to provide an example of its popular unacceptability, or rather to demonstrate the immorality of false religion, Webb provoked an intense reactionary response, and an opportunity for Barrows to exclude Roberts from the Main Hall in the parliament, and thus exclude Mormonism.

Not unexpectedly, Roberts's exclusion provoked defensive responses, some exaggerated and some quite legitimate. The *Chicago Herald* noted the parliament's "decided opposition to a free discussion of polygamy" and criticized "the managers of the religious congress," asserting that "Elder Roberts, of Salt Lake City, had good ground of complaint. . . . The gathering at the Art Institute [which housed Columbus Hall] is a parliament of religions—not a parliament of Christians or a parliament of monogamists."[105] Merwin-Marie Snell, president of the Scientific Section, who befriended Roberts, declared with significant exaggeration Roberts's exclusion to be the "darkest blot in the history of civilization in this country." Snell argued that "the Mormon Church had suffered through the preposterous ignorance and prejudice of other religious bodies," comparing prejudice against Mormonism to that of his own Roman Catholic faith. Snell added, "No one would exclude the church of the latter day saints from the family of the world's religions who had caught the first glimpse of its profound cosmogony, its spiritual theology and its exalted morality."[106] Following the fair's closure, Roberts aired his complaints by means of a newspaper article in the *Chicago Inter-Ocean*, calling out Barrows and the other organizers of the parliament to explain themselves and their prejudices and hypocrisy in the unfair exclusion of Mormonism within an event that claimed structures of inclusion.[107] However helpful these outlets were in providing a public platform to Roberts's exclusion from the parliament, Snell and the *Herald*'s protests do not represent wholesale defense of Mormonism or a massive shift in public opinion. Snell was marginal and the news press was limited. Most liberal Christians as well as scholars of the social sciences still dismissed—if not disdained—Mormonism, finding little interest in the incident. Rather than using progressive visions to break down the walls of prejudice, the new scientific rhetoric of the era gave new life and lent new respectability to the earlier theological arguments which were turned into scientific arguments against polygamy and Mormonism. Nonetheless, Higginson's western rationality in support of sympathy for other religions had the consequence (intended or not) of bringing about a new ambivalence toward other religions, even if it retained earlier prejudices and assumptions of Christian supremacy that pervaded the institutional makeup of the larger parliament. The peculiar variable of Mormonism's exclusion reveals the frightening implications of these new definitions of religion, demonstrating a continued rejection of Mormonism, yet a weakening in these earlier justifications behind that exclusion.

In the paper prepared to be given at the Parliament of Religions which he later published, Roberts stated that Mormonism was a unique faith that has "attracted more attention and awakened more universal interest than any religious body of modern times."[108] In an attempt to provide an intellectual framework that would reflect the parliament's interest in modernity, Roberts ignored the topic of polygamy and vigorously projected Mormonism as an important American religion that had something to contribute to the nation's emergent problems when it came to the role of religion in society. Mormonism stood as "one of the potent religious forces of the age," and thus held the "claim upon the respect and thoughtful considerations of mankind . . . and as such claims the right to be heard in this Parliament." Roberts further argued that Mormonism had answers for many of the current problems plaguing Christianity, including the growing secular disaffection toward Christianity and the challenge of sectarianism. Mormonism was thus "progressive," and if further evidence is what a skeptical scientific age needs to believe in God, then "'Mormons' have double the amount of evidence of God and the truth of the gospel than other people possess." In an argument that would have created discomfort for the parliament officials, Roberts proposed that the widely ridiculed *Book of Mormon* provided additional proof of the divine authorship of the Bible and the miracles of Christ, and hence should be seen as a defense against the excesses of biblical criticism. "'Mormonism' has an especial mission," he maintained, "to prepare the earth for the coming and reign of Messiah." In the spirit of the ecumenical vision of the parliament, Roberts argued that the kingdom was not to be brought forth in opposition to the belief of other Christians, but actually joining together in the "fundamental truth of all religions," namely "faith in God," or, as others described it, a shared universal "aspiration." [109]

Roberts's response and the sequence of omission, reluctant inclusion, and final exclusion from Columbus Hall of the Latter-day Saint religion is particularly important in light of one of the parliament's declared aims: to create a "Christian brotherhood." For parliament organizers, Mormonism was neither a "great Historic Religion of the world" nor even part of the body of Christianity, and Roberts represented little more than an obnoxious, out-of-place apologetic of Christian devolution and immorality, and a disrupting and untrustworthy example of human aspiration for the divine. The parliament was thus effectively and "rigidly purged of cranks," as there was "neither time nor fitness for minor sects." [110] However, the main emphasis of Roberts's speech was to explain how Mormonism established faith in God with greater clarity, power, and authority than any other religion. In short, Roberts declared that the American kingdom of God was a Mormon engagement—an appropriation and extension of Christianity itself. Such religious exceptionalism clearly challenged the imposed and rationalized Protestant claim to the kingdom that currently had enough problems of its own, but also illuminated the new challenges and necessary limitations of religious pluralism in a new era of liberalism and increased tolerance.

As witnessed with the parliament and its exclusion of Mormonism, the study of religion was deeply contested, and not easily submitted, as envisioned, to scientific concepts as they applied to national progress. Turner's thesis, for all its cracks, blind spots, and falsely imagined realities, changed how many thought about morality, Mormons, and the frontier, and though the Mormons were treated unfairly in the Parliament of Religions, the Mormons still came away from the World's Fair with a different vision of themselves as well as the nation. For one, there was a very successful "Utah Day" at the fair, in which Utah citizens, particularly Mormons, were presented as hardworking, cultured, and progressive Americans—in line with Turner's Frontier Thesis. Moreover, since the frontier was now considered closed, Mormon barbarism, including polygamy, was potentially part of this past era—even a relic of the frontier. However lawless and crude Mormonism had appeared throughout much of the century, Turner now opened up the idea that Mormons could now be redefined in uniquely American terms which grew into a new national mythology that had progressed against the old ways and assumed new ways—in industry, science, and even religion.[111]

It was within this air of American progressivism and a transformed Mormonism that religious pluralism and the American character was being defined, and it would be by way of this more sanitized form of Mormonism that American modernity would be constructed and in which Mormonism found its place. Religion, as seen from within this dynamic, had shifted for Mormonism, allowing for the creation of a more apolitical and thus separate expression of the kingdom from the nation-state's vision of legitimate power and appropriate belief. The next two chapters will consider how Mormons saw, understood, and took advantage of this new national mood and understandings of the frontier. The church engaged with this new era of character building and progress and began efforts to successfully redefine itself as similarly progressive at both the World's Fair in Chicago, and, ten years later, by means of the Reed Smoot hearings in Congress. This and later chapters thus demonstrate the metamorphosis of religion within American society, which transformed American power and helped fashion a new relationship for religion within that power.

# CHAPTER 5

## The Inclusion of Mormonism at the Chicago World's Fair, 1893

A musical performance also softens hard hearts, leads in the humor of reconciliation, and summons the Holy Spirit.

—Hildegard von Bingen, *Scivias*

The World Columbian Exposition offered significant and unexpected consequences for how Americans perceived themselves and their religious institutions—as well as how such perceptions redefined ideas of Americanism and its meaning in national progress. Mormons were not exempt from these consequences and innovating perceptions—moreover, the Mormons were, to a degree, participants in this unintended effect of the exposition. Though sidelined and humiliated at the Parliament of Religions, the secular Mormon presentation at the Utah exhibit revealed that its faith, culture, and adherents were in some ways in step with the progressive times and thus engaged with the national narrative of providential and progressive determinism. Public response to the Mormons' secular presentation of themselves as a frontier people promoted understanding of a growing phenomenon of industrialized times, namely, the force of public opinion and its related value systems that allowed for the transcending of the church's former offending and exclusionary practices. This new power of public opinion helped guide the church's educational, theological, spiritual, and missiological efforts as the church prepared to enter the twentieth century by adopting broader national tendencies toward bureaucratic corporate centralization and correlation.[1]

In some ways, this was no sudden shift on the part of the Mormons, or of Utah, or for the country. During the era framed by post–Civil War memories and the secularization struggles of the late nineteenth century, there was anxiety over the role of religion in the protection and upholding of constitutional government, concerns which fueled Mormon rhetoric, particularly in response to earlier antipolygamy rulings and legislation. In important ways, Mormon leaders adopted a less religiously rooted perspective and orientation in response to federal laws, but the Mormons and Utah were not exempt from the march of industrialization and its effects on transportation, communication, and consumption, all of which challenged traditional religious responses. Thus, in arguing for a bill in support of Utah statehood, Utah's territorial representative Joseph L. Rawlins (Dem.) explained that "polygamy was dying from natural causes, and in a short time would cease to exist altogether." Similar to Missouri senator George G. Vest's argument that polygamy had ended as a result of the natural disintegration of Mormon religiosity due to the forces of modernity and the closure of the frontier, Rawlins assured, "The people were not as credulous now as in former years; and, while they believed forty or fifty years ago in Divine approval of polygamy, and Divine protection for those who practiced it, they were more enlightened now."[2] This national boom in technological and material advancement inspired a new sense of optimism and boldness toward secular progress, directly influencing how Americans observed themselves and their once-deemed-backward neighbors. While controversy yet swirled around the religious institution and certain practices, the territory of Utah had developed its agricultural and mineral resources. Railroads had been built, and an important line ran through Salt Lake City. Telephone wires were now connecting the desert metropolis with the rest of the country, and it was anticipated that Utah would soon be granted statehood.[3]

Many were hearing of and investing in Utah's significant agricultural, mineral, and land development potential.[4] The specter of polygamy and theocracy were fading as the church upheld its promise to release its grasp on Utah politics and its renunciation of polygamy, and Utah's land and resources proved worthy of outside speculative investment. Indeed, one contributor for the *New York Times* wrote of how the territory of Utah seemed to be transcending Mormonism. Revealing his confidence in the civilizing power of the receding frontier, the *Times* declared with speculative interest that Brigham Young's "reign" had been reduced to merely a "Mormon quarter—a curiosity to be visited, but no longer part and parcel of the life of the place." Moreover, because of its mineral wealth, Salt Lake City's identity was now projected as a secular marketplace, rather than the center of religious Mormonism. Surely, as here indicated, the church and its polygamous practices had given way "to mammon and plutocracy"—meaning that Mormonism had succumbed to worldly influences and was thus being "brought into line."[5] These observations were in light of the diminished place of America's rural agricultural dream as a consequence of land monopolists and booming corporate privilege. In the same way that America's farmers were becoming tenants and laborers, it was supposed that Mormons were likewise surrendering their isolationist independence.[6] Furthermore, it was argued, Mormonism was "doomed from the time the civilization of the country closed around the Mormon community in Utah and began to pervade it with the social, educational, and industrial influences of modern progress."[7] The *Times* went on to report that Utah's bid for statehood was only opposed by prejudiced non-Mormon ministers, who were overreacting since polygamy and Mormon peculiarities were "undoubtedly dead and cannot be revived." Though perhaps a bit overly dismissive of Mormonism's continued wildness, this article spoke presciently about Mormonism and Utah engaging with the forward thrust of industrialization and of their becoming more Americanized. Indeed, beyond these regional changes, the church was soon to engage with external functions and events in Chicago and would take public opinion into consideration. In so doing the church commenced to separate their institutions into religious and secular identities, thereby furthering the growing idea of religion as private and separate. This new faith in modernity and the closed frontier communicated national confidence in the irresistible power of technological and economic progress and the power of the frontier in the creation of America. It also demonstrates the resonance Turner's Frontier Thesis had as Mormons began to reintroduce themselves to the nation in these progressive and outwardly nonreligious terms at the fair.

These major shifts were not simply caused by Mormonism going to the fair in 1893 during a particular moment in history, but were aided and abetted by the church's experience there. B. H. Roberts projected their religious beliefs (not very successfully) and Utah's fair commission projected the territory's secular progressivism (very successfully). As has been reviewed in the previous chapter, the Mormon presence at the fair nearly did not happen. Mormon historian Davis Bitton described the Mormon efforts at the Parliament of Religions as "lukewarm" and "belated," owing to church authorities who generally failed to discern its importance. Mormon participation at the fair came about largely by the efforts of the energetic thirty-six-year-old Mormon General Authority Brigham H. Roberts who argued as early as 1891 for Mormon inclusion "in such an important gathering." Despite a specially organized committee's judgment that involvement in the fair was "unimportant," Mormon leaders came around to Roberts's belief by the summer of 1893.[8] As it turned out, efforts to participate in the Parliament of Religions fell short and Roberts and his speech were ultimately rejected. It's not surprising, then, that Bitton termed the event "not exactly edifying," and the incident was largely forgotten within the collective Mormon memory.[9]

In taking account of both Mormonism's presence at and exclusion from the fair, we can better understand how religious minorities negotiate and navigate their inclusion into American acceptability, despite their limitations. Such an approach toward group agency offers a better perception of these larger cultural structures and their own metamorphosis that such resistance and efforts at accommodation and assimilation brought to light.[10] Placing the near-absence and the presence of the Mormons at the religious and secular venues of the fair allows us to appreciate not just the academic side of the equation, but the dynamism of the Protestant hegemony itself as it struggled over its own relevance at the fair. Furthermore, understanding Mormon participation at the more secular area of the fair provides broader insight into national shifts in popular understanding of religion and its relation to political power, and how Mormonism realigned itself with this new national understanding. By these means and others, Mormons would realign themselves not by abandoning their faith but by developing a religious vision and public presentation that expanded (or perhaps narrowed) their understanding of religion, their own religion's place in American society, and its place in the newly reenvisioned American frontier.

As previously reviewed, the World's Parliament of Religions sought first and foremost to unify a deeply divided Christendom and reclaim its waning authority over American culture and thus extend Christianity's ideals more effectively throughout the world. It was intended as an institutional and contemporary manifestation of the modern creed of unity through universal brotherhood and the scientific study of comparative religions—though this creed was screened through Christian triumphalism. However, many events, such as the fair staying open on Sunday, reveal that many Americans were no longer deeply concerned with Christian polity and piety, which provided some new territory to American thought—such as providing more space to previously excluded groups. Nevertheless, it would be claiming too much to see this as an unqualified acceptance of American religious diversity, rather than a new ambivalence and powerlessness toward rendering it invisible. Indeed, Americans, as the century advanced in industrial and corporate might, were given a new set of rules to define the American character—rules by which minority groups could more clearly protest their exclusions as well as forge more acceptably American identities—identities based upon character over theology.[11] Minority groups were presented with two ways of doing this: by domesticating themselves under a liberalized banner of Christian brotherhood and/or by engaging in American secularism.

Mormons, even if it might not have been always deliberate, directly engaged with American secularism by renouncing plural marriage and participating in more acceptable political and economic practices. In so doing, the church domesticated its religious identity into one more acceptable to the United States and its increasingly diverse population. Second, the church was revealing itself, by this change and in other ways, to be in step with a new liberal progressivism and a more tolerant Progressive Era. The church did not fully succeed at the Parliament of Religions as Roberts, a practicing polygamist, sought to uphold LDS exceptionalism. But the church, in its joining with those not of their faith to celebrate Utah Day in the other part of the fair, had a more positive experience and created a kind of precedent, and a model, in which religious diversity could participate in the United States' belief and culture. It was here, then, that the necessary groundwork was laid in which unorthodox religion and the state could coexist, and in which a particular style of religious pluralism began to emerge and take shape.

## DIVINE SANCTION AND THE SPIRIT OF PROGRESS

Symbolized by George Washington Gale Ferris Jr's innovative 264-foot-high Ferris wheel, the World's Fair of 1893 directly correlates to the beginning of what historians have referred to as the Progressive Era (roughly 1890 to 1910s). Marking this era as one of explosive technological and medical innovation and increased efficiencies, together with shifting attitudes toward the frontier, politics, and religion, American sensibilities concerning the world began to be reimagined. Not least among these reimaginations was that of Mormonism itself, and its potential relations with and contributions to the rest of the country. Following statehood, a "Salt Lake City Letter" to the *Baltimore Sun* explained that Mormons were "affected by the incoming of the Gentile world," such as the adoption of the two-party political system and Utah's advancements in industry and society.[12] In many ways, continued the letter, "Mormon and Gentile are thrown together," thus ending Mormon isolationism, thanks to the receding frontier and its accompanying railroad, telegraph, and the electric car. On top of this, Mormon assimilation was further assured as "Mormon boys marry Gentile girls and Gentile boys marry Mormon girls." Consistent with the assurance that frontier barbarism could not endure the closure of the frontier and the overwhelming forces of civilization and modernity, the article concluded that in this "face to face" encounter with "the civilization of America," Mormonism's incongruity "with Christianity and America" will soon be as 'a tale that is told.'"[13]

As part of this new optimism toward the future place of Mormons in the country and its economic investment potentials, the Fourth District Court declared the Idaho test-oath law unconstitutional in October 1892, reintroducing 25,000 Mormon votes into Idaho politics.[14] "It seems that the Republicans of Idaho," reported the *New York Times*, "are undergoing a change of heart in respect to the Mormon inhabitants of their State, which we are pleased to see and only wish it extended to the entire Republican Party."[15] Though a limited and reluctant amnesty was given by rigid Presbyterian and U.S. president Benjamin Harrison on January 4, 1893, to those who upheld the antipolygamy manifesto of 1890 President Grover Cleveland offered that next year an even more liberal amnesty that paved the way for statehood.[16] As Brigham H. Roberts suggested, Harrison's amnesty demonstrated little if any shift in attitude toward the LDS Church, whereas Cleveland's amnesty, coming after the events of the World's Fair, reflects this shifting stance. In 1896, under the promise that polygamy was dead and Mormon leaders separated from local and national politics, Utah achieved its long-awaited status as a state.

Some indices of change were more architectural and symbolic, but just as profound for the internal workings of the Mormon sense of national stability and presentation. Nationally heralded as "the most remarkable building in the country," the completion of the Salt Lake Temple was the most visible expression of Mormon architectural sophistication. Estimated to have cost almost $3.5 million to complete, the April 6, 1893, dedication of the Salt Lake Temple (whose construction began under Brigham Young almost half a century earlier) provided a strong continuity with the Mormon past as well as a new determination to present the Mormon faith and people in more public and acceptable ways. In response to positive international acclaim for the Mormon Tabernacle Choir's performance at this temple dedication, Mormon leaders, still grappling with the aftershocks of the severities of federal prosecutions of the 1880s, found promise, however hesitant, in putting their choir before the world just a few months later at the Columbian Exposition. This participation by the choir became what Reid Neilson refers to as the catalyst for Mormonism's transformation into a "public relations juggernaut."[17] Beyond this, however, the Chicago World's Fair of 1893 stands as a pivotal moment in the coevolution of both the national and Mormon conceptions of the kingdom of God, the millennial meaning of America, and the shifting role of religion in the nation more broadly.

Chosen over proposals of New York and St. Louis, Chicago symbolized "the imperial city of the American West," becoming a fitting model of how the country sought to present itself, both visually and aesthetically. Built on a swampy outpost on the southwest shores of Lake Michigan, and following the devastating Chicago fires from two decades earlier, Chicago and its transformation into the White City, notes Richard Seager, symbolically portrayed the victory of civilization over the savage forces of the frontier. As a way of introducing Chicago to visitors at the fair, the *Religious Herald* mentioned that though America lacked ancient monuments, Americans, compelled by the force of circumstances, were uniquely connected to their frontier past in a way that inspired devotion and a vivid imagination toward their national future. With Chicago springing forth "like magic," its existence gave credence and boldness to this vivid American frontier imagination.[18] Chicago was, as seen by many at the time of the fair, both a New Rome and a New Jerusalem, and even the last word of the European Enlightenment.[19] This great frontier city stood in the center of the Columbian myth of America, which Seager explains as a fusion of symbols (e.g., patriotism, Christianity, and the Greco-Roman classical traditions) that informed an Anglo-Protestant religion of civilization in mainline American churches, and of which the Mormon Choir now placed Mormonism within.[20] Not unlike Mormon anticipations over the Salt Lake Temple, Chicago's White City stood as a type of world temple, being a visible display of a more internal anxiety over Christianity's progress and global leadership amidst new challenges of the modern world. Indeed, Chicago in 1893 did not just represent a better model for public relations as Mormons adopted this Columbian mythos, but also highlighted these redefinitions of American society and power structures that made this Mormon redefinition as part of the American West possible in the first place.

Mormons looked to the dedication of the Salt Lake City Temple with similar cosmic importance that many Protestants looked to the World's Fair. *The Atlanta Constitution* observed that Mormons flocked from far and near, "with bed and babies in arms," so as not to miss some great revelation or other divine manifestation and holy blessing. "The ancient Hebrew looked not to the sky with more expectancy from the base of fiery Sinai than did the Mormon peasantry at their temple gates today."[21] Just two days prior, at the semiannual general conference, as reported by the *Los Angeles Times*, senior Mormon apostle Lorenzo Snow felt the need to caution against overzealous expectations at the Thursday conference and dedication, such as the hope of Christ's Second Advent. Snow explained that Christ may not return that Thursday as many had anticipated, but rather that it could take ten, twelve, or even twenty years before the saints would be prepared for such an event.[22] For Mormons, the year 1890 represented the end date of a type of millennial countdown, which with the completion of the Salt Lake Temple made it all the more real, since Christ was predicted to usher in the millennium by coming to the temple, a hope now being cautiously downplayed. It was a subtle but profound theological and millennial shift from just a few years earlier, one that matched a broader national trend to spiritualize the significance of the kingdom of God and the coming millennium, which failed to materialize for both Mormon and Protestant alike. Though still holding to an imminent return of Christ and his kingdom, Mormon leaders began to imagine the kingdom as synonymous with the church itself and encourage expectations of a less imminent return, and thus began to ponder more long-term realities.

These new long-term expectations and concessions had much to do with the friends Mormons were now trying to win over and the transformations then necessary for the church to not just survive, but thrive within American society. Those in the throes of progress do not seek the destructive fires and judgments from heaven, but rather divine endorsements of their path of progress. Though most influential Americans still disliked Mormonism, these new developments within the church and the nation made the Utah-based church look less threatening and thus more prone to the transformative features of the frontier environment. Typical of these frontier expectations, national leaders like Missouri senator George G. Vest (1830–1904) declared in late 1893 that "the death blow to Mormonism has already been struck. It can never flourish in this country again." The reason polygamy had ended was not because Mormonism chose to end it, argued Vest, but because "the religious sentiment of the Latter Day Saints is not strong with them," having reference to the secularization of the general membership of the church and their new integration into American society. Being an important "part of their religion," Mormon leaders may hate to see plural marriages go, "but there is no help for it."[23] Though Vest's theory of Mormon declension does not adequately explain Mormon transformation, nor the actual underground continuation of the practice of polygamy, his thesis that Mormons were losing and compromising vital aspects of their faith was part of this divine affirmation. That year the church lay in serious debt due to the consequences of the antipolygamy crusades and negligent budget keeping, but these problems were compounded by the misfortune of the 1893 national financial panic, which had also hit Utah. These developments threatened a sense of deep crisis regarding church independence and solidarity (principles that defined Mormonism until then), at a time when the church had to redefine itself within these new "progressive American" terms, and thus stood in need of its own divine affirmations, which came by way of this new acceptance.[24]

Political transformations in Utah were an important part of these external and internal shifts, but they had immediate consequences to the internal unity of the Mormon community, something held as anathema to the Mormon sense of divine acceptance.[25] This division along political party lines had been necessary in alleviating an earlier crisis brought on by the national concern about Mormon political unity (inspiring national legislation to break it up). Elections like the one in Logan in 1892, which the national press heralded as the initiation of Mormons into the national political process, were deeply contested and bitterly fought, leaving more than a few with bitter words and feelings for their fellow Mormons.[26] In preparation for the Salt Lake Temple dedication, the Mormon First Presidency sent out a circular letter to officers and members of the church on March 18, 1893. "During the past eighteen months," the letter announced, "there has been a division of the Latter-day Saints upon national party lines." Feelings had been intense, inspiring actions on the part of members toward one another that "have been very painful to us and have grieved our spirits." Restricting attendees of the temple dedication to those whose conduct was befitting such pretentions of unity was important in not just establishing the edifice as a visible reminder of an invisible commitment of solidarity to the community, but affirming their cosmic legitimacy and religious exceptionalism amidst significant political and religious change.[27]

## THE LDS PRESENCE AT THE CONGRESS
## OF STATES AND TERRITORIES

In juxtaposition with their disappointing exclusion at the Parliament of Religions, but in line with these broader changes in Utah, the church, and the United States, Mormonism found ways to be celebrated in the fair's Congress of States and Territories. Granted the coveted Lot 38, the territory of Utah and its exhibit was grand, large, and centrally located, becoming a secular back door by which the church entered upon the stage of national legitimacy, thereby setting forth the frameworks of national acceptability that Mormons would interpret within divine terms.

This granting of Lot 38 was not accomplished without controversy. Many were surprised that this prized lot was given to Utah and not unexpectedly demands were made that Utahns be dispossessed; one unnamed state commissioner resigned over the incident. The site was desired and contested by other states, and Utahns were understandably thrilled over "one of the best, if not the best lot assigned to any state or territory." The lot was one of the largest ones; indeed, it was double the size of the lots given to Idaho and Arizona, and larger than the lots given to Delaware and Massachusetts, two of the original thirteen states. Officiators of the Congress of States and Territories were noticeably avoiding privileging older states at the expense of newer states and territories.[28] Moreover, the central location of the lot made it the most

A MAN FROM UTAH BRINGS HIS FAMILY.

FIGURE 5.1. "Mormon and Gentile: Join Hands Heartily on Utah Day." *Sunday Herald* (Chicago), September 10, 1893. In depicting Mormon visitors at the World's Fair, popular mediums such as this commonly observed them as a backward curiosity, something the larger fair took great interest in.

convenient for the curious passerby. Seeing possession as nine-tenths of the law, it was no wonder that one of the Utah fair commissioners and long-time publisher of the *Salt Lake Tribune*, Patrick H. Lannan, on the day of lot assignment "was found sitting on a log in the center of the coveted lot, under an umbrella, industriously smoking a cigar, while the rain came down in torrents."[29]

On September 9, the Utah Commission made cautious use of its space and of its allotted time for Utah Day. The exhibit and the speakers steered away from religious controversy that could negatively influence the visitor's interest in the territory of Utah, long a center of religious concern. The commission had as its central aim to be inclusionary—and thus counteract the "widespread prejudice against Utah and her citizens." Rather than attempting to expound upon its unique religion—the commission ignored it altogether. The Utah Commission desired to "obliterate" negative impressions of Utah "among the masses" of people and instead hoped that the "good seed sown [on Utah Day] will continue to bear fruit for years to come." The exhibit portrayed a Utah characterized by its great potential as a valuable future state with exemplary human and mineral resources. The commission's objective appealed to both Mormons and those unaffiliated with the church. With the opportunity to publicly display to a mass audience their material and artistic abilities, all Utahns were united in the thought that "Utah must, under no condition, fail to be represented at the Exposition."[30] Utah Day thereby became a rare event at which all Utahns could come together, be they Mormon, Protestant, or Catholic. These positive developments, however, were far more significant than merely causing improved feelings; they actually spoke to an opening market economy that Utah was now becoming a part of, suggesting an end to the earlier cooperative ideal as it related to Utah's economy.

The old ritual of going west in search of the individual agrarian dream and utopia, had by the 1890s become more about tapping into a new retail context. If this first age of conquest had ended with the imagined closure of the frontier, then a new one had opened that commodified both the natural resources of the West as well as its unique, if romanticized, heritage. "Indian" trinkets were sold, Wild West circuses were widely attended, dime novels brought frontier heroes (and villains) to life, and capitalist investors and boosters encouraged propaganda and urban development that heightened their investment and wealth.[31] Monopoly capitalism, which emerged after the Civil War and endured deep into the twentieth century, was characterized by the development of urban markets and the exploition of natural resources from new territories, which in the 1890s became characterized by the imperial development of international markets.[32] When Utah presented itself as a willing participant in these national and international markets, rather than a force against them, it generated great interest. Mormons and Utah were staking a place within the evolving American corporate imperial world, with Utah claiming important natural and domestic cultural resources to sell to this newly interested nation. No longer a kingdom within a kingdom, the church was becoming a competitive corporation within the national corporate economy.

For a territory whose fame (or infamy) was the obstructionist Mormon religion, projecting itself as a relevant and modern state with a thriving and inclusive multicultural urban center, while retaining the integrity of its frontier past, was a difficult task, though the challenge was taken up by Utahns of all persuasions. To overcome forty years of opprobrium attached to Utah by its association with Mormonism, Mormons and non-Mormons of both genders sought to remove or at least alleviate the Mormon stigma. The church's recent institutional reforms promoted cooperation and allowed for an active and purposeful re-presentation of the Mormon people as good neighbors and cooperative Utahns—rather than as mere passive pawns of Mormonism's deviant, anti-American, and irreligious schemes.

As promoted by a new vision of the frontier as introduced by Frederick J. Turner, the Mormons could now be seen as separate from their religious institution and its isolationist past, and therefore more American. Headed by Robert Craig Chambers, president of the Utah World's Fair Commission, organizers of the Utah exhibit set out to demonstrate Utah's strengths and its secular progress by presenting exhibits of its agriculture, mines, manufacturing, fine arts, ethnology and archaeology, education, and women's work, as well as a bureau of information to address and answer the many questions posed by curious spectators.[33] The display further promoted pride of place in Utah's social, cultural, and material wealth, effectively projecting Utah in its most attractive, secular, and progressive light, and making Utah a beacon to attract potential settlers and speculators which would spur further growth.[34]

There were five particularly notable features of Utah Day and events surrounding it. The first emerged with Utah's territorial governor, anti-polygamist and confederate Civil War veteran Caleb W. West (1886–1889 and 1893–1896), in his address to the crowds of Utah Day which minimized Utah's religious distinctiveness and distanced the contemporary secular territory from its religious past. In positioning Mormons within the frontier narrative, West argued that Mormon pioneers were "made of sterling stuff," being unique men and women who "encountered dangers untold, and endured hardships" that entitled them "to the highest honors that can be accorded the first settlers of any country." West then drew attention to the elephant, only to mention its departure from the room: "In times past there have been struggles and differences, and I mention these only to say that they exist no more." In light of these differences that had prolonged Utah's repeated petitions for statehood for nearly half a century, Governor West argued that such "have been buried and now we bespeak for Utah simply justice."[35] Notably, in describing the settlement of Utah pioneers, West ignored their religious motivation and presented them in frontier terms of loyal pioneers and patriots, and as such archetypal developers and urban pioneers of the American West. Not unlike Columbus, "These pioneers of Utah blazed the way for the Westward course of empire, and at the time of their first entrance into the valley of the Great Salt Lake planted the flag of the union on foreign soil," assuring that Utahns received deserved recognition as fellow contributors to American colonization and Manifest Destiny.[36]

As far as Governor West was concerned, national fears over the several accounts of treason Mormons had been accused of were an error in perception, "for our flag has never ceased to float over the land that was then taken possession of, from that day until now."[37] Governor West helped set the trend, as seen with William "Buffalo Bill" Cody's similar assessment just a few years later, that past Mormon troubles with the country were largely that of misinformation and misunderstanding. The Utah War, for example, was more of a "spirited resistance" against the "President's political chess-board" than it was an act of treason or rebellion. In citing the "farcical demonstration on part of the government," there appeared "no genuine basis" for sending troops to Utah in 1857, except perhaps "to the clamour of other religious sects against what they held to be an unorthodox belief." Indeed, far from deserving public derision, Salt Lake City contains "all the adjuncts of our most modern civilization. Rich in its architecture, progressive in its art, with a literature that is marvelous," and when the "conditions from which it has sprung are seriously considered, the Mormon community meets all the demands of our ever advancing civilization."[38] By assuring Americans that Mormons were fellow nation builders, Governor West and Buffalo Bill Cody fully appropriated Mormons into an overall national identity and narrative, allaying any past or current fears of a separate Mormon kingdom. This process of *remembering* Mormonism's pioneer heritage thus came as a simultaneous *forgetting* of Mormonism's polygamous, economic, and political heritage, together with the widespread religious anxieties of the Protestant kingdom Mormons had long challenged and provoked.

The second feature of Utah Day emerged with church president Wilford Woodruff and his ability to recast himself and his fellow Utahns in terms of independent pioneers and even frontier men and women. At the administration building on September 8, just one day before Utah Day, President Woodruff spoke before the National Commission of the World Columbian Exposition, following its president, former Senator Thomas W. Palmer's cancellation of normal committee proceedings. Following Governor Caleb West's speech before the committee, Woodruff was asked to speak to them as a pioneer, which he readily did. The next day at Festive Hall on Utah Day, the eighty-six-year-old Mormon leader spoke again with a strong voice as one of Utah's oldest living pioneers, rather than as a Mormon prophet—a speech that was noted to have been "listened to attentively."[39] As he had before the committee, Woodruff again refrained from taking polygamy or persecution as his theme and spoke rather of the faith and determination of the pioneers, a narrative that resonated with the experiences, memories, and national narrative of many non-Mormons and their romantic visions of the frontier and the nation's own heroized pioneers.

Just two days earlier, Woodruff attended Buffalo Bill's Wild West show at the fair, which was subtitled "Congress of Rough Riders of the World." Impressed by the "finest shooting" of both Buffalo Bill and Annie Oakley, Woodruff noted their large herd of buffalo on hand to shoot at and sat with Cody afterward in his tent. This aged president of the Mormon Church had had a friendly meeting with Cody a year earlier in Salt Lake City, and it seemed this was a continuation of that amiable relationship. Now on Utah Day as Woodruff spoke before the attentive crowd, he drew attention to his own version of what it meant to be a "rough rider" of the frontier. Indeed, as he and other Mormon pioneers traveled to Utah in the summer of 1847, Woodruff detailed unique frontier experiences such as having to wait for three days and three nights as a massive herd of wild buffalo passed by. Being among the first to make this pilgrimage westward, it was they who had to build the roads and bridges, which became important for later travelers and settlers. In speaking of their initial entrance to the Salt Lake Valley, Woodruff noted before the crowd that plowing was nearly impossible, since the soil was so hard and dry, forcing them to develop efficient irrigation systems that allowed for the production of things such as Utah's "world-famed potatoes." As Governor West argued in his own speech, these Mormon pioneers were "made of sterling stuff" and deserved recognition.[40] Mormon pioneers thus epitomized, not the hopeless barbarism of the frontier that needed eradication, but instead the frontier roughness that laid out important frameworks for the progress of American civilization and empire.

President George Q. Cannon, Woodruff's counselor, also spoke, and similarly avoided controversy. Rather, he too directly connected Mormonism with the broader American narrative of the frontier and its quest toward conquest and liberty. In Mormon thought, he explained, Columbus was "raised up and inspired by Divine Providence" to discover America, a land reserved for white Europeans who had, with the help of Providence, made it a home of liberty, "where the oppressed of all lands might find refuge." Contributing to the myth of white American civilization, Mormons, led by the "noble pioneer" Brigham Young, "proceeded to build up a commonwealth, consecrated to religious liberty and the rights of man." Indeed, Cannon made the case that the Mormon trek west to "the then unknown and uninhabited, the vast and forbidding West" in search of religious liberty, was parallel to that of the "Pilgrim Fathers and all the early colonists who came out from the Old World in search of that freedom of conscience which is the inalienable right of human kind"; "for Utah, too, was founded by men who held to these same views and were actuated by the same high resolves."[41] This was not a complaint of injustice or protest against "liberties denied," an accusation Cannon had become nationally known for just a few years prior; or a proclamation of religious exceptionalism as attempted by Roberts at the Parliament. Rather, this was a more nuanced plea to be embraced as fellow contributors to the national pioneer narrative of freedom, liberty, and human discovery that was then the object of celebration at the Columbian World's Fair. *The Deseret Weekly News* reported that "President Woodruff, Cannon and Smith, the heads of the Mormon Church, made speeches. If anybody attended with the expectation of hearing the Mormon faith expounded they were disappointed, as the great exponents of Mormonism were full of other subjects relating to what they had seen since their arrival in Chicago."[42]

Third, the Ladies Board also assisted in the repositioning of Utah as a secular progressive territory, creating a display that not only credited the women of Utah, but women in general.[43] A subset of the Utah World's Fair Commission, the board worked especially hard to present Utah's women, long thought of as ignorant dupes and slaves of their lazy, if well-organized sociopathic Mormon male masters, as citizens of one of the first territories to grant female suffrage, a right that most states had not yet extended. Thus having linked arms with female suffragists as early as 1871, Utah women were credited as a vital element in the national feminist movement.[44] Now at Utah Day, Mormon suffragist and president of the Utah Board of Lady Managers, Emily Sophia Richards, drew attention in her speech not only to the efforts of Mormon women at the great exhibition, but to the fact that Utah women were coworkers with men "in all the walks of life." Several years before the World's Fair, Mormon women leaders enthusiastically allied the church's Relief Society and YLMIA (Young Ladies' Mutual Improvement Association) into the national feminist movement (ICW—International Council of Women, 1888; NCW—National Council of Women of the United States, 1891), a relationship that endured until 1987.[45] Indeed, and in contrast to Roberts's rejection at the Parliament of Religions, leaders of the Women's Branch of the World's Congress Auxiliary sent invitations to Mormon female leaders to attend the World's Congress of Representative Women at the Chicago's World Fair. Aside from speaking at Utah Day, Emily Richards was invited to speak before the auxiliary Women's Branch of the World's Parliament of Religions, while Mormon Relief Society leader Emmeline B. Wells was invited to act as honorary president over one of the sessions in the Art Palace's Hall of Columbus, the very building where Roberts found himself excluded.[46]

At the event, female Mormon leaders similarly avoided religious issues and instead concentrated on the secular topics of pioneers, child education, entertainment, patriotism and their deep connections to their sisters in New England and their commitment to national female suffrage. Their secular interests extended to the domestic as silk curtains and piano scarves assisted in adorning the interior of the Columbian Exposition's Woman's Building; the representatives were also invited to a luncheon in honor of the officers of the International Council of Women (ICW).[47] Reid Neilson has explained that such a female presence at the fair "privileged feminist values over religious beliefs," and that although nearly all were Protestant, these women's groups conducted themselves as a "women's organization—not a Christian association."[48] However, the presence of Mormon women via the Ladies Board and their broader participations at the fair were now revealed as potent agents within the Mormon faith and worthy of the respect of prominent secular and religious feminist leaders, who had by this time become more inclusive in ways that paralleled popular trends then utilized with the scientific study of comparative religion. As extolled by prominent feminist leader Susan B. Anthony, who had befriended Mormon women like Emily Richards, the female platform, as witnessed by the fair—and by extension Utah Day—was understood to be "broad and inclusive, equally welcoming Jew or Christian, Protestant or Catholic, Gentile or Mormon, pagan or atheist."[49] In summary, again in stark contrast to Roberts's experience at the Parliament of Religions, national feminists recognized and upheld Mormon women and their participation, effectively casting a halo of progressivism around LDS women officers.

Also notable as a fourth point was Dominick "Don" Maguire (1852–1933), knowledgeable mineralogist, and a Catholic from Ogden, Utah, who spoke on Utah Day at Festival Hall, extolling Utah's mineral wealth as unique. Head of the Department of Mining, Ethnology, and Archaeology, Maguire claimed that within its boundaries, "the territory of Utah contains . . . a greater variety of minerals than any other state or territory of the Union."[50] At no time during his talk did he steer his audience's attention toward Utah's religious peculiarities, rather presenting Utah as an area on the verge of great economic development and wealth. Indeed, as a willing supplier of the growing needs of a new industrial society, Utah was now accepted as part of this exploitation and commodification of the natural resources of the American West.

Finally, there was the Mormon Tabernacle Choir whose power in representing the church—and Utah—and assisting shifts in opinion cannot be overestimated. Moreover, the Tabernacle Choir negotiated the difficult meeting ground of Utah's inescapable religious identity with more national-secular identities by presenting rousing renditions of music ranging from Handel's Hallelujah Chorus to "The Star-Spangled Banner." Unsurprisingly, there were some difficult moments. The choir had been invited to sing at the fair as early as 1891, but Mormon authorities were uncertain of it making such an appearance as a mere public relations gesture. This attitude left the choir's participation in Chicago in doubt just months before its anticipated performance in September 1893. Threatening not to compete in the choral competition unless some arrangements were made, the choir managed to get certain accommodations from the fair's general-director, George R. Davis, including correlating the competition with Utah Day and granting those traveling with the choir passes to the fair in order to allay costs. Word of the Tabernacle Choir's appearance was sent out via telegraph all over the nation, generating much interest.[51]

Suggestive of the irony such new perceptions could raise, national newspapers took note of the choir's appearance and laudations in Missouri en route to Chicago, the state where violent mobs in the 1830s made refugees of Mormon settlers and whose governor issued the infamous 1838 Extermination Order. Being "immensely applauded" following a brief stop and performance, the *Kansas City Times* playfully published a long celebratory article titled "This Time a Friendly Mob."[52] The mayor of Independence, Missouri, Col. Joseph W. Mercer, had lost an arm in the battle of Pine Bluff during the Civil War on the side of the Confederacy, but gave Wilford Woodruff his other arm to hold while they were together. While on a short pilgrimage to Independence on Friday, September 1, Woodruff recalled that the last time he had been there was in 1834 as a missionary, hiding from mobs who sought his life. Now, however, Woodruff was greeted by a delegation of citizens and the mayor "with the warmest reception," and, as Woodruff noted in his journal, "How Great the Contrast."[53]

Back in Kansas City later that day, the choir sang to a packed crowd at the Grand Music Hall, ending with the patriotic hymn, "My Country, 'Tis of Thee," to which the *St. Louis Post Dispatch* remarked, "Whatever the choir might lack it was not power. . . . The time and taste manifested was remarkable. . . . The choir acquitted itself in a most admirable manner and the large audience manifested its appreciation by frequent bursts of applause." Given a final reception just prior to their departure on Saturday at the Merchants' Exchange Building in St. Louis, the entire choir was brought to the floor of the Exchange and introduced by Mayor C. P. Walbridge, who spoke of Utah's settlement as one of the great achievements of the century, having not only caused the western frontier to "blossom as a rose," but was able to produce such a high quality of musicians now able to compete on the world stage.[54] Arriving in Chicago on September 3, the choir serenaded director-general Davis as an expression of gratitude for his hospitality and generosity. Davis was "visibly affected" by the choir's honoring of him by special performance and the gift of a cane made from the wood of the Great Salt Lake Tabernacle, followed by cheers from "the followers of Brigham Young."[55]

The 250 voices from Utah performed on Friday, September 8, in Festival Hall the day before Utah Day, as part of the Columbian Exposition's choir contest. The competition was against three professional choirs, two from Scranton, Pennsylvania, and the Western Reserve Choir from Ohio. The judges had a hard time determining the victor, finally deciding the Scranton choristers were nearer perfection in two points than the Tabernacle Choir; and the Utah choir received second place. Though accepted peaceably, the judgment prompted partisan expression that the Utahns had been discriminated against, with some of the Scranton choristers even claiming that the Utah choir had sung better than their competitors.[56] Wilford Woodruff confided in his diary, "I think without Doubt that our Quire was the Best & should have had the first Prize But the Quire that took the first Prize was Welsh and the Welsh furnished the Money And it Could hardly be Expected that they would give it to a Mormon Quire Though one of the Judges said the Salt Lake Quire ought to have it."[57] The *Deseret News* recorded proudly that a noted organist, one Professor Radcliffe of the Congregationalist Church, had also given an opinion to an unnamed reporter that the Mormon Choir should have won first place.[58] Beyond this, the choir was celebrated as an important aspect of the World's Fair itself. In what Neilson has defined as the Mormon "Cinderella moment," the choir was invited to provide the dedicatory music for the official placement of the iconic Liberty Bell at the Columbian Exposition.[59] That afternoon at Festival Hall, the choir sang again as part of the Utah Day celebration. Performing before a curious audience of between three and four thousand, the large choir, according to the *Chicago Sunday Herald*, did not disappoint: "Festival Hall has echoed with the music of many famous organizations, but it never witnessed more enthusiasm than followed the Mormon choir's 'Star-Spangled Banner' at the opening of the exercises. The three Mormon leaders glowed with pride as the audience burst into applause when their pet choir finished."[60] As on the previous day, the audience "went wild with enthusiasm" and demanded an encore, with some shouting "Three cheers for the Mormons!"[61]

Whether the choir was discriminated against in the judging of the competition is unclear, but what is clear is that it had enormous impact on those in attendance, and that the church and all of Utah—and the West—were proud of it. The Utah Commission reported the Tabernacle Choir "to be almost if not quite equal to the best talent the country could produce was something for the West to be proud of."[62] The accolades the choir received left little room for disagreement regarding the correctness of the authorities' decision, however slow and hesitant, to allow participation. As the *Herald* noted, in addition to the judicious and harmonious tactics of the varied speakers representing Utah, the Mormon Tabernacle Choir was an important element in the program's success. It is uncertain to what extent the audiences perceived the choir as Mormon or simply as talented and gifted fellow citizens, but the choir resonated with their fellow Americans as expressing in their music both American patriotism and Christian faith. Arguably, the choir seems to have been the most important and effective tool used to gain national and even international acceptance for Utah, establishing the precedent for the Tabernacle Choir to become a global phenomenon. Standing on the middle ground of art and culture, it linked religious and secular interests, while lending itself to both—and in so doing demonstrated, somewhat ironically, how the divisions between the two at the fair were less than clear. James Turner notes that this linkage between art and spirit comes from a very old "cult of the heart" tradition, forming a powerful aspect of Victorian religion, particularly as it had among American Protestants. Such spiritual engagements of art and emotion had the tendency for its participants to pull "God out of transcendence" and actually push "Him more fully into the human sphere."[63] Chicago's own Apollo Choir closed the Parliament of Religions by singing Handel's "Hallelujah Chorus" from *Messiah*. "To the Christians who were present," noted Barrows, "it appeared as if the Kingdom of God was descending visibly before their eyes."[64] Together with the American flag, millenarianism, and the Goddess of Liberty, Richard Seager indeed spoke of such musical expression as making up a single yet crucial component of a larger "American myth." This myth directly informed the World's Fair and its various auxiliaries and their handlings of different groups, becoming a site of a new and positive dynamic encounter between the Mormons and the United States, ushering them into the Anglo-Protestant mythology of American civilizations—well underscored by the choir's selections, from Handel's *Messiah* to patriotic songs.[65]

The day following the Utah Exhibition, the *Chicago Sunday Herald* reported that something "unique" was happening. "Mormons and gentiles came together as friends." Be it the music of the choir or the oratory of Governor West, "something made all the people from Utah friends and all their guests happy."[66] Whether part of an orchestrated strategy or not, the Utah Exhibition and the Women's Congress contributed to further uniting Mormonism with more modern concepts of religion and thus defining Mormonism with more secular and nationally acceptable terms. Utah's participation in the fair both represented the finding of and the creation of common ground that had not existed before. As they found, their religious goals were not so separate from their secular goals. Mormons were not the sole organizers of the Utah exhibit, but they took full advantage of it. After the crushing severity of the antipolygamy crusades throughout the 1880s and the parliament's dismissal of their faith, Mormons intentionally tapped into the popular agendas of success, wealth, and equality and presented their faith in ways that Americans could sympathize with and appreciate in their practice and praise of scientific discovery, music, women's rights, and westward expansionism.

Leaving explicit evangelizing behind, new Mormon policies avoided even the appearance of proselytizing and stirring up old controversies, seeking instead to bridge differences and assuage enmities. Mormons revealed themselves to be more open to all Americans and gave Americans excellent opportunities to demonstrate their own new ideals of tolerance in an era of progress.

Whether part of an orchestrated strategy or not, the Utah Exhibition, the Women's Congress, and the Mormon Tabernacle Choir succeeded in two ways: further uniting Mormonism with more acceptable approaches to religion, particularly in separating religion from structures of power, and redefining the church within more secular and nationally accepted terms. Utah's participation in the fair represented the finding of—and certainly the creation of—common ground that had not previously existed, and Mormons had much to gain in calming popular fears about them. In other words, Mormons found value in how others regarded them—as well as finding value in how they regarded others—and in doing so, reflected a growing phenomenon in the industrialized and increasingly scientific Anglo-European civilization.

In a relevant international survey over the meaning and history of public opinion, philosopher Jürgen Habermas expressed the idea that during the nineteenth century, public opinion was part of the public sphere that had become an important element in checking state dominance over society. By the end of the century, as the press and politicians closed the gap between the social sphere and the new American market economy, their powerful influence over public opinion grew in support of special interests—exemplified here by Governor West's oratory, rewriting Mormon-American relations in support of Utah's financial growth. Life, growth, and the public's perceptions of things were already being fashioned by the media, of which the World's Fair was a massive organ. Walter Benjamin noted that these American fairs were "sites of pilgrimages to the commodity fetish," and as part of this fetish, each fair was, explains fair historian James Gilbert, a "progress report on the rapid expansion of consumer culture," attracting millions of patrons.[67] The power of these fairs to influence public opinion, as well as to move commodities, was rivaled by none. According to Habermas, such an event would have been a "public sphere in appearance only." Religions of the world as presented at the parliament, for example, would not have been a true or accurate depiction of global diversity, but as we've seen, rather a carefully laid-out and editorialized vision of a liberal Protestant worldview. Public opinion had become a type of commodity of powerful elites and activist groups, manipulating public conformity toward particular ends, thus helping explain the importance of Mormonism's exclusion.[68] The emerging liberal ideal of religious plurality and tolerance was thus not a blanket acceptance of this diversity, but rather an insistence on a particular version of that diversity that did not upset current structures of American privilege and power, but rather sought to improve them. However, the church, and Utah, took advantage of the same kind of media exposure and its reach on the public sphere to further themselves in improved public perception and economic advantage, which in itself was a sort of manufactured consensus of American progress.

These points about influencing public opinion for Mormons reached the level of scandal at the Louisiana Purchase Exposition, or St. Louis World's Fair, in 1904. Having taken great pride in earlier awards and positive publicity in Chicago, Mormons in St. Louis, notes Reid Neilson, won so many medals and ribbons in mining, agriculture, education, and irrigation, among others, that leaders of other states levied complaints before the fair's International Jury of Awards committee.[69] Upon investigating the Utah Commission's accounts, a special committee from the lower house of the Utah state legislature found irregularities, including forgeries of vouchers aggregating $2,100 by John Q. Cannon, secretary of the Utah Louisiana Purchase Fair Commission and son of George Q. Cannon. Though allowing Utah to keep their honors, the official report of the investigation offered a "unanimous" conclusion that the "so called awards" given under the authority of the Louisiana Purchase Exposition were "an immense and gigantic fraud." As an advertising gimmick, official awards were sold for commercial advertising purposes, while legitimate medals were held back by exposition management in order to promote and traffic these fraudulent awards. Under the authority of the Louisiana Purchase Exposition, one agent from the St. Louis official ribbon committee admitted to having sold one award "of special merit" for $500, explaining that other awards sold for as much as $20,000, such as one bought by a manufacturing company in order to boost its product. With warrants out, Cannon fled Utah to avoid arrest, but on July 19,

1905, was arrested in Lethbridge, Alberta, Canada, on charges of forgery and uttering fraudulent papers.[70]

## AFTER CHICAGO

In speaking before the large crowd assembled on Utah Day in Chicago 1893, one fair official candidly confessed that he had visited the Utah Exhibit out of duty, rather than desire. "Deep down in my heart," he said, "there was a strong prejudice against the people of Utah." However, "after listening to the music of your great choir I have changed my mind." He emphatically claimed that this change of heart was no mere "enthusiasm of the moment," but instead he could "not find it in my heart to mistrust a people possessed of such musical ability, which is certainly the outgrowth of refinement and noble aspirations." He added that his feelings were not unique as "I am only one of thousands here to-day whose sentiments in regard to Utah and her people have changed."[71] Governor West was clearly optimistic that the "widespread prejudice against Utah and her citizens" was now in the past. Thanks to the fine effects of the Utah exhibit and the choir, the "feeling among the masses of the people" had been obliterated, "and the good seed sown will continue to bear fruit for years to come."[72] Of course, mistrust of Utah and its citizens was far from obliterated; nevertheless, the optimistic expressions did reflect changing public perceptions of the territory and the people living there, Mormon and non-Mormon alike. Moreover, there was a new sense that Mormons were being identified with both an identifiable if amorphous religious Americana and the new secular quality of the territory and economically prosperous future state of Utah. The fact that Brigham Roberts was excluded from the Parliament of Religions, yet secular Utah was accepted and even welcomed at the fair, was not lost on Mormon leaders.

George Q. Cannon, speaking to the church after his return from the exposition, ignored the affront offered to Roberts and instead focused on the acceptance the church found in "The White City." "At Chicago everything went off in the most pleasant manner," he said, emphatically. As had the Mormon women leaders at the fair, Cannon positioned Mormonism squarely in the progressivism increasingly characterizing

American society. "I am thankful," Cannon continued, "to see people free from prejudice; to see them look at the Latter-day Saints as they truly are; to see us in our true light, and recognize the fact that we are struggling, with them, in our way, to advance the human family and to make progress."[73] Lorenzo Snow, upon the closure of the Columbian Exposition, similarly remarked to the Mormon people that "a great change had come over the feelings of the people of the world in reference to us—especially with the people of our nation."[74] Eighty-six-year-old President Woodruff recorded with satisfaction in his journal: "This is the Last of the year of 1893. . . . Their [sic] has been the Greatest Changes taken place Concerning the Church of Jesus Christ of Latter Day Saints during the year 1893 Ever known since its Organization."[75] Apostle Heber J. Grant, age forty-six, said, "The prejudice, the bitterness, and the animosity that a few years ago existed in the hearts of the people of this country against the Latter-day Saints, because of the outpouring of the blessings of the Lord upon us had almost entirely disappeared."[76] Grant also called for the renewed vigor in accomplishing the goals of the kingdom as now conflated with the church, of admitting past follies, and moving forward in both progress and humility. "If these things were not foremost in our hearts," said fifty-three-year-old apostle Francis M. Lyman, "then all Israel had need of reformation in this regard."[77]

These sentiments in regard to how the world was now beginning to perceive them also extended to how Mormons should receive the world within and outside of Utah. Though mixed in their success, the Parliament of Religions ideals were extended to Asian religions: Hinduism, Buddhism, Jainism, and Confucianism were worthy of Mormon respect. "They are not," stated President Cannon, "so imperfect and heathenish as we have been in the habit in this country of believing." Though astonished at the level of tolerance extended toward the Mormon Church at the fair, Cannon himself, after having met "the heathens who are representing themselves at the Fair," was newly convinced of their possession "of much more truth and intelligence than we credit them with having."[78] At the parliament, Methodist Charles Little commented that "people expected pagans. And pagans, they thought, were ignorant and impotent of mind, with no reasons for their worship and no brains in their theology. To them the Parliament was a stunning revelation."[79] As it was, the earlier binary of conflict that upheld America's sense of self as that of purity and innocence, had revealed itself as more multifaceted and complex, thereby inspiring new levels of understanding of America's marginal religious groups. Indeed, it became clear that morality, character, and inspiration were not limited to any single religion. To borrow from a speech by Hindu reformer Vivekananda, Cannon believed that if the Parliament of Religions revealed anything, it was "that holiness, purity, and charity are not the exclusive possessions of any church in the world, and that every system has produced men and women of the most exalted character."[80]

Clearly, the Columbian Exposition of 1893 had significant and unexpected consequences for the Mormons and other Americans in how they saw each other, how they saw themselves and their religious institutions, and how such visions redefined notions of Americanism. This is not to say that changes in practices, particularly among the Mormons, or changes in perception immediately resulted in the shift from religious to secular perspectives. However, the fair created a space in which, to a degree, these two terms evolved and became operational in the realm of popular thinking. As religion and secularism separated and defined themselves through juxtaposition with the other, and this separation became acceptable to people's ways of thinking, it helped impel the trend toward the United States' secular ideals of centralization, bureaucratization, urbanization, and industrialization. Faith, no matter whose, was transforming the needs and opportunities of a monopolistic corporate economy, and Utah's statehood became an imminent possibility, operationalized in similar fashion, assuming a more fully American identity that did not interfere with a religious identity. In other words, Mormons could now balance and even synthesize their religion and citizenship, and not feel torn. To return to the remarkable performance of the Tabernacle Choir at the World's Fair, whose singing of "The Star-Spangled Banner" thrilled the audience, the choir demonstrated one of Carrie Bramen's two modalities of syncretism: coming in "from below" as opposed to "coming in from above." The choir's grand singing of the American national anthem demonstrated that they of the Mormon faith were not at odds with America's new sense of secular progress. Roberts's approach was not quite so; he sought to fuse with other faiths but retained his own brand of Mormon exceptionalism and made a claim of religious supremacy and leadership over other religions.[81] The choir's performance celebrated a joint American religious exceptionalism that was as secular as it was religious.

Following the fair, this method, or rhetoric, was used and developed to support the separation between religion and Utah's political affairs, however ambivalent it remained. In an important point of analysis, David Chidester demonstrates how Americans produced a unique "negotiation of the sacred," allowing them to negotiate what is normally considered sacred for nonreligious purposes. In looking at American football or even Coca-Cola, Chidester shows Americans doing "real religious work in forging a community, focusing desire, and facilitating exchange in ways that look just like religion."[82] In similar ways, as Mormons reintroduced themselves to the country "from below," they demonstrated a "negotiation of the secular." With the closed frontier and the beckoning of the twentieth century, development and progress were the new powerful forces to be reckoned with, rather than religion. Mormons, by these successful ways and means, came to understand their secular participation as not all that different from their larger religious goals. Mormons did not discard their religious elements as they filtered them through these more secular environments, but rather negotiated within these new environments for deeply religious purposes. Jonathan Z. Smith explains, "We have not been attendant to the ordinary, recognizable features of religion as negotiation and application but have rather perceived it to be an extraordinary, exotic category of experience which escapes everyday modes of thought." Human life, and, we could add, Mormonism's transformation toward the secular, "is not a series of burning bushes."[83]

The choir represented its own call back to the idea of the transformative power of ordinary events. The fact that Mormons had their own choir was not particularly noteworthy, but the effects of this choir at the World's Fair were extraordinary, which Mormon leaders effectively utilized in their attempt to rebrand Mormonism. Building off their accrued social capital from the fair, Mormons pushed for their choir to "not only maintain the high reputation it has earned at home and abroad, but become the highest exponent of the 'Divine Art' in all the land." In a letter to choir director Evan Stephens and members of the choir, the First Presidency, consisting of Wilford Woodruff, George Q. Cannon, and Joseph F. Smith declared that musicians and poets were to be stimulated by this choir "until its light shall shine forth to the world undimmed, and nations shall be charmed with its music." With its "perfection in the glorious realm of song," it was anticipated that

> it may unstop the ears of thousands now deaf to the truth, soften their stony hearts, and inspire precious souls with a love for that which is divine. Thus removing prejudice, dispelling ignorance and shedding forth the precious light of heaven to tens of thousands who have been, and are still, misled concerning us.

Seen as a type of sacred ritualistic enterprise, music was to be a "noble work, a glorious cause, worthy of your earnest efforts."[84] Considering their initial hesitancy, this new emphasis is impressive. "It has often been remarked since the choir left here," explained George Q. Cannon upon his return from the fair, "that their visit would be productive of greater good than almost any number of missionaries."[85] As the First Presidency wrote to Conductor Evan Stephens (a Welsh convert) and the members of the choir less than two years after the fair, "Members of the Tabernacle Choir are really acting as missionaries, called for their special work."[86] The choir had quickly become, due to its secular appeal, one of the church's greatest auxiliaries "for the cause of Zion" and its singers some of its best and most effective missionaries.

The church also negotiated new relationships with politics. Notably, just before the fair, at the April 1893 General Conference of the church, the *Los Angeles Times* reported that Brigham Young Jr. made the statement that "politics are as important to the Latter Day Saints as religion, and should be so considered by the Mormon church."[87] A few years later, in 1896, a "Political Manifesto," subscribed to by twenty-four of the highest authorities of the church, including Brigham Young Jr., declared in "the most positive and emphatic language" that the church and its leaders had never attempted or even desired that the church "in any manner encroach upon the rights of the State" or to unite "in any degree" the function of either upon the other.[88] However inaccurate this statement was and however mixed politics remained with the church, and however disingenuous many outside and inside the church felt this manifesto to be, this new negotiation with politics was an important strategic shift by Mormon leaders.[89] As indicated by its decision to end polygamy (however much it remained in effect), Mormons were adopting a less religiously rooted perspective and orientation, which ultimately legitimated the federal government's right to assert itself into their religion's marital practices.

This negotiation can also be observed in the realm of church education in the 1890s. On June 1, 1893, the church sent out a circular letter in response to national and international strides in secular education which "seemed to demand like progress in the methods employed in our Sunday Schools in imparting the most important part of all true education," namely, "God and His Laws." The stated policy was to "make haste slowly" in furthering a church-wide training course for teachers centered at Brigham Young Academy (now Brigham Young University). These teacher-training courses were deemed experimental, but, notably, attendance was considered by the First Presidency to hold "the same weight and importance and be accounted in the same light as a foreign mission."[90]

That same year, in an attempt to promote intellectual credibility, the church established the Church University, which was to become "the head of our Church School system." The hope was that Mormon youth could gain just as high an education within Utah as they could in the rest of the country. But the overlap and competition in Salt Lake City between this church-based school and program with the University of Utah proved problematic and the Church University was closed in 1894. Following its closure, the First Presidency called upon Latter-day Saints to "faithfully devote their influence and energy" to the University of Utah. In promoting and furthering explicit goals toward nationally competitive and professional instruction, the church endorsed the "purely secular instruction" of Utah's state institution of higher learning, which avoided "any species of sectarian religious instruction." Interestingly, Latter-day Saints' Colleges were developed in close proximity with the University of Utah's programs, though the colleges' objectives were to fulfill the spiritual and theological training of LDS university students. This modeled the church's later seminaries and institutes of religion adjacent to high schools, colleges, and universities worldwide.[91] Following World War I, the church again reevaluated its secular education program as it became too expensive to remain competitive with state-funded schools. Centralizing its colleges and handing over its academies to the state, the church dramatically expanded its successful religious education program.[92] These developments demonstrate the continued relationship the Mormons now had with the state and its secular agenda of progress and intellectual advancement. Such policies were not devoid of important lessons of secular progress and public relations as learned in Chicago in 1893, revealing the church's attempt to be seen as in step with the rest of the United States' agenda of progressivism, intellectual advancement, sophistication in education, and the separation of church and state, and its implied privatization of religion.

The church's commitment to advancement in education and the modern presentation of itself in an industrializing and Progressive Era as an equally progressive faith can also be seen in the previously mentioned political manifesto made by the church in 1896. Despite significant controversy among high-profile Democrats B. H. Roberts and Moses Thatcher, who believed the church to have influenced elections against them and their party in 1895, the First Presidency, in "the most positive and emphatic language," denied church involvement or influence in Utah politics. An "era of peace and good-will seemed to be dawning upon the people, and it was deemed good to shun everything that could have the least tendency to prevent the consummation of this happy prospect."[93] While there was significant weight behind concerns and accusations of continued church influence within Utah politics, the rhetoric among church leaders was decidedly for separation.

Along similar lines of encouraging a better public image for the church, the First Presidency called for "more enlightened" expounders of the gospel. In an 1894 letter to President Lorenzo Snow and the Twelve, the First Presidency brought awareness to the fact that a "great proportion of those who go out" on missions do "not do justice to the message of which they are bearers," and whose lack of knowledge was not synchronized with "the great work of the last days that one would naturally expect them to possess in view of their high calling and of the exalted origin of the Priesthood which they bear." The letter went on to declare that "a different class of people" were now interested in the church, and it was "very desirable that something be done, if possible, to make a better impression upon the world through the medium of our elders." Many elders from the past, the letter pointed out, "were taken from the plow, the anvil, the shoemaker's shop and carpenter's bench";

furthermore, some "could scarcely read or write."

> But since those days a great change has taken place in America as well
> as in European land. Education has become very general, and in many
> countries compulsory. There is no reason now why any one should be
> ignorant of book learning, and it seems necessary that our elders should
> keep pace in this respect with the rest of the world.

Despite the tone of alert preparedness in this letter, such appropriations of the secular world, its concerns, and the growing importance of
presentation were not taken without concern by the Mormon leaders.
The late nineteenth century's increasing levels of literacy and intellectual sophistication and resulting secularism were not to ignore more
religious goals. Indeed, this same letter closed with the warning that
attempts to catch up with the world of learning "should be entirely free
from any tendency likely to check the Spirit of the Lord or cause men
to depend upon their own learning instead of the guidance of the Holy
Ghost."[94] President Wilford Woodruff, in a discourse delivered at the Salt
Lake City Tabernacle on Sunday, April 18, 1894, similarly emphasized
that changes within the church could not forsake the Holy Ghost: "We
should now go on and progress," but such progress was to be framed by
an "assistance of the Holy Ghost."[95]

However, by 1893, and following the footsteps of a Protestant kingdom now conceived in social terms of progress, Mormon leaders had
begun to realize that if they hoped to accomplish their goals as a religious people—which now included social progress as well as the building of a more internal spiritualized kingdom of God—they could not
do so without better organization and an acceptable public persona to
take their place in a world that was growing smaller, more organized,
more rational, and more bureaucratic, imperialist, and corporate. For
Protestants at this time, being "reconciled to God," argued H. Richard Niebuhr, "now meant to be reconciled to the established customs
of a more or less Christian society," where revivals were often utilized
to "enforce the codes of capitalist industry, to overcome the rebellion
of workers and to foster the bourgeois virtues on which the success of
the industrial system depended."[96] In line with these trends to enforce
prevailing standards, the First Presidency strongly upheld the side of

corporate bosses and condemned the idea of worker unions in 1896 as "contrary to our religion, and contrary to good citizenship." At the start of the Spanish-American War in 1898, the First Presidency informed Utah's governor, Heber M. Wells, of the church's preference for peace, but with the call to war with Spain, members had been admonished to support and enlist in America's imperialist efforts in Cuba without hesitation.[97] In contrast to the self-imposed isolationism and rejectionism of conservative Protestants, it became clear to the First Presidency, which now sided with liberal progressives, that they could no longer sell themselves while plagued with popular, persistent caricatures of their peculiar religious doctrines and exclusionary practices that had provoked no less than war, federal pressures, and failed cases in the Supreme Court. Nor could Mormons achieve these critical ends without becoming more sophisticated as a people and practitioners of a religious belief that no longer emphasized distinctive practices and theological peculiarities. Hoping to demonstrate themselves as on the right side of the frontier line, Mormons highlighted their shared history of progress and their full support of U.S. imperialistic engagement, and revealed the same goals of everyday citizens. Seeking inclusion with other American citizens, who believed in intellectual progress and social reform, their own church's growing bureaucratization and corporate form of worship contrasted powerfully with a more decentralized America and its multiple volunteer societies that Mormonism so heavily clashed with in an earlier evangelical era. Unqualified support for American military efforts also presented a strong contrast with earlier Mormon beliefs about the country and the millennium, which had served to justify earlier LDS noninvolvement and even condemnation of the U.S. military and its misled wars.[98] With these internal and external shifts, Americans watched as the frontier appeared to "work its magic." Mormons now moved gladly toward the respectability of national acceptance, a state more closely associated with proper religiosity, rather than one that inspired marginalization and stigmatization.

However, the new agenda competed with old agendas, and such was revealed by Roberts in his undelivered paper to the Parliament of Religions: though affirming that Mormonism was progressive, Roberts also described Mormonism as "destined to be the religion of the age"— which stood in contrast with the parliament's professed objectives of progressivism and unity, as directed by white Protestantism. Perhaps for this reason Barrows directed Roberts to read his defense of Mormonism in the margins of the parliament; in any case, he prevented Roberts from participating in the larger dialogue of the parliament and thereby rendered invisible the idea that Mormonism was the religion of the age or even shared anything in common with true religion—leaving Roberts dejected and bitter. As has been seen, Mormonism gained a degree of acceptance in the secular venues of the same fair, riding in on a wave of progressive presentations of economic and mineral wealth, ecumenism, feminism, and glorious music that united patriotism and religion, thereby setting the stage for Mormonism in the new era.

By 1900 Mormons increasingly downplayed their claims of global leadership and of being the religion of the age, and instead presented themselves as ordinary yet exceptional Americans whose past was indeed not irreproachable, and were willing to bend the knee, repent of past sins, and become, as President Cleveland had once remarked, "more like us." Growing ideals of religious tolerance demanded that the religious majority accept the minority, however conditional upon a standard of loose conformity. In order to fit these national ideals, Mormonism had to demonstrate itself as apolitical and less theological in its approach to public matters. The kingdom of God itself, preached new church president Joseph F. Smith in the first few years of the twentieth century, was now understood as none other than the "organization of the Church of Jesus Christ of Latter-day Saints," over which "the Son of God presides, and not man."[99] Such were the limits of American tolerance and the forming image of pluralism, and such was the new interpretation of Mormonism and the kingdom. Of course, suspicion of Mormonism continued; however, Turner's ready-made Frontier Thesis and narrative of national progress secularized the old covenant agenda of the earlier Puritan "city on the hill" motif. Within this new narrative, Mormons were no longer hopeless heretics and idolatrous worshippers of Dagon, but pioneers and reformed citizens now willing to fall into line with the nation's progressive patriotic codes, or covenant of proper apolitical and monogamous behavior. Turner's frontier allowed Mormons to be conditional allies of the existent status quo and direction of progress. This may have required a surrender of former claims to morality, the kingdom, and Americanism within earlier Mormon structures, but it offered placement into the confines to true Americanism. With the closure of the American frontier, Mormonism's earlier peculiar beliefs and practices became enshrined as a part of the savage frontier that was overcome by this new form of progressivism and had been changed or exchanged for a better future. Such a domestication of Mormonism fed into the myth of the frontier and new world of secular scientific belief in progress. "God's pedagogy," which had once justified heavy governmental action against sin (i.e., polygamy), was now, as reflected in part by Mormonism's assimilation, recast as a natural outcome of the American frontier.[100]

New challenges awaited this assumption of the Mormons into the national frontier narrative. Though Mormons wholeheartedly adopted Turner's thesis of progress and the frontier, they read it in a very different light than other Americans. For example, as Americans saw in the closing of the frontier the inevitable end to frontier barbarism and savagery (which Mormonism formerly epitomized), Mormons celebrated the waning bigotry and prejudice against them and their religion. In 1903, Mormon apostle Reed Smoot was elected to the U.S. Senate and the Mormons and their religion found themselves once more under heavy national scrutiny. The question was once again posed: "Can Mormons also be good Americans?" Smoot's victory decided in the affirmative, but only after Smoot's religion and role as an apostle within that religion were demonstrated to be impotent forces within American public life. As will be discussed in the final chapter, the Smoot hearings demonstrated that the Christian moral establishment, for however populous and powerful it yet remained, no longer retained sufficient support from the political and popular realm, and thus previously marginal religious groups found means of participation on the national stage. The Mormon Church's decision to participate at the World's Fair, as well as the Reed Smoot hearings, both reveal in secular ways a faith that still retained a more traditional and multidimensional perspective toward religion, one that did not easily separate the crossover of the two, thereby allowing them to play out in broader ways in the furtherance of these Mormon aims. This shift holds even broader significance in the scientific study of religion and its contributions to religious pluralism, as it was only when the element of Mormonism was removed from the discussion, that pluralism and Mormonism's place within it was granted.

# CHAPTER 6

## Embracing the Closed Frontier:
## The Reed Smoot Hearings, 1904–1907

And here let me add, the feelings of pure and unalloyed loyalty to our government which were deep-seated in the hearts of the Mormon people then, are still a part and parcel of our very being now, and indeed could not be otherwise, for the simple reason that as a community, we are an integral part of the nation itself, and the God whom we worship is the God of this nation.

—Joseph F. Smith, 1907[1]

This final chapter in the examination of the place and the placing of Mormonism in the national narrative of the United States and its shifting Protestant hegemony focuses on the election of Mormon apostle Reed Smoot to the U.S. Senate from Utah, on January 20, 1903—and the subsequent protests and congressional hearings over Smoot's qualifications to assume his seat. This was one of the final high-profile and national confrontations between Mormonism and Protestantism and between the Church of Jesus Christ of Latter-day Saints and the United States; the background and era of this confrontation reflected the secular progressivism that both sides learned from and engaged in.

Following his election to the Senate by the Republican and Mormon majority of the Utah State Legislature, there followed immediate protests, prompting Senate hearings against Smoot that began on January 16, 1904, and endured until June 6, 1906, when the Senate Committee on Privileges and Elections advised to reject Smoot. On February 20, 1907, the full Senate voted, failing to uphold the suggestion by the Senate Committee to deny Smoot his seat, which allowed Smoot to serve in the Senate for another three decades. Brigham H. Roberts had been denied his seat in the House of Representatives just a few years earlier, in 1897, because he was a polygamist; but as a monogamist, Smoot proved more difficult and dangerous, with opponents citing, beyond polygamy, treasonous oaths against the government, continued religious influence in politics, and, making things worse, Mormon insincerity behind their promises to end polygamy. Incited and fueled by businessmen, Protestant ministers, numerous denominations, and various Christian organizations, Smoot's opposition amounted to an unprecedented popular nationwide and interdenominational crusade, not solely against Smoot, but against the perceived slippage of the Christian hegemony within American power and the meaning of what it meant to be American, together with this new and uneasy inclusion of those deemed unworthy of this sacred national privilege.

Convened some ten years after Mormonism's participation at the Chicago World's Fair in 1893, the Reed Smoot hearings were similarly dramatic in representing Mormonism to the country—as well as providing insight into how Americans, including the church, were beginning to redefine religion and political participation as the frontier was declared closed and the twentieth century dawned. The hearings capped decades of turmoil and further inspired progress for the church and its alignment with the Republican Party, bringing forth important lessons. The antipolygamy crusades and accompanying legislation taught Mormons how "not to behave" as a religious body, while the Columbian World's Fair taught Mormons how "to behave." The highly publicized Reed Smoot hearings of the Mormon apostle and his religion firmly committed Mormons to these earlier-learned lessons, offering an even more stark contrast between the two. Indeed, the hearings for Reed Smoot represent more of a checkup of what had already been established between the Mormon religion and the country since Utah achieved statehood in 1896. Beyond being held accountable for verified breaches of earlier promises in the achievement of statehood, the case became more complex as Mormon leaders were also forced to respond to these new inconsistencies that faced the entire nation as religion was increasingly understood to be a private affair, rather than a public one.

While Protestant influence had been significantly weakened in American politics by 1903 by secularism and the growth of the progressive movement, it remained a potent social and cultural force, as witnessed by its volunteer religious societies that were still very much intact, and which came out in massive numbers against Smoot. As the Smoot Senate victory in 1907 reveals, Protestant churches and associations retained their distrust of Mormonism but, as is argued here, were no longer in a position to altogether marginalize Mormons from American public life. With its new emphasis on merit and reason over theology, the Progressive Era brought forth a new level of uncertainty, ambivalence, and powerlessness for the American Protestant movement that had earlier defined American politics and the placement, or nonplacement, of religious minorities. The ultimate failure to stop Smoot by a heavy-handed theological-political assault is a powerful testimonial that these cultural shifts were no longer taken for granted in American politics and popular culture. As suggested in the *Washington Post* at the beginning of the outcry against Smoot, there was a growing Jeffersonian sentiment that insisted Smoot's religion was "nobody's business but his own."[2] Although this new popular understanding of religion allowed for broader religious participation in the nation at the opening of the twentieth century, it should also be remembered that this expansion of American religious pluralism, which now included Mormonism, furthered a set of exclusionary definitions of religion as articulated by Smoot himself, that the separation between his religion and his Senate seat would be absolute. Josiah Strong's fear that "religion has been made an adjunct" of American public life had become, with Smoot's success, a reality.[3]

Mormonism accepted this progressive notion of religious privatization that not only opened doors for Mormon political participation but minimized traditional religious forces against it. However, as noted by Kathleen Flake, the waning Protestant homogeneity and hegemony was being forced to accept or at least acknowledge a new reality: unwanted groups could no longer exile themselves or be exiled to the "apparently limitless American frontier."[4] Without the existence of the frontier, such groups had to be acknowledged and reconciled as part of the nation and its new sense of secular identity and inclusiveness. Connectedly, the geographic frontier became an internal symbolic struggle that hinged upon the development of one's individual character as an American, a theme Smoot sought to emulate and project on his Mormon faith. As an important part of this inclusiveness, the Progressive Era caused a reassessment of previous understandings of the world—a world that was rapidly changing with the growth of cities, industrialism, economic expansion, and an explosion in technology that would drive a new modern economy, from Gottlieb Daimler's first high-speed internal combustion engine, to Thomas Edison's lightbulb, kinetoscope, and larger system of electricity generation and measurement.[5] "It is a new century," Henry Adams wrote in 1900, "and what we used to call electricity is its God."[6] The latter was rhetorical yet it provides an understanding of how previous conceptions of religion had shifted, and how the modern American nation-state was separating itself from a largely religious identity to one more secular, scientific, pluralistic, and diverse.

In this new Progressive Era that prized tolerance and separation, Smoot's opponents unintentionally revealed in their opposition powerful religious influence in politics that belied new progressive views of modern governance, appearing out of place as well as both hypocritical and prejudiced. The certainty of national stewardship with which Americans once held evangelical Protestantism had now become less sure amidst the progressive currents of modernity and the growth of pluralism and secularism. Indeed, as Charles Taylor explained, modern factors removed people out of an earlier context and brought the nation into a new secular age, one where old religions no longer felt at home, and where new and diverse religious forms responded, thereby expanding our sense of modernity and its new and multiple definitions. Classical understandings of religion as a public institution were in decline as a new form of privatization encouraged religious bureaucratization, allowing for a more efficient, competitive edge within a new world of nationalist pride and capitalist power.[7] As such, the Smoot case demonstrates not only a coming of age for the Mormon religious institutional church by way of its adaptation to this closed frontier, but simultaneously, one for the secular republic itself and the Christian modernists who embraced and helped define it. Conservative Protestants, on the other hand, defined themselves over and against these new liberal trends, thus setting the stage for their own marginality and creating a new fundamentalist form of religion. The Smoot hearings reveal more than a struggle between the newly emergent categories of the secular and the religious at the turn of the twentieth century, but also the influence either would wield within American society. In exposing their initial hazy separation, the hearings helped formulate these very categories that would preserve their social relevance in ways that would become normative and taken for granted in the twentieth century.

The crisis posed by Smoot was not just about the nation adopting a more liberal sense of participation for all including Mormonism, but indicated a shift in the very definition of the nation and the role of religion itself. Although Protestants retained considerable influence within American culture by way of volunteer societies, there was, in the words of William Hutchison, a new "modernist impulse" which now framed American institutions of power as separate from religious influence.[8] Furthermore, popular shifts in how Americans perceived the American spirit, which had always been understood in particularly religious terms, were now, with the redefinition of the frontier in more "closed" and secular terms, made disturbingly apparent to those who wished to deny it.

## Background of the Smoot Hearings

The details of the Smoot hearings touched on above do little justice to the forces propelling and directing them in how they played out. Smoot was not the first Mormon authority to aspire to high public office; Joseph Smith, Mormonism's founder, made a bid for the White House in 1844, just prior to being assassinated by a mob while imprisoned in Carthage, Illinois. Brigham Young was appointed Utah's first territorial governor in 1850 and served until he was deposed by President Buchanan during the Utah War of 1857–1858. George Q. Cannon of the First Presidency served as Utah's territorial delegate in Congress for ten years before his seat was declared vacant by the Edmunds Act (1882)—and before his face appeared on Wanted posters for his arrest. Brigham H. Roberts of the First Council of the Seventy, elected in 1895, was denied his seat in the U.S. House of Representatives after a brief fight in Congress because of his polygamous status and national fears of Mormon political influence. Given this unsuccessful track record, perhaps it is no surprise that many prominent Mormons initially questioned the wisdom of Apostle Reed Smoot's run and were nervous about his election.[9] However, LDS president Joseph F. Smith assured Smoot and others that God was behind these events. Prior President Lorenzo Snow believed in the providence of human progress, and Smith upheld Smoot's election as a revelation and a manifesto of progress that would carry the modernizing church successfully into the twentieth century. However, it was also no surprise when a harsh national spotlight again glared on Mormonism with the election of Smoot to the Senate. Despite achieving statehood, finding success at the World's Fair, being described in the press as "intense Americans" by high-profile figures,[10] and adopting new ideas and strategies in the struggle over being American, earlier fears and new concerns came together to pose an old question—can a Mormon be trusted to be a good American?

Such perceptions became clear almost immediately after Smoot's election. Non-Mormon Utah political and business figures and Protestant ministers immediately came together to protest Smoot's election. Six days after Smoot's election, former U.S. district attorney in Utah Edward B. Critchlow, and Dr. William M. Paden, pastor of the First Presbyterian Church of Salt Lake City and representative of the Salt Lake City's Ministerial Association, filed the first petition, signed by sixteen other prominent men from Salt Lake City, challenging the legitimacy of the election. Among other reasons, this petition based its opposition upon Smoot's high position of authority within the church, and the war Mormonism has waged "upon the home—the basic institution upon whose purity and perpetuity rests the very Government itself."[11] The month following the filing of the Paden and Critchlow petition in the Senate, Julius C. Burrows, Republican senator from Michigan, introduced a Citizens Protest to the Senate on February 23, 1903, that turned the case over to the Committee on Privileges and Elections, which he chaired. John L. Leilich, superintendent of Missions of the Utah District for the Methodist Episcopal Church, and signer of the original petition, joined his own petition to Paden and Critchlow's two days later, on February 25.[12] However, his sensationalist accusations which wrongly declared Smoot a practicing polygamist backfired. It helped to discredit Smoot's opposition as overzealous religious bigots, and induced the threat of a libel suit against him by Smoot. It also brought severe criticism from the Ministerial Association and on March 21, twenty out of twenty-five pastors of the Methodist churches in Leilich's jurisdiction asked his superior in Denver to move him to another field.[13] Nevertheless, Leilich's false claims helped bolster popular sentiment against Smoot, fueling anti-Smoot assemblies and religious rallies. Many thus saw within their opposition to Smoot, a larger symbolic struggle over everything Mormonism was imagined to represent. In justifying his vote against Smoot, Senator Henry C. Hansborough (R-North Dakota) argued: "Were I to fail to do otherwise, I should feel that I had condoned every offense ever committed against good morals and the written laws of the country by the Mormon Church."[14] A fight against Mormonism represented a fight for America and the sanctity of the American home and family. While Smoot understood the weight of his victory for the Mormon people and their own political ambitions, the question went much deeper.[15]

On a broader canvas, the Reed Smoot hearings, though held within the nation's highest political venue, were deeply theological and helped express a continued framing of the American myth of civilization—a myth that equated civilization with white Protestantism. The hearings exposed a fusion of Christian theology and politics that were so tight that Smoot's major offense is apparent. These popular nationwide crusades, as led by ministers and Christian groups, not only reveal the deep roots Protestantism still held over American sources of power, but also demonstrate its waning influence within this new era. Criticizing the "absurd clamor" over Smoot's opponents, the *Hartford Courant* posited that if the same arguments were used across the board that were now used against Smoot, they would also work to "shut Jews, Catholics or other religionists out."[16] But as seen in a public meeting later that year by the Inter-Denominational Congress of Women of Washington, it wasn't just that Mormonism was an unorthodox religion that contradicted hegemonic Protestant norms, but rather, Mormonism's direct affront to the American home and family that victimized and threatened "every form of religion based upon the Bible."[17] By the opening of the twentieth century, the preservation of the family had become a rally cry for Protestants against this new Mormon presence, allowing for the concealment of religious motivations behind popular volunteerism within a more secular-sounding framework. Being monogamous, Smoot found this new framework easier to navigate than that of false religion, and one that Mormons themselves adopted as a way to prove their Americanness. More than anything else, however, the exposure of continued polygamy within the church nearly lost Smoot his seat and relegated Mormonism in the minds of many to the status of being antifamily, and therefore un-American and unmanly.

With such mixed interest in Smoot's struggle in the Senate, Mormons latched onto new ideas that connected Mormon millennialism with those of the Progressive Era. Though remaining technically premillennial in theological orientation in particular ways, such progressive leanings certainly represented practical appropriation of the spirit of progress, and actually assisted with postmillennial ideas of a more perfected society prior to Christ's return—a society Mormons could help direct. Unlike their more conservative evangelical cousins, Mormons at the beginning of the twentieth century were not retreating from this increasingly secularized society, but rather found in it religious vision and societal opportunity, particularly as it brought forth a new sense of inclusion as envisioned in the newly formulated ideals of religious pluralism. As such, Mormons were now participating from *within* a nation that was redefining itself as separate from religion, further encoding this secularization process as a new presumption of the nation-state. Thus, the national stage that Smoot had stepped onto was one of growing division and uncertainty, for both the Senate and the church. Mormonism entered the conversation about national change and this assisted in the formation of new boundaries of American pluralism. As had other American religious institutions, the Mormon Church had developed during this period a more sophisticated bureaucracy and promoted the ideal of individualism—which moved the church against its earlier ideals of cooperation and the country against those of broad religious volunteerism.[18]

Though these new attitudes and changes had their roots in the World's Fair, they were powerfully framed in an address in the Tabernacle on January 1, 1901, by then-Mormon president Lorenzo Snow. This address ushered in Mormon modernity by way of celebrating secular progress as a sort of revelation from God, thereby Mormonism's purposeful and official integration of it. In his welcoming of the new century, President Snow did not anticipate the immediate return of Christ, but rather explained in his officially released "Greeting to the World" that the progress as seen during this new era was not purely a human accomplishment, but was "prompted by His Spirit which before long will be poured out upon all flesh that will receive it."[19] This announcement amounted to an enthusiastic embrace of progress by the Mormon people and their leaders at the opening of the century and was echoed by Mormon leader Emmeline B. Wells who declared, "The spirit of progress of this age is the work of God."[20] Though not without some qualifications, the Mormons were expanding their religious vision and attending societal opportunities to create a new sense of national inclusion and participation.

In their broadened vision, the church declared the year 1904 to be a "building era." This was given to the world in an annual Christmas greeting (or pastoral epistle), issued by members of the LDS First Presidency. Lorenzo Snow, in his last conference address in 1901 as president of the church, continued his earlier theme of progress in his realization that "we are not expected to do the work of the days of our youth, but to do greater, larger, and more extensive work."[21] Following Snow's death later that year, his successor, Joseph F. Smith, declared this last address the "word of the Lord to us all," and that the way forward "is too zealously and arduously labor to successfully accomplish all that is required at our hands."[22] In 1906, near the end of the Smoot hearings, the First Presidency commented in a similar Christmas greeting that "a healthy, progressive spirit has been manifested in almost every part of Zion." Latter-day Saints found themselves better organized internally, pushing forward with social improvements that affected communication, architecture, agriculture, transportation, and medical care.[23] There were also improvements in education, ecclesiastics, business, politics, and proselytizing. Within the religious realm, the church was refining itself socially, theologically, and ecclesiastically; illiterate missionaries were no longer being sent out in 1894; non-tithe-payers were kept from the Temple, and a budgeting committee was initiated in 1899; the importance of serious and accurate recordkeeping was reemphasized in 1902; stake presidents were advised in 1903 to be more selective in the choosing of their stake patriarchs; congregational "floating" (where congregants "floated" from one congregation to another) was condemned in 1902; by 1905 non-church attendance was rebuked and members who did not adhere to the Word of Wisdom (i.e., abstaining from alcohol) had their memberships threatened.[24] This embracing of progressive aims at health and self-improvement were not so much to reformulate a peculiar self-identity as a chosen people (particularly since the demise of polygamy), but rather to demonstrate their chosen status by being more American than other Americans. That is, they were peculiar because they were quintessentially American, and thus sought to exemplify American progress and character building at a time of new national fixation on the body, self-discipline, and health. Shipps accurately expressed this shift to reveal a new focus on the individual over a larger Mormon "corporate identity," but we also see here the Mormon embrace of the larger American corporate identity that demanded new roles for the individual in economics and politics, as well as the new national emphasis on codes of health and nutrition.[25] Such a refocusing by the church reveals an acceptance or even appropriation by the church of important themes within Turner's frontier visions of an American national identity and character—not one that was in opposition to the nation and its direction of progress, but one that sought to lead the way. Though this more centralized system of Mormon power prohibited a more dynamic approach that was needed for a more global outreach, Mormonism's increasing identification with Americanism allowed Smoot to retain his seat in 1907. This success helped contribute to a feeling of profound change within the church and its perception of the place and role of Mormonism in the nation, and would help color how Mormons would look to the rest of the world.

However, a great deal of the nation had its own perceptions of the place and role of Mormonism within the nation, and the election of Reed Smoot propped up old fears. It can be said that many—including Theodore Roosevelt—adjusted and expanded their thinking about Mormons, based on personal observation and an internalized sense of the frontier, together with a sense of tolerance toward religious difference and a new willingness to listen. Roosevelt's presidency throughout the hearings provided a critical framework for progressives in their new formulations of what it means to be American. For many, however, the conventional wisdom of the day was that one could not simultaneously be an American and a Mormon.

### Voices against Smoot

The center of gravity of this controversy centered not just on the church's continued political influence, but on the issue of polygamy and its suspected endurance following the church's promises to end it in 1890. National outrage broke out following the candid admissions of church president Joseph F. Smith and president of the Quorum of Twelve Francis M. Lyman that they had both personally continued to illegally cohabit with their polygamous families. These revelations, however, worked to cover more troublesome realities that both men adamantly denied before the Senate Committee, that both Smith and Lyman—not to mention other high-ranking leaders, including President Lorenzo Snow and Apostles Marriner W. Merrill, Matthias F. Cowley, John W. Taylor, John Henry Smith, Heber J. Grant, Abraham O. Woodruff, and George Teasdale, among others—had and continued to secretly condone, defend, and perform new plural marriages long after 1890.[26] Hoping to save Smoot's seat and allay growing suspicions, Smith presented a second manifesto on April 6, 1904, which prescribed excommunication as the penalty for newly formed polygamous unions. Joseph F. Smith continued to covertly authorize and encourage new plural marriages while simultaneously denouncing new marriages in public meetings, but it was Apostles Matthias Cowley and John W. Taylor who refusal to appear before the Senate Committee that set the nation on edge and put Smoot's seat into serious question.[27] National fears that Mormon leaders were not to be trusted in keeping their promises continued to boil over in 1904 and 1905 in light of Cowley and Taylor, and all claims of adopting Protestant forms of marriage and being trustworthy rang hollow. Moreover, growing division and confusion among church leadership over the secretive continuation of polygamy and its public denouncements revealed institutional and personal difficulties and contradictions inherent in such a dramatic policy/doctrinal change.

As rumors of new marriages circulated, and these "renegade" apostles retained their position in the same ecclesiastical body with Smoot, national outrage and suspicion increased, threatening a crisis akin to the antipolygamy crusades twenty years earlier. Smoot's attorneys reminded President Smith that if the church could not quickly prove its sincerity by strong action, not only would Smoot lose his seat, but a "constitutional amendment and perhaps confiscation" of church property were already being discussed in Congress.[28] Church leadership added their voices to calm the backlash both in Washington and at home in Utah. As president of the Twelve, Lyman vigorously scolded his colleagues in the Quorum to "sustain the stand taken by President Smith" and to not "talk or act at cross purposes" with his testimony in Washington, however false they seemed. As Lyman observed, not only was this confusion "shaking the confidence of the Latter-day Saints" at home, but it was justifying outside accusations that Mormons were "two-faced and insincere."[29]

Smoot found himself in the middle of one of the oldest charges against Mormonism and its leaders, which was that Mormons were inherently dishonest. Or, as Presbyterian missionary to Utah Dr. S. E. Wishard explained to a group of Methodist ministers, "It is easier for a Mormon to lie than it is to tell the truth, as they do not recognize it as wrong to lie."[30] Due to precedent and swirling suspicions, such accusations were hard to shed. Smoot wrote letters to friends and church colleagues concerning the consequences of Mormon dishonesty before the country. In a letter to his wife, Allie, Reed wrote:

> There is an awful bitter feeling against the church, more so, I believe, than since its organization. I am worrying over adverse legislation more than over my chances to retain my seat. It would not surprise me to see a constitutional amendment adopted embracing or incorporating the Idaho Test oath, which virtually disfranchises every Mormon. This is the result aim to be accomplished by Burrows and [Fred T.] Du Boise and I am afraid that most of the Senators will approve of it. They are disgusted with our double dealing and they say they are going to put a stop to it.[31]

Historically, dishonesty among church leaders to the outside world had been a way of protecting the interests of the church itself or even just the public reputation of its leaders, but now the question of honesty was recognized as connected to public relations, something that Chicago a decade earlier taught church leaders to take seriously. As the hearings drew out, these Mormon leaders' refusal to appear before the Senate Committee had become a public relations nightmare, which even Mormons in Utah found difficult to reconcile, on top of all the other disturbing disclosures of church duplicity.[32] The Smoot controversy illuminated a church and leadership beset by external and internal criticisms and challenges, providing momentum to those seeking to hurt Smoot and, by extension, the church itself.

The Ministerial Alliance of Salt Lake City, led by William Paden, became a major player in this local attempt to embarrass the church and expel Smoot from office.[33] As a "saving grace" of a divided Christendom, Mormonism provided a powerful common enemy in which political and religious unity could be found. Paden also benefitted from timing: in May 1903, as Paden was commencing his crusade, a large number of Presbyterian ministers from eastern states were passing through Salt Lake City by train en route to a conference in Los Angeles. Soliciting their cooperation, the Salt Lake Ministerial Alliance distributed several pamphlets that focused on the more sensational and threatening aspects of the "Mormon Question." According to Mormon apologetic B. H. Roberts, the ministers took more than a thousand of these pamphlets which they distributed at the General Assembly. These pamphlets were subsequently taken back and presented at the Baptist Conference in Buffalo, New York; the Congregational Conference in Portland, Oregon; the Women's Christian Temperance Union (WCTU); the YWCA and YMCA conventions; and the Inter-Denominational Association of Women.[34] So successful was this church-related national distribution of anti-Smoot literature and its influence to action that the *New York Times* found it noteworthy that the thirty-second annual conventions of the New York and New Jersey Evangelical Lutheran Synod adjourned without passing a resolution against Smoot.[35] Finally, Protestant volunteer societies heightened the rhetoric and the importance of Reed Smoot into that of an emotion-fueled national preoccupation and crisis.[36]

Women's organizations, including the National Congress of Mothers and the Inter-Denominational Congress of Women of Washington, led these national efforts against Smoot.[37] Hannah Schoff, president of the Congress of Mothers, declared in March 1905 that Mormonism was "a menace to every home in America." In the same assembly, a woman named Mary E. James declared the church's origins as "one of fraud and duplicity."[38] One month later the Daughters of the American Revolution passed a resolution stating that the Mormon "hierarchy" not only stood as an offense to the modern family, but sought "the overthrow of the government."[39] One Marion Bosnall of Minneapolis, who had visited Utah for two months, declared in July 1905 that Mormon Utah was "practically a bit of foreign territory in the midst of our country" and a greater menace than previously thought.[40] One of the more disconcerting protests against Smoot came from the Interdenominational Council of Women for Christian and Patriotic Service. This group warned in February 1903 that Mormons took secret oaths to "avenge upon the Government of the United States the death of Joseph and [Hyrum] Smith," thus associating Smoot with treason.[41]

So efficient were these efforts against Smoot and his religion that Burrows, the chairman of the Senate Committee of Privileges, remarked that it was "impossible for the committee to hear all the protestants."[42] These protests were said to have come from every state and territory in the nation, in "hundreds of thousands of documents."[43] In the halls of Congress, in which these hearings were to take place, senators were fearful of Mormon complicity. The chief counsel of the Senate Special Committee, Robert M. Tayler, a former Ohio House representative who had chaired the House Special Committee that had successfully thwarted B. H. Roberts's seating in the House only five years earlier, now assumed his role as chair of the committee to expel Smoot and did not feign impartiality. Not reticent in expressing his opinion that Mormonism threatened the "sacred pledges of the past," Tayler saw his appointment as counsel for the complaints against Smoot as both a patriotic and a religious obligation. Assuring the committee that his motivations were not "hysteria" or "anti-church" bigotry, Tayler declared himself to be the voice of liberty.[44] Tayler went on to evoke the "foundation of democracy of Thomas Jefferson" and the "republicanism of Abraham Lincoln" in opposition to Reed Smoot and Mormonism. Thus, Tayler helped direct protest against Smoot away from being a narrow political concern within American government and into a near-cosmic struggle that combined the frontier spirit with the larger religious fight that stood "as deep as the human soul, as broad as life." Despite growing trends to romanticize the noble frontier pioneers that opened space for Mormonism to reframe itself, Tayler repositioned the Mormon religion in theological and digressive terms which questioned its ability to become Americanized, despite the frontier. In bringing to remembrance Mormonism's distrusted heritage, Tayler brought back old arguments that Smoot's church "assumes to exercise, supreme authority in all things temporal and spiritual, civil and political." Due to imposed sacred and treasonous covenants made in Mormon temples, Mormons were barred from the democratizing effects of the frontier, which Smoot himself "was bound to accept and obey." As such, being a member of the mountain-based church made it impossible for Smoot to separate church and state (or "things spiritual or things temporal"), which Joseph F. Smith was quick to deny in testimony before the committee.[45]

Smith purposefully downplayed and attempted to contradict earlier and still present fears of Mormonism, namely its hierarchical male despotism, its obfuscating of human agency, its enslavement of women, and its uniting of church and state. Smith even went so far as to deny having received revelation in his leading of the church and made the case that one could still be a "good Mormon," even while in dissent from following essential life-saving teachings of the church—such as polygamy. All in all, Smoot and other members of the church faced a formidable array of questioners from the Congress, while two apostles failed to appear, reigniting national distrust.[46] While Tayler's arguments were ultimately unsuccessful in ousting Smoot, they did uphold and solidify popular notions of Mormon discursiveness and distrust in American eyes, representing a struggle that would long outlive Smoot's tenure in Washington.

The anti-Smoot crusade was rooted in many causes, ranging from legitimate suspicion, to willful prejudice, to deeply intertwined notions of Americanism and religious influence that provoked widespread concern. Through it all, Smoot insisted that he had broken no law, local or national, nor was he guilty of any practices destructive to home or family. He declared his election proper, his identity as independent of his private faith, and himself endowed with "the patriotism and loyalty expected and demanded from every United States Senator."[47] Smoot's attempt to redefine this national personality, which he attempted to separate from his religion, directly placed him within this new progressive myth of the early twentieth-century American—a myth created via frontier expansionism, monogamous fidelity, and the privatization of religion. This American myth was further legitimated by the new progressive view, as articulated by Senator Albert J. Hopkins (D-Illinois) in defense of Smoot, that Mormonism "was undergoing a radical change for the better, and that Senator Smoot represented the higher and better Mormonism."[48] Nevertheless, though Smoot was acutely aware of the broader religious and constitutional significance of the controversy, he seemed unaware of how his continued public experience of Mormonism applied to his identity as an apostle of the Mormon Church. As Tayler indeed indicated, Smoot similarly found it difficult to separate his patriotic duty from his larger religious destiny and that of his church, and Smoot perhaps had a difficult time seeing this religious dynamic within the new private redefinition of Mormonism. As Smoot told his friend John McQuarrie, public scrutiny of the arguments given by religious ministers would reveal that this isn't a "fight against Reed Smoot, but that it is a fight against the authority of God on earth and against the Church of Jesus Christ of Latter-day Saints."[49] Indeed, Smoot's apostolic authority directly contributed to his political influence and success in Utah, providing for him a preset organizational arm of political support made up of stake presidents, bishops, and prophets, many of whom rallied popular Mormon support for Smoot and the Republican Party, including Roosevelt's presidential run in 1904.[50]

Smoot retained faith in the constitutional fidelity of the American people, particularly as many were beginning to draw clearer lines around signs of overt religious bigotry in the beginning of a new and more tolerant century. In January 1903 U.S. President Theodore Roosevelt dismissed Mormonism's religious claims, particularly its temple ordinances, as "foolishness," and had advised against Smoot's nomination as "very unwise," due to his position as Mormon apostle, something Roosevelt never warmed to. Relying on personal observations of Smoot, however, as well as those of close friends, Mormonism was for Roosevelt, "simply an aberrant sect," which, however odd, posed no real threat.[51] These sentiments marked the larger tenor of the hearings, as noted by historian Harvard Heath, where "pro-Smoot speeches . . . appealed to reason and common sense while the heated fulminations of the anti-Smoot senators seemed too mean-spirited to have much credibility."[52] Indeed, Smoot's opposition struck many as the sole fight of prejudiced ministers and religious zealots than that of a reasoned political investigation committee, however accurate and popular some of the accusations were, particularly concerning the continuation of plural marriage.[53] For this and other reasons, the new century, notes Thomas Alexander, had become more conciliatory and open, providing better opportunities for the church to launch "concerted efforts to explain the Latter-day Saints to the outside world."[54]

Thus Smoot could, with some confidence, expect that the religious motivations behind the opponents' attacks would ultimately prove counterproductive in this new secularized, masculinized frontier mentality that had defined the political realm as severed from that of the emotional, and, at least explicitly, from that of the religious.

## VOICES FOR SMOOT

A particularly notable example of how these new privatized ideals of religion affected the potency of religious protest in politics, took place in the Presbyterian General Assembly in May 1904. The assembly opened with a prayer that God would expel Smoot from office, and during its time in session slanderous reports were made against the Utah senator. John I. Platt, the ruling elder from New York and chairman of the Committee on Polity, created some pandemonium when he, from the floor of the assembly, opposed what was going on. "Hold on gentlemen," he insisted, "I have a right to my opinion. I hold this as a political question with which this Assembly has nothing to do."[55] Platt went on to say that the assembly was not attacking Mormonism, but it was attacking by its actions and words the principle of the separation of church and state. Platt spoke as a minority in the assembly but his view represented the changing beliefs about the role of religion in American society and the inappropriateness of religious bodies setting or steering political standards for the rest of the country. Having mingled with and befriended Mormon women at the World's Fair in Chicago, Susan B. Anthony spoke out against women's organizations that opposed Smoot, particularly on the grounds of polygamy, calling their efforts "a small way for our country to be acting."[56] According to the *Washington Post*, such women's groups had gained over a million individual petitions, with millions of signatures.[57] The National Congress of Mothers had originally hoped the national efforts against Smoot were to be "entirely an affair of women," but eventually accepted the help of male ministers and politicians, while appealing to "all women" whose hearts yearned for "the interests of American womanhood." Following the patriarchal theme of ignoring the female voice, Senator Albert J. Hopkins (D-Illinois) added his voice, stating, "I do not think the ladies thoroughly understand the points involved," but declared he said this based on his experiences as a lawyer: evidence was lacking. Smoot was both "above reproach" and a "Christian gentleman" who had lived "a singularly pure and upright life." If the Senate were to expel him due to the sins of his religion, then under the same standard, and in light of the entirety of Christian history, "where is the Christian gentleman in this body who would be safe in his seat?"[58] Smoot's wife, Alpha (Allie) May Eldredge, lamented in a nationally published letter that if "all the enemies of Mormonism could visit our home in Utah," they would end such "ignorant prejudice" against Smoot and his religion. President Theodore Roosevelt himself dismissed the idea that "a case has been made out against Smoot," becoming Smoot's most powerful ally and critic against such "persecution."[59]

According to historian Milton Merrill, it was Smoot's alliance with the progressive reformer Roosevelt that made his victory in the Senate possible. The significance of this support, however, extended beyond Roosevelt's high political position, emerging also from his simultaneous status as the nation's foremost archetype and expression of America's frontier spirit and manhood. As seen in Roosevelt's idealizing of the "strenuous life," the frontier line that had long inspired conflict between the barbarian and the civilized, was also a deeply internal struggle over character and what it meant to be a man. For many, Roosevelt did not just articulate and advocate, but embodied the new progressive reformist struggle and determinism of this new era, bringing his friend Frederick J. Turner to reference him as "the most important single force in the regeneration of this nation in his day." Equally inspired by Turner, Roosevelt continually pointed to the Frontier Thesis as a "certain definite order," detailing in his own multivolume work *The Winning of the West*, America's conquest over the unruly frontier and its related American character. As consistent in other writings, Roosevelt understood that as settlers conquered and transformed the American frontier, "the wilderness in its turn created and preserved the type of man who overcame it." "Nowhere else on the continent" has so sharply defined a "distinctively American type" as has "been produced as on the frontier."[60] The frontier represented a masculine place of "constant warfare" between the settler and his environment, one that brought into existence a defiant and even belligerent self-sufficiency and independence that outlined a "peculiar American spirit" that carried into reality the nation's "manifest destiny." Citing Daniel Boone and Davy Crockett as the perfect male ideals and even heroic examples, the frontiersman was strong and virile, "certain to make their weight felt either for good or for evil."[61] Smoot was no Crockett, but as noted by Roosevelt concerning Crockett's descendants, Smoot was a Republican, and though Mormons may have been characterized as rude, violent, and even belligerent toward outside intervention and critique, such "manly" characteristics were no longer deemed not representative of what it meant to be American, particularly of those from the frontier. The idea of the closed frontier at this time, wrote Michael Johnson, inspired a new impulse to prove the national vitality, being expressed through various "postfrontier sublimations," including Wild West shows, rodeos, dude ranches, Roosevelt's "strenuous life" of "sheer gusto," Boy Scouts and Girl Scouts, and organized sports teams whose team names and mascots included Indians, Bears, Cowboys, etc.[62] As Mormons appeared to be adopting this postfrontier progressive impulse, Roosevelt hoped that the Mormons would turn in large numbers to the Republican Party. Indeed, in his conditional support of Smoot, Roosevelt brought the Republican apostle-pioneer into his own masculine-progressive nationalist vision of the country, marking an important beginning of Mormonism's ironic yet close relationship with the Republican Party, and its twentieth-century vision of itself as a manly, progressive and even quintessential American faith.

As a committed progressivist, Roosevelt looked to the new Social Gospel movement, which practiced a form of active religious piety for social betterment that sought to solve the ills of an increasingly secular and urbanized society.[63] Roosevelt's progressivism, then, was not separate from his Protestant religion, but was instead integral to it. Though adopting a type of male-centrism that granted undue privilege to a particular form of American progress and identity, Roosevelt appropriated a brand of social Darwinism that idealized righteous action over theological belief. Such action encouraged a form of religious piety that was rooted in external and public forms of faith, such as helping the weak and destitute, despite their sectarian preference. Roosevelt quoted James 2:18 as his creed: "I will show my faith by my works," and he and others looked to deeds and merit for religious sanction.[64] Support for Smoot, then, was partly political opportunism, as it encouraged a certain level of collective Mormon political solidarity toward him and the

Republican brand, but more profoundly, this support for Smoot and the Mormons represented an important aspect of Roosevelt's Square Deal creed that judged people based upon merit over religious creed, thus helping to bring forth a new sense of social inclusivity and tolerance to American politics, similar to Roosevelt's secularization push in public education. At the same time, progressive views of merit and tolerance were understood from within this postfrontier mythology, where a certain level of white-male religious privilege was assumed, built upon, and protected. For Roosevelt, the question of racial and religious bigotry and intolerance remained an urgent one for the country, as was the progressive motto, but as would be expected in early twentieth-century politics, many contradictions continued and many remained hidden.[65]

In important ways, this Square Deal meshed with Roosevelt's view of the effects of the frontier on individuals, as well as its relevance to those in the perhaps overcivilized and emasculated industrial East. An asthmatic Harvard alum from New York, Roosevelt held a strong romanticism for the now-closed American frontier as a place where a more solid American manly character of self-reliance and determination could be cultivated. In writing the history of his own involvement and leadership in the Spanish-American War, Roosevelt referenced himself as every bit as much a product of the frontier as those cowboys and mountain hunters of the Northwest. Roosevelt believed that the time he spent on the frontier prepared him for the bravery and diligence that was then needed as lieutenant colonel of the First United States Volunteer Cavalry—a.k.a. "Rough Riders," named after the rough riders of Buffalo Bill's Wild West show, as prominently featured at the 1893 World's Fair in Chicago.

Roosevelt presented these Rough Riders in the historical record as a visible symbol of an invisible struggle over the savage frontier, together with its social unifying effects on both frontier cowboy and Harvard quarterback, of wilderness hunter and Yale tennis champion. Though of diverse backgrounds, all men in Roosevelt's cavalry were united in the common traits "of hardihood and a thirst for adventure. They were to a man born adventurers, in the old sense of the word." The now-closed frontier line that had long marked the division between the civil and savage, also took place in the inner soul and one's new struggle to become a sculpted American, with all of its spiritual and physical characteristics. At the same time, there were new frontiers to be subjugated and explored beyond the American continent, making Roosevelt an ardent expansionist in search for new colonies, often comparing Filipinos to Apaches and condemning anti-imperialists as "Indian lovers."[66] However real the frontier and however romanticized by Roosevelt as an actual site of intrinsic conflict, Roosevelt celebrated the unifying characteristics of the war effort in Cuba against Spain, and the need of cultivating among American citizens this new self-reliance and efficiency as presented by his own Rough Riders, whom he felt embodied this idealized patriotic manhood.[67] If Buffalo Bill turned the myth of the frontier into a romanticized entertainment franchise, noted Western historian Robert Hine, then Turner and Roosevelt brought it intellectual respectability.[68] With the frontier now perceived to be closed, its expression as its own religious mythology and its relationship with the state became immortalized into the fabric of what it meant to be American, however transformed. Traditional religion may have been relegated to the feminine private sphere, but this old frontier religion had become enshrined into the public manly garb of the new Progressive Era.

Having internalized the Americanization effects of the frontier, Roosevelt believed that the best way to assimilate wayward groups was to offer "fair treatment," building a "community of interest among our people," thereby making ethnic and racial differences wane in importance.[69] In befriending Mormons and building on mutual interests, Roosevelt fully expected Mormons to be well on their way to being properly Americanized. Within such a context, Roosevelt became upset over Senator Frederick T. Dubois's anti-Smoot efforts that appeared to only incite trouble in Idaho and threatened these Americanization efforts in the West.[70] As part of his progressive responsibilities, Roosevelt led the charge to bring religious, racial, and ethnic minorities into the folds of the Republican Party, not just Mormons, but Catholics, Jews, and African Americans, as well as Irish and German immigrants.[71] Following President Roosevelt's controversial White House dinner with prominent African American Booker T. Washington, Smoot caused a local controversy in inviting black guests to a banquet he and his wife organized for members of the Utah Legislature and state officials: "If President Roosevelt isn't too good to entertain a colored man at the White House, I don't see why I shouldn't have colored people as my guests."[72]

This progressive social gospel, however patronizing at times toward the "weak," had unintended consequences as it exposed elites, notes William Hutchison, "to minorities and their problems. Quite often, it involved exposure to their religious forms and religious experience."[73] Roosevelt's personal associations with Utah and its leaders were important in how he came to view Smoot. In 1900, when Roosevelt was campaigning for William B. McKinley in Utah, he was struck by Mormonism's pioneer past and, as seen with the Mormon Church–sanctioned support of the Spanish-American War, came to celebrate Mormon soldiers and pioneers for their part in upholding America's imperialist destiny. Roosevelt was particularly impressed with Mormon pioneer irrigation strategies in their desert basin, which he helped frame into national irrigation laws, further upholding this frontier idealism and its national importance for these contributing pioneers of American progress.[74] Beyond his own personal observations, Roosevelt sent his close friend and journalist Jacob Riis to Utah with an investigating committee. Following his trip, Riis assured his friend there was nothing to fear from Mormons. Presenting a stark contrast to President James Buchanan's lack of investigation prior to his hasty decision to dispatch military forces to Utah in 1857, Roosevelt took C. E. Loose, an important Utah politician with no direct ties to Mormonism, aside in a private meeting. His questions were simple and direct: "Is Smoot a polygamist?" and "Are Mormons good Americans?" Loose readily denied the former but affirmed the latter.[75] Admittedly, as polygamist apostles Matthias F. Cowley and John W. Taylor continued to evade testifying before the Senate committee, Roosevelt's relations with Smoot cooled. After Taylor and Cowley were removed from the Quorum of the Twelve, however, Roosevelt once again threw his support behind Smoot.[76]

Not surprisingly, as had his sit-down with Washington, Roosevelt's support for Smoot generated wide controversy; women's groups, including the Council of Mothers, for whom Roosevelt had served as advisory committee chairman, decried his support.[77] Some national newspapers editorialized against his beliefs, noting that Roosevelt's friends found his actions "extremely unfortunate" and were "believed to have alienated powerful friendships for the party."[78] Frederick T. Dubois, a member of the Senate committee, believed he spoke for the majority of the committee in his attacks against Roosevelt. Idaho's Democratic

senator and a former antipolygamist federal marshal, Dubois has been
described by Smoot biographer as the "most vindictive enemy Smoot
and the Church ever had." His wife, Edna M. Whited, was equally vocif-
erous against Roosevelt's support for Smoot and the Mormons. Dubois
charged Roosevelt with using the influence of high office to befriend
Smoot and his "law-defying and un-American organization" in a "high
conspiracy" that would supplant American affairs of state with Mormonism. This religion, he declared, had been marked as a menace by
"Presidents Buchanan, Johnson, Grant, Hayes, Garfield, Arthur and
Cleveland," and yet "Mormonism is more insidious, more dangerous,
and a greater menace to our Government and civilization to-day than
it was at any particular period."[79] To Dubois, Roosevelt was selfishly
courting the Mormon vote at the expense of the national welfare and
he blasted Roosevelt for doing what "no president heretofore" had done,
namely, to make national security "a matter of partisan politics."[80]

Though Dubois ignored Lincoln in his list of presidents who saw
Mormonism as a national threat, Roosevelt would reference him for his
willingness to stick up for the "plain people" and to defend them against
demagoguery.[81] Also, to Roosevelt, Lincoln was exemplary of masculine Christianity, which Roosevelt had embraced from Boston's Trinity
Church when he was a student at Harvard.[82] Emphasizing the manly
and aggressive aspects of Christ's ministry, masculine Christianity constructed proper piety as both active and aggressively involved in the social
world. Manliness no longer referred to one's civility as a gentleman as it
had in an earlier Victorian era, but instead, as expressed by Clifford Putney, that "raw male power needed to combat disruptive changes in society." For many during the Progressive Era, a new progressive model for
manhood emerged, "one that stressed action rather than reflection and
aggression rather than gentility."[83] Following the imagined closure of the
frontier, this new model of gender and its implied manly characteristics
comfortably informed how Roosevelt and other progressives saw both the
direction of the country and Mormonism's new place within it. At a particular moment in frontier intellectual history, these new definitions of
gender transcended their own creation, becoming seen as ahistorical and
universal and placing themselves outside critique. Like the Frontier Thesis itself, this new myth of gender transformed itself into timeless dogma
that directly affected the mode of transitions for both Mormonism and

the country at large. Finally, these shifts in gender perceptions directly contributed to Roosevelt's distrust of Smoot's heavily religious female antagonists, as they appeared rooted in what was seen as more womanly, emotionally driven paranoia than manly reason.

Roosevelt dismissed the female voice and the original accusations against the Mormon religious institution as being "without so much as the smallest basis in fact" and similarly dismissed the women's organizational outcry as being "hysterical persecution."[84] To Edna Whited's hyperbolic claims that Mormonism was a "treasonable organization" and an "even greater blot than was slavery," and reports that Mormon children were taught to "spit upon the American flag," Roosevelt retorted, "You don't know what you are talking about."[85] Beyond dismissing this female voice as mere emotionalism and hysteria, he was equally dismissive of any organizations that accused Mormons of being un-American. In some ways, misrepresentation not only countered the fair treatment of Roosevelt's Square Deal but appeared personal. Responding to "malicious inventions" and "deliberate falsification" about his own family, Roosevelt severed all connections between the *Boston Herald* and all federal departments in Washington in November 1904.[86] He also publicly defended and even praised Mormons, in an article he wrote for *Collier's Magazine*, for "unusually high" standards of sexual morality.[87] Finally, as indicated previously, Roosevelt, who was a historian of the American West in his own right, also perceived Mormons as among the finest representatives of pioneers and the American frontier, as they had proven themselves successful in the rugged American West and its demand for the strenuous life.

For the American pioneer more generally, Roosevelt stereotyped them as courageous, loyal, and patriotic, but "as a whole" were poor and "not over scrupulous of the rights of others." As part of these masculine characteristics of the frontier, pioneers were intense in their emotions and persistent in accomplishing their wishes. "There was little that was soft or outwardly attractive in their character; it was stern, rude and hard, like the lives they led; but it was the character of those who were every inch men, and who were Americans through to the very hearts core."[88] The frontier and its identity of conflict and strenuous living idealized and even romanticized these new gender norms that underlined Roosevelt's support of Smoot, which Joan Smyth Iversen explains as coinciding with an understanding of sexuality that was compatible with the new secularism of the Progressive Era.[89] The secularization of American society was associated with these new presumed gender norms, relegating the feminine as private (religion, emotion, gentleness), and the masculine as public (aggression, reason, roughness). As new beliefs in the worldly and even strenuous life filled in the secular spaces of American culture and power, this growing sense of the enormous impact of the frontier on the pioneer heritage on the American experience served Roosevelt well, and he in turn served Smoot, and thus Mormonism's status as American to the heart's core. Roosevelt's adaptation of the secular in his support of Smoot was not so much devoid of religion as it was implicitly religious—in contrast to an earlier era where American politics followed more explicit forms of religious precedent.

## CRUSADE IN THE HALLS OF CONGRESS

Reed Smoot had reasons to hope that ill-founded popular prejudice against Mormonism would not rule the investigations. In this, not surprisingly, he was doomed to disappointment, as seen with prominent religious voices such as Charles Parkhurst of Madison Square Presbyterian Church. Parkhurst was quoted at the start of the Smoot hearings in the *New York Times* as claiming that Mormons were affecting our children at school by distributing literature on polygamy; that they were seducing women by secretly attending Protestant services to win over unsuspecting females; and, finally, that the Mormon Church was a sworn enemy of the state and was using Smoot "as a means to its eventual overthrow."[90] On the floor of the Senate, Smoot and his supporters were publicly accused of threatening the Christian family and of potentially bringing the country to ruin. Republican Chairman Burrows, who was on the investigative committee, declared that allowing Smoot to retain his seat would drag "the churches of this land, Jew and Gentile, down to the level of abomination." Listening from the galleries, women, who made up the majority and who, according to the *New York Times*, even "invaded the reserved precincts of the men's galleries," applauded this forceful statement. Even after Smoot had been voted to retain his seat, Dubois accused Senator Hopkins, who had voted in support of Smoot, of placing the Mormon Church above all other Christian organizations, demonstrating a certain anxiety over the place of religion in this new era.[91]

The extremity of such an outcry makes visible the deeper issues at stake in the Smoot case. To Smoot's Protestant opponents, the issue was not necessarily his presence in the Senate, but rather it was more the country's fading fidelity to religious orthodoxy and its Christian identity, imagined by Protestants during the nineteenth century to have been enshrined at the country's founding. As a Mormon apostle, Smoot's very presence in the Senate threatened to alter the definition and tone of who and what was American. Although overshadowed by the inevitable issue of—and fascination with—polygamy, Mormon theology and ritual practices were inquired into, particularly in how they influenced longstanding political and religious beliefs of free will, and the role of Mormon leaders within that individual agency.

On March 3, 1904, attorney Robert Tayler questioned President Joseph F. Smith about the nature of God in Mormon thought and how such related to free will. Smith explained that, although the leaders of the church declared that they have divine authority to speak for God, "there is not, and can not be, any possible restraint held over the members of the Church of Jesus Christ of Latter-day Saints except the restraint which people themselves voluntarily give." The exchange between Tayler and Smith continued:

> Mr. Tayler: In your conception of God then, He is not omnipotent or omniscient?
>
> Mr. Smith: Oh yes; I think He is.
>
> Mr. Tayler: But do you mean to say you, at your pleasure, obey or disobey the commands of Almighty God?
>
> Mr. Smith: Yes sir.
>
> Mr. Tayler: Communicated to you?
>
> Mr. Smith: I obey or disobey at my will.
>
> Mr. Tayler: Just as you please?

Mr. Smith: Just as I please.

Mr. Tayler: And that is the kind of a God you believe in?

Mr. Smith: That is exactly the kind of a God I believe in.

In this exchange, Tayler highlighted the principle of man's will over God's will in Smith's theology in an attempt to highlight the important inconsistency between Smith and popular protests against Smoot. Senator Joseph B. Foraker (R-Ohio), after this exchange, reminded Tayler that this doctrine of free will, or, in his words, "free moral religion," was the same that "every good Methodist believes in."[92] Moreover, in contradiction to an earlier Calvinist notion of predestination, and as a consequence of the frontier experience, such "moral agency" over God's sovereignty had become a core philosophical issue among early twentieth-century progressives. In this new century, people were their own free agents rather than mere tools of a higher divine purpose. Questioned along these same lines, Smoot took it even further by stating that if God commanded him to break American law, he would personally dismiss God's command.[93] This progressive line of thinking did not, of course, aim to contradict God's omniscience in the affairs of humanity, but rather acknowledged the limitations of humans in tapping into that omniscience, and in the context of Mormon revelation and prophetic leadership, limitations in conveying it and encouraging others to follow it. With such responses to Tayler and the Senate committee, Smith and Smoot countered the accusation that Mormons were controlled by church leaders (thus feminine), thereby placing Mormonism directly in line with other notable national figures and their perceptions of manly agency, including Woodrow Wilson and Theodore Roosevelt.[94]

The next morning, March 4, Senator George F. Hoar (R-Massachusetts) continued this challenge of Smith and the Mormon worldview by using the Bible as his means of inquiry. Of course, this creates the ironic situation in which, in the midst of concern over whether Mormonism had separated church from state, a senator was using sacred literature and an explicit scriptural model to size up Smoot's fitness. Polygamy, though perhaps not explicitly, was at the heart of the confrontation between Smith and the committee, as revealed by Hoar's selection of

1 Timothy 3:2, which states that a bishop must be the husband of at least one wife. The senator pursued the familiar verse used by Protestant ministers to discredit plural marriage:

> Senator Hoar: I understood—and I am not sure I understood you aright—that it [the injunction of polygamy] was permissive, but did you mean to say that or do you mean to say that it is obligatory, so far as a general principle of conduct is concerned, but not mandatory under the circumstances?
>
> Now I will illustrate what I mean by the injunction of our scripture—what we call the New Testament.
>
> Mr. Smith: Which is our scripture also.
>
> Senator Hoar: Which is your scripture also?
>
> Mr. Smith: Yes, sir.
>
> Senator Hoar: The apostle says that a bishop must be sober and must be the husband of one wife.
>
> Mr. Smith: At least.
>
> Senator Hoar: We do not say that. [Laughter] The bishop must be sober and must be the husband of one wife. I suppose that is generally construed to enjoin upon bishops the marriage relation. But I have known several bishops, two in my own State, of great distinction, who were bachelors.

Such scriptural interpretation and theological commentary continued during the course of the hearings to promote or deny Smoot's fitness for the Senate. Not all members of the committee found such lines of questioning relevant to whether Smoot should retain his seat. Such questions appeared off-base if not unnecessary, and this was summed up by Senator Beveridge: "I do not think questions as to what are his conceptions of God, or his private, personal duty, are competent."[95] In taking another approach on April 26, Tayler hoped to expose Mormonism's incompatibility with American political and social culture, this time steering his questions down more secular and political lanes: Mormon manhood and patriotism, and church members' lack of individual choice.

For this tactic, Tayler called Mormon apostle Moses Thatcher as witness, whom Tayler presented as the heroic embodiment of individuality and manly independence—he had been deposed as an apostle for standing up against the powerful church hierarchy and opposing the church's interference in local politics.[96] This depiction enabled Tayler to remind the committee of Mormonism's breach of the separation of church and state as well as its dominance over individual free will. Thatcher's case was an interesting one. In April 1896, Thatcher indeed lighted the fires of controversy in Utah when he refused to sign the Political Manifesto, which required church officials to seek permission for a leave of absence prior to running for public office. In light of his refusal, the members of the Twelve brought forth evidence that Thatcher was not in harmony with his brethren, and had hurled heavy public "insults and hard language" against President George Q. Cannon's ecclesiastic, business, and political endeavors; that he was lethargic in his duties as an apostle; and that he refused to put forth any real effort to promote good-will with his colleagues of the Twelve.[97]

Following the failed attendance at his own hearing with the Twelve on November 19, 1896, Thatcher was dropped from the Quorum. After this removal was made public that same day in the church-owned *Deseret News*, Thatcher declared himself to be "in the position of a victim," and accused the Twelve of not taking his refusals seriously.[98] The Political Manifesto which Thatcher refused to sign quickly became the center of public debate, and Thatcher stood as a democratic hero who defied hierarchical control over individual political conscience. Thatcher lost his bid for the U.S. Senate by a narrow margin in February 1897 (state legislature election was in 1895, U.S. Senate election was in 1897), and then accused church authorities of influencing the election outcome in favor of the Republican Party and cited the Political Manifesto as another attempt by the church to control local politics.[99] In the following April General Conference, Cannon condemned those who supported Thatcher, calling upon them to "repent in the name of the Lord Jesus" and warning them that if they did not, "God will withdraw His Spirit from them and they will go down into darkness."[100] In August, Thatcher was brought to trial for "apostasy and un-Christian like conduct"—and at this time he had a change of heart and reconciled with both his church and the manifesto.[101] Judge Calvin Reasoner, a gentile editor of the Utah-based periodical *Men and Women* and a Republican friend of Thatcher, self-published a tract in 1896 detailing the Thatcher controversy. This document Tayler placed into the official Senate record as evidence against Smoot and the church's influence in politics.

Reasoner's tract provides broad insight into the stakes involved, not just for Mormons, but for non-Mormons in Utah who continued to be unconvinced of the church's separation from local politics and thus useful, to a degree, to Tayler. This tract laid down the fact that by defying the Twelve, Thatcher stood for individualism, progressivism, and masculine Americanness. Reasoner praised Thatcher for being unwilling to sign the manifesto and for refusing "to be made a subservient tool in the hands" of his ecclesiastical superiors who required of him a "full renunciation of his rights and manhood as an American citizen." Then, quoting Lorenzo Snow, who dispensed Thatcher from the Quorum for his "rebellious spirit," Reasoner contrasted Snow's prophetic claims to those of Thatcher, who was being punished for his progressive American spirit and honest patriotism. Thatcher's individualistic heroism and patriotic manhood were the direct antithesis of "unmistakable indications of narrowness, prejudice, and injustice," which were incompatible with characteristic of modern Americanism.

Having established Mormonism as an obstructive force against the Jeffersonian frontier spirit of democratic progress, Reasoner wrote that Thatcher's personal falling-out with his Mormon colleagues placed him at the center of this so-called frontier spirit. The men that Thatcher defied represented "a priestly junta" comparable to the Jesuits who imposed a kind of "serfdom" on the masses, thus conflating fears of Mormonism with those of an illegitimate public form of religion—namely Roman Catholicism. "Of all the Mormon high priesthood, Moses Thatcher is the one that stands for the principles of Jefferson and Lincoln as the American people understand those principles." In what was interpreted by Reasoner as a refusal of the religious authorities, Thatcher surrendered his position in the church on the basis of an "emasculated manhood and civil agency," making him, in Reasoner's words, "a humble instrument in His Omnipotent hand."[102] Reasoner's articulation did not leave out God's mind from his own analysis of the situation. Mormonism, as seen by Thatcher's example, obstructed divine designs by being "inimical to liberty, and the genius of American citizenship." Furthermore, now that the Progressive Era had well advanced, the church was clearly "opposed to the true spirit of progress" that it had "solemnly pledged itself against." "Thatcher's war with the Church was not a religious or personal one," but rather "a war with the individuality and independent manhood required by the Declaration of Independence. . . . Everyone [in Utah] relinquishes his individuality. He no longer acts from the dictates of his own will, but from the will of the Church."[103] After declaring the church to be inimical to these basic tenets of the modern American character and its sense of manhood,[104] Reasoner went on to predict national ruin if Mormon dictation of politics continued: "In the end there will be violence and loss of life; the whole State will be storm-swept," resulting in the "end of Jeffersonian Democracy in Utah."[105]

Though this tract was an obscure piece of literature outside of Utah, it embodied popular fears surrounding Smoot's emergence onto the national stage, and Tayler sought to exploit Reasoner's words by Thatcher's own testimony. Fortunately for Smoot, the opposite occurred, with Thatcher putting to rest concerns over Mormon clerical influence as little more than an unfortunate misunderstanding. In response to Waldemar Van Cott, Smoot's attorney, Thatcher testified that the Political Manifesto "left all the officers of the church absolutely free as an American citizen to exercise my rights as such," with the main caveat being that "it simply applied to the higher authorities of the church [as opposed to rank-and-file members], to which I had no objection."

> Mr. Van Cott: Mr. Thatcher, as that rule [regarding the political manifesto] was interpreted by the high council of the Salt Lake stake of Zion, and your acceptance of it, did that meet with your free and voluntary judgement, or not?

> Mr. Thatcher: Entirely so, for the reason that that was the contention. You will notice in the correspondence which is now filed for record that my objection to the political manifesto was in reference to the fact that it was not definite, that it might be applied to all officers in the church, and seriously I objected to that. I would object to it to-day just as seriously, because I apprehend that under such a condition it would absolutely put the state in the power of the church. That was my objection; but when an authoritative tribunal, holding coordinate jurisdiction with that of the

twelve apostles, decided that that was not the meaning—that there was no conflict between the former announcements and the political manifesto itself—I accepted that decision on those grounds, and held that that would be the finding, and it would be the understanding throughout Utah. Whether it was or not, it was my understanding, and I am left perfectly free to stand where I have stood in all that discussion, barring any unkind references while under that misapprehension to my friends in and out of the church.

Brigham H. Roberts was also questioned in relation to the Political Manifesto. Roberts had run for the House of Representative in Utah's first elections as a state in 1895. He too noted his initial misunderstanding of the manifesto's implications, wrongly thinking it was applicable to all Mormons, rather than a unique requirement for Mormon leaders. When asked if he felt bested by his church in this affair, Roberts stated that he had been "enlightened . . . in reference to their purposes," which echoed Thatcher's statement that nothing had "come to my knowledge" that indicates that "the church had ever undertaken to dominate the political affairs of Utah."[106] If Roberts and Thatcher had earlier felt betrayed by their ecclesiastical colleagues and political opponents, they were now willing to stand behind them, as these arguments were less about vindicating their initial complaints against particular events and leaders, but rather the unfitness of Mormonism itself to form a part of the new era.

The confused perceptions and motivations became clear when Frank J. Cannon, son of church president George Q. Cannon, was excommunicated on March 15, 1905, following a series of spirited criticisms and denunciations of Joseph F. Smith and his testimony as printed in the *Salt Lake Tribune* during the Smoot hearings. This incident endowed the younger Cannon with the persona of hero for Tayler and other anti-Mormon groups. Turning excommunication into a true demonstration of American patriotism, the Mother's Congress on March 18, 1905, declared him, upon being "expelled by the Mormon hierarchy," to be "welcomed into the ranks of loyal, law abiding citizens as a brave defender of home and purity"—either not knowing or ignoring his drinking habits and his engagement with prostitutes though being a married man. While it appeared that Mormons could prove themselves "manly American citizens" and of "valuable service" to the nation by dissenting from their church, even if by mistake, it was also clear that the suggestion, or even intention, was to reveal that one could not be a good member of the church and a good American at the same time.[107]

However ultimately time-absorbing these hearings proved, there was a benefit to having the debate on the national stage, a debate on the place of religion within the state as the country launched into an industrialized Progressive Era that propounded questions of freedom and the rights of citizens. The Smoot hearings had gone on for three years before the Senate Committee on Privileges and Elections, ending with the suggestion to expel Smoot due to his position as a Mormon apostle. This was an official end of the hearings, but its peculiar debate, and the questions it brought to the nation, continued to inform American politics as it related to religion. A new emphasis on the rational over the emotional, the masculine over the gentleman, and moral action over proper belief had swept the nation, but battles continued to rage in Congress over the proper framework of religion, specifically whether it retained a more implicit or explicit function. On the day before the final Senate plenary debate and vote, Smoot addressed the president and the Senate in a prepared thirty-minute speech. Smoot spoke against the false claims made against him—one, that he was a polygamist, and second, more important, that he could not be a Mormon official and a national legislator: "I owe no allegiance to any church or other organization which in any way interferes with my supreme allegiance in civil affairs to my country—an allegiance which I freely, fully, and gladly give."[108] With the support of Theodore Roosevelt, the final Senate vote on February 20 was positive: 28 voted for the resolution to oust Smoot; 42 voted against it. Requiring a three-fourths vote to unseat Smoot, this tally left Smoot in his seat. Thus was set the standard for non-Protestant populations engaging in American politics, as well as setting a precedent for religious minorities as they enunciate what it means for them to separate their religious beliefs from their political identity. Such claims of privatized faith and separation applied differently to Protestant politicians like Roosevelt who often emphasized their faith in public, though in more implicit ways than earlier politicians. However, Smoot's approach to religion in this new secularized nation was one of complete separation, which forcefully reappeared on the national stage later with Catholic presidential nominees Alfred E. Smith (1928) and John F. Kennedy (1960), and more recently, Mormon candidate Mitt Romney's national run for the presidency in 2008 and 2012. The individual non-Protestant citizen who chose to engage in high politics was no longer thoroughly identified by their faith—as long as they practiced the proper relationship between the two, a relationship that Smoot helped define and, to a degree, that is still being defined and debated.

Of course, Smoot's victory was both celebrated and decried; both sides indicated that old beliefs of exceptionalism and paganism still existed. In celebration of Smoot's victory, and by extension, the church's victory, Joseph F. Smith and his counselors issued "An Address to the World," which was read in General Conference and unanimously adopted by the church on April 5, 1907. This letter emphatically declared Mormonism to be a pure "Christian church"—indeed, "the most distinctively American church." While conciliatory in spirit, the letter seemed to affirm a form of Mormon exceptionalism in ways not unlike Robert's speech for the Parliament of Religions. Not surprisingly, there was a response from members of the Ministerial Association of Salt Lake City, which issued its own review of "An Address to the World." The association strongly discredited such claims by the church and declared that until church authorities themselves radically changed, "there can be no peace between them and pure Christianity." Furthermore, until the church's doctrines were radically altered, Mormonism could "never establish a claim to be even a part of the Church of Jesus Christ."[109] Likewise, the *Salt Lake Tribune* criticized the letter for its evasions and dishonesty. The *Tribune* further accused its authors of "half-hearted efforts . . . to make the world believe in their patriotism, their piety, their selflessness." Mormon leaders could not have believed in their own letter, for they knew "their own corruption, treason, blasphemy and corroding selfishness, avarice, lusts of power, and of the flesh." The *Tribune* described the Ministerial Association's response as "calm, deliberate, and temperate in tone," characterizing it as a type of revelation, and announced that it was "warmly welcomed and approved by the loyal citizenship of Utah."[110]

From the perspective of its authors, the address advanced a deep intention on the church's part to affirm its belief that Mormonism was both Christian and American, and by its reckoning, quintessentially so. The debate over the seating of Reed Smoot provided an occasion for an intense debate over the belief above. This debate involved the highest levels of political power in defining the meaning—and cost—of American inclusivity and the meaning—and again the cost—of American citizenship. The debate's outcome indicated that both the nation's and the church's official position on American inclusion and cooperation were changing, and thus offered new ways and options for imagining a new secular self in a new era of progress. Indeed, the very framework of congressional inclusion and action that had presupposed the implication of God's law as found in the Bible, which stood above the U.S. Constitution and was referred to as the higher law, was now criticized as unworkable, particularly as it pertained to exclusionary actions such as those waged against Smoot.[111] During the plenary debate preceding the final Smoot vote, Senator Foraker justified his support for Smoot by recognizing the dilemma, even contradiction, between the higher law and the oath of office as established by the U.S. Constitution, together with new sensibilities of the Progressive Era concerning the secularization of American polity and the privatization of religion.

> This higher law we all appreciate. The Senator from North Dakota [Mr. Hansbrough] is not the only man who thinks of the higher law; we all think of it; but the trouble about following the higher law is that every man writes the higher law to suit himself. [Laughter.] What we are here to follow and to be governed by and to observe—and we violate our oaths of office if we do not do it—is the Constitution of the United States in its requirements.[112]

The debate in some ways crowned a remarkable journey that Americans, which, with the waning of the higher law, now included Mormons. This journey from the Protestant hegemony and its kingdom to a broader sense of religious inclusion and separation brought new kinds of identity and a broader sense of the secular and modern. This new dynamic between religion and the state transformed what it meant to be an American, and religion's place in this new, recently constructed secular definition of the state and its influence of the closed frontier.

The relationship between the secular and religious, manliness and womanhood, the private and public, together with the idea of the open and closed frontier at the time of Smoot, was that of creation and contestation, rather than that of the already created. This creation and alignment of how public America was to be understood, led to many contradictions

and complications in how Americans defined themselves and their relationship with the state. Mormon leaders such as Reed Smoot and Joseph
F. Smith set themselves and their religion as part of the manly-Chris-
tian progressive nationalism of Roosevelt and the popular politics of the
Republican Party, adopting and taking advantage of these new definitions
of the secular and progressive. As seen during the World's Fair in Chicago
in 1893, Mormon leaders understood these new workings of the secular
and the frontier as linked to their own religious goals, even as Roosevelt
understood his approach to politics and the effects of the frontier as a
direct outgrowth of his own social gospel motive and creed. As always, the
secular and religious were not so easy to disentangle as they intersected
in these multidirectional ways, especially as these complicated definitions
wrapped themselves in the mythical and romanticized cloth of the closed
frontier, and lay between the growing struggles that tore apart modernist
and conservative Protestant churches. Those who opposed Smoot, such
as the well-organized and culturally powerful women's movements and
reform associations, together with politically powerful Robert Tayler and
Frederick Dubois, similarly pointed to progressive and religious themes
in order to uphold their voice, citing liberty, the American family, manly
civilization, and freedom, though ultimately appearing prejudicial and
misinformed. The significance of these contested voices, despite their failure to end Smoot's political career and mark Mormonism as un-American, was that they stood for an enduring voice that looked critically on
Mormonism and its existence as defined conversely to what it meant to
be American, and the new progressive form the nation was to take in this
new century.

Many voices against Smoot also cried out against the loss of this
explicit religious reference point in determining the shape and contours of American society, particularly along the lines of what it meant
to be American and how church and the Bible were supposed to continue to fit into that definition. Rather than this case answering the
question concerning the new role of religion in the twentieth century, it
demonstrated its cultural and religious disunity, however strong these
new trends toward secularism and the privatization of religion were.
Secularism then, as dealt with throughout the Smoot hearings, was
not understood by many Americans as a call to erase religion from the
state, but instead to redefine and control it within acceptable Protestant

boundaries. These boundaries either followed the "modernist impulse" then redefining Protestantism as less dogmatic and more based on manly character, or they followed along more conservative lines that emphasized an exclusionary identity that retained and celebrated more traditional ideals in the public realm. As progressive reformers gained momentum in the public arena as evidenced by Smoot, or among intellectuals as seen by Turner and his Frontier Thesis, or in the popular imagination as celebrated at Chicago's Exposition and Buffalo Bill's Wild West shows, the perimeters of those who could now participate in American society had enlarged and had enshrined a particular frontier narrative into the American public imagination. All this represents the creation of American secularism at the beginning of the twentieth century, its contested relationship with religion, and the genius behind Mormonism's entrance into genuine Americana and the new division within the nation that gave rise to both the Social Gospel in Protestantism and its fundamentalist counterpart.

# CONCLUSION

## Reopening the Frontier

An important focus of the coevolution of Mormons and Protestants into more secular or privatized forms of faith, has been to trace how both perceived and then redefined their relationship to the state. The conflicts that arose from 1857 to 1907 between these two religious camps demonstrate a conundrum often overlooked: both groups shared a millennial worldview that was complicated by each having a similarly idealized vision of the American kingdom of God, the frontier, and its shifting relationship to civil governance. Both were challenged as America was transformed by industrialization, urbanization, and the resulting measures of secular progressivism. In telling this story, the temptation is strong to contrast an irrational, two-dimensional Mormonism with that of the more rational, multidimensional republic, framed at times by white Protestantism, but more often by the secular forces of individualism, liberty, and progress. However, both sides came of age in terms of religion and its relation to the modern state, with Mormonism's coming of age inevitably linked to its surrender of polygamy, as well as other economic and political practices and attitudes. Nonetheless, as this study has revealed, Mormonism and the nation mirrored each other—for both, modernity broke down and challenged old practices and beliefs, leading to internal upheaval and schism, yet these new modern selves refashioned themselves within trusted frameworks of an earlier era.

The secularized form of Americanism that Mormonism successfully adopted and adapted itself to, most visibly and visually at the 1893 Columbian World Exposition, and then following Smoot's victory in 1907, simply did not exist in 1857 when the two groups nearly came to blows. In five decades immense changes to the American intellectual and cultural landscape occurred, inspired by new technologies and increased ease of travel, opening new physical connections and causing important shifts in popular worldview regarding American belonging and the role of the frontier in that belonging. Questions that continually emerged during this research largely addressed what it meant to be an American—and where minority groups, both religious and racial, fit within that challenged and changing understanding. This understanding was controlled in part by the changing of the guard of American elites for that of a new generation of more secularized-progressive leaders.

In looking at these transformations within both Mormonism and Protestantism from midcentury to the turn of the century, each chapter highlighted a particular critical point of development. In highlighting those points, it has been important to pay attention, not just to how other minorities were similarly challenged in light of their racial identifications as American and their (non)ability to participate in the politics of the state, but also to their definitions of being religious, be it Native American ghost dances or African American ring shouts.[1] Definitions of what it means to be an American, and to be a religious American, were contested and made dynamic in such minority encounters with the overwhelming Protestant hegemony. Mormons likewise stood outside these narrow national categories of race and religion, and were thus denied the status of full Americanism by the Protestant hegemony and its accepted sense of religion. However, Mormons eventually became perceived as being more American, but not without significant abandonment of crucial concepts of what it meant to be Mormon, an ironic loss that justified the initial need for that loss. Equally important, this achievement was not the result of a more tolerant and accepting Protestant hegemony, but rather the fracturing of that hegemony as part of its own struggle with these larger national shifts. Emerging from this is how Americanism was—and is—a particularly narrow and historically positioned term whose framework, though once deciphered through Protestant white-male America, was now redefined by those with more liberal and inclusive secular understandings of religion.

What lessons can be learned by these dynamic encounters between the dominant group and the smaller groups, particularly those who challenge and contest the narrow identities forced upon them? In this study, one stands out: however successful the evangelical and secular ages were in inspiring Mormonism to become a new American expression of religion, such success was not devoid of simultaneous exploitative agendas and expressions of Mormon agency in appropriating those agendas for their own benefit. American progress and religious pluralism were situational and framed in local prejudices (be it racial or religious), thereby exposing the deep cultural particulars in which American identity was dependent—as opposed to this identity being universal and unchanging as many argued during the nineteenth century, or even the product of some larger invisible force of the frontier as theorized by Turner.[2] As seen with Smoot, progress was not unidirectional, as the concept of a waning frontier assumed, but rather moved in oppositional directions simultaneously. Mormonism's own metamorphosis to become American paralleled this national metamorphosis, and could not have taken shape as it did independent of it, allowing this larger context to do more than just broaden understanding of the American past, but actually help detail the contours and boundaries of these changes in the nation and in Mormonism.

The crucial question concerning whether a Mormon could be a good American was reopened at the World's Fair, the same event that oversaw the intense clashes among Protestants over the meaning of America and its new relationship with the rest of the nation and the world. These fights and divisions continued to take root throughout the Progressive Era and helped to create national visions and boundaries of American religious plurality in the United States, a vision still struggling toward completion and boundaries still contested. Indeed, the journey from being un-American to quintessentially American does not simply portray a pluralism success story about a minority faith that finally learned how to behave; rather, this journey is a testimonial to the level of tolerance of a nation which demanded and accepted such modification. In many ways, this narrative is less about Mormonism than it is about a transformed popular sense of Americanism and its new impositions and limitations on religion, which Mormons wholeheartedly embraced and adopted. Through reading the records of the Utah War, antipolygamy crusades, and the experiences of Mormons at the World's Fair and the Smoot hearings, this work defines, by inverse, American idealism and national identity which established themselves in sectarian and parochial ways by way of these dynamic encounters. It was in these sectarian and parochial ways that Mormonism and Americanism made their transitions into a more secular modern world, which both were transformed by and both helped to invent.

This approach to Americanism was uniquely put on public display at the Columbian World's Fair which celebrated and legitimized earlier mythologies in new modern, secular forms. With the fair, Americans took part in an unprecedented celebration of Columbus and his adventurous spirit of discovery, and remained uncritical and even accepting of its more unsavory undercurrents. This spirit of discovery was not only highlighted by new technologies that made such deep-sea voyages possible in the late fifteenth century, but also spurred on by a strong quest for wealth and power and religious energy, a quest that not only inspired the Catholic Spanish monarchy to support this zealous Italian explorer in 1492, but that same year to expel its Muslim and Jewish populations. Indigenous populations in the Americas fared little better under Spanish influence and control. In some ways the Columbian Fair, as the explicit four-hundred-year anniversary of Columbus and the symbolic rise of Christianity in the West and the attendant global colonial enterprise, helped solidify the eradication of the religious pluralism that had existed in America (and Spain) prior to Columbus in its quest to celebrate a particular brand of Christian triumphalism and progress. European expansionism was part of this triumph, justifying both polarization and genocide.

With such connections to Columbus and this new status for Christian power at its Parliament of Religions, the organizers of the World's Fair articulated Columbus's "discovery of the New World" as a vital aspect of the American mythology of progress for the modern era. Turner's thesis of the frontier, together with the newly established comparative study of religion and other intellectual and even popular trends, embraced these darker realities as the price of progress, and an outcome and consequence of basic and unavoidable social evolutionary forces. American expansionism, evangelism, and indigenous subjugation were important aspects of this new American contribution to social and religious progress for the world, as celebrated and put forth at the fair, within which Mormonism was now embraced. Only a few years following the fair, Colonels Henry Inman and William F. ("Buffalo Bill") Cody lauded Salt Lake City as a "monument to the ability of man to overcome almost insuperable obstacles," expressing the creation of Salt Lake City as "the product of a faith equal to that which inspired the crusader to battle to the death for the possession of the Holy Sepulcher."[3] Like the European Christian crusades before the Renaissance, Columbus's voyage of discovery was thus an archetype and even model of the new American involvement with modernity and the context for American religious pluralism for the next century. As highlighted throughout the fair, Americans were not just demonstrating their contribution to an expanding Christendom, but rather were proposing a model that would help affect the progressive potentials, as they believed, of the entire human race throughout the world.

Of course, the Parliament of Religions employed a more liberal, less violent, and more ecumenical version of this earlier Christian expansionism and triumphalism by attempting to bring together and create the first global gathering of the world's major religions. Understood through this new modern understanding of religion, this new comparative model of religion became a blueprint for American as well as world religious pluralism and Christian ecumenism. The parliament's triumphalist Christian vision was furthered—and challenged—by its appropriation of this new scientific method of comparative study. In bringing various religions together onto a single world stage under a new rubric of comparative difference, American Christianity was critiqued as lacking moral authority and called out in its arrogance for assuming global supremacy and leadership—yet it recovered a sense of plurality that had been lost since Columbus. By way of comparative demonstration, it was learned that Asians were not as heathenish as believed, women were not so silent as expected, blacks were intelligent and could articulate, and Mormons were not so easily marginalized—and white Protestant supremacy was not so intuitive and universally apparent as previously entertained. The parliament witnessed a broader and more expansive form of ecumenical unity and plurality that emerged as an outcome of the event itself, from both a response to the new scientific study of comparative religion, and, just as importantly, challenges to that structure. By the fair's conclusion, helped by the powerful presence of secular Mormon presentations, the Tabernacle Choir, and Utah's mineral and artistic wealth, together with this more liberal conception of religious pluralism and the secular, Mormons were no longer castigated for their opposition to the traditional national narrative of America frontier progress, but rather were being celebrated for their significant contribution to it. The fair allowed for a powerful platform for Americans to celebrate their colonial sameness, despite their many theological differences.

On the secular front, helped on by the Reed Smoot hearings, a new mythology came into place: It was increasingly less common for the major parties to unite in their dislike of unpopular religious groups; rather, political figures promoted the secular virtues of religious toler-ance and the new "Melting Pot" ideal—an ideal that still insisted on a certain level of religious uniformity, conformity, and exclusivity. How-ever, this emphasis on American diversity revealed a national trend toward an old ideal of progress and tolerance, but this time more in line with then-current trends of scientific evolutionary thought. Histo-rian Albert Bushnell Hart, who wrote in the Turner-influenced era, in his *National Ideals Historically Traced* (1907) observed and advocated a "steady progression from one condition to another." In a tribute to Charles Darwin, civilization's "great historical master," Hart celebrated Darwin for teaching Americans how to think about biological as well as institutional and historical advancement. Following the laws of nature, the placement of the United States was "not a miracle," but instead the product of "a steady and measurable growth, still enlarging, still to put forth new branches for the world's advantage." Hart goes on to point out that during this era the role of religion in society itself had declined, ref-erencing the decline of religious tests for voting and holding office and the marginalized influence churches held over American politics and public education. With such a division of religion and the state and the dwindling potency of public religion, tolerance as a virtue was upheld as unquestioned and absolute. Hart summed up this changing reli-gious environment of America: "Doctrine has decayed, but the appeal to character, to the ennoblement of the human soul, still continues and is as active a principle as it has ever been at any time in the history of the nation."[4] Turner's model stood as an example of this new focus on character building over doctrine, providing a new central theme for the twentieth-century church to frame its new identity around. Undeniably, this new emphasis within American society at the beginning of the twentieth century had a powerful consequence in Smoot's eventual acceptance into the U.S. Senate and the means by which Mormons could stake their American claims. Both positively and negatively, Mormons, no longer considered a threat to the national narrative on religion, were now accepted, or, as Turnerian-influenced historian Hart would have it, at least ignored.[5]

How does all this charged historiography and dwindling theology, together with an emergent secular vision of national progress and its enlarged acceptance of minority groups into the national narrative, finally achieve meaning in Turner's Frontier Thesis? In short, Turner's thesis popularized and intellectually enshrined the secularization model that allowed Americans to move past earlier theological interpretations, for one that provided a new and secular path toward reimagining a shared American character not limited to white Protestantism. It is posited by Klaus Hansen that for Mormon historians of the early twentieth century, Turner's thesis provided a "ready-made vehicle for the Americanization of the Mormon past" in ways that could establish and legitimate its presence in America. Turner's thesis was applied to Mormon history with such zeal in the first few decades of the twentieth century, noted Klaus Hansen, that "several of these [Mormon] scholars probably would have invented Turner had he not existed." Early Mormon historians followed these more popular historiographical trends and thus rewrote their past in a way that emphasized Mormonism's contribution to a twentieth-century white triumphalist Americanism while minimizing more embarrassing themes that contradicted, such as the political kingdom of God, polygamy, and economic cooperatives, thus sanitizing or ignoring "the social implications of past struggles between the Mormons and non-Mormons."[6] By these means, Mormon-U.S. struggles, such as the Utah War and the antipolygamy crusades, amounted to little more than "another episode in the American West's development." Entirely lost, not just for historians but for the larger Mormon memory, were the important and even crucial elements these themes served throughout the nineteenth century. Historian Ethan Yorgason agrees that Mormonism, as portrayed by these new Turnerian Mormon historians, became "yet another brick in building the nation."[7]

Thomas S. Kuhn has considered how this paradigm shift affected

Mormon thought: the Progressive Era and the noteworthy events during this era taught Mormons how to *think* like Americans. Focusing on this new frontier ideal of character building and manly cultivation, as epitomized by their early and strong involvement with the new Boy Scouts of America organization, Mormons thus began to see their story as indeed an important component of the patriarchal Anglo-Saxon myth of civilization that itself tapped into this earlier Columbian American myth of progress.[8] To use colonial terms, Mormons and their historians thus embraced in indigenous ways this foreign narrative of American progress and masculinity that once targeted and excluded them, thereby providing an important entry point into this new conformist secular-imperial world, a world that only began to be seriously challenged in the last half of the twentieth century with the rise of the social revolutions and civil rights legislations of the 1950s, 1960s and 1970s—much of which the church found challenging.[9]

What was gained by these new inclusionary tactics also helped to obscure or diminish Mormon creative agency as played out throughout the nineteenth century. The story of *Reynolds* in the 1870s and the half-masting of the flag on the Fourth of July in 1885 to protest "liberties denied" is an example of how Mormonism generally forced the nation to define what it meant to be religious and American, but was then lost to Mormon collective thought as Mormons adopted a more "American" expression of themselves from within this new frontier mythology. The Mormon element was thus simplified and reduced to little more than a supportive example of the progressive American myth of increasing rationality and liberty as framed within the frontier and postfrontier narrative, making it difficult to come to terms with and explore the needs of Mormonism—and the Protestant influence on Mormonism in that century.[10] These recognitions require a rewriting and rethinking of the past for both Protestantism and Mormonism, and, more important, a recognition of the enormous power and influence of the Protestant kingdom nationally, and the Mormon kingdom regionally, prior to the postfrontier secular revolution that challenged and provided new opportunities for both.

Within this context of how the Frontier Thesis both tamed and concealed distinctive aspects of Mormon history, religion scholar David Chidester articulated that a prematurely closed frontier has additional import. The American frontier should not be considered an "in-between space" where savagery met civilization (as suggested by Turner, Roosevelt, and others), but instead one of significant contestation and struggle between the colonial intruder and the indigenous. In his *Savage Systems*, Chidester describes how this imagined closing of the frontier presumes moral victory over barbarism and how this perceived act upheld the exploitative colonial structures of power in apartheid South Africa. With relevance to the American frontier and its own apartheid-like structures, the Frontier Thesis contrasted the idea of what now was with the way things are supposed to be, and thereby provided a moral compass that celebrated the accomplishments of the powerful at the expense of the less powerful on the imagined frontier. As seen at the World's Fair and again at the Smoot hearings, the idea of the closed frontier did not bring in others on their own terms, but solidified as superior one particular set of terms—those of the already powerful.

Chidester's discussion of the British frontier in South Africa works equally well when applied to the indigenous populations of North America, where the frontier, while opened, determined that Native Americans, as it did Africans, had no religion, thus demonstrating the need of both to be subjugated by a white dominating power. Once subjugated, the frontier was determined on both continents to be closed, and as such, both Native Americans and South Africans were compensated for their loss of political and cultural independence by being acknowledged as having a religion.[11] As already visited in this work, frontier Mormonism was also deemed "not a religion" by the American courts and legislatures in the 1870s and 1880s while the frontier remained open, and the Mormon practice of plural marriage "was not a religious practice."[12] With the announced closing of the frontier in 1893, Mormonism was met with a new ambivalence at the same World's Fair in which such a claim was made. Convinced that Mormonism's metamorphosis in the 1890s and first few years of the 1900s had made Mormonism less of a threat, the four-year hearings of Reed Smoot determined Smoot's religion as valid and his entrance into national power legitimate. The national acceptance of Mormonism had as much to do with the increased embrace of religious pluralism in this new era, as it did with the ability of Mormon elites to convince the nation that they were now co-conquerors of the frontier, rather than a force needing to be conquered.

In his work, Chidester challenges scholars to rethink such rational-ized frontier closures, in South Africa and by extension in the United States, as built on coercive conformity, and to "once again" find them-selves "on the frontier."[13] The more we tell ourselves "barbarism [was] progressively conquered by rationality and freedom," as the triumphal-ist liberal state likes to consider itself, explains William Cavanaugh, "the more we are capable of ignoring the violence we do in the name of reason and freedom."[14] Tomoko Masuzawa extended these ideas to caution modern historians who celebrate the 1893 Parliament of Reli-gions as a harbinger of what we have become (that is, pluralistic and nonsectarian) unknowingly tap into exclusionary notions of progress that informed the liberal Protestant ideals of the parliament's organiz-ers.[15] As argued throughout this book, the expansion of secular religious tolerance embodied at the fair not only allowed Mormonism's entrance into American acceptability but simultaneously drew clear moral boundaries to that toleration. Informed by these ironic ideas and those who challenged them, nineteenth-century Mormonism represents one among many minority groups that were simultaneously advantaged and disadvantaged and redefined in the service of the new master narrative of the rational-secular nation-state.

This study of religion and its changing relations to an American identity and political practice, has focused on important themes that have been neglected in both Mormon and American religious histo-riography—namely, the shared world of both Mormons and Protes-tants. Going back to the open frontier allows us to question its religious authority and its overly simplistic and historically placed definitions of morality and progress. Reopening the frontier thus reopens the contes-tations between Mormons and the nation in a way that reimagines the American religious ideal and its connection to state power as far more central to early Americans as might be imagined in our more secular age. The status and role of religion in America, frequently if benevo-lently dismissed as a nonissue in the history of the United States and its quest for liberty and progress, is far more than the generic theopolitical rhetoric and superficial public rituals of Robert Bellah's "civil religion," as best seen among contemporary politicians' invoking of "God" during times of national mourning. Such a twentieth- and twenty-first-century secularized and privatized understanding of religion obscures the public efficacy of religion when it comes to the motives of nineteenth-century America. This secularized vision of the past altogether neglects the political and social ramifications of the frontier and its connected kingdom of God ideal as they related to American power for all involved in these earlier struggles over national identity and belonging. Both Mormon and general religious historiography have thus neglected to place Mormonism within these larger national trends and transitions or have wrongfully contrasted fanatical Mormonism with a more rational, civil Protestantism or rational secularism. These chapters have challenged such assumptions and have sought to bring together both Mormon and popular notions of religion as it relates to the state into a single narrative that sheds light into three areas: the common religious roots of both Mormon and Protestant, their conflicts and seeming resolution in the secular and progressive age, and Reed Smoot's position and importance in the shifting national religious and political narrative.

This work has not sought to produce a narrative that is either exhaustive or conclusive. In focusing this study as I have, the aim has been to challenge old assumptions and open new questions, as well as to provoke further study of the dialectic between the minor and the major faiths as they transitioned over time and circumstances. Beyond this attempt to rethink that relationship, this work has attempted to better imagine the influence such dialectics had on society and on particular groups and the ways in which we think about religion, the environment, and their relations to the modern secular state. These dialectics and related transitions have not been isolated, nor have they come about without coercive violence or compromises of religious values and principles dearly held by both minority and majority groups. Rethinking religious inclusion and the Mormon placement in U.S. history, both secular and religious, can reconfigure the narrative and, by implication, reevaluate what it means to be an American, and religious, both in the nineteenth and twenty-first centuries.

# NOTES

## CHAPTER 1

1. William James, *The Varieties of Religious Experience: A Study in Human Nature* (New York: Simon & Schuster, 1997 [1902]), 59.

2. Clifford Geertz, *The Interpretation of Cultures* (New York: Basic Books, 1973), 90; Richard Wentz, *The Culture of Religious Pluralism* (Boulder, CO: Westview Press, 1998), 98.

3. W. Paul Reeve, *Making Space on the Western Frontier: Mormons, Miners, and Southern Paiutes* (Urbana: University of Illinois Press, 2006), 10, 19–20.

4. Joseph Smith Jr., *History of the Church of Jesus Christ of Latter-day Saints* (Salt Lake City: Deseret Book Co., 1960), 1:28; D. Michael Quinn, *The Mormon Hierarchy: Origins of Power* (Salt Lake City: Signature Books, 1994), 6–7.

5. Though initially framing his new church as part of this larger Christian world that united believers more based on devotion to God rather than an institutional structure of priests and ordinances, Smith's revelations toward additional scripture, priestly authority, economic consecration, plural marriage, and hotel and temple building soon took his church well beyond it. Richard Lyman Bushman, *Joseph Smith, Rough Stone Rolling: A Cultural Biography of Mormonism's Founder* (New York: Knopf, 2005), 112.

6. Horace Bushnell, *Barbarianism the First Danger: A Discourse for Home Missions* (New York: William Osborne, 1847), 32.

7. In defining religion, William James provides further insight to this new focus on the "invisible kingdom of Christ": "Whoever possesses strongly this sense comes naturally to think that the smallest details of this world derive infinite significance from their relation to an unseen divine order," establishing powerful focus and motivation. James, *Varieties*, 292.

8. George Rogers Taylor, ed., *The Turner Thesis: Concerning the Role of the Frontier in American History* (Lexington: D. C. Heath, 1972), 3.

9. Henry Nash Smith, *Virgin Land: The American West as Symbol and Myth* (Cambridge: Harvard University Press, 1975), 4, 251, 257.

10. As an early standard guidebook to the West, see Robert Baird, *View of the Valley of the Mississippi; or, The Emigrant's and Traveler's Guide to the West* (Philadelphia: N.p., 1834), 100–3; Baird, *Religion in the United States of America; or, An Account of the Origin, Progress, Relations to the State, and Present Condition of the Evangelical Churches in the United States, with Notices of the Unevangelical Denominations* (New York: Arno Press & The New York Times, 1965 [1844]), 35–43.

11. Alexis de Tocqueville, *Democracy in America*, trans. Henry Reeve (New York: Bantam Classic, 2000 [1835]), 337–38.

12. Edwin Lawrence Godkin, *Problems of Modern Democracy: Political and Economic Essays* (New York: Charles Scribner's Sons, 1896), 25–26. To be sure, the immediate dangers and difficulties of the frontier inspired various forms of collectivism and cooperation among settlers, but it would be the individualism and independence that would be emphasized in this new nineteenth-century American mythology. By way of example of this collectivism and cooperation in the supplying of immediate needs on the frontier, see Joseph Doddridge, *Notes on the Settlement and Indian Wars* (Pittsburgh: N.p., 1912), 110–15.

13. For an in-depth study of this literature, see Smith, *Virgin Land*, chapter 9, "The Western Hero in the Dime Novel."

14. Schaff, *America*, 262–63. Robert Baird's "most strenuous endeavour has been to promote the extension of the Messiah's kingdom in the world," by way of producing his early historical text of American religion. Baird, *Religion in America*, ix.

15. H. Richard Niebuhr, *The Kingdom of God in America* (New York: Harper & Brothers, 1959), 45–49, 56, 89–92.

16. Ernest L. Tuveson, *Redeemer Nation: The Idea of America's Millennial Role* (Chicago: University of Chicago Press, 1968), 29.

17. John Taylor, *The Government of God* (Liverpool: S. W. Richards, 1852), 87.

18. Plymouth governor William Bradford explained that the Puritans were profoundly motivated, despite their hardships, by a "great hope and inward zeall" to lay the physical and legal foundations of the "gospel of the kingdom of Christ in those remote parts of the world." William T. Davis, ed., *Bradford's History of Plymouth Plantation* (New York: Charles Scribner's Sons, 1920), 54–55. See also Sydney E. Ahlstrom, *A Religious History of the American People*, Vol. 1 (New York: Image Books, 1896), 120.

19. As quoted in Lewis A. Dunn, "Past as Prologue: American Redemptive Activism and the Developing World," *World Politics* 27, no. 4 (July 1975): 617.

20. Leonard Bacon, *Thirteen Historical Discourses, on the Completion of Two Hundred Years, from the Beginning of the First Church in New Haven, with*

*an Appendix* (New York: Gould, Newman & Saxton, 1839), 31.

21. Walt Whitman, *Drum-Taps* (New York, 1865), 53–54, 64–65; Walt Whitman, *Passage to India* (Washington, DC, 1871), 6–10; Smith, *Virgin Land*, 44–48.

22. Smith, *Virgin Land*, 183, 259–60.

23. Baird, *Religion in America*, 179, 182; According to John Corrigan, Old Testament themes such as "Amalekites" were utilized by Protestants in North America against Roman Catholics, Quakers, Jews, and Native Americans as a way of attributing to them as "deserving of the penalty of extermination that God long ago had ordained as judgment on those who, in spite of their kinship with a people favored by God, betrayed their relatives." John Corrigan and Lynn S. Neal, eds., *Religious Intolerance in America: A Documentary History* (Chapel Hill: University of North Carolina Press, 2010), 21. As John Winthrop had put it centuries earlier, just as Saul, the ancient Israelite king, lost his kingdom due to his negligence to destroy Amalek, so too stood "the cause between God and us." Indeed, in light of biblical prophecy (specifically Deuteronomy 30), the early Reformed Protestant colonists in North America saw themselves as more than a religious society hoping for God's favor, but rather as an already chosen society that stood on the edge of "life and good and death and evil." John Winthrop, *A Modell of Christian Charity (1630)*, Collections of the Massachusetts Historical Society (Boston, 1838), 3rd series 7:31–48.

24. Ahlstrom states, "Many long-hidden implications became explicit affirmations, while old informal working arrangements were enacted into law and custom." Ahlstrom, *A Religious History*, 1:34, 464–65.

25. Baird, *Religion in America*, 284–85.

26. David Sehat, *The Myth of American Religious Freedom* (New York: Oxford University Press, 2011), 17–21; Edwin Gaustad and Leigh Schmidt, *The Religious History: The Heart of the American Story from Colonial Times to Today*, rev. ed. (New York: HarperSanFrancisco, 2002), 131; Baird, *Religion in America*, 262, 284–85.

27. Stephen Colwell, *The Position of Christianity in the United States, in Its Relations with Our Political Institutions, and Specially with Reference to Religious Instructions in the Public Schools* (Philadelphia: Lippincott, Grambo, 1854), 32–33, 36, 53, 57. For more on religious privilege within early state constitutions, see Kenneth D. Wald and Allison Calhoun-Brown, *Religion and Politics in the United States*, 5th ed. (New York: Rowman & Littlefield, 2007), 71–73. For more details on how religion played a role in these early state constitutions, see Edwin S. Gaustad, *Faith of the Founders: Religion and the New Nation, 1776–1826* (Waco, TX: Baylor University Press, 2011), Appendix B.

28. Baird, *Religion in America*, 179, 253, 261–62. As Sidney Mead noted, disestablishment was not understood by American Protestants as an open "competition between those of rival faiths, but competition between those holding divergent forms of the same faith." Mead, *The Lively Experiment*, 130.

29. Niebuhr, *The Kingdom of God*, 48, 97; Vernon L. Parrington, "The Puritan Divines, 1620–1720," in *Cambridge History of American Literature* (New York: G. P. Putnam's Sons, 1917), 1:32, 41–42.

30. "Now," remarked Robert Baird, "none of Mr. Jefferson's admirers will consider it slanderous to assert that he was a very bitter enemy to Christianity, and we may even assume that he wished to see not only the Episcopal Church separated from the state in Virginia, but the utter overthrow of everything in the shape of a church throughout the country." Baird, *Religion in America*, 230.

31. See Sidney Mead, "Timothy Dwight and Disestablishment," as reprinted in Richard Wentz, ed., *The Unfinished Experiment: Essays of Sidney E. Mead* (Tempe, AZ: Scholargy Custom Publishing, 2004), 45; Timothy Dwight, *Virtuous Rulers a National Blessing, A Sermon Preached at the General Election, May 12th, 1791* (Hartford: Hudson and Goodwin, 1791).

32. In the cosmic time that marks the Protestant worldview, such democratic advances were seen as linked to unchecked vice and hindered the encouragement of virtue, thus attributing such work of "political atheism" to the Antichrist and misled French revolutionary fanaticism. Nathan O. Hatch, *The Democratization of American Christianity* (New Haven: Yale University Press, 1989), 184.

33. Mead, "Timothy Dwight," 50.

34. Mark A. Noll, *America's God: From Jonathan Edwards to Abraham Lincoln* (New York: Oxford University Press, 2002), 44, 75.

35. Barbara M. Cross, ed., *The Autobiography of Lyman Beecher* (Cambridge, MA: Harvard University Press, 1961), 253.

36. Sehat, *Myth of American Religious Freedom*, 37, 50, 54–58.

37. Hatch, *Democratization*, 5–10, 29–33, 46, 81.

38. Stephen R. Graham, *Cosmos in the Chaos: Philip Schaff's Interpretation of Nineteenth-Century American Religion* (Grand Rapids, MI: Wm. B. Eerdmans, 1995), 120.

39. Colwell, *The Position of Christianity*, 68–69; Winthrop Hudson, *Religion in America: A Historical Account of the Development of American Religious Life* (New York: Charles Scribner's Sons, 1981), 157. In this unchecked Protestant reign, constitutional checks against majoritarian tyranny in the United States was thus obfuscated. Alexis de Tocqueville observed in his American travels, "I do not say that tyrannical abuses frequently occur in America at

the present day, but I maintain that no sure barrier is established against them." Tocqueville goes on to suggest that religion has a deep and pervasive hold on American society, both direct and indirect in ways more powerful than the theocracies of Europe. *Democracy in America*, 304, 351–53.

40. Sehat, *Myth of American Religious Freedom*, 65.

41. Lyman Beecher, "A Plea for the West (1835)," in *The Fear of Conspiracy: Images of Un-American Subversion from the Revolution to the Present*, ed. David Brion Davis (Ithaca: Cornell University Press, 1971), 86.

42. Hudson, *Religion in America*, 152.

43. Niebuhr, *Kingdom of God*, 123.

44. As quoted in Hudson, *Religion in America*, 152.

45. Schaff, *America*, 90–91; Baird, *Religion in America*, 273, 372; Sarah Barringer Gordon, *The Mormon Question: Polygamy and Constitutional Conflict in Nineteenth-Century America* (Chapel Hill: University of North Carolina Press, 2002), 8, 10. Outlining the attendant anxieties to these religious standards on society: "God's Church, God's Book, and God's Day," wrote Philip Schaff "are the three pillars of American society." "Without them," we "must go the way of all flesh, and God will raise up some other nation or continent to carry on his designs." Philip Schaff, "Progress of Christianity in the United States of America," *Princeton Review* 2 (July–December 1879): 214.

46. Tocqueville, *Democracy in America*, 515; Noll, *America's God*, 197. As articulated by Mark Noll, mainstream publishers, foreign observers, immigrants, and general Protestants in America "always singled out [Protestant Christianity] as a (if not the) driving force of the culture." Jonathan D. Sarna, ed., *Minority Faiths and the American Protestant Mainstream* (Urbana: University of Illinois, 1998), 193. Paradoxically, the power of this religious establishment came from its very denial, as noted by historian David Sehat. Sehat, *Myth of American Religious Freedom*, 159.

47. Colwell, *The Position of Christianity*, 13–14, 54. For studies on how this dynamic played out in the public educational system in the nineteenth century, particularly concerning Jews and Catholics, see David M. Reimers, *White Protestantism and the Negro* (New York: Oxford University Press, 1965). John R. G. Hassard, *Life of the Most Reverend John Hughes. . .* (New York: Appleton & Co., 1866), 230–32. Abram S. Isaacs, "What Shall the Public Schools Teach?" *Forum* 6 (October 1888): 207–8. John T. McGreevy, *Catholicism and American Freedom: A History* (New York: W. W. Norton), 7–8.

48. Baird, *Religion in America*, 255.

49. Niebuhr, *The Kingdom of God*, 112, 120, xiii. As explained by Reverend J. M. Williams late in the nineteenth century in the *New Englander and*

*Yale Review,* efforts toward establishing moral law via invisible efforts was "identical with *love,* the great imperative of that law." J. M. Williams, "Virtue, From a Scientific Standpoint," in *New Englander and Yale Review* 43, no. 183 (1884): 759.

50. Nancy Towle, *Vicissitudes Illustrated, in the Experience of Nancy Towle, in Europe and America* (Charleston, SC: James L. Burges, 1832), 221.

51. Bushnell, "Barbarism," 28–29; Baird, *Religion in America,* 210.

52. Wald and Calhoun-Brown, *Religion and Politics,* 44.

53. William J. Cooper Jr. and Thomas E. Terrill, *The American South: A History* (New York: McGraw-Hill, 1996), 437; George M. Marsden, *Fundamentalism and American Culture,* 2nd ed. (New York: Oxford University Press, 2006), 13. Tocqueville, *Democracy in America,* 515. Charles Taylor noted that this "background" emerges "as soon as we take account of the fact that all beliefs are held within a context or framework of the taken-for-granted, which usually remains tacit, and may even be as yet unacknowledged by the agent, because never formulated." Taylor, *A Secular Age,* 13. The process of "secularization" within the American environment depended upon a shift in this background, from one of cosmic time, to that of the natural.

54. Tocqueville, *Democracy in America,* 355; Sehat, *Myth of American Religious Freedom,* 287; Hatch, *Democratization,* 7. For more on these establishments, see Marsden, *Fundamentalism,* 12–13, and Gaines M. Foster, *Moral Reconstruction: Christian Lobbyists and the Federal Legislation of Morality, 1865–1920* (Chapel Hill: University of North Carolina Press, 2002), 6, 12, 43.

55. Justice Shea wrote in 1882, "Our own government, and the laws by which it is administered, are in every part—legislative, judicial, and executive—Christian in nature, form, and purpose." As quoted in Josiah Strong, *Our Country,* ed. Jurgen Herbst (Cambridge: Belknap Press of Harvard University Press, 1963 [1885]), 97. Robert Baird, *Religion in America,* 410–11.

56. Randall M. Miller, Harry S. Stout, and Charles Reagan Wilson, eds., *Religion and the American Civil War* (New York: Oxford University Press, 1998), 113, 118.

57. Charles C. Starbuck, "The Sects and Christianity," *New Englander and Yale Review* 49, no. 225 (December 1888): 416, 420–21.

58. Ibid., 424.

59. William R. Hutchison, *Religious Pluralism in America: The Contentious History of a Founding Ideal* (New Haven: Yale University Press, 2003), 4–5, 21.

60. As found in Tracy Fessenden's "Race," in *Themes in Religion and American Culture,* ed. Philip Goff and Paul Harvey (Chapel Hill: University of North

Carolina Press, 2004), 142; Jon Butler, *Awash in a Sea of Faith: Christianizing the American People* (Cambridge: Harvard University Press, 1990), 3, 256.

61. Schaff, *America*, 97, 250, 260–63, 272.

62. The perpetuation of intensive religious revivalism on the American frontiers during the formative years of the nation, however, did not so much unify but expanded upon many of these differences within American religion. At the same time, we also see it simultaneously helping to initiate a form of religious creativity and innovation that influenced national policy that helped control, via marginalization and intimidation, this diversity within the newly formed institutional frameworks of national and state power. Butler, *Awash in a Sea of Faith*, 216–17, 223–24. Though progress was assured, church historians continued throughout this century to look at history as "the record of a world-wide, time-filling, and veritable conflict between right and wrong, God and Satan." Samual M. Jackson, ed., *Papers of the American Society of Church History: First Annual Meeting in Washington D.C.*, December 28, 1888 (New York: Knickerbocker Press, 1889), 2:77.

63. Beecher, "A Plea for the West," 11ff.

64. Beecher spoke of this loss of birthright in terms of a "morsel of meat," which had direct reference to the Biblical account of Isaac's son Esau and his foolish selling of his birthright to his brother Jacob. Because of this thoughtless act on the part of Esau, he became symbolic of surrendering your divine potentials in exchange for petty worldly desires; see ibid., 87–94.

65. Baird, *Religion in America*, 38.

66. Bushnell, "Barbarism," 27.

67. Reeve, *Making Space*, 10–20.

68. Bushnell, "Barbarism," 5, 26.

69. Ibid., 20.

70. According to western historian Ferenc Morton Szasz, such fears over the fabled "Wild West" were not altogether unjustified. See chapter 2, "The Wild Ones, c. 1865–1882," in Szasz, *The Protestant Clergy in the Great Plains and Mountain West, 1865–1915* (Lincoln: University of Nebraska Press, 2004).

71. Following the Civil War, historian Gaines M. Foster shows how a powerful Christian lobby fought for these moral reforms against national sin, depending no longer on individual volunteerism, but instead the strong arm of government, be it on the executive, congressional, or judicial level. Foster, *Moral Reconstruction: Christian Lobbyists and the Federal Legislation of Morality, 1865–1920* (Chapel Hill: University of North Carolina Press, 2002), 12, 77–78, 234.

72. Bushnell, "Barbarism," 16.
73. Horace Bushnell, "Our Obligations to the Dead," in *Building Eras in Religion* (New York: Charles Scribner's Sons, 1910), 325–28.
74. For Brigham Young in Utah, Mormon theocracy was the ideal form of political unity and republican government. See Young, "Remarks," *Deseret News*, September 23, 1857.
75. Young's biographer, John G. Turner, describes Young's justification of extralegal frontier violence as a point of theology, or "spiritual charity." For certain transgressions, sometimes it was best to kill a person. According to Young, this is what Jesus had in mind with the great command in "loving our neighbor as ourselves." Turner, *Brigham Young: Pioneer Prophet* (Cambridge: Belknap Press, 2012), 258–62. While the Council of Fifty focused upon practical concerns of the Mormon state, questions of law and necessary violence were present in council meetings. Joseph Fielding wrote in his journal the following: "Others also were spoken of in the Council as being worthy of Death and as the Kingdom is now being established which is as a Shield round about the Church and as Judgment is in the Hands of the Members thereof it is incumbent upon them to cleanse it inside of the Platter, in short we feel ourselves to be in different Circumstances as to respo[n]sibility to what we were ever in before, because the Lord has placed us where we can execute his Laws." As reprinted in Jedediah S. Rogers, ed., *The Council of Fifty: A Documentary History* (Salt Lake City: Signature Books, 2014), 172.
76. As Michael Quinn shows, Joseph Smith and other early followers initially imaged the "church" to be no more than a body of believers, independent of authority and ordinances. Later, in 1829, Smith began to embrace the idea of authority and ordinances, leading to the practice of altering earlier revelations to reconcile these different understandings of church. Quinn, *The Mormon Hierarchy*, 5–7.
77. Such connections to the iconic Old Testament prophet and the Exodus story were common and were typically used by Young himself to encourage Mormon settlement building. John Williams Gunnison, *The Mormons, or, Latter-Day Saints, in the Valley of the Great Salt Lake: A History of Their Rise and Progress, Peculiar Doctrines, Present Conditions, and Prospects, Derived From Personal Observation, During a Residence Among Them* (Philadelphia: J. B. Lippincott, 1857), 23; Leonard Arrington, *Brigham Young: American Moses* (Urbana: University of Illinois Press, 1986), 174.
78. Joseph Smith, *History of the Church*, 7:515.
79. Taylor, *Government of God*, 16–19, 57, 58, 62, 92.
80. Rogers, *Council of Fifty*, 43, 83.

81. Taylor, *Government of God*, 89–90, 95, 104–5.

82. Donald Worster, *Rivers of Empire: Water, Aridity, and the Growth of the American West* (New York: Oxford University Press, 1985), 4, 47. For examples of this centralized control exerted by Mormon ecclesiastical leaders, see examples of Lot Smith and Brigham Young. Brigham Young said of his role in the kingdom, "It is my right and duty to do it—were it not, I should not say it. I have never sought but one thing in this kingdom, and that has been to get men and women to obey the Lord Jesus Christ in everything. I do not care what they say of me, if they will live so as to help build up his [the Lord's] kingdom." Arrington, *Brigham Young*, 360. The totalitarian rule of stake president Lot Smith of the Arizona colonization efforts is expounded on in Charles S. Peterson, *Take Up Your Mission: Mormon Colonizing along the Little Colorado River 1870–1900* (Tucson: University of Arizona Press, 1973), 114–22.

83. Graham, *Cosmos in the Chaos*, 130. John Taylor remarked, "But in this, as in Church matters, there must be an entire absence of individuality, covetousness and selfishness, and we must operate, under God, in the interests and for the benefit of all with whom we associate; for we are building up a kingdom that will stand forever." John Taylor, "AN EPISTLE to the Presidents of Stakes, High Councils, Bishops and other Authorities of the Church," in James R. Clark, comp., *Messages of the First Presidency* (Salt Lake City: Bookcraft Publishers, 1966), 2:338. Brigham Young asked what would happen if everyone went their own way? "What confusion, what discord, what discontent, what hatred would soon creep into the bosom of individuals, one against the other?" Using the example of a family whose child rose up to dictate, Young set up the problematic scenario of the child saying, "'I have as much power in this family as my father or mother.' If the mother says to one, 'you go and make the beds,' and to another, 'Wash up the dishes,' the girls would disobey her orders and think they had as much right to dictate as she had." Brigham then added, "Are we the Church and Kingdom of God? The family of Heaven? Yes. . . . We have made no bargain to gather up to Zion to raise confusion." See Arrington, *Brigham Young*, 360.

84. Joseph Smith, for example, spoke of all forms of human government, including monarchical, aristocratic, and republican, as doomed to be "prostrated in the dust." Rogers, *Council of Fifty*, 376–77.

85. Bushman, *Rough Stone Rolling*, 520–21; see also Leonard J. Arrington, Feramorz Y. Fox, and Dean L. May, *Building the City of God: Community and Cooperation among the Mormons* (Urbana: University of Illinois Press, 1992), 5.

86. In light of this dynamic, Josiah Strong went on to quote M. W. Montgomery's *The Mormon Delusion* to make his larger point: "The public has not yet grasped the proportions of this problem," and the "present laws and Christian forces at work in Utah" have much to do to eradicate such national threats." Strong, *Our Country*, 109, 115.

87. Orson Pratt, ed., *Journal of Discourses, by Brigham Young, President of the Church of Jesus Christ of Latter-day Saints, His Two Counsellors, the Twelve Apostles, and Others* (London: Latter Day Saints' Book Depot, 1856), 3:72.

88. Rogers, *Council of Fifty*, 376–77; *Journal of Discourses* 7:9–15.

89. Taylor, *Government of God*, 57–63.

90. Leonard Arrington provides an example of how this rule of obedience played out: "During the early years of the church, the priesthood not only had an interest in temporal affairs, but claimed the right to command in temporal affairs, and this tendency prevailed after the Mormons arrived in the Great Basin. As one bishop expressed it, 'the Priesthood [had the right] to dictate to the people all kinds of duties to perform. The Lord spoke to Brigham, Brigham to the Bishops, and the Bishops to the people.' In obedience to ecclesiastical authority men established new settlements, set up sawmills, opened general stores, operated ferries, and transported immigrants. And if the call involved selling all their possessions and moving their families to a new and perhaps inhospitable location, the vast majority of them accepted the call as a command." Leonard J. Arrington, *Great Basin Kingdom: Economic History of the Latter-Day Saints, 1830–1900* (Cambridge: Harvard University Press, 1958), 29–30. Turner, *Brigham Young*, 199–200; Rogers, *Council of Fifty*, 10, 13, 352–53; Quinn, *Mormon Hierarchy*, 124; Taylor, *Government of God*, 104–5.

91. Arrington, *Great Basin Kingdom*, 30. Though again underplaying the duration of this dynamic, Arrington writes, "In the first few years of Mormonism the government of the church was also the government for the kingdom. This was handled by organizing the bulk of the male members into two lay 'priesthoods' or governing bodies: the Melchizedek and the Aaronic. The Melchizedek priesthood, consisting of High Priests, Seventies, and Elders, governed the church in spiritual matters; the Aaronic, consisting of Priests, Teachers, and Deacons, supervised the temporal. Each was divided into local groups or 'quorums,' with leaders appointed by general church authorities, with the consent of the quorum." Arrington, *Great Basin Kingdom*, 29.

92. Rogers, *Council of Fifty*, 170–71, 379–81. As President George Q. Cannon similarly wrote while editor of the *Juvenile Instructor*: "Undoubtedly all this [the political 'Kingdom of God'] has reference to the time spoken of by St. John in *Revelation* when he said: 'And the seventh angel sounded; and there

were great voices in heaven, saying, The kingdoms of this world are become the kingdoms of our Lord, and of his Christ; and he shall reign forever and ever.'" Smith, *History of the Church*, 7:382.

93. Turner, *Brigham Young*, 204; Doctrine and Covenants 132:29–33.

94. Joseph Smith, *History of the Church*, 2nd ed. rev. (Salt Lake City: Deseret Book Company, 1976), 4:210–12; Todd Compton, *In Sacred Loneliness: The Plural Wives of Joseph Smith* (Salt Lake City: Signature Books, 1997), 27–28; John Taylor, *An Examination into and an Elucidation of the Great Principle of the Mediation and Atonement of Our Lord and Savior Jesus Christ* (Salt Lake City: Deseret News Company, 1882), 120–23.

95. David L. Bigler and Will Bagley, *The Mormon Rebellion: America's First Civil War 1857–1858* (Norman: University of Oklahoma Press, 2011), 272.

96. Klaus Hansen, "The Political Kingdom of God as a Cause for Mormon-Gentile Conflict," in *BYU Studies* 2, no. 2 (1960): 3, 7–8, 11. See also Gustive O. Larson, *The "Americanization" of Utah for Statehood* (San Marino: Huntington Library, 1971), 1, 4–7, 29–31, 273. This emphasis on the kingdom often equated Joseph Smith and later Brigham Young in Utah with that of monarch. Turner, *Brigham Young*, 185, 200. Rogers, *Council of Fifty*, 29–32, 49, 75–76. Quinn, *Mormon Hierarchy*, 120–26.

97. Rogers, *Council of Fifty*, 27, 32–33, 48, 72–73, 172.

98. Clark, *Messages*, 2:49, 82.

99. Ibid., 2:40.

100. Ibid., 2:67, 98, 113, 206. Such utopianism in the coming kingdom paralleled Bushnell's utopian hopes that America's destiny was that of "a nation of free men, self-governed, governed by simple law, without soldiers or police." Bushnell, "Barbarism," 29. This Protestant ideal, beginning with Martin Luther, was that if believers were truly repentant, there would be little need for either church or state. All would resist evil and love goodness, and there would be "no need of courts, laws, police, military establishments." Niebuhr, *Kingdom of God*, 35.

101. By way of example of this Promised Land obstructionism by American Canaanites and Hittites, together with their eventual eradication, see William Hubbard, *A General History of New England, from the Discovery to MDCLXXX*, 2nd ed. (1848; rpt., New York: Arno Press, 1972), 60.

102. As quoted in Matthew Frye Jacobson, *Whiteness of a Different Color: European Immigrants and the Alchemy of Race* (Cambridge: Harvard University Press, 1998), 206.

103. Conrad Cherry, ed., *God's New Israel: Religious Interpretations of American Destiny* (Chapel Hill: University of North Carolina Press, 1998), 115; Clark, *Messages*, 2:197, 203.

104. Bushnell, *Barbarism*, 27.

105. Smith, *Virgin Land*, 176–78.

106. Strong, *Our Country*, 9, 42, 194 (emphasis in original). Outlining the supremacy of the West and its Anglo-Saxon developers in regard to the "world's last hope," Strong unabashedly identified the perils of the West that then threatened this hope—immigration, Romanism, and Mormonism.

107. "Utah—The Louisville Journal Comments upon the Situation," *Weekly Vincennes Gazette*, April 22, 1857.

108. J. W. Mendenhall, "The Mormon Problem," *The Ladies Repository: A Monthly Periodical, Devoted to Literature, Arts, and Religion* 1, no. 4 (April 1875): 312.

109. Marsden, *Fundamentalism*, 27. As Hutchison observed, this enforcement of proper religious beliefs came in various forms in the handling of various groups. Some groups were harmless, requiring an amused yet condescending tolerance. Others were more annoying, requiring mockery and tolerance; but then there were the dangerous others, those that required intolerance and violence. This informal Christian establishment pushed to either make all Americans alike, or to push out the unwanted. Hutchison, *Religious Pluralism in America*.

110. Schaff, *America*, 243–46, 249–50. Schaff, "Progress of Christianity," 221.

111. Baird, *Religion in America*, 649.

112. *Journal of Discourses*, 5:99. For the story of the Midianites whom the Israelite army defeated, see Judges 7:5–25.

113. Herman Melville, *White-Jacket; or, The World in a Man-of-War* (London, 1850), chapter 36.

114. Marsden, *Fundamentalism*, 86.

## Chapter 2

1. K. Jack Bauer, *The Mexican War, 1846–1848* (New York: Macmillan, 1974), 1–3. See also Robert Glass Cleland, where the western settler and President Polk (himself a westerner) had become "almost fanatical in his belief in manifest destiny and the expansion of the United States to the Pacific." *From Wilderness to Empire: A History of California* (New York: Knopf, 1960), 86–87, 104–5.

2. See Bigler and Bagley, *The Mormon Rebellion*, 7, 17; William MacKinnon, ed., *At Sword's Point, Part I: A Documentary History of the Utah War to 1858* (Norman, OK: Arthur H. Clark, 2008), 44; David Bigler, *Forgotten Kingdom: The Mormon Theocracy in the American West 1847–1896* (Logan: Utah State University Press, 1998), 15–16, 87.

3. Juanita Brooks, *The Mountain Meadows Massacre* (Stanford: Stanford Uni-

versity Press, 1950); Ronald W. Walker, Richard E. Turley Jr., and Glen M. Leonard, *Massacre at Mountain Meadows* (New York: Oxford University Press, 2008). Jan Shipps correctly inquired in response to an earlier manuscript of Turley's book: "Where has all the religion gone?" See Jan Shipps et al., *A Preliminary Look Inside* Tragedy at Mountain Meadows: *A Panel Discussion*, Proceedings of Mormon History Association, Salt Lake City, Utah, 2007.

4. Sarah Barringer Gordon and Jan Shipps, "Fatal Convergence in the Kingdom of God: The Mountain Meadows Massacre in American History," *Journal of the Early Republic* 37, no. 2 (Summer 2017): 310.

5. Szasz, *Protestant Clergy*, ix, 3; Kerstetter writes, "Historians, then, have covered the government's political, economic, social, and to an extent cultural role in creating the West in its own republican image, but they have largely neglected the religious implications of this creative effort." Todd M. Kerstetter, *God's Country, Uncle Sam's Land: Faith and Conflict in the American West* (Urbana: University of Illinois Press, 2006), 5.

6. Kevin M. Schultz and Paul Harvey, "Everywhere and Nowhere: Recent Trends in American Religious History and Historiography," *Journal of the American Academy of Religion* 78, no. 1 (March 2010): 132.

7. "Modern Millenarianism," *The Princeton Review* 25 (1853): 66–71, 73. Concerning the millennium in connection with both the kingdom and the "ultimate evolution of government," see also Strong, *Our Country*, 155. Josiah Strong perhaps best makes this connection in his defense of the funding of public schools, which were based upon Protestant religious teachings and tradition. He argued that the teachings of Protestant morality were essential if society hoped to remain civil and to continue to evolve towards God's kingdom. Catholic schools, of course, should not receive similar established state support, because the consequences of their teachings could only result in a corrupt and degraded society. Protestant Christianity, then, as sponsored on the federally funded level, "is to make good citizens." Similar to Catholicism, Mormonism in the public schools could not be tolerated, for such naturally influenced society into tyranny, antirepublicanism, corruption, and the degradation of women. The best way to attack them was to set up Protestant schools in their midst. The natural outgrowth of both Catholicism and Mormonism was thus: "True religion" produced civil and religious life, whereas "false religion" brought forth death. See Strong, *Our Country*, 90, 101, 111, 113, 116.

8. "Modern Millenarianism," 69–70.

9. Ibid., 71–72, 83.

10. O. A. Kingsbury, "A Christian Daily Paper," *New Englander and Yale Review*

47 (September 1887): 182; Mark Noll in *America's God* effectively outlined the growth and development of this relationship. For example, see pp. 32, 114, 208.

11. "Modern Millenarianism," 77.

12. J. C. Welling, "The Science of Politics," *North American Review* 80, no. 2 (April 1855): 358.

13. Ibid., 357; Patrick Edward Dove, *The Theory of Human Progression, and Natural Probability of a Reign of Justice* (Boston: Sanborn, Carter and Bazin, 1856), 498.

14. Dove, *Theory of Human Progression*, 496.

15. Tuveson, *Redeemer Nation*, 24.

16. Robert V. Hine and John Mack Faragher, *Frontiers: A Short History of the American West* (New Haven: Yale University Press, 2007), 80–86.

17. Norman Graebner, ed., *Manifest Destiny*, The American Heritage Series (Indianapolis: Bobbs-Merrill, 1968), lxiii, lxvi.

18. Albert K. Weinberg, *Manifest Destiny: A Study of Nationalist Expansionism in American History* (Baltimore: The John Hopkins Press, 1935), 174, 190.

19. "President's Message," *National Era*, December 9, 1858.

20. Henry F. Bond, "Cuba and the Cubans," *North American Review* 79, no. 1 (July 1854): 113–16, 134.

21. Henry Nash Smith pointed out that this creating of heroes through the imagined barbarism of the frontier actually helped formulate this American mythology of the frontier. Smith, *Virgin Land*, 85.

22. Winthrop Sargent, "M. Gironiere and the Philippine Islands," *North American Review* 78, no. 1 (1854): 67, 75–76.

23. William Walker, *War in Nicaragua* (New York: S.H. Goetzel, 1860), 251–52, 256, 259, 272.

24. Banco de America, *The War in Nicaragua as Reported by Frank Leslie's Illustrated Newspaper, 1855–1857* (Managua: Editorial San Jose, 1976), 43.

25. Andrew F. Rolle, *California: A History* (New York: Thomas Y. Crowell, 1969), 256–57.

26. Americans had long attributed their own racial supremacy as a mixture of northern European Protestant races, taking in what they perceived to be the best characteristics of all; racial crossover with Africans and the indigenous however was seen as corrupting, rather than purifying. In his presidential address before the Senate on December 8, 1857, Buchanan complained that as long as the slave market remains open, "there can be no hope for the civilization of benighted Africa. Whilst the demand for slaves continues in Cuba, wars will be waged among the petty and barbarous chiefs in Africa for the purpose of seizing subjects to supply this trade. In such a condi-

tion of affairs, it is impossible that the light of civilization and religion can ever penetrate these dark abodes." It is noteworthy the signification that the term "civilization" merits in this statement by the president to the Senate—where barbarism exists, religion and civilization are not. Of course, "religion" as used by Buchanan, was Protestant Christianity. U.S. Congress, *Message of the President of the United States to the Two Houses of Congress at the Commencement of the First Session of the Thirty-Fifth Congress, Vol. II*, 35th Cong., 1st sess. Cong. Doc. 2 (Washington, DC: William A. Harris, Printer, 1858), 15.

27. Laurence Oliphant, *Patriots and Filibusters; or, Incidents of Political and Exploratory Travel* (Edinburgh: William Blackwood and Sons, 1860), 209–10.

28. Cooper and Terrill, *The American South*, 231.

29. Walker, *War in Nicaragua*, 278.

30. One example of the violence Walker brought to Nicaragua can be seen in his own written account of events. Referring to Guatemalan troops as "half drunk with aguardiente," as well as lacking military experience, they "exposed themselves without reason" near the American line. Walker supporters then "poured a deadly fire into the foolish and ignorant Indians" that were sent to fight Walker in Nicaragua, "and it was with a feeling almost of pity for these forced levies that the Americans were obliged to shoot them down like so many cattle. The Guatemalan officers cared no more for their men than if they were sheep; and when they finally drew off their troops the ground was thickly strewn with the dead and the wounded." William Walker, *The War in Nicaragua* (New York: S. H. Goetzel, 1860), 407.

31. Frank P. Blair argued: "The bottom of this whole movement" was slavery. He then continued, "There is a party in this country who go for the extension of Slavery; and these predatory incursions against our neighbors are the means by which territory is to be seized, planted with Slavery, annexed to this Union, and, in combination with the present slaveholding States, made to dominate this Government and the entire continent; or, failing in the policy of annexation, to unite with the slave States in a Southern slaveholding Republic." As reprinted in "Speech of Hon. Frank P. Blair, Jr. of Missouri," *National Era*, May 13, 1858.

32. "Welcome to General Walker," *New York Daily Times*, June 12, 1857.

33. Ibid.

34. Robert A. Pastor, *Not Condemned to Repetition: The United States and Nicaragua* (Cambridge, MA: Westview Press, 2002), 17.

35. As quoted in Miller, Stout, and Wilson, *Religion and the American Civil War*, 22.

36. Ibid., 120.
37. As quoted in Bigler and Bagley, *The Mormon Rebellion*, 260.
38. On March 12, 1854, one Mr. Everett presented a protest to the Kansas-Nebraska Act that was signed by 3,050 clergymen from New England, out of a total of 3,800 sects, and sent it to Congress. Though supporters of the bill marked such clergy influence over the state as a "desecration of the pulpit," there were many in Congress who heartily defended the memorial and the memorialists. Frederick W. Seward, *Seward at Washington, as Senator and Secretary of State: A Memoir of His Life, with Selections from His Letters 1846–1861* (New York: Derby and Miller, 1891), 225.
39. Nichole Etcheson, *Bleeding Kansas: Contested Liberty in the Civil War Era* (Lawrence: University Press of Kansas, 2004), 27.
40. "Kansas—The Mormons—Slavery," *New York Times*, June 23, 1857.
41. Ibid.; see also W. Paul Reeve, *Religion of a Different Color: Race and the Mormon Struggle for Whiteness* (New York: Oxford University Press, 2015), 161–63.
42. As printed in the "Causes of Increase in Population," *Brooklyn Eagle*, January 22, 1857; for an expansion of this binary of freedom and despotism as negatively applied to Roman Catholicism, see William M. Shea, *The Lion and the Lamb: Evangelicals and Catholics in America* (New York: Oxford University Press, 2004), 60.
43. Andrew P. Peabody, Review of *Samuel Eliot's History of Liberty, Part II*, by Samuel Eliot, *North American Review* 78, no. 2 (1854): 348, 357–58.
44. The *Times* declared the impossibility of a "peaceful solution" to the Mormon "problem before us, with these facts staring us in the face." Under Young, Mormons have emulated the "followers of MAHOMET," and thus, not a crusade, but a war against them was necessary. The new "Governor of Utah," the *Times* argues, "will need at his back an armed force large enough to strike terror at once to the heart of Mormondom." "War with the Mormons," *New York Daily Times*, May 13, 1857.
45. For a fuller examination of this connection between Mormonism and race, see Paul Reeve's excellent monograph, *Religion of a Different Color*, especially chapter 1, "The New Race."
46. Jacobson, *Whiteness*, 30.
47. Baird, *Religion in America*, 35.
48. Jacobson, *Whiteness*, 206. Significantly, Sidney Mead notes that the United States had two religions, or a syncretism of the same form of a Protestant ideology, namely "the religion of the denominations," and the "religion of the democratic society and nation." Rooted in the rationalism of the Enlightenment, this democratic (self-regulated by the people) society was "articulated in terms of the destiny of America, under God, to be fulfilled by perfecting

the democratic way of life for the example and betterment of all mankind. This was a calling taken as seriously as ever a Christian saint had taken his peculiar vocation." Wentz, *Religion in American Life and Thought*, 135.

49. Etcheson, *Bleeding Kansas*, 29.

50. Kenneth M. Stampp, *America in 1857: A Nation on the Brink* (New York: Oxford University Press, 1990), 5.

51. Etcheson, *Bleeding Kansas*, 72.

52. "President's Message," *National Era*, December 9, 1858.

53. Marsden, *Fundamentalism*, 22.

54. Debby Applegate, *The Most Famous Man in America: The Biography of Henry Ward Beecher* (New York: Doubleday Broadway, 2006), 281–82.

55. Boston clergy had great influence within society, as in 1829, when Boston clergy incited the fears of the lower classes against Catholics, inspiring various attacks on individual homes and the stoning of churches. See Ray Allen Billington, *The Protestant Crusade 1800–1860: A Study of the Origins of American Nativism* (Chicago: Quadrangle Books, 1964), 70.

56. Beecher, "A Plea for the West," 85–94.

57. Davis, *Images*, 95.

58. "One of the Army Contracts," *Weekly Vincennes Gazette*, May 12, 1858.

59. See Robert Baird, *Religion in America*, 442. Daniel Dorchester spoke of these revivals as "one of the most remarkable revivals of a century full of wonders of grace." Daniel Dorchester, *Christianity in the United States from the First Settlement Down to the Present Time* (New York: Hunt and Eaton, 1889), 694. Kathryn Long refers to these urban revivals as "the closest thing to a truly national revival in American history." Major Protestant denominations stunningly increased memberships by almost half a million between the years 1856–1859. Kathryn Teresa Long, *The Revival of 1857–58: Interpreting an American Religious Awakening* (New York: Oxford University Press, 1998), 7, 9, 48.

60. Marsden, *Fundamentalism*, 86–87. As Long noted, even the *Journal of Commerce*, a financial paper, urged its readers to "steal awhile away from Wall Street and every worldly care, and spend an hour about mid-day in humble, hopeful prayer." Noon prayers had the explicit goal of focusing businessmen during the day on their religious obligations. Long, *The Revival*, 52, 128.

61. Damuel Irenaeus Prime, *The Power of Prayer: Illustrated in the Wonderful Displays of Divine Grace at the Fulton Street and Other Meetings in New York and Elsewhere, in 1857 and 1858* (London: Sampson, Low, Son, 1859), 72. Famed revivalist Charles G. Finney wrote in his memoir that the 1857 and 1858 revivals "swept over the land in such a tremendous manner, that for

some weeks it was estimated that not less than fifty thousand conversions occurred per week." Indeed, between 1856 and 1859, nearly half a million Americans entered the fold of the revivalist Christian gospel. Garth M. Rossell and Richard A. G. Dupuis, eds., *The Original Memoirs of Charles G. Finney*, rev. ed. (Grand Rapids, MI: Zondervan, 2002), 405.

62. Leonard I. Sweet, "'A Nation Born Again': The Union Prayer Meeting Revival and Cultural Revitalization," in *The Great Tradition: In Honor of Winthrop S. Hudson, Essays on Pluralism, Voluntarism, and Revivalism*, ed. Joseph D. Ban and Paul R. Dekar (Valley Forge, PA: Judson Press, 1982), 210.

63. Long, *The Revival*, 100.

64. John Corrigan, *Business of the Heart: Religion and Emotion in the Nineteenth Century* (Berkeley: University of California Press, 2002), 15–18, 45–46.

65. In language that would have been familiar to Puritan adherents of covenant theology and its corollaries, Col. Patrick Connor argued for the "annihilation of this whole people [of Mormonism]," positing: "If the present rebellion [Civil War] is a punishment for any national sin, I believe it is for permitting this unholy, blasphemous, and unnatural institution [Mormonism] to exist almost in the heart of the nation, ignoring its horrid crimes and allowing it to extend its ramifications into every grade of society in defiance of laws human and divine." He added, "The sooner we are rid of the evil, and the nation of the stigma, the better it will be for us." As quoted in E. B. Long, *The Saints and the Union: Utah Territory During the Civil War* (Chicago: University of Illinois Press, 2001), 149.

66. Hine, *Frontiers*, 80; Reeve, *Religion of a Different Color*, 163.

67. U.S. Congress, *Utah: Message from the President of the United States, Transmitting Information in Reference to the Condition of Affairs in the Territory of Utah*, by Lemuel G. Brandebury, Perry E. Brocchus, and B. D. Harris, 32nd Cong., 1st sess. Cong. Rept. 25 (Washington, DC, 1852), 20 (hereafter *Utah: Message*). It was under such suspicions against Mormons that President Fillmore gave territorial officials private instructions to watch the movements of the Mormons and their leaders, and that likely emboldened Buchanan to heavily react to federal reports from Utah disparaging Mormons. Ibid., 29–30.

68. "What Shall We Do with the Mormons?," *New York Times*, April 21, 1857.

69. "War with the Mormons," *New York Daily Times*, May 13, 1857.

70. "The War Department and the Utah Expedition," *New York Times*, December 10, 1857. Religious historian George Marsden notes that antebellum mainstream evangelicals tended to view God's kingdom in a worldly

framework, rather than one otherworldly. Therefore, Protestant evangelicals "generally regarded almost any sort of progress as evidence of the advance of the kingdom." Prior to the Civil War, evangelicals continued to view history as "a cosmic struggle between the armed forces of God and Satan and that these supernatural powers might directly intervene at any moment." George Marsden, *Fundamentalism*, 50. Mormonism's continued and ever-growing existence presented one of the greatest frustrations among evangelicals, whose views of the kingdom held no place for Mormons. This was especially alarming as the West was considered by influential religious thinkers like Lyman Beecher to be America's last hope in the establishment of the American kingdom, and the Mormons had planted themselves right in its heart. Josiah Strong's analysis best demonstrates this, for not only did the presence of Mormons hamper Protestant democracy in the West, but were a general threat to a peaceful society nationally. Strong's observation was not whether Mormonism is to be attacked and killed, but how best to do it. Strong, *Our Country*, 110–16.

71. U.S. Congress, *Message of the President of the United States to the Two Houses of Congress at the Commencement of the Second Session of the Thirty-Fifth Congress*, 35th Cong., 2d sess. Cong. Doc. 1 (Washington, DC: William A. Harris, 1858), 6, 161; U.S. Congress, *Message of the President, First Session*, 24–25.

72. Norman F. Furniss, *The Mormon Conflict, 1850–1859* (New Haven: Yale University Press, 1960), 74–75; U.S. Congress, *Message of the President, Second Session*, 7.

73. In analyzing American anti-Mormon fiction, Terryl L. Givens makes a similar argument concerning the "rhetorical strategies that must be deliberately and ingeniously applied, in order to maintain intact the underlying value system of pluralism and religious toleration while the aberrant group is proscribed." This rhetorical strategy to remove groups "out of the sphere of religion" allowed them to be placed in "conflict with a republican people and their institutions." Givens, *The Viper on the Hearth: Mormons, Myths, and the Construction of Heresy* (New York: Oxford University Press, 1997), 21–22.

74. Turner, *Brigham Young*, 268; U.S. Congress, *Message of the President, Second Session*, 7.

75. Diary of Captain Phelps, as reprinted in *Mormon Resistance: A Documentary Account of the Utah Expedition, 1857–1858*, ed. Leroy R. Hafen and Ann W. Hafen (Lincoln: University of Nebraska Press, 2005 [1958]), 90, 101, 131; Marsden, *Fundamentalism*, 28.

76. Schaff, "Progress of Christianity," 221. Following this privileged nar-

rative of the Protestant mainstream, Ferenc Szasz notes that the Mormons created a "distinctly hostile environment" against the nation and their "Gentile" neighbors, making Utah so different and foreign from the rest of the nation that missionaries felt "as if they had been serving in Asia or Africa." It was to the credit of "three generations of Protestant missionaries," Szasz writes, that we have to thank for helping "the Saints . . . appear more and more like another 'conservative' denomination." Szasz, *Protestant Clergy*, 154, 174. For similar assessments of Mormonism within developments of American religious pluralism, see also Hutchison, *Religious Pluralism in America*, and Kerstetter, *God's Country, Uncle Sam's Land*.

77. For this reason, Schaff explained, "All religious associations, which do not outrage the general Christian sentiment and public morality (as the Mormons, who, for their conduct, were driven from Ohio and Illinois), enjoy the same protection and the same rights." Schaff, *America*, 115–16, 246, 249–50.

78. James W. Alexander, "The Holy Flock," in *The New York Pulpit in the Revival of 1858: A Memorial Volume of Sermons*, ed. Samuel Irenaeus Prime (New York: Sheldon, Blakeman, 1858), 28–29.

79. Roy Franklin Nichols, *The Disruption of American Democracy* (New York: Macmillan, 1948), 99, 101, 179; Henry Inman and William F. Cody, *The Great Salt Lake Trail* (Topeka: Crane, 1914), 121.

80. Nichols, *American Democracy*, 99. Walker, Turley, and Leonard, *Mountain Meadows*, 75.

81. Nash, *Virgin Land*, 166–67; Reeve, *Religion of a Different Color*, 46–50.

82. U.S. Congress, Joint Congressional Committee on Inaugural Ceremonies, *Inaugural Addresses of the Presidents of the United States: From George Washington to George W. Bush* (Washington, DC: US Government Printing Office, 1976); U.S. Congress, *Message of the President, First Session*, 27.

83. Frederic L. Paxson, *History of the American Frontier 1763–1893* (Boston: Houghton Mifflin, 1924), 346.

84. Bushnell, "Barbarism," 27.

85. Paxson, *History of the American Frontier*, 570.

86. Cooper and Terrill, *The American South*, 302; Hine and Faragher, *Frontiers*, 109, 118.

87. Gerald M. Capers, *Stephen A. Douglas: Defender of the Union* (Boston: Little, Brown, 1959), 81.

88. As quoted in Donald Moorman, *Camp Floyd and the Mormons: The Utah War* (Salt Lake City: University of Utah Press, 2005 [1992]), 17.

89. Stampp, *America in 1857*, 199.

90. John Bassett Moore, ed., *The Works of James Buchanan: Comprising His Speeches, State Papers, and Private Correspondence* (Philadelphia: Washington Square Press, 1911), 330–33.

91. For the Mormon perspective of why Mormons rejected these federal appointees, see Edwin B. Firmage and Richard C. Mangrum, *Zion in the Courts: A Legal History of the Church of Jesus Christ of Latter-day Saints* (Chicago: University of Illinois Press, 2001 [1988]), 1–17. See also Clark, *Messages*, 2:98, 113, 155.

92. Federal officials often left Utah in the 1850s with feelings of mutual bitterness. Four officials, Secretary Broughton D. Harris, Chief Justice Lemuel G. Brandebury, Associate Justice Perry E. Brocchus, and Indian Subagent Henry R. Day all left Utah in 1851 due to the lack of cooperation from Utah Mormons. See Thomas G. Alexander, *Utah: The Right Place* (Salt Lake City: Gibbs Smith, 2008), 119–20; Rogers, *Council of Fifty*, 246.

93. "News of the Day," *New York Times*, April 21, 1857; "How Aliens Were Naturalized in Utah—Letter from Judge Drummond," *New York Times*, August 24, 1857.

94. "While kingdoms, governments, and thrones, are falling and rising; revolutions succeeding revolutions; and the nations of the earth are overturning; while plague, pestilence and famine, are walking abroad; and whirlwind, fire, and earthquake, proclaim the truth of prophecy, let the Saints be faithful and diligent in every duty, and especially in striving to stand in chosen places, that they may watch the coming of the Holy One of Israel." First Presidency, October 12, 1849. Clark, *Messages*, 2:37. "I have been taught from early life that the day would come when republican institutions would be in danger in this nation and upon this continent, when, in fact, the republic would be so rent asunder by factions that there would be no stable government outside of the Latter-day Saints; and that it is their destiny as a people, to uphold constitutional government upon this land." George Q. Cannon, April 3, 1881, *Journal of Discourses*, 23:122–23. Drummond's conclusions regarding the Mormon threat were based in paranoia, but his questions, at least in part, were based in reality. Though Mormons anticipated an eventual wasteland of American society and government, the secretive Council of Fifty understood itself as having "full authority to build up the Kingdom of God on earth, that His will might be done on earth as it is in heaven," and were at one point given assignment to disperse "abroad in the nation." Those of the Council spoke of themselves as independent from and superior to both the U.S. Constitution and Congress itself, spoke of building Mormon cities throughout the United States, pushed forth its own political leaders on the national

     level, and anticipated a certain level of dominion as a consequence of their success. Rogers, *Council of Fifty*, 48–49, 53, 58.

95. Clark, *Messages*, 2:117.

96. David M. Pletcher, *The Diplomacy of Annexation: Texas, Oregon, and the Mexican War* (Columbia: University of Missouri Press, 1973), 334, 609–11.

97. "Still Later from Utah: W. H. Drummond," *New York Daily Times*, May 20, 1857.

98. On December 29, 1856, Mormons raided the office of George P. Stiles, a territorial associate justice, destroying over a hundred of his law books. Matthew J. Grow and Ronald W. Walker, *The Prophet and the Reformer: The Letters of Brigham Young and Thomas L. Kane* (New York: Oxford University Press, 2015), 204. However exaggerated by frontier officials Mormon tendencies toward violence in early Utah was, it is understood by even the more sympathetic of Mormon historians that Brigham Young encouraged an attitude that furthered a culture of violence and fear that gave credence to some of these claims. See Walker, Turley, and Leonard, *Mountain Meadows*, 127–28. For more examples of a culture of violence in Utah, see Bigler, *Forgotten Kingdom*, 131–36; MacKinnon, *At Sword's Point*, 298–328; Rogers, *Council of Fifty*, 149, 161, 165–66, 171; Quinn, *The Mormon Hierarchy*, 112–13. An important reference work outlining Brigham Young's role in Utah's scene of violence, together with him being an accessory to the massacre at Mountain Meadows after the fact, is Will Bagley, *Blood of the Prophets: Brigham Young and the Massacre at Mountain Meadows* (Norman: University of Oklahoma Press, 2002). In outlining the significance of the term "fanaticism," historian of religion Spencer Fluhman noted that its use emphasized "Mormonism's tyrannical and violent potential," namely the propensity for putting into action one's delusion, which with accounts such as this, stood in antithesis of what was then idealized as the philanthropic efforts of Christian "Love." Fluhman, *"A Peculiar People,"* 86.

99. In a letter to President Millard Fillmore, one judicial officer wrote on September 20, 1851, "This kind of feeling [fanatic intolerance] I found pervading the whole community, in some individuals more marked than in others" (*Utah: Message*, 5). In a report of Brandebury, Brocchus, and Harris to the president, Mormons were characteristically "ignorant and credulous." In this same letter, Harris testifies that the "violent exhibition of [Brigham Young's] temper and abuse" towards territorial officials "were rife throughout the community." *Utah: Message*, 9–10, 14–15, 21. In a letter to Secretary Floyd, Powell and McCulloch acknowledged that they were informed that "many were dissatisfied with the Mormon Church, and would leave it whenever they could with safety to themselves," upon which they informed

them to go back to their homes and that they would protect them from their religion. U.S. Congress, *Message of the President, Second Session,* 173; US Congress, *Proclamation of President of United States to People of Territory of Utah,* by James Buchanan, 35th Cong., 2d sess. Cong. Doc. Vol. 2 (Washington, DC: U.S. Government Printing Office, 1858), 69–71. These accusations by Drummond of violence were of course unfair distortions of the affairs in Utah, but they were not altogether unfounded. As Mormon historian William P. MacKinnon pointed out in his recent study of the Utah War, within the ambiguity of borderland Utah, "simple ageless acts of murder, plundering, and vengeance unfolded." Indeed, the military campaign against Utah was not an unprovoked or bloodless confrontation, but a military campaign that had spawned in part by a Mormon "territorial culture of violence." MacKinnon, *At Sword's Point,* 296–97. Will Bagley provides the number of forty men, thirty women, and seventy children who were involved in the massacre. Only seventeen children were spared since they were considered too young to tell the story. Bagley, *Blood of the Prophets,* 4–5.

100. As quoted in "The Utah Question," *National Era,* July 1, 1858.
101. Ibid.
102. As reprinted in "Polygamy and Slavery," *National Era,* December 24, 1857.
103. The use of territorial posts as payment for political debts, marks Furniss, further reduced "the possibility of selecting suitable men for public service." Men like Perry Brocchus and W. W. Drummond "could only exacerbate the difficulties" between Utah and the United States. See Furniss, *The Mormon Conflict,* 13. Young argued that such appointees were in the habit of "setting up gambling shops, and drinking, and carousing, and stirring up strife, and hatching up law-suits," and then, after wreaking such local havoc, "ran home, and raised the cry, 'Mormon disturbances,' 'Mormon rebellion,' 'Mormon war,' and 'Treasoners.'" As quoted in a master's thesis by Laura Cruse, "American Republicanism as Shown through Mormon-Federal Conflict, 1846–1890" (Master's thesis, Northeast Missouri State University, 1994), 47. These complaints coming from Utah's territorial officials tapped into these providential designs and anxieties toward America's destiny. In 1835, Lyman Beecher outlined, in his extremely popular "Plea for the West," that the religious makeup of the West held the key to survival of the nation and the world. Much was at stake in the West, for if it was lost, "our race" would have a short journey "from the cradle to the grave." As one of New England's leading ministers, Beecher's greatest goal was to bring forth Jesus Christ's millennial glory by evangelizing the West. Beecher, "A Plea for the West," 85–57. Regarding territorial officials sent to

Utah, Brigham Young's complaints were not without merit. "This is the case with most men sent to the Territories," noted army officer Major Van Vliet, in response to Young's complaints. "They receive their office as a political reward, or as a stepping-stone to Senatorship; but they have no interest in common with the people. . . . This people [the Mormons] has been lied about the worse of any people I ever saw." As reprinted in Hafen and Hafen, *Mormon Resistance*, 45. For more on Drummond and these officials, see Grow and Walker, *The Prophet and the Reformer*, 200–5.

104. For more on Brigham Young and his responses to these federal officials, see Turner, *Brigham Young*, 202–4; Grow and Walker, *The Prophet and the Reformer*, 205.

105. As reproduced in "By Telegraph," *Weekly Vincennes Gazette,* December 30, 1857; *Utah: Message*, 27.

106. As reprinted in "The Mormon Question—Its True Solution," *Brooklyn Eagle*, May 2, 1857.

107. As quoted in Turner, *Brigham Young*, 279.

108. Richard D. Webb, ed., *The Life and Letters of Captain John Brown* (London: Smith, Elder, 1861), 273–74; Applegate, *Most Famous Man in America*, 283. At his death, Brown became, according to the words of his earliest biographer, "the latest and bravest martyr to the teachings of the Bible and the American idea." James Redpath, *The Public Life of John Brown* (Boston: Thayer and Eldridge, 1860), 406. John Brown had become, as continued by twentieth-century historian Louis Ruchames, "devoted to the highest ideals of equality and democracy, influenced by the best in the Judeo-Christian tradition and all that was good and noble in the thoughts and actions of the Founding Fathers." Louis Ruchames, "John Brown and the American Tradition," in *The Age of Civil War and Reconstruction, 1830–1900: A Book of Interpretive Essays*, ed. Charles Crowe (Homewood, IL: Dorsey Press, 1966), 212. Cultural icons Ralph W. Emerson, Henry W. Beecher, and Henry D. Thoreau hailed Brown as a saint, when he was put to death in 1859, comparing his hangman's noose with the cross of Christ. Emerson wrote, "Some eighteen hundred years ago Christ was crucified; this morning, perchance, Captain Brown was hung. These are the two ends of a chain which is not without its links. He is not Old Brown any longer; he is an angel of light." As quoted in Ruchames, "John Brown," 210. Beecher wrote of Brown's imprisonment: "Let no men pray that Brown be spared. Let Virginia make him a martyr. Now, he has only blundered. His soul was noble, his work miserable. But a cord and a gibbet would redeem all that, and round up Brown's failure with heroic success." Thomas W. Knox, *Life and Work of Henry Ward Beecher:*

*An Authentic, Impartial and Complete History of His Public Career and Private Life, from the Cradle to the Grave* (Kansas: S. F. Junking, 1887), 155.

109. *Weekly Vincennes Gazette*, "Thirty-Fifth Congress: First Session," March 10, 1858.

110. James Buchanan, *Great Speeches of the Honourable James Buchanan: Delivered at the Mass Meeting of the Democracy of Western Pennsylvania, at Greensburg, on Thursday, Oct. 7, 1852* (Philadelphia, 1852), 9. The context of this quote concerning religion and its mingling with the state concerns Buchanan's outrage that a presidential candidate would insult another's religion, in this case Roman Catholicism, for personal political gain. In his own 1856 run for president, however, against Republican John Charles Fremont, Buchanan's campaign moved to discredit Fremont's bid for the presidency by calling him a Canadian, gambler, thief, and scoundrel, as well as a Catholic and apostate. Corrigan, *Business of the Heart*, 54.

111. Caleb Sprague Henry, *Politics and the Pulpit: A Series of Articles Which Appeared in the Journal of Commerce and in the Independent, During the Year 1850 . . .* (New York: William Harned, 1851), 6.

112. For more on these schisms, see Moses N. Moore Jr., "Black Presbyterians and the Schism of 1837," *Union Seminary Quarterly Review* 54, nos. 3–4 (Spring 2000): 57, 63, 68, 81–82. See also Moore, "History and Historiography: Revisiting the Presbyterian Schism of 1837," in *AME Church Review* (October–December 2005); George M. Marsden, *The Evangelical Mind and the New School Presbyterian Experience: A Case Study of Thought and Theology in Nineteenth-Century America* (New Haven: Yale University Press, 1970), 76–80.

113. William Hosmer, *The Higher Law, in Its Relations to Civil Government: With Particular Reference to Slavery, and the Fugitive Slave Law* (Auburn, NY: Derby & Miller, 1852), 85.

114. "The Bible is the Higher Law, in fact and in form. It is a formal announcement of the Divine will as the Divine will." Ibid., 1, 24, 85; Henry, *Politics and the Pulpit*, 9–11.

115. Harney was a skilled but excessively violent commander, gaining a reputation for torturing and mutilating enslaved African-Americans; was court-marshaled four times by the army; and had earned the title "Squaw Killer" for massacring eighty-six Sioux, including men, women, and children, in 1855. Beyond this, following his appointment, Harney requested appointment as Utah's governor, "with full powers to declare martial law," giving him the "power to compel" obedience. See Walker et al. *Mountain Meadows*, 37, 46. Bigler and Bagley, *Mormon Rebellion*, 130, 132.

116. See MacKinnon, *At Sword's Point*, 152. As would be seen in the Civil War, such missionaries/army chaplains found little distinction between the extension of U.S. power and that of their own Christian faith and missionary efforts. One clergyman illuminated the importance of such "men of God" in 1865: "Patriotism demands that the sanctions of our holy religion be given to [the government's] combat for humanity, freedom, unity, and stable peace; and the vigorous arms of its soldiery must not be palsied, their earnest hearts must not be chilled with doubts as to the righteousness of their vocation." Joseph Horner, "Christianity and the War Power," *Methodist Quarterly Review* 60 (April 1865): 185.

117. Being Episcopalian, the term "the one Catholic Church" as used here does not have reference to the Roman Catholic Church, but instead that of a larger invisible Christian family inclusive of all Protestant denominations. Gunnison, *The Mormons*, 165.

118. L. U. Reavis, *The Life and Military Services of Gen. William Selby Harney* (St. Louis: Bryan, Brand, 1878), 276–79. Rumors were afloat in Utah that Harney's army was operating under orders to exterminate the Mormons. Moorman, *Camp Floyd*, 126–27.

119. "Utah and the Union," *New York Times*, November 13, 1857.

120. U.S. Congress, *Proclamation of President Buchanan*, 25.

121. MacKinnon, *At Sword's Point*, 35, 43–44, 77–82, 97, 100; Turner, *Brigham Young*, 266, 299.

122. Though Buchanan had grave hesitations about Kane's involvement, he finally accepted Kane's proposal. Colonel Kane traveled to Salt Lake City and convinced an angry Governor Brigham Young to comply with military orders and to step down as governor. This represented the first attempt at diplomacy with Utah and it was successful. Moorman, *Camp Floyd*, 28–38; Grow and Walker, *The Prophet and the Reformer*, 242, 247.

123. Besides the letters given to Kane from Buchanan, Bernhisel equipped Kane with a letter for Brigham Young that expressed the belief of Kane's divine guidance. It was also this feeling of providence that allowed Kane's wife, Elizabeth, to accept her husband's dangerous mission to go to Utah and "bring peace to those lost sheep of Israel." Grow and Walker, *The Prophet and the Reformer*, 235–38.

124. As printed in "President's Message," *National Era*, December 9, 1858.

125. Following amnesty, Mormon claims of patriotism were difficult to embrace. Floyd argued that the apparent demonstration of Mormon patriotism was a mere façade, as "patriotism is the last resort of a villain." "Affairs in Utah," *New York Times*, March 2, 1860.

126. In a report from Council Bluffs, "General Johnston," who had led the troops

to Utah and suffered the winter of 1857–1858 near burned-out Fort Bridger, "seemed in bad humor towards the Governor and mankind generally, at the peaceful indications being made." Similarly upset, Col. Charles Ferguson Smith spoke of his desire to "see every damned Mormon hung by the neck." See "Colonel Kane Returns to the States," *Crescent City Oracle*, June 11, 1858. Hafen and Hafen, *Mormon Resistance*, 289–92; Moorman, *Camp Floyd*, 44, 51.

127. Furniss, *Mormon Conflict*, 175.
128. For an analysis of the Civil War as a conflict over national theology, see Mark Noll, *Civil War as a Theological Crisis* (Chapel Hill: University of North Carolina Press, 2006).
129. Ibid., 28.
130. Marsden, *Fundamentalism*, 24, 49–50, 86–87.

### CHAPTER 3

1. U.S. Congress, Message of the President, First Session, 25.
2. Gordon, *The Mormon Question*, xiii, 5–7. This supports American scholar Ann Taves's approach to religious experience as embedded and connected, rather than abstracted and disconnected from other things, such as politics and culture. See Ann Taves, *Fits, Trances, & Visions: Experiencing Religion and Explaining Experience from Wesley to James* (Princeton: Princeton University Press, 1999), 360–61.
3. Dorchester, *Christianity*, table of contents.
4. Davis, "Some Themes of Counter-Subversion," 208–9, 215, 224.
5. This model of seeing Mormonism as a national cultural construct follows that proposed by Jenny Franchot in her analysis of Roman Catholicism in the United States. See Franchot, *Roads to Rome: The Antebellum Protestant Encounter with Catholicism* (Berkeley: University of California Press, 1994), 6, 350–51, 361. In seeing how these themes intermingle with Islam, see Tammy Heise, "Marking Mormon Difference: How Western Perceptions of Islam Defined the 'Mormon Menace,'" *Journal of Religion and Popular Culture* 25, no. 1 (Spring 2013): 82–97.
6. Arrington, *Great Basin Kingdom*, 257–58.
7. Firmage and Mangrum, *Zion in the Courts*, 139.
8. As quoted in Davis Bitton, *George Q. Cannon: A Biography* (Salt Lake City: Deseret Book, 2004), 272.
9. "The Mormon Insult to the Flag," *Brooklyn Eagle*, July 7, 1885.
10. Jacobson, *Whiteness of a Different Color*, 77–78; Reeve, *Making Space*, 6–7.
11. "Anti-Chinese Testimony," in *Living History America: The History of the United States in Documents, Essays, Letters, Songs and Poems*, ed. Erik Bruun and Jay Crosby (New York: Tess Press, 1999), 497.
12. Jean Pfaelzer, *Driven Out: The Forgotten War Against Chinese Americans*

(Berkeley: University of California Press, 2008), xxv, 31, 47–54. For more on American violence against Chinese immigrants, see Alexander Saxton, *The Indispensable Enemy: Labor and the Anti-Chinese Movement in California* (Berkeley: University of California Press, 1971); Paul Crane and T. A. Larson, "The Chinese Massacre," *Annals of Wyoming* 12, no. 1 (1940): 47–55; 12, no. 2 (1940): 153–60.

13. Pfaelzer, *Driven Out*, 302–4.

14. Sarna, *Minority Faiths*, 307–8.

15. Jacobson, *Whiteness of a Different Color*, 59–63; Pfaelzer, *Driven Out*, 54.

16. For more on the policies that were designed to tear apart Indian communities and tribal lands, including the 1887 Dawes Act, which quartered sections of tribal lands for individual families with the aim of turning them into boarding-schooled Christian farmers in the hopes of "killing the Indian" in order to "save the man," see Michael L. Johnson, *Hunger for the Wild: America's Obsession with the Untamed West* (Lawrence: University Press of Kansas, 2007), 198–99. By the time of the Gold Rush in California (1849), there were an estimated 150,000 to 300,000 Native Americans in California, a number which by 1860 had dwindled to 32,000 due to extermination, malnutrition, disease, and the seizure of land. Newspapers called for "a war of extermination until the last red skin of these tribes has been killed," while others stated, "It is a mercy to the red devils to exterminate them, and a saving of many white lives. Treaties are played out—there is only one kind of treaty that is effective—cold lead." See Pfaelzer, *Driven Out*, 19. On January 29, 1863, Col. Patrick Connor attacked the resistant Shoshone Indians at Bear River, in what is now Idaho, killing an estimated 300 men, women, and children in what Scott Christenson labeled a "wholesale slaughter." Christenson, *Sagwitch: Shoshone Chieftain, Mormon Elder 1822-1887* (Logan: Utah State University Press, 1999), 52. For the American military, this massacre represented a "signal victory," establishing American authority in the northern Rockies and essentially terrorizing Native tribes into submission, bringing forth Conner's promotion to brigadier general for his "heroic conduct" at Bear River. Long, *The Saints and the Union*, 139–41.

17. Hine and Faragher, *Frontiers*, 90–93; Johnson, *Hunger for the Wild*, 139.

18. Again, generals were promoted and soldiers were given Medals of Honor for their bravery and service to their country. Native resistance was broken, the American frontier was considered closed, and progress was assured. Jeffrey Ostler, *The Plains Sioux and U.S. Colonialism from Lewis and Clark to Wounded Knee* (Cambridge: Cambridge University Press, 2004), 345, 361–62.

19. Schaff, *America*, 53; Baird, *Religion in America*, 13.

20. For a similar analysis on this point, see Todd M. Kerstetter, *Inspiration & Innovation: Religion in the American West* (Somerset, NJ: John Wiley, 2015), 163–64.

21. John Hope Franklin and Alfred A. Moss Jr., *From Slavery to Freedom: A History of African Americans*, 7th ed. (New York: Alfred A. Knopf, 1994), 249–50.

22. Legislative and judicial rulings supportive of the Anglo-Protestant majority were crucial in returning white supremacy to a war-torn South. In response to the imagined problem of "lazy blacks" following the emancipation of slavery, infamous Black Codes were initiated throughout the South. Targeting blacks, the Mississippi code forced "all other idle and disorderly persons" (i.e., blacks) to involuntary labor, often at the hands of former slaveholders. Mississippi law ordered that all blacks were to be courteous, dutiful, and diligent employees to their new white employers, in support of a system that kept blacks landless and poor, and once again dependent upon white masters. Cooper and Terrill, *The American South*, 395. In United States v. Reese (1875), the Supreme Court declared that the Fifteenth Amendment did not guarantee suffrage to anyone, while United States v. Cruikshank declared the Enforcement Act of 1870, which guaranteed black suffrage, unconstitutional. Together, these court decisions opened the way for the South to settle its own problems regarding voting standards. Mississippi led the way as it wrote into its constitution a suffrage amendment discouraging the black vote, including a poll tax, literacy tests, and a property ownership standard. Louisiana added a "grandfather clause" to its constitution in 1898 which limited suffrage to those whose fathers or grandfathers could vote before January 1, 1867, essentially disenfranchising all blacks. Tennessee outlawed racial intermarriage in 1870, and in 1875 initiated the first set of Jim Crow laws. In banning the Civil Rights Act of 1875, the Supreme Court further extended the ban on blacks in public space. Furthering laws on segregation, the Supreme Court upheld segregation as constitutional in the landmark Plessy v. Ferguson decision (1896), legitimating the "separate but equal" doctrine. Franklin explains, "The laws, the courts, the schools and almost every institution in the South favored whites," essentially establishing white supremacy into law, and ensuring a racial definition of "American." Franklin and Moss, *From Slavery to Freedom*, 254, 260, 262–63.

23. Franklin and Moss, *From Slavery to Freedom*. Time and again throughout the nineteenth century, legal interpretations limited the American sense of belonging and public participation to that of white Protestants, allowing

for the reinforcement of a particular religious idealism within American society. Jacobson, *Whiteness of a Different Color*, 302–6. Such idealisms were likewise pushed forth through scientific thought: expanding on his scientific view of natural selection in light of American progress, Charles Darwin argued in a way that would be repeated by minister historians, that history too was marked by natural selection, and that human progress included the survival of the fittest. As he demonstrates, nineteenth-century science complemented both social and political thought. "There is apparently much truth in the belief that the wonderful progress of the United States, as well as the character of the people, are the results of natural selection; for the more energetic, restless, and courageous men from all parts of Europe have emigrated during the last ten or twelve generations to that great country, and have there succeeded best." Darwin then quotes minister Foster Barham Zincke (a vicar, author, and traveler) to further his point on this new American race: "'All other series of events—as that which resulted in the culture of mind in Greece, and that which resulted in the Empire of Rome—only appear to have purpose and value when viewed in connection with, or rather as subsidiary to, the great stream of Anglo-Saxon emigration to the West.'" Charles Darwin, *The Descent of Man: And Selection in Relation to Sex*, 2nd ed. (London: John Murray, 1888), 1:218–19.

24. James Russell Lowell, "Democracy" [1884], in *Essays, Poems, and Letters*, ed. William Smith Clark II (New York: Odyssey, 1948), 147.

25. John J. Appel, "From Shanties to Lace Curtains: The Irish Image in Puck, 1876–1910," *Comparative Studies in Society and History* 13, no. 4 (October 1971): 369–70.

26. Erika Lee, *At American's Gates: Chinese Immigration during the Exclusion Era, 1882–1943* (Chapel Hill: University of North Carolina Press, 2003), 6.

27. Sehat, *The Myth of American Religious Freedom*, 288.

28. Givens, *Viper on the Hearth*, 136–37.

29. William Mulder, "Immigration and the 'Mormon Question': An International Episode." *Western Political Quarterly* 9, no. 2 (June 1956): 417.

30. Brigham H. Roberts, *A Comprehensive History of the Church of Jesus Christ of Latter-day Saints, Century I* (Provo, UT: Brigham Young University Press, 1965), 6:141.

31. Civil liberty and spiritual Christianity, argued Strong, were the two major forces which, "in the past, have contributed most to the elevation of the human race, and they must continue to be, in the future, the most efficient ministers to its progress. It follows, then, that the Anglo-Saxon, as the great representative of these two ideas, the depositary of these two greatest blessings, sustains peculiar relations to the world's future, is divinely commis-

sioned to be, in a peculiar sense, his brother's keeper." Strong then pointed out that, although the Anglo-Saxon race (which he now uses broadly to include all English-speaking peoples) comprises only "one-thirteenth part of mankind, now rules more than one-third of the earth's surface, and more than one-fourth of its people." Strong, *Our Country*, 200–2.

32. Jacobson, *Whiteness*, 23, 68–75.

33. Davis, "Some Themes of Counter-Subversion," 213.

34. Roberts, *Comprehensive History*, 6:141.

35. Mrs. T. B. H. Stenhouse, *"Tell It All": The Story of a Life's Experience in Mormonism, An Autobiography* (Hartford: A. D. Worthington, 1875); by way of examples, see pp. 130, 135, 139, 251, 310–15, 364, 508; *Ann Eliza Young, Wife No. 19; or, The Story of a Life in Bondage, Being a Complete Expose of Mormonism, and Revealing the Sorrows, Sacrifices and Sufferings of Women in Polygamy, by Ann Eliza Young, Brigham Young's Apostate Wife* (Hartford, CT: Dustin, Gilman, 1876), 11, 32, 92–95, 98, 102, and chapter 8, "Troubles Under the New System."

36. Young, *Wife No. 19*, 32.

37. Stenhouse, *Tell It All*, 247; Young, *Wife No. 19*, 7, 400.

38. Mark Twain, *The Innocents Abroad and Roughing It*, ed. Guy Cartwell (New York: Literary Classics of the United States, 1984), For an account of these tales, see pp. 611–16.

39. Givens, *Viper on the Hearth*, 117–30.

40. U.S. Senate, Committee on Education and Labor, Notes of a Hearing before the Committee on Education and Labor, United States Senate, May 7, 1886, on the Proposed Establishment of a School under the Direction of the Industrial Christian Home Association of Utah, to Provide Means of Self-Support for the Dependent Classes in That Territory, and to Aid in the Suppression of Polygamy Therein, by Henry W. Blair, 49th Cong., 1st sess., S. Rept. 1279 (Washington, DC: US Government Printing Office, 1886), 1; Ward Platt, ed., *Methodism and the Republic: A View of the Home Field, Present Conditions, Needs and Possibilities* (Philadelphia: Board of Home Missions and Church Extension of the Methodist Episcopal Church, 1910), 329.

41. *Notes of a Hearing*, 4, 10, 15. This incident illuminates the deep underlying assumptions and prejudices behind the Americanization project that moved to bring into conformity groups deemed inconsistent with prevailing notions of Christian civilization, with Mormonism being its archetype. Religious agendas worked hand in hand with the powers of the state.

42. Ibid., 19.

43. Ibid., 30.

44. Ibid., 43.

45. Ibid., 4.
46. Ibid., 44.
47. Such can be found in the "Minutes of Woman's Mass Indignation Meeting," January 19, 1870, as printed in Roberts, *Comprehensive History*, 5:233.
48. *Notes of a Hearing*, 45–46.
49. "Our Pictures," The Wasp, August 29, 1885.
50. Firmage and Mangrum, Zion in the Courts, 161–62, 199, 201, 235, 239, 242, 256, 329.
51. *Journal of Discourses*, 10:188.
52. See Jeffrey Nichols, *Prostitution, Polygamy, and Power: Salt Lake City 1847–1918* (Urbana: University of Illinois Press, 2002), 13. Taylor and Cannon wrote, "Where in this broad land is the virtue of women so amply guarded or so jealously protected as here? No cry of hungry, naked or outraged humanity has ever ascended to heaven from our borders against the men whom the courts are now so busy in sending to prison and treating as criminals. There was a time in these mountains when adultery, fornication, whoredom and illegitimacy were almost unknown." George Q. Cannon and John Taylor, "AN EPISTLE from the First Presidency: To the Officers and Members of the Church of Jesus Christ of Latter-day Saints," in Clark, *Messages*, 3:38. Mormons were adamant that it was not they that brought lawlessness and sexual immorality to Utah, but non-Mormons, whom they termed "Gentiles." Clark, *Messages*, 3:67.
53. As Brigham Young's biographer John Turner put it, "Brigham Young, who had feared for his life while on the margins of Illinois society, created a climate in which men and women on the margins of Mormon society lived in a similar state of fear." For examples of this violence against sexual deviance and the related Mormon doctrine of "Blood Atonement," see John Turner, *Brigham Young*, 187, 258–59, 262–64. Kathryn M. Daynes, *More Wives Than One: Transformation of the Mormon Marriage System 1840–1910* (Urbana: University of Illinois Press, 2001), 200–2; Clark, *Messages*, 3:39; Gordon, *Mormon Question*, 59, 127; Bigler and Bagley, *The Mormon Rebellion*, 95; Rogers, *Council of Fifty*, 161, 171–72.
54. Strong, *Our Country*, xvii.
55. *Journal of Discourses*, 1:203. Councilor Lorin Farr of the Council of Fifty warned that it wasn't just the U.S. government whose time was short, but warned his quorum members that if they were not awake, the kingdom could very well be taken from them and given to another people. See Rogers, *Council of Fifty*, 280.
56. Lee, *At America's Gates*, 29.
57. It is the struggle between this duality and its linguistic exchange, marks

philosopher Michel Foucault, which informs our governing institutions as pertaining to group classification. See Edward W. Said, "Michel Foucault, 1926–1984," in Jonathan Arac, *After Foucault: Humanistic Knowledge, Postmodern Challenges* (New Brunswick: Rutgers University Press, 1988), 1–12; Michel Foucault, *The Order of Things: An Archaeology of the Human Sciences*, ([1971]; rpt., New York: Pantheon Books, 1994), xxi.

58. U.S. Congress, Enforcement of the Anti-Polygamy Act, Letter from the Secretary of the Interior, Transmitting Certain Petitions for Enforcing Anti-polygamy Act of 1862, by Samuel J. Randall, 45th Cong., 3d sess., H. Doc. 58 (Washington, DC: US Government Printing Office, 1879), 1–6.

59. Firmage and Mangrum, *Zion in the Courts*, 239.

60. Because of the virtual "blank check" given to territorial officials by Congress as a result of the Edmunds law, and the significant boost in manpower, what Mormon historians call "the Raid" against the Mormon people had begun. For more on this, see Arrington, *Great Basin Kingdom*, 359. In this raid, windows were peeped in, homes were broken into, men and women were pulled from their beds and arrested, women were forced to describe sexual relationships with their alleged husbands, and children were confronted by city officials to reveal the relationships of their parents. Polygamous men, or even those under suspicion of polygamy, were forced into hiding for fear of unfair conviction. Firmage and Mangrum, *Zion in the Courts*, 172, 173.

61. U.S. Congress, Committee on the Judiciary, Suppression of Polygamy in Utah, by John Randolf Tucker, 49th Cong., 1st sess., H. Rept. 2735 (Washington, DC: US Government Printing Office, 1886), 6–7.

62. Arrington, *Great Basin Kingdom*, 358; Rogers, *Council of Fifty*, 13–14n41.

63. Arrington, *Great Basin Kingdom*, 279–93, 313–22; Arrington, Fox, and May, *Building the City of God*, 85, 90.

64. Arrington, Fox, and May, *Building the City of God*, 82, 151, 269.

65. In a pamphlet sent out in 1875 to the general membership of the church by Mormon authorities, it was noted, "One of the great evils with which our own nation is menaced at the present time is the wonderful growth of wealth in the hands of a comparatively few individuals." This pamphlet continues that the very freedom our fathers fought for are challenged by this trend. Cooperative enterprises were formed to combat this very danger, at least in part. Clark, *Messages*, 2:268. This policy would soon change, however much attempts were made to retain the underlying sentiment. In 1882, President John Taylor wrote an epistle to the various leadership branches of the church: "A feeling had been manifested by some of our brethren to branch out into mercantile business on their own account," and the idea was presented that "if people would be governed by correct

principles, laying aside covetousness and eschewing chicanery and fraud, dealing honestly and conscientiously with others as they would like others to deal with them, that there would be no objection on our part for our own brethren to do these things; that it was certainly much better for them to embark in such enterprises than our enemies." Taylor then continued, "Our cooperative institutions generally had done very well in subserving the interests of the people; and if other institutions should be introduced in the various stakes by wise, honorable, just and honest men, who had at heart the spirit of co-operation, and who practiced the principle and carried it out, there would be no objection to their calling upon the people to sustain the same principle in anything that they might introduce by way of financial enterprises among themselves." In short, though cooperation was ideal, it was only now acceptable to engage in market capitalism so long as one retained a cooperative heart. Ibid., 2:334–39.

66. Firmage and Mangrum, *Zion in the Courts*, 165.

67. For more on John R. Tucker and his efforts against Mormon polygamy, see Patrick Q. Mason, *The Mormon Menace: Violence and Anti-Mormonism in the Postbellum South* (New York: Oxford University Press, 2011), 91; Foster, *Moral Reconstruction*, 63, 130. See also Larson, *"Americanization" of Utah*, 208.

68. U.S. Congress, Suppression of Polygamy, 10.

69. As quoted in Arrington, *Great Basin Kingdom*, 358.

70. As quoted in Roberts, *Comprehensive History*, 6:60.

71. As related in Bitton, *George Q. Cannon*, 252–53.

72. Explained Mormon president John Taylor, "When this infamous Edmunds law was passed, I saw that there were features in that which were contrary to law, violative of the Constitution, and contrary to justice and the rights and the freedom of men. But I said to myself I will let the law take its course; I will place myself in accordance with it, so far as I can. Did I do it? I did." *Journal of Discourses* (February 1, 1885), 26:151. See also Larson, *"Americanization" of Utah*, 126.

73. Associated Press interview as quoted in Roberts, *Comprehensive History*, 6:152.

74. John Taylor and George Q. Cannon, "AN EPISTLE of the First Presidency to the Church," in Clark, *Messages*, 3:69.

75. Clark, Messages, 3:32; *Journal of Discourses* 23:110–11.

76. Hatch, *Democratization*, 71. This "American Passover" was a day laden with deep symbolism, evoking with the flag what theorist Catherine Bell described as a "summarizing symbol" that conflated identity with history and a deeper core value system, inspiring under a more visible banner an

emotion that evokes a "collective sense of 'we'—as in 'our' flag." Catherine Bell, *Ritual: Perspectives and Dimensions* (New York: Oxford University Press, 1997), 157.

77. "Would to God, both for your sakes and ours," noted Douglass, that the "great principles of political freedom and of natural justice, embodied in that Declaration of Independence, extended to us." The Fourth of July "reveals . . . more than all other days of the year, the gross injustice and cruelty to which he is the constant victim. To him your celebration is a sham; your boasted liberty an unholy license; your national greatness, swelling vanity; your sounds of rejoicing are empty and heartless; your denunciation of tyrants, brass-fronted impudence; your shouts of liberty and equality, hollow mockery; your prayers and hymns, your sermons and thanksgivings, with all your religious parade and solemnity, are to him mere bombast, fraud, deception, impiety, and hypocrisy—a thin veil to cover up crimes which would disgrace a nation of savages. There is not a nation of the earth guilty of practices more shocking and bloody than are the people of these United States at this very hour." Frederick Douglass, "What, to the Slave, Is the Fourth of July?," in *Lift Every Voice: African American Oratory, 1787–1901*, edited by Philip S. Foner and Robert Branham, rev. ed. (Tuscaloosa: University of Alabama Press, 1997), 255–58.

78. The association declared, "Yet we cannot forget, even in this glad hour, that while all men of every race, and clime, and condition, have been invested with the full rights of citizenship under our hospitable flag, all women still suffer the degradation of disfranchisement." See National Woman Suffrage Association, "Declaration and Protest of the Women of the United States by the National Woman Suffrage Association" Philadelphia, July 4, 1876 (Pdf, https://www.loc.gov/item/rbpe.16000300/).

79. As found in Gary L. Bunker and Davis Bitton, *The Mormon Graphic Image, 1834–1914: Cartoons, Caricatures, and Illustrations* (Utah: University of Utah Press, 1983), 54.

80. As printed in Roberts, *Comprehensive History*, 6:160–61.

81. Bunker and Bitton, Graphic Image, 54.

82. "Salt Lake Treason," *Western Rural and American Stockman: A Weekly for the Farm, Field & Fireside* 23, no. 29 (July 18, 1885): 456.

83. Larson, "Americanization" of Utah, 140–41.

84. As recorded in Roberts, *Comprehensive History*, 6:161–62.

85. Larson, "Americanization" of Utah, 140–41.

86. "The 'Mass' Meeting," *Deseret News*, July 22, 1885.

87. William E. Moore, comp., *The Presbyterian Digest of 1886: A Compend of the Acts and Deliverances of the General Assembly of the Presbyterian*

*Church in the United States of America, compiled by the Order and Authority of the General Assembly* (Philadelphia: Presbyterian Board of Publication and Sabbath Work, 1886), 608.

88. Albert Barnes, *The Church and Slavery* (Philadelphia: Parry & McMillan, 1857), 37.

89. Larson, *"Americanization" of Utah*, 140.

90. Bunker and Bitton, *Graphic Image*, 55; Larson, *"Americanization" of Utah*, 142.

91. Taylor et al., "AN ADDRESS to the Latter-day Saints in the Rocky Mountain Region and Throughout the World," in Clark, *Messages*, 3:20.

92. John Taylor and George Q. Cannon, "TO THE PRESIDENTS OF STAKES and their Counselors, the Bishops and their Counselors, and the Latter-day Saints Generally," in Clark, *Messages*, 3:16.

93. Leonard Woolsey Bacon, "Polygamy in New England," *Princeton Review* 2 (July–December 1882): 41.

94. Bitton, *George Q. Cannon*, 178.

95. *Journal of Discourses*, 23:210.

96. Ibid., 26:144.

97. Ibid., 23:210, 242, 264, 267; 25:70; 26:104; Clark, *Messages*, 3:17, 29, 34, 37, 49, 69, 75, 110, 143. The optimism that Mormon leadership hailed to its general membership amidst this period of severe governmental oppression is best stated in the First Presidency epistle read in General Conference April 8, 1887, at Provo: "Such periods appear to be necessary in the progress and perfecting of all created things, as much so in the history of peoples and communities as of individuals. These periods of transition have most generally their pains, perplexities and sufferings. The present is no exception to the rule. But out of apparent evil, Providence will bring abundant good, and the lesson which the signs of the times should teach us is one of patience, endurance, and calm reliance on the Lord. The result will be that we shall be stronger, wiser, purer, happier, for the experience gained, and the work of the Lord, delivered by His Omnipotence from all the snares set for its retardation, or plans laid for its destruction, will yet triumph gloriously over all its foes, and the infinite atonement of the Redeemer will accomplish its perfect work. The final victory of the Saints is certain; after the trial comes the reward." Clark, *Messages*, 3:127. These sentiments paralleled Mormon scripture: "It must needs be, that there is an opposition in all things. If not so, . . . righteousness could not be brought to pass." Book of Mormon: 2 Nephi 2:11.

98. Clark, *Messages*, 3:173–76. Mormons anticipated an imminent fulfillment of their own literalist visions of the kingdom and their anticipated prom-

inent role within it. Apostle Franklin D. Richards said in General Conference in 1882, "While this is upon the nation and until they wash their hands of it [deaths of Joseph and Hyrum Smith], we can but look upon them with sorrow and apprehension and dread for thus acquiescing in breaking and overriding the fundamental laws of the land." *Journal of Discourses* 23:112. With continued resentment toward the injustices done against them in Missouri and Illinois, Mormons in the 1880s were not interested in national reconciliation, but instead looked toward its annihilation through Christ's return to Earth. Concerning this return, many Mormons, including Wilford Woodruff, were promised through their Patriarchal Blessings that they could look forward to about the year 1890 for the grand event. See B. Carmon Hardy, *Solemn Covenant: The Mormon Polygamous Passage* (Urbana: University of Illinois Press, 1992), 151–52. For further examples of this prophecy, see H. Michael Marquardt, ed., *Early Patriarchal Blessings of the Church of Jesus Christ of Latter-day Saints* (Salt Lake City: Smith-Pettit Foundation, 2007), 74, 143; Henry Ballard, Henry Ballard Journal, 1852–1885, Joel E. Ricks Collection of Transcription (Logan: Library of the Utah State Agricultural College), 1:67. Special thanks to Joe Geisner for bringing these sources and this "1890 countdown" to my attention.

99. *Journal of Discourses* 25:350. President Wilford Woodruff records this revelation in his journal on November 24, 1889: "The wicked are fast ripening in iniquity, and they will be cut off by the judgments of God. Great events await you and this generation, and are nigh at your doors. . . . I the Lord will deliver my Saints from the domination of the wicked in mine own due time and way." Wilford Woodruff, Wilford Woodruff's Journal, 1833–1898: Typescript, ed. Scott G. Kenney (Midvale, UT: Signature Books, 1985), 9:69–70, 75.

100. Clark, *Messages*, 3:176–78.

101. Samuel Harris, "The Millenarian Conference," in *New Englander and Yale Review* 38, no. 148 (January 1879): 114, 145.

102. Marsden, *Fundamentalism*, 51, 54.

103. Ibid., 86–89.

104. Sehat, *Myth of American Religious Freedom*, 179.

105. Mendenhall, "The Mormon Problem," 306, 311, 314.

106. Further details of these events can be found in Bitton, *George Q. Cannon*, 218–21.

107. Ibid., 218.

108. Reynolds v. United States, 98 U.S. 145 (1879), 150, 165.

109. Gordon, *Mormon Question*, 140; Thomas Laycock, "Manhood and Womanhood," *Appleton's Journal: A Magazine of General Literature* 1, no. 10

(June 5, 1869): 312; Reynolds v. United States, 166. Such comments by Lieber were conservative and widely embraced. According to Nancy Cott, "The founders learned to think of marriage and the form of government as mirroring each other." Cott argued that Enlightenment thinker Montesquieu "initiated what became a formulaic Enlightenment association of polygamy with despotism. The harem stood for tyrannical rule, political corruption, coercion, elevation of the passions over reason, selfishness, hypocrisy—all the evils that virtuous republicans and enlightened thinkers wanted to avoid. Monogamy, in contrast, stood for a government of consent, moderation, and political liberty." Nancy Cott, *Public Vows: A History of Marriage and the Nation* (Cambridge, MA: Harvard University Press, 2000), 10, 22.

110. Reynolds v. United States, 163, 165.

111. Sehat, *Myth of American Religious Liberty*, 170–71.

112. Reynolds v. United States, 168.

113. *Journal of Discourses*, 23:73.

114. Ibid., 23:67.

115. Ibid., 23:73.

116. Firmage and Mangrum, *Zion in the Courts*, 234–35. See also Gordon, *Mormon Question*, 224–28.

117. Davis v. Beason 133 U.S. 333 (1890), 8.

118. Ibid., 5.

119. Ibid., 5–6.

120. In what legal expert Winnifred F. Sullivan explained as an act that rendered the disestablishment clause of religion obsolete, the Court took upon itself to define religion so as to demonstrate when its free expression is breached—thus excluding the possibility of religion to define itself, thereby rendering religious freedom an "impossibility." Its reference to Mormonism's loss of religious liberty in the Reynolds v. United States (1878) case is significant. Winnifred F. Sullivan, *The Impossibility of Religious Freedom* (Princeton: Princeton University Press, 2005), 8, 26, 29, 136–37, 151, 159. Kenneth R. Craycraft went so far as to argue that "the establishment of religious freedom" itself, and not just the Court's tendency to define religion, "is necessarily in the establishment of certain exclusionary claims about religion," thus making religious freedom itself a myth. Craycraft, *The American Myth of Religious Freedom* (Dallas: Spence, 1999), 27.

121. Robert G. Ingersoll was a well-known secularist-agnostic who ran for president in 1880. His push for the privatization of religion included even Protestant Christianity. Ingersoll's platform was: "TOTAL SEPARATION OF CHURCH AND STATE, to be guaranteed by amendment of the United

States Constitution: including the equitable taxation of church property, secularization of the public schools, abrogation of Sabbatarian laws, abolition of chaplaincies, prohibition of public appropriations for religious purposes and all other measures necessary to the same general end." See Philip Hamburger, *Separation of Church and State* (Cambridge: Harvard University Press, 2002), 327.

122. *Journal of Discourses*, 24:42–43.

123. Foster, *Moral Reconstruction*, 65.

124. Late Corporation of the Church of Jesus Christ of Latter-Day Saints v. United States, 136 U.S. I (1890), 49, 63–64.

125. Concerning these challenges: These two decades represented a time when such presumptions over the family and home were being questioned and doubted, not just by Mormons, but by the more radical wing of the feminist movement as led by Elizabeth Cady Stanton, together with an 1886 study on marriage by Congress and the Evangelical Alliance that found the institution of marriage under duress. See Sehat, *Myth of American Religious Freedom*, 139, 146.

126. Late Corporation v. United States, 63, 65.

127. A related point of contention that Mormons had with the Supreme Court and the rest of mainstream America was when and to what degree polygamy was rendered unconstitutional. The church was emphatic that Reynolds had only upheld the Morrill Act of 1862, leaving some technical wiggle room when it came to the constitutionality of polygamy, legitimating the continued Mormon opposition to it while simultaneously calling for obedience to the laws of the land. It was not until the Supreme Court decision of 1890 in Late Corporation v. United States that the Mormon Church was forced to acquiesce and finally accepted the constitutionality of anti-Mormon legislations. For a detailed argument between Mormon president Joseph F. Smith and Attorney Tayler on this question, see U.S. Senate, Committee on Privileges and Elections, Proceedings before the Committee on Privileges and Elections of the United States Senate in the Matter of the Protests against the Right of Hon. Reed Smoot, a Senator from the State of Utah, to Hold His Seat, by Julius C. Burrows and Joseph Benson Foraker, 59th Cong., 1st sess. S. Rept. 486 (Washington, DC: U.S. Government Printing Office, 1906), 101–5 (hereafter Smoot Hearings). Consequently, as Mormons understood themselves to be law-observant citizens, as argued in the Woodruff Manifesto of 1890 (which essentially ended new contracts of plural marriage), other Americans pointed to nearly three decades of defiance toward all branches of government, be it judicial, legislative, or executive.

128. Reeve, *Making Space*, 6–7.

129. Inspired by theorist and philosopher William James, cultural historian Ann Taves admonishes an approach to the study of American religious experience that focuses "our attention from the study of religion per se to the processes by which religious and nonreligious phenomena are made and unmade." As such, we "lose a sense of religion (or not-religion) as a substantive thing." See *Taves, Fits, Trances, & Visions*, 360–61.

130. Sehat, *Myth of American Religious Freedom*, 180.

131. Foster, *Moral Reconstruction*, 91.

132. This position stands in direct contrast to more popular historiographical portrayals of the American West. For example, Ferenc M. Szasz and Margaret Connell Szasz suggest that "with a few notable exceptions, tolerance and openness characterized the world of western faiths." "Religion and Spirituality," in *The Oxford History of the American West*, ed. Clyde A. Milner II, Carol A. O'Connor, and Martha Sandweiss (New York: Oxford University Press, 1994), 360.

## CHAPTER 4

1. Richard D. White Jr., *Roosevelt the Reformer: Theodore Roosevelt as Civil Service Commissioner*, 1889–1895 (Tuscaloosa: University of Alabama Press, 2003), 117; Hine and Faragher, Frontiers, 178, 191.

2. Josiah Strong, *The New Era; or, The Coming Kingdom* (New York: Baker and Taylor, 1893), x–xiii, 143, 344–45.

3. In a tone of prophetic utterance and in response to the new city working class, Strong cautioned that if the churches did not "awake to their duty and their opportunity," then the "present tendencies will continue until our cities are literally heathenized." Calling out the tendency to appear as a type of indifferent "religious coterie of 'steepled club,' existing expressly for 'our sort of folks,'" Strong condemned the popular elitist snobbery of many Protestant churches. Reverend De Witt Talmage of the Central Presbyterian Church in Brooklyn best exemplified this disgust of the working class, warning against "mixing up the common people with the uncommon." As Talmage continued, such a course would "keep one-half of Christians sick at their stomach. If you are going to kill the church thus with bad smells, I will have nothing to do with this work of evangelization." Ibid., 201, 209–11, 253, 255. See also Paul F. Boller, *American Thought in Transition: The Impact of Evolutionary Naturalism, 1865–1900* (Chicago: Rand McNally, 1969), 118–19.

4. Taylor, *A Secular Age*, 1.

5. Benedict Anderson, *Imagined Communities: Reflections on the Origin and Spread of Nationalism*, rev. ed. (New York: Verso, 1991), 5–7, 12.

6. Historian of religion and American culture George M. Marsden argues the failure of postmillenarianism when challenged by modernity. *Fundamentalism*, 50–55. As such, the more "socially responsible" postmillennialism was abandoned for a more isolationistic and pessimistic premillenarianistic worldview of politics. Ferenc M. Szasz, *The Divided Mind of Protestant America, 1880–1930* (Tuscaloosa: University of Alabama Press, 1982), 72–75, also offers an important overview of the bible conferences that continued to grow since 1876, popularizing a form of premillennialism that would continue to define itself against the growing tides of both modernity and liberal Christianity. Adherents of this reactionary movement against modernity and liberalism soon self-titled themselves the "Fundamentalists."

7. Marsden, *Fundamentalism*, 49; Historian Grant Underwood, *The Millenarian World of Early Mormonism* (Urbana: University of Illinois Press, 1993), 3–5, 8, 41, 74, recognized that the "simplistic differentiations about whether Christ will come before (pre-) or after (post-) the millennium are hardly sufficient to distinguish these two schools of thought." The eschatology of Mormonism, for example, "is thoroughly premillennial," despite its postmillennial evangelical drive, its social sense of responsibility, and its heavy political aspirations. As a general rule, premillennialists are literalists, while postmillennialists were more allegorists. Mormonism, however, represented a mix of figurative, literal, and allusive tendencies in their biblical interpretations. Therefore, the major differences between the two camps can be seen as differences of scriptural interpretation on such key points as what the kingdom will look like, humanity's role (or non-role) in bringing forth this kingdom, the need for evangelism, and, importantly, the relation of the state in this coming messianic millennial kingdom.

8. For an important resource dealing with the religious underpinnings of the American progressive movement and its competing implicit and explicit engagements with religion, see Robert M. Crunden, Ministers of Reform: The Progressives' Achievement in American Civilization, 1889–1920 (New York: Basic Books, 1982). Throughout this text, Crunden demonstrates that progressivism, despite its complicated relationship with religion, largely gained its moral compass from within an earlier religious framework. These moral frameworks were then brought forth to sacralize progressive reform efforts to better human society.

9. Taylor, *A Secular Age*, 1–3.

10. Strong, *The New Era*, 70.

11. Nineteenth-century Protestants in America allied themselves with the American philosophy of Francis Bacon, who had established that careful

observation and classification of the facts presented the avenue toward scientific truth. This approach was connected to the popular notion of "common sense realism," which asserted that things were just as they appeared to be to the common observer. As Marsden, Fundamentalism, 7, 14–15, notes, far from excluding religion, as the next century would do, scientists could focus on theology as well as geology, needing only to classify the certainties of the latter and avoid speculative hypotheses. "The Bible, of course, revealed the moral law; but the faculty of common sense, which agreed with Scripture, was a universal standard. According to Common Sense philosophy, one can intuitively know the first principles of morality as certainly as one can apprehend other essential aspects of reality." See also pp. 24, 50, for more on Beecher and the larger theological connection between science and the kingdom of God, which was to be a literal historical event, taking place "in this world," not otherworldly, but "here and now." Tuveson, Redeemer Nation, 29–30, had earlier argued that redemption of society had its appointed progression, and natural laws could not be ignored. Upon similar grounds of social progress, Henry Ward Beecher would take up the topic of evolution and its compatibility with religion in his *Evolution and Religion* (Boston: Pilgrim Press, [1885]).

12. Strong, *The New Era*, 11, 12, 22, 30.

13. Stanley J. Tambiah, *Magic, Science, Religion, and the Scope of Rationality* (New York: Cambridge University Press, 1990), 17; J. Edward Larson, *Summer for the Gods: The Scopes Trial and America's Continuing Debate over Science and Religion* (New York: Basic Books, 2006), 23.

14. Strong, *The New Era*, 123–24.

15. Boller, *American Thought in Transition*, 22. For more on Hodge and his contempt for this animosity toward religion by men of science, see James Turner, *Without God, Without Creed: The Origins of Unbelief in America* (Baltimore: Johns Hopkins University Press, 1985), 123.

16. German philosopher Friedrich Nietzsche, following his intellectual forerunners Karl Marx and Ludwig Feuerbach, tore apart traditional notions of good and evil in 1887. He questioned the very value of values, noting that morals are all manufactured to oppress lower classes, priests being the worst offenders and classifying "all religions" as being "at bottom systems of cruelty." Friedrich Nietzsche, *The Birth of Tragedy* and *The Genealogy of Morals*, trans. Francis Golffing (New York: Anchor Books, 1956 [1870–71] [1887]), 167, 192. According to sociologist Christian Smith, editor of *The Secular Revolution: Power, Interests, and Conflict in the Secularization of American Public Life* (Berkeley: University of California Press, 2003), 1, 4, 62, this drastic societal shift can be attributed to the "Secular Revolution,"

which occurred between 1870 and 1930. The secularization of American public life represented more of a "contested revolutionary struggle than a natural evolutionary progression."

17. Pointing to attempts by Lyman Beecher and the "godly Beecher family" to adapt to the new social, economic, and intellectual standards, James Turner argues that it was American Protestant leaders who exposed the inadequacy of their own arguments and thus strangled God out of American public life, rather than those of the "godless Robert Ingersol." Turner, *Without God*, xiii, 179, 181, 199–202, 225.

18. George Marsden, historian of American Christianity, shows that as the popularity of premillenarianism rose near the end of the century, postmillenarianism did not disappear, but rather transferred hope for the kingdom from this world to the heavens. Although the Social Gospel movement, which emphasized Christianity's liberal responsibility over society, demonstrates a continued interest in a type of here-and-now amelioration, postmillennialism in general became secularized in the sense that it dropped many earlier supernatural expectations, reimagining the kingdom as more figurative and spiritual than literal and tangible. Marsden, *Fundamentalism*, 48–51. For early controversies surrounding Darwinism and religion, see Bert J. Loewenberg, "The Controversy over Evolution in New England 1859–1873," *New England Quarterly* 8, no. 2 (June 1935): 232–57.

19. C. T. McIntire, "Transcending Dichotomies in History and Religion," *History and Theory*, Theme Issue 45, no. 4 (December 2006): 83, 86; Michael Lambek, "Provincializing God? Provocations from an Anthropology of Religion," in *Religion: Beyond a Concept*, ed. Hent de Vries (New York: Fordham University Press, 2008), 121.

20. Eric J. Sharpe, *Comparative Religion: A History* (La Salle, IL: Open Court, 1986), 1, 46–48, 56–57, 82–83, 89; Sydney E. Ahlstrom, *The American Protestant Encounter with World Religions, The Brewer Lectures on Comparative Religion* (Beloit, WI: Beloit College, 1962), 10–12, 25.

21. John H. Barrows, ed., *The World's Parliament of Religions: An Illustrated and Popular Story of the World's First Parliament of Religions, Held in Chicago in Connection with the Columbian Exposition of 1893* (Chicago: Parliament Publishing, 1893), 2:1198, 1201. Indeed, as Ahlstrom notes, church historians and bible critics were "the real groundbreakers and methodological pioneers of the history of religions." Ahlstrom, *American Protestant Encounter with World Religions*, 8.

22. Ahlstrom, *American Protestant Encounter with World Religions*, 10–12.

23. David Goldfield et al., *The American Journey: A History of the United States* (Upper Saddle River, NJ: Prentice-Hall, 1998), 2:594; Reeve, *Making Space*, 8.

24. Henry Warner Bowden, *Church History in the Age of Science: Historiographical Patterns in the United States 1876–1918* (Carbondale: Southern Illinois University Press, 1991 reprint), xiii, 8–9, 14, 43, 49, 51, 226.

25. For a discussion of history as Kant's "prophetic history of humanity," see Jergen Habermas, *The Structural Transformation of the Public Sphere: An Inquiry into a Category of Bourgeois Society*, trans. Thomas Burger (Cambridge: MIT Press, 1989), 113–17.

26. Wilbur R. Jacobs, ed., *Frederick Jackson Turner: The Frontier in American History* (Tucson: University of Arizona Press, 1986), xvii.

27. After reading Turner's Frontier Thesis, Woodrow Wilson called for new frontiers in the Indies and Far Pacific, being sentiments upheld by another Turnerian imperialist, Theodore Roosevelt. Hine and Faragher, *Frontiers*, 198. Turner notes Wilson's acceptance of his views here, *Frederick Jackson Turner, The Frontier in American History* (New York: Henry Holt, 1921), 1n1.

28. John P. Burris, *Exhibiting Religion: Colonialism and Spectacle at International Expositions 1851–1893* (Charlottesville: University Press of Virginia, 2001), 122–23, 137. See also Tomoko Masuzawa, *The Invention of World Religion; or, How European Universalism Was Preserved in the Language of Pluralism* (Chicago: University of Chicago Press, 2005), 126. Although her entire book expounds on this connection in the creation of the study of "world religion," chapter 4, "Buddhism, a World Religion," demonstrates that Buddhism was rather born in a European workshop in ways that allowed European colonialists to control it and mark important boundaries of power and religious legitimacy. See also Randall Styers, *Making Magic: Religion, Magic, & Science in the Modern World* (New York: Oxford University Press, 2004), 16; David Chidester, *Savage Systems: Colonialism and Comparative Religion in Southern Africa* (Charlottesville: University Press of Virginia, 1996). The Columbian Exposition of 1893 was an example of this complex interweaving of the natural sciences and colonial power, as it graphically juxtaposed the fruits of modern human progress and racial supremacy with carefully selected examples of human depravity and ignorance.

29. Smith, *Virgin Land*, 89, 99, 107, 111, 192.

30. "It was the nationalizing tendency of the West that transformed the democracy of Jefferson into the national republicanism of Monroe and the democracy of Andrew Jackson." The focus, then, was on the tendencies of the western frontier, due to its unique geographic dynamics, and how those tendencies brought actual visible social, economic, and political change. The historian's focus, then, was that of the observable and empirical. Turner, *The Frontier*, 28–29.

31. For more on this cultural transition in regard to the American frontier, see

Johnson, *Hunger for the Wild*, 190.

32. Turner, *The Frontier*, 4.

33. Ibid., 28–29; Hofstadter, *The Progressive Historians*, 109.

34. *Picturesque Chicago and Guide to the World's Fair Issued by the Religious Herald, and Presented to Its Subscribers as a Souvenir of Fifty Years Publication of the Paper* (Hartford: D. S. Moseley, 1893), preface.

35. Richard Hughes Seager, *The World's Parliament of Religions: The East/West Encounter, Chicago, 1893* (Bloomington: Indiana University Press, 2009), 25. Utah's official recorder of the fair wrote of the Midway, "For many, the Midway provided necessary psychological comfort, as it restored feelings of superiority amidst intimidating innovations and ideas, as well as challenging and disorienting worldviews and cultures. The lessons of the Midway were valuable, aside from the amusement they afforded. One could learn a great deal about the strange peoples who inhabit other portions of the globe. But for the Midway, many men, and women, too, would have gone from the Exposition to an insane asylum. It furnished rest and recreation to the mind, which it would have been impossible to obtain in any other way. Many weary mortals entered the portal of the Midway after having tramped for hours among the bewildering scenes of the Exposition proper until they were so confused that they could not realize what they were doing, and suddenly remembered that they were on the earth and at the World's Fair. Whereas, if they had gone directly home, their rest would have been broken, their minds confused, resulting in many mental wrecks. It was the change of scene and the amusement which the Midway afforded that was absolutely necessary to restore rational thought and regulate the machinery of the mind so that it would resume its normal condition." E. A. McDaniel, *Utah at the World's Columbian Exposition* (Salt Lake City: Press of the Salt Lake Lithographing Co., 1894), 164.

36. This Auxiliary included 224 General Divisions within twenty Departments. Seager, *Parliament of Religions*, xx; Richard H. Seager, ed., *The Dawn of Religious Pluralism: Voices from the World's Parliament of Religions, 1893* (La Salle, IL: Open Court Publishing, 1993), 4.

37. The Parliament of Religion itself housed forty-six General Divisions, being a seventeen-day-long event that attracted an estimated seven hundred thousand visitors. Charles C. Bonney, *World's Congress Addresses* (Chicago: Open Court Publishing, 1900), iii; Seager, *The Dawn of Religious Pluralism*, 4; Burris, Exhibiting Religion, 98–99.

38. Quoted in Barrows, *World's Parliament of Religions*, 1:39.

39. Seager, *The Dawn of Religious Pluralism*, 6–7.

40. John Henry Barrows, *Parliament of Religions at the World's Fair* (New York:

Funk and Wagnalls, 1892), 458; "Religious Forces at the Fair," *New York Times*, July 11, 1892.

41. Barrows, *World's Parliament of Religions*, 1:24–25, 39, 60.

42. Judith Snodgrass, *Presenting Japanese Buddhism to the West: Orientalism, Occidentalism, and the Columbian Exposition* (Chapel Hill: University of North Carolina Press, 2003), 46–47; Carrie Tirado Bramen, *The Uses of Variety: Modern Americanism and the Quest for National Distinctiveness* (Cambridge: Harvard University Press, 2000), 259, 265.

43. Snodgrass, *Presenting Japanese Buddhism*, 51.

44. Barrows, *World's Parliament of Religions*, 1:60.

45. As quoted on the front of Barrows' two-volume history and speech compilation of the parliament, World's Parliament of Religions.

46. Strong, *The New Era*, 16.

47. Barrows, *World's Parliament of Religions*, 1:36, 56.

48. Burris notes that for Swedenborg, Bonney's source of inspiration, "irreligion" meant "lack of religion." As he explained, "To be religious meant 'to acknowledge God, and to refrain from evil because it is contrary to God.' These two acts 'make religion to be religion.'" To be able to "acknowledge God," however, was a possibility open only to certain cultural groups, leaving others altogether incapable of such and thus unable to "refrain from evil." Such groups would have been necessarily sidelined, as was Mormonism. See Burris, *Exhibiting Religion*, 147–48.

49. Richard Hughes Seager, "The Two Parliaments, the 1893 Original and the Centennial of 1993: A Historian's View," in *The Community of Religions: Voices and Images of the Parliament of the World's Religions*, ed. Wayne Teasdale and George F. Cairns (New York: Continuum, 1996), 25.

50. Bonney, *World's Congress Addresses*, 6–7; Barrows, *World's Parliament of Religions*, 1:18; Seager, *Dawn of Religious Pluralism*, 4.

51. Bonney, *World's Congress Addresses*, 5–7.

52. Quoted in Leigh E. Schmidt, *Restless Souls: The Making of American Spirituality, From Emerson to Oprah* (Berkeley: University of California Press, 2005), 106–7; Walter R. Houghton, ed., *Neely's History of the Parliament of Religions and Religious Congresses at the World's Columbian Exposition*, 3rd ed. (Chicago: F. T. Neely, 1893), 364.

53. As Higginson understood it, science provided means whereby one could get beyond traditional "methods of authority" and thereby strip religion down to its core "essence," in which even the "humblest individual thinker" could grasp and learn from, having "not only one of these vast faiths but all of them at his side." J. W. Hanson, ed., *The World's Congress of Religions: The Addresses and Papers Delivered before the Parliament and an Abstract of the*

*Congresses Held in the Art Institute, Chicago, Illinois, U.S.A., Under the Auspices of The World's Columbian Exposition, Profusely Illustrated* (Chicago: International Publishing, 1894), 265.

54. For a description of this "rationality," see Tambiah, *Magic, Science, Religion*, 115; Russell T. McCutcheon argues that those who create this measuring rod in which to compare religion become themselves manufacturers of the phenomenon itself, rather than mere observers and interpreters of the phenomenon. McCutcheon, *Manufacturing Religion*, 14. For more on this artificial construction of religion as an outgrowth of the Enlightenment, see William T. Cavanaugh, *The Myth of Religious Violence: Secular Ideology and the Roots of Modern Conflict* (New York: Oxford University Press, 2009); Fitzgerald, *Ideology*; Talal Asad, *Formations of the Secular: Christianity, Islam, Modernity* (Stanford: Stanford University Press, 2003).

55. Cavanaugh, *Myth of Religious Violence*, 81.

56. Richard Wentz explains, "In other words, the modern understanding of 'secular' is satisfied with a world of observable data—the thingification of existence. 'Secular,' therefore, came to stand for the world unto itself (whatever that may mean)." As Wentz further elaborates, "There is no 'conflict' [between the religious and the secular] in a traditional society because there is no 'science,' no 'religion.'" Wentz, *Culture of Religious Pluralism*, 78, 87.

57. Wilfred Cantwell Smith, *The Meaning and End of Religion* (Minneapolis: Fortress Press, 1991), 51.

58. Houghton, *Neely's History*, 364–67.

59. This observation closely follows that of McIntire, "Transcending Dichotomies," 89.

60. Ahlstrom, *The American Protestant Encounter with World Religions*, 26.

61. "Study of Comparative Religions," *Chicago Daily Tribune*, September 14, 1893.

62. Barrows, *Parliament of Religions*, 452.

63. Philip Schaff, *History of the Apostolic Church: With a General Introduction to Church History*, trans. Edward D. Yeomans (New York: Charles Scribner, 1853), 678; Bowden, *Church History*, 62.

64. Barrows, *Parliament of Religions*, 452–56.

65. Sabbath observance was a key component of American "common law" and part of Richard Seager's identification of the "Anglo-Protestant religion of civilization": the Sabbath as an external performance of an internal commitment to God, epitomizing Christian America and its continued status before God as a chosen nation. Seager also noted several other debates that took shape at the World's Fair as part of this attempt to conserve this Puri-

tan covenant, such as the restriction of nudes on display in the Palace of Fine Arts and the prohibition of alcohol sales on the fairgrounds. Seager, *Parliament of Religions*, 4, 6, 18–19; Sehat, *Myth of American Religious Freedom*, 58–59, 170–75.

66. As quoted in Foster, *Moral Reconstruction*, 96. See also Sehat, *Myth of American Religious Freedom*, 62.

67. Foster, *Moral Reconstruction*, 101.

68. Barrows, *World's Parliament of Religions*, 1:58.

69. "Wide Open on Sundays," *Chicago Times*, September 7, 1893. See also Seager, *Parliament of Religions*, 18.

70. Barrows, *Parliament of Religions*, 451.

71. According to John Burris, the fair's attempts "to separate religious concerns from secular ones proved unfeasible. The secular encroached upon the religious determinedly in the exposition setting, finally leaving even the Sabbath in its wake." Burris, *Exhibiting Religion*, 139, 176.

72. For more on this theological and cultural crisis that began to be discerned in the 1890s and contributed to a sense of increased religious powerlessness, see Hutchison, chapter 5, "A Prophetic Minority: Liberal Perceptions of Cultural Crisis, 1900–1914," in William R. Hutchison, *The Modernist Impulse in American Protestantism* (Durham, NC: Duke University Press, 1992).

73. H. B. Hartzler, *Moody in Chicago; or, The World's Fair Gospel Campaign: An Account of Six Months' Evangelistic Work in the City of Chicago and Vicinity During the Time of the World's Columbian Exposition, Conducted by Dwight L. Moody and His Associates* (Chicago: Fleming H. Revell, 1894), 52–53.

74. Hartzler, *Moody in Chicago*, 252, 254.

75. See James Gilbert, *Perfect Cities: Chicago's Utopias of 1893* (Chicago: University of Chicago Press, 1991); Hartzler, *Moody in Chicago*, 101. This growing distrust of modernity, modern popular culture, and its fixations on the external (if not increasing hostility and polemicism) furthered the religious divide between conservative and more culturally accommodating liberal Protestants, later culminating in what scholars would term the "The Fundamentalist Controversy," which grew in parallel with these new social, intellectual, and scientific developments. Ahlstrom, *The American Protestant Encounter with World Religions*, 16–17, 25–28. Impressively, even some of the writers of the conservative "fundamentals" of the 1900s and 1910s saw Darwinism as an important link in understanding God's creative forces in the world. For a discussion on this, see Larson, Summer of the Gods, 19–25.

76. Barrows, *World's Parliament of Religions*, 1:26; Richard Hughes Seager,

"Pluralism and the American Mainstream: The View from the World's Parliament of Religions," *Harvard Theological Review* 82, no. 3 (July 1989), 315, 321. Richard Seager articulated that although many conservatives avoided and denounced the parliament, doctrines that later marked the Holiness and Fundamentalist movements were heard throughout the conference presentations. Though divisions were in an early state, the parliament proved divisive for Protestantism in America.

77. Barrows, *World's Parliament of Religions*, 2:1243–49. For more by way of evangelical presentation on this more "seamy side" (i.e., negative and unfair) of non-Christianity, as Barrows called it, see speeches by Dr. Pentecost, Joseph Cook, Mr. Mozoomdar, Mr. Nagarkar, Dr. Post, Mr. Candlin, Mr. Gordon, Mr. McFarland, Dr. Clark, and Dr. Dennis.

78. Ibid., 2:1250–51.

79. For an overview of these developments within American Protestantism, see chapter 4, "But Why Christianity? Liberal Extension and Apologetics in the 1890s," in Hutchison, *The Modernist Impulse*.

80. For more on social evolutionism at the fair, see Burris, "Social Evolutionism and International Expositions: A Cultural History," chapter 3 in *Exhibiting Religion*.

81. Barrows, *World's Parliament of Religions*, 2:1293.

82. Ibid., 2:1138–40 (emphasis in original).

83. Chidester, *Savage Systems*, xiii. For further discussion of the links between colonialism and the study of religion, see Masuzawa, Invention of World Religion; Talal Asad, *Genealogies of Religion: Discipline and Reasons of Power in Christianity and Islam* (Baltimore: Johns Hopkins University Press, 1993); Richard King, *Orientalism and Religion: Postcolonial Theory, India and "The Mystic East"* (New York: Routledge, 1999); Bruce Lincoln, *Theorizing Myth: Narrative, Ideology, and Scholarship* (Chicago: University of Chicago Press, 1999); Styers, *Making Magic*.

84. Barrows, *Parliament of Religions*, 452–56.

85. According to Reid Neilson, both Barrows and Bonney "were uniquely positioned to act on their anti-Mormon prejudice." Having preached and published against Mormonism during the 1870s and 1880s, Barrows saw Mormon doctrine as "abominable" and argued that the system itself "ought to be wiped out." Barrows called for Christianization efforts to "heal this plague spot" in Utah by "touching it with pure gospel instruction." In 1900, while president of Oberlin College, Barrows became a founding member of the Utah Gospel Mission Executive Committee, who's stated purpose was to mount "a national crusade against Mormonism." As Neilson explains, "Barrows wore his anti-Mormonism on his sleeve as a badge of evangelical

courage and Christian orthodoxy. He was likely the chief agitator within the organizing committee who lobbied against Latter-day Saint participation in the congress." For more information and a collection of important resources, see Reid L. Neilson, *Exhibiting Mormonism: The Latter-day Saints and the 1893 Chicago World's Fair* (New York: Oxford University Press, 2011), 152–55.

86. Roberts, *A Comprehensive History*, 6:238.

87. Bitton, "B. H. Roberts at the World Parliament of Religion 1893 Chicago," *Sunstone* 31 (January–February 1982): 47–48.

88. First Presidency, [Wilford Woodruff, George Q. Cannon, and Joseph F. Smith], letter to Charles C. Bonney, July 10, 1893, as reprinted in Clark, *Messages*, 3:249.

89. Roberts, *History of the Church*, 6:237–38; and Brigham H. Roberts, "The Church of Jesus Christ of Latter-Day Saints at the Parliament of Religions: 'Christian Treatments of Mormons,'" *Improvement Era* 2, no. 10 (August 1899): 754; Barrows, *World's Parliament of Religions*, 1:44.

90. Roberts, *History of the Church*, 6:240.

91. Roberts, "The Church at the Parliament of Religions," 752–53.

92. Brigham H. Roberts, *Defense of the Faith and the Saints* ([1907 and 1912]; rpt., Provo, UT: Maasai Publishing, 2002), 1:2.

93. Roberts, *History of the Church*, 6:237, 239; Truman G. Madsen, *Defender of the Faith: The B. H. Roberts Story* (Salt Lake City: Bookcraft, 1980), 205.

94. Roberts, *Defense of the Faith*, 1:2; Roberts, "The Church at the Parliament of Religions," 755.

95. Houghton, *Neely's History*, 1:187.

96. "The Religious Congress," *Deseret Semi-Weekly News*, October 3, 1893.

97. Webb's biographer speculates, "Since Barrows chaired the first session, it is quite possible that Barrows himself prompted Webb to begin his speech by addressing the issue of polygamy." See Umar F. Abd-Allah, *A Muslim in Victorian America: The Life of Alexander Russell Webb* (New York: Oxford University Press, 2006), 238, 240.

98. Barrows, *World's Parliament of Religions*, 1:127. Americans had been patient and even celebratory with criticism from foreign speakers, such as Protap Chandra Majumdar, but as noted by Bramen, Webb was not an outsider and thus not an authentic "other," and the audience was therefore less forgiving. Bramen, *Uses of Variety*, 270, 274.

99. Barrows, *World's Parliament of Religions*, 1:127.

100. "The Religious Congress"; Barrows, *World's Parliament of Religions*, 1:127; Houghton, *Neely's History*, 1:460. One of the foremost historians of the parliament, Richard Seager, points out that newspapers indicated significant

approval from the audience, "with applause outnumbering hisses and boos three to one (indeed, twice hisses and cries of 'shame' were heard together with applause.)" Seager, *Dawn of Religious Pluralism*, 279–80.

101. Houghton, *Neely's History*, 1:460. Webb's biographer notes that, although Webb was no advocate of polygamy, he had argued "that Westerners were ignorant of how it was actually practiced in the Muslim world and that their categorical condemnation of it was self-righteous and hypocritical in view of the problems that surrounded the marital and sexual practices of their own societies." See Abd-Allah, *Muslims in Victorian America*, 239–41.

102. By way of example of the overt prejudice against Islam at the parliament, Rev. P. Phiambolis of the Greek Church of Chicago explained at the congress that Islam retarded the advancement of Christianity. The motto of "Mohammedanism" was "'Kill the Infidels,' because every one who is not a Mohammedan, according to the Koran of the Prophet, is an infidel, is a dog." Fitting Philip Schaff's assessment that Islam is the "inveterate foe" of Christianity, Phiambolis spoke of the sufferings of Christians and especially the dishonoring of "Christian virgins" in the Orient under Muslim "Turkish tyranny." In the Orient, "Christian virgins are dishonored by the followers of the Moslem Prophet, and the life of a Christian is not considered as precious as that of a dog." Barrows, *World's Parliament of Religions*, 2:1129. For more on this Muslim-Mormon connection, see Arnold H. Green, "Mormonism and Islam: From Polemics to Mutual Respect and Cooperation," *Brigham Young University Studies* 40, no. 4 (2001): 199–203; Green's essay "The Muhammad-Joseph Smith Comparison: Subjective Metaphor or a Sociology of Prophethood?" in *Mormons and Muslims: Spiritual Foundations and Modern Manifestations*, ed. Spencer J. Palmer (Provo: Religious Studies Center at Brigham Young University, 2002), 111–33; and Timothy Marr, *The Cultural Roots of American Islamicism* (New York: Cambridge University Press, 2006), chapter 4, "'Turkey Is in Our Midst': Mormonism as an American 'Islam.'"

103. As quoted in Gordon, *Mormon Question*, 140; Laycock, "Manhood and Womanhood," 312.

104. John H. Barrows, *Christianity, the World-Religion* (Chicago: A. C. McClurg, 1897), 104–5. In the mind of Barrows, polygamy proved an important symbol of immorality, and thus a hindrance to progress. "The permissions of the Koran in respect to polygamy, concubinage and divorce; the sanction of slavery and holy war, the example of Mohammed himself, the adoption of the principle that the end justifies the means—thereby consecrating every form of deception and lying, every sort of persecution and violence to the cause of religion—these things effactually block the wheels of progress in

ethical spheres, so that Moslem nations have hardly ever reached even the planes of moral purity occupied by the most degenerate Christian nations." Quoting E. M. Wherry, *Islam; or, The Religion of the Turk*, 59, in Barrows, *Christianity*, 364.

105. *Chicago Herald*, September 26, 1893.

106. Roberts, "The Church at the Parliament of Religions," 756–57; Hanson, *World's Congress of Religions*, 818.

107. Roberts, "The Church at the Parliament of Religions," 757–66.

108. Ibid., 758–59.

109. The full speech is published in Roberts, *Defense of the Faith*, 1:3–13.

110. Barrows, *World's Parliament of Religions*, 1:18, 2:1561.

111. However lawless and crude Mormonism appeared throughout much of the nineteenth century, Turner opened up the possibility in 1893 that Mormons, in light of these conflicts, could be redefined in uniquely American terms—as it were, the vices of the frontier and their inevitable eradication that ultimately defined an "American character" that left its mark on "language, and literature, not soon to be effected." Turner, *The Frontier*, 32–33n49.

## CHAPTER 5

1. For further insight into these bureaucratic and centralizing shifts within Mormonism and the introduction of twentieth-century correlation, see Thomas G. Alexander, *Mormonism in Transition: A History of the Latter-day Saints 1890–1930* (Urbana: University of Illinois Press, 1996), 93–115; Matthew Bowman, *The Mormon People: The Making of an American Faith* (New York: Random House, 2012), 152–215; Ethan Yorgason, *Transformation of the Mormon Culture Region* (Urbana: University of Illinois Press, 2003), 130–70.

2. "Utah Wants to Be a State," *New York Times*, December 13, 1893; "Mormonism Waning," *Atlanta Constitution*, December 20, 1893. Newspaper headlines such as "Mormon Influence Waning," "Polygamy Dead in Utah," and "Mormonism Done For" were common in the early 1890s.

3. Mormons had largely been isolated from fellow Americans as a result of geography and the lack of transportation that would later make traveling doable for most Americans. As Reid Neilson wrote about nineteenth-century Mormons, "few" Americans "ever saw, heard, smelled, or touched a Mormon with their own eyes, ears, noses, or hands." Neilson, *Exhibiting Mormonism*, 22. With such unfamiliarity and distance, it was easy for rumors and fantasies to spread unchecked and mythologies to emerge regarding the qualities and characteristics of Mormons in Utah, particularly as a consequence of the peculiar practice of polygamy. As Americans encountered their Mormon

neighbors at the World's Fair, the fact that they were not so strange and different was a point of surprise and changed sentiment for many.

4. McDaniel, *Utah at the World's Columbian Exposition*, 44.

5. "Notes of a Winter Trip," *New York Times*, May 2, 1892.

6. For more on how land monopolists killed the dream of the Yeoman farmer, and thus transformed how Americans viewed the West, see Smith, *Virgin Land*, 247–48.

7. "Is Utah Fit for Statehood?," *New York Times*, February 16, 1893.

8. From Abraham H. Cannon's journal on April 6, 1893: "It was decided on the recommendation of J. H. Smith and myself who were appointed a committee to consider the matter, to send B. H. Roberts and Ben E. Rich to Chicago [Illinois] to represent us at the World's Fair, and to do missionary work wherever possible." Edward Leo Lyman, ed., *Candid Insights of a Mormon Apostle: The Diaries of Abraham H. Cannon, 1889–1895* (Salt Lake City: Signature Books, 2010).

9. Bitton, "B. H. Roberts," 50. Aside from Reid Neilson's recent monograph *Exhibiting Mormonism*, the Mormon incident at the fair remained largely ignored or limited to Richard Seager's terse summation that the "Mormons were simply not invited." Seager, *Dawn of Religious Pluralism*, 6. For more on this historiographical neglect, see Joseph Kitagawa, "The World's Parliament of Religions and Its Legacy" (Eleventh John Nuveen Lecture, Chicago: University of Chicago Divinity School, 1983), and Seager, "Pluralism and the American Mainstream."

10. The idea of taking into account both presence and nonpresence at the fair comes from John Burris, *Exhibiting Religion*, 157.

11. By way of example of these protests, historian Keith Naylor demonstrates how the African Methodist Episcopal (AME) Church turned the event into a "world court of opinion regarding racial equality," directly challenging the "state of mind of the Fair planners and Fair-goers" when it came to definitions of diversity and implied notions of religious, racial, and cultural and even gender superiority. D. Keith Naylor, "The Black Presence at the World's Parliament of Religions, 1893," *Religion* 26, no. 3 (1996): 249, 253. Hirai Kinzo, second speaker for the Buddhist delegation, similarly challenged Barrows's narrow religious vision by condemning Christianity and its missionaries in Japan for its "abusive, high-handed, self-righteous, bigoted, and racist attitudes" toward his native home and people. As explained by Carrie Bramen, Asian representatives "altered the Christian logic of the event, transforming a potentially Orientalist spectacle into an anti-colonial critique." Bramen, *The Uses of Variety*, 255. For more on Barrows attempt to silence such critiques, see Seager, *Parliament of Religions*, 74, Neilson,

*Exhibiting Mormonism*, 160; Snodgrass, *Presenting Japanese Buddhism*, 184; Bramen, *The Uses of Variety*, 271–72.

12. In the early 1890s, national political parties (Democrat and Republican) replaced Utah's more polemical Liberal (anti-Mormon) and People's (pro-Mormon) Parties. For a discussion of this political shift in Utah, see Alexander, *Mormonism in Transition*, 37–50; Edward L. Lyman, *Political Deliverance: The Mormon Quest for Utah Statehood* (Chicago: University of Illinois Press, 1986), 153–81; Roberts, *Comprehensive History*, 6:297–301.

13. "The Future of Mormonism," *New York Times*, September 12, 1898.

14. "A Victory for Mormons: Judge Stockslager Says They May Vote in Idaho," *New York Times*, October 9, 1892.

15. A recent platform of the Republican convention went as follows: "We congratulate the Mormon Church on the recent declaration abandoning polygamy and divorce of Church and State in all political concerns, and, accepting this declaration as sincere, we pledge the party that, with the continuance of the evidences of this sincerity, we will at the next ensuing session of the Legislature restore to its members the free political privileges of citizenship secured to all others." As reported in "The Mormons in Idaho," *New York Times*, September 5, 1892.

16. Harrison's amnesty was in response to an 1891 petition by leaders of the Mormon people on behalf of all those "under disabilities because of the operation of the Edmunds-Tucker law" of 1887. Roberts, *Comprehensive History*, 6:288–89; Lyman, *Political Deliverance*, 191, 206–7; "These culminated in the passage of the Edmunds (1882) and Edmunds-Tucker (1887) acts, which disfranchised all polygamists, took control of Utah's Mormon-dominated public school system, abolished the territorial militia, disfranchised Utah women, provided for imprisonment of those practicing plural marriage, and confiscated virtually all the church's property." Alexander, *Mormonism in Transition*, 4.

17. "Cost of the Salt Lake Temple," *Deseret News*, March 23, 1895. Neilson, *Exhibiting Mormonism*, 7, 116.

18. *Picturesque Chicago*, 1–2.

19. Seager, *Parliament of Religions*, 10–11, xxii; Snodgrass, *Presenting Japanese Buddhism*, 28; Hine and Faragher, *Frontiers*, 165.

20. Seager, *Parliament of Religions*, 4–6.

21. "The Great Temple of the Mormons Was Formally Dedicated Yesterday," *Atlanta Constitution*, April 7, 1893.

22. "Saint and Sinner: Mormons and Gentiles Journey to Salt Lake City," *Los Angeles Times*, April 5, 1893.

23. "Mormonism Waning: Senator Vest States That Polygamy Is on The

Decline," *Atlanta Constitution*, December 20, 1893.

24. For thorough details on the final situation of the church following the Edmunds-Tucker law of 1887, see Arrington, *Great Basin Kingdom*, 360–79. Arrington concludes his chapter thus: "The Raid had finally culminated in the long-sought goal of statehood, but had produced capitulation in many areas of Mormon uniqueness, not the least of which was the decline in the economic power and influence of the church. The temporal Kingdom, for all practical purposes, was dead—slain by the dragon of Edmunds-Tucker."

25. As testified by one of the most quoted verses of Mormon scripture throughout the nineteenth century, "I say unto you, be one; and if ye are not one ye are not mine." Doctrine and Covenants 38:27.

26. With the March 9, 1892, Republican victory in the Democrat stronghold of Logan, Utah (home of both apostle and politician Moses Thatcher and Utah's delegate to Congress, John T. Caine), the *New York Times* wrote that the outcome "effectually disposes of the question of Mormon Church influence in the political field." The Times quoted a *Salt Lake Tribune* editorial that said: "We congratulate Logan on having a genuine American election, and we say, 'Good for Logan!'" "Mormon Influence Waning: A City Election In Utah Over Which It Had No Control," *New York Times*, March 10, 1892.

27. Calling offense toward each other to be a breach of their covenant, the letter from the First Presidency called for member reconciliation. Before church members could consider themselves worthy to attend the dedication, they were to "divest ourselves of every harsh and unkind feeling against each other; that not only our bickering shall cease, but that the cause of them shall be removed, and every sentiment that prompted and has maintained them shall be dispelled." Demonstrating the "supreme importance" of this, the First Presidency admonished bishops not to give recommends to those not "at peace with all his or her brethren and sisters," even going so far as to threaten disfellowshipment and excommunication for the unworthy who did attend. Thus, at a time when political parties in Utah were in serious flux and heated polemics, Mormon leaders were seeking to remind their membership of Mormonism's higher-kingdom principles of unity. Clark, *Messages*, 3:241–44.

28. McDaniel, *Utah at the World's Columbian Exposition*, 11–12.

29. Ibid.

30. Ibid., 14, 27, 41, 43.

31. Paxson, *History of the American Frontier*, 108, 190–91; Charles N. Glaab, "Historical Perspective on Urban Development Schemes," in *Social Science and the City: A Survey of Urban Research*, ed. Leo F. Schnore (New York: Praeger, 1968), 219.

32. For more on monopoly capitalism, see Ernest Mandel, *Late Capitalism*, trans. Joris De Bres (London: Humanities Press, 1975), 594–95.

33. Hubert Howe Bancroft, *The Book of the Fair* (Chicago: Bancroft Company, 1893), 832.

34. With secular work such as Mormonism's engagement in iron missions, Leonard Arrington notes that Mormon leaders considered such work as holding "quite as much importance as preaching the Gospel." Various levels of mining and industrial development programs were understood to be part of a divine work, whose workers were often called and whose organizations and finances were directly correlated through church offices under the influence of the priesthood. See *Great Basin Kingdom*, 33, 112–30, 155. Arrington considered this work the "spiritualization of temporal activity," but it is important to note that such an Eliadean dichotomy of the sacred and the profane had not been clearly defined throughout much of the nineteenth century, and many Protestant Americans understood their temporal work in the extension of the nation as altogether insignificant to their spiritual worldview. Abolitionism, the Civil War, volunteer and benevolent societies, militia movements, etc., all testify to this fact. Robert Baird, for example, understood the colonizing efforts of America's Anglo population to be directly related to the ultimate realization of Christ's kingdom. Manifest Destiny, a term coined in 1845 by American journalist John Louis O'Sullivan in his promotion of the U.S. annexation of Texas and Oregon, expressed the faith of many Americans in the divine destiny behind their growing empire. According to Paul Reeve, mining represented an indispensable part of the mission of Western civilization itself, which was interwoven with religious expectation. Reeve, *Making Space*, 20–21. *Harper's New Monthly Magazine* made the connection in 1858 that the fundamentals of American democracy developed directly from the Protestant idea of God's kingdom, and that God's "Providence in national affairs is primarily due to the moral spirit which Christianity awakens in the heart," and that it is the spirit, which acts through the intellect, which "reads the manifestations of God in the outward world, and discerns His going forth in the events of the age." Historian Ernest L. Tuveson explains that "mission" is a term that extends beyond the building of churches, into the building of the nation. Part of this "mission" was to "establish a great territorial 'empire,' even though much of it, like the Promised Land, might at first be under the Philistines," where nineteenth-century authors continually conflated political and spiritual and moral elements. See Tuveson, *Redeemer Nation*, 125–36. "Editor's Table: Providence in American History," Harper's New Monthly Magazine 17 (1858): 697. It is an exaggerated position, however

prevailing among American historians, that Mormons were altogether unique in the spiritualizing of the profane.

35. "Mormon and Gentile: Join Hands Heartily on Utah Day," *Sunday Herald* (Chicago), September 10, 1893.

36. McDaniel, *Utah at the World's Columbian Exposition*, 53.

37. Ibid., 52–53.

38. Inman and Cody, *The Great Salt Lake Trail*, 111, 131.

39. Woodruff, Wilford Woodruff's Journal, 9:262–63.

40. Ibid., 9:230, 262; McDaniel, *Utah at the World's Columbian Exposition*, 53, 56–57.

41. McDaniel, *Utah at the World's Columbian Exposition*, 54–56.

42. "Utah's Day at the Fair," *Deseret-Weekly*, September 16, 1893.

43. For more on the important role Mormon women had at the World's Fair, see Neilson, *Exhibiting Mormonism*, chapter 3, "Mormon Matriarchs: LDS Ladies at the World's Congress of Representative Women."

44. McDaniel, *Utah at the World's Columbian Exposition*, 23, 37; Jill M. Derr, Janath R. Cannon, and Maureen U. Beecher, *Women of Covenant: The Story of Relief Society* (Salt Lake City: Deseret Book, 1992), 134–47.

45. Derr, Cannon, and Beecher, *Women of Covenant*, 138–39; McDaniel, *Utah at the World's Columbian Exposition*, 52.

46. May Wright Sewall, ed., *The World's Congress of Representative Women: A Historical Resume for Popular Circulation of the World's Congress of Representative Women, Convened in Chicago on May 15, and Adjourned on May 22, 1893, Under the Auspices of the Women's Branch of the World's Congress Auxiliary* (Chicago: Rand, McNally, 1894), 84; Neilson, *Exhibiting Mormonism*, 100–101; Andrea G. Radke-Moss, "'Truly Her Soul Rejoiced in Helping the Helpless: Emily Sophia Tanner Richards (1850–1929),'" in *Women of Faith in the Latter Days*, ed. Richard Turley and Brittany A. Chapman (Salt Lake City: Deseret Book Company, 2014), 3:139.

47. See Etta L. Gilchrist, "The World's Fair," *Ashtabula News Journal*, May 23, 1893, reprinted in *Woman's Exponent* 21, no. 24 (June 15, 1893): 177–78; Neilson, *Exhibiting Mormonism*, 93–102.

48. Neilson, *Exhibiting Mormonism*, 78.

49. Among these national leaders were Susan B. Anthony, Isabella Beecher Hooker (of the famed Beecher family—father Lyman Beecher, sisters Harriet Beecher Stowe and Catharine Beecher, and brothers Henry Ward Beecher and Edward Beecher) and Clara Thatcher (wife of Chicago World's Fair commissioner Solomon Thatcher Jr.). Even Rosetta Luce Gilchrist, who published the anti-Mormon fiction "Apples of Sodom: A Story of Mormon Life" (1883), became close friends with Mormon female leaders at the

fair. See Derr, Cannon, and Beecher, *Women of Covenant*, 140; Ida Husted Harper, *The Life and Work of Susan B. Anthony* (Indianapolis: Bowen-Merrill, 1898), 2:631; Neilson, *Exhibiting Mormonism*, 82–83, 102–3.

50. McDaniel, *Utah at the World's Columbian Exposition*, 14, 20–23, 29.

51. "Serenaded by the Mormon Choir," *Chicago Times*, September 7, 1893.

52. "This Time a Friendly Mob," *Kansas City Times*, September 1, 1893; "In Jackson County!," *Deseret Semi-Weekly News*, September 5, 1893. "Upon returning to Utah from Chicago, President Woodruff spoke on the kind treatment and enjoyable time he and his companions had enjoyed at the Fair. He also referred to their reception at Independence, Mo, where the mayor and citizens now turned out to meet them, whereas in 1834 he and his companion who traveled through that section of country had to hide by day and travel by night in order to escape the death which the inhabitants had intended to inflict upon them." Lyman, *Candid Insights*, 417–18.

53. Woodruff, Wilford Woodruff's Journal, 9:260.

54. "Mormon Singers," *St. Louis Post Dispatch*, September 3, 1893; "Received on 'Change,'" *St. Louis Post Dispatch*, September 2, 1893.

55. "Serenaded by the Mormon Choir."

56. McDaniel, *Utah at the World's Columbian Exposition*, 46–48, 59.

57. Woodruff, Wilford Woodruff's Journal, 9:262. Abraham H. Cannon wrote in his journal on September 13, 1893: "The Tabernacle choir returned this morning early from its trip to the World's Fair at Chicago. They bring with them the second prize of $1,000. awarded for choir singing at the Fair, though it is said by those who are thought to be competent to judge that they should really have been awarded the first prize. They had a pleasant trip." Lyman, *Candid Insights*, 415.

58. "Utah's Big Choir," *Deseret Semi-Weekly News*, September 22, 1893.

59. Neilson, *Exhibiting Mormonism*, 138.

60. "Mormon and Gentile."

61. McDaniel, *Utah at the World's Columbian Exhibition*, 51; "The Great Contest," Deseret Semi-Weekly News, September 12, 1893.

62. McDaniel, *Utah at the World's Columbian Exposition*, 60.

63. Turner, *Without God*, 253.

64. Barrows, *World's Parliament of Religions*, 1:172–73. Music played no small role in the enthusiasm of the fair: *The Chicago Daily Tribune* termed response to the Apollo Choir as a greater "storm and uproar" than had "never before shaken the Hall of Columbus." It then added, "The great Parliament of Religions had come, and dying, like a swan it kept its sweetest music to the last." "In Word of Praise," *Chicago Daily Tribune*, September 28, 1893.

65. Seager, *Parliament of Religions*, 3–8.

66. "Mormon and Gentile." It described Robert C. Easton as a "tenor of rare training." Following a speech by Governor West, Easton sang the favorite Mormon hymn written by Eliza R. Snow, "O, My Father," accompanied by Professor Krouse on the piano. This solo, given by special request, is recorded as being listened to by the crowd "in breathless silence by all that great audience. Mr. Easton was at his best and never sang better." The crowd "broke forth in a round of most hearty applause, and would not be contented until the distinguished soloist responded with another song." At the closing of Utah Day, Easton sang an encore entitled "Annie Laurie." He was then followed by the entire Mormon Tabernacle Choir singing Handel's "Hallelujah" Chorus. Though Mormons largely avoided presenting their own peculiarities for the sake of building bridges, they seem to have gotten away with a few, such as with the hymn "O, My Father," which references the Mormon belief in heavenly parents, inclusive of a heavenly mother. See McDaniel, *Utah at the World's Columbian Exposition*, 53–54.

67. James Gilbert, *Whose Fair?: Experience, Memory, and the History of the Great St. Louis Exposition* (Chicago: University of Chicago Press, 2009), 17.

68. Habermas, *The Structural Transformation*, 133–34, 140, 171, 184–85, 213. Neilson, Exhibiting Mormonism, 102–4. For more on polygamy, women's suffrage, and Mormon women at the Chicago World's Fair, see Andrea G. Radke-Moss, "Polygamy and Women's Rights: Nineteenth-Century Mormon Female Activism," in *The Persistence of Polygamy: From Joseph Smith's Martyrdom to the First Manifesto, 1844–1890*, ed. Newell G. Bringhurst and Craig L. Foster (Independence, MO: John Whitmer Books, 2014).

69. Neilson, *Exhibiting Mormonism*, 182.

70. "Fraud at the World's Fair," *Chicago Daily Tribune*, March 13, 1905; "World's Fair Awards," Los Angeles Times, March 13, 1905; "John Q. Cannon Arrested," *Washington Post*, July 20, 1905.

71. McDaniel, *Utah at the World's Columbian Exposition*, 52.

72. Ibid., 59, 42–43.

73. "Remarks by President George Q. Cannon," *Deseret Semi-Weekly News*, October 3, 1893.

74. Lorenzo Snow, "General Conference," *Deseret Semi-Weekly News*, October 10, 1893.

75. Woodruff, Wilford Woodruff's Journal, 9:278–79.

76. Heber J. Grant, "General Conference," *Deseret Semi-Weekly News*, October 10, 1893.

77. Francis M. Lyman, "General Conference," *Deseret Semi-Weekly News*, October 10, 1893.

78. "Remarks by President George Q. Cannon"; Lyman, *Candid Insights*, 417–18.

79. Seager, *Parliament of Religions*, 211.

80. Reprinted in ibid., 82.

81. Bramen, *Uses of Variety*, 277.

82. David Chidester, *Authentic Fakes: Religion and American Popular Culture* (Berkeley: University of California Press, 2005), viii, 19.

83. Jonathan Z. Smith, *Map Is Not Territory: Studies in the History of Religions* (Chicago: University of Chicago Press, 1993), 308. In some ways, this fair was a type of "burning bush." As reported of the enchanted aura of the fair itself, where at the fair's opening ceremony on May 1, Chicago's *Daily Inter-Ocean* spoke of such portrayals of modernity as the realization of a "self-conscious spirituality" that had been in preparation ever since Columbus four hundred years earlier. Indeed, President Grover Cleveland, "like a magician with his wand, touched an electronic button which signaled the formal opening of the World's Columbian Exposition," bringing forth earth's re-creation "by a great burst of sound, 'And there was light!'" "Our Day of Triumph," *Daily Inter-Ocean*, May 2, 1893.

84. Clark, *Messages*, 3:267–68.

85. "Remarks by President George Q. Cannon."

86. Clark, *Messages*, 3:267.

87. "A Hard Road," *Los Angeles Times*, April 6, 1893.

88. Clark, *Messages*, 2:31; 3:274.

89. By way of example of the distrust toward this manifesto, the *New York Times* warned that such manifestos have been a common Mormon practice against protests of their religious influence in politics, but that Mormons had always neglected to follow through. Tapping into older stereotypes, Mormons were accused of being disingenuous. The article argued that this new political manifesto came only after the Democratic Party forced the issue, and that Mormon leaders included within it a loophole that still allowed them political prominence. George Q. Cannon was a "wily politician" and "the statement that the leaders do not desire to unite Church and State is worthless." "The Mormon Manifesto," *New York Times*, April 17, 1896.

90. Clark, *Messages*, 3:246–48.

91. Ibid., 3:261–63.

92. James B. Allen and Glen M. Leonard, *The Story of the Latter-day Saints*, 2nd edition (Salt Lake City: Deseret Book, 1992), 503–6.

93. Clark, *Messages*, 3:274–75. For a summary of events involving Roberts and Thatcher leading up to this "political manifesto," see Roberts, *Comprehensive History*, 6:330–36; Lyman, *Political Deliverance*, 268–75; J. D. Williams,

"The Separation of Church and State in Mormon Theory and Practices," *Journal of Church and State* 9, no. 2 (Spring 1967): 247–48.

94. Clark, *Messages*, 3:265–66.

95. Ibid., 3:252–55.

96. Niebuhr, *Kingdom of God*, 181, 183.

97. Clark, *Messages*, 3: 278–79; 298–99.

98. Alexander, *Mormonism in Transition*, 13.

99. Joseph F. Smith, "Opening Address," Seventy-Seventh Semi-Annual Conference of the Church of Jesus Christ of Latter-day Saints, October 1906, 9; Joseph F. Smith, "Opening Address," Seventy-Second Annual Conference of the Church of Jesus Christ of Latter-day Saints, April 1902, 2.

100. For a deeper analysis of this shift from "God's pedagogy" to natural consequence, see Taylor, *A Secular Age*, 679.

## CHAPTER 6

1. Joseph F. Smith, Letter to Reed Smoot, February 23, 1907, in Clark, *Messages*, 4:141.

2. "The Storm Will Soon Die Out," *Washington Post*, January 19, 1903. The Post then comments: "That is a correct view of the matter. The constitutional qualifications of the Senator do not require that he shall be equipped with any particular set of opinions on religious subjects. A Senator may be a Christian or an atheist, or entertain any other views that suit him or have no religious views at all. Some of the ablest men who have ever served the country in the Senate have been decidedly non-Christian. What a man believes is nobody's business but his own. What a man does, if he be an applicant for a seat in Congress, may be the public's business. Mr. Smoot is charged with no unlawful or immoral act."

3. Strong, *The New Era*, 123–24.

4. Flake, *American Religious Identity*, 17.

5. Arthur M. Schlesinger Jr., ed., *The Almanac of American History* (New York: Barnes & Noble Books, 2004), 371–77; Gary Cross and Rick Szostak, Technology and American Society: A History (New Jersey: Prentice Hall, 1995), 153, 160.

6. Quoted in Boller, *American Thought in Transition*, 227.

7. Taylor, *A Secular Age*, 281, 436, 443. For more on this as it pertains to the secularization of America, see pp. 13–15. Though an early speculative work on the question of secularization and religion, Peter Berger provides important questions and insight concerning the loss of the social influence of religion in this secularized era, and its move toward that of the more private and bureaucratic. See *The Sacred Canopy: Elements of a Sociological Theory of Religion* (New York: Anchor Books, 1967), chapter 6.

8. See the preface of Hutchison, *The Modernist Impulse*, in which the author claims that this "impulse" was perhaps "the single most important [force] informing and shaping Protestant liberalism over a period of about 120 years." It was the position of many in the 1880s that there was no line between the secular and religious, but by 1920, liberal ideas had become both accepted and respectable by more than a third of Protestant pulpits, and more than half of those pulpits associated with institutions of higher learning. Pp. 3, 8.

9. Roberts, *Comprehensive History*, 6:390; Milton R. Merrill, *Reed Smoot: Apostle in Politics* (Logan: Utah State University Press, 1990), 8.

10. "Sees a Bright Outlook for Utah," New York Times, July 23, 1894.

11. Roberts, *A Comprehensive History*, 6:390–91; Flake, *American Religious Identity*, 13; Merrill, *Reed Smoot*, 30–31; Smoot Hearings, 1:25.

12. Smoot Hearings, 1:26–30; Merrill, *Reed Smoot*, 34.

13. "Attack on Smoot's Accuser," *New York Times*, March 22, 1903; "Ministers Act on Smoot," *New York Times*, March 1, 1903.

14. "Senate Refuses to Oust Smoot," *New York Times*, February 21, 1907.

15. As Smoot expressed to his close friend John Q. McQuarrie, president of the Eastern States Mission headquartered in New York, "If they can expel me from the Senate of the United States, they can expel any man who claims to be a Mormon." Reed Smoot, Letter to John G. McQuarrie, December 16, 1902, quoted in Merrill, *Reed Smoot*, 31.

16. "The Absurd Clamor About Smoot," *Hartford Courant*, January 27, 1903.

17. "Protest Against Smoot," *New York Times*, December 14, 1903; Smoot Hearings, 1:1.

18. Alexander, *Mormonism in Transition*, 126.

19. Lorenzo Snow, "Greeting to the World," January 1, 1901, in Clark, *Messages*, 3:335.

20. Alexander, *Mormonism in Transition*, 96.

21. Lorenzo Snow's "last address" from Conference Reports, October 1901, Clark, *Messages*, 4:11.

22. Roberts, *Comprehensive History*, 6:389–90.

23. First Presidency "Christmas Greeting," December 17, 1904, in Clark, *Messages*, 4:92–98; First Presidency "Christmas Greeting," December 15, 1906, in ibid., 4:128–32.

24. These developments are identified in various First Presidency statements during the period. Clark, *Messages*, 3:265, 266, 288, 315; 4:12, 35, 58, 64, 100, 130, 185. See also Alexander, *Mormonism in Transition*, 99.

25. Concerning this new national religious focus on the importance of a healthy and strong body (which had been denied in the nineteenth cen-

tury), see R. Marie Griffith, *Born Again Bodies: Flesh and Spirit in American Christianity* (Berkeley: University of California, 2004), 1–10; Clifford Putney, *Muscular Christianity: Manhood and Sports in Protestant America, 1880–1920* (Cambridge: Harvard University Press, 2001), chapters 1–2; Jan Shipps, *Mormonism: The Story of a New Religious Tradition* (Urbana: University of Illinois Press, 1985), 125, 128. For more on this shift from the communal to the individual, see also Alexander, *Mormonism in Transition*, 109–15.

26. See also Smoot Hearings, 1:129–31. Reports like "Law of 1890 Violated," *Hartford Courant*, March 5, 1904, were common, repetitively declaring that Mormons were still engaging in plural marriages, that Smoot knew all about them, and that President Smith would raise revelation above the nation's law. See also Michael Harold Paulos, "Under the Gun at the Smoot Hearings: Joseph F. Smith's Testimony," *Journal of Mormon History* 34, no. 4 (Fall 2007): 181–225. During Brigham H. Roberts's contestation over the retention of his House seat in 1898, it was apparent that he was still practicing polygamy, justifying it as an interpretation of the 1890 Manifesto. For him, the manifesto spoke against future marriages and did not invalidate already established families. See Madsen, *Defender of the Faith*, 247. Mormon dishonesty became apparent at the hearings. In Smith's words: "Let me say to you, Mr. Senator—I have said it, but I repeat it—there has not any man, with the consent or knowledge or approval of the church, ever married a plural wife since the manifesto [1890]." And again, "I wish to say again, Mr. Chairman, that there have been no plural marriages solemnized by and with the consent or by the knowledge of the Church of Jesus Christ of Latter-Day Saints by any man. I do not care who he is." Smoot Hearings, 1:148, 177. As multiple historians have noted, Taylor and Cowley were offered up as sacrifices to save the church's duplicity on plural marriage but were no guiltier than Joseph F. Smith and other high officials who taught and performed plural marriages post-1890. See Jonathan H. Moyer, "Dancing with the Devil: The Making of the Mormon-Republican Pact" (PhD diss., University of Utah, 2009), 373, 500–502; D. Michael Quinn, "LDS Church Authority and New Plural Marriages, 1890–1904," *Dialogue: A Journal of Mormon Thought* 18, no. 1 (Spring 1985): 97–98.

27. Clark, *Messages*, 4:84–85; Hardy, *Solemn Covenant*, 141–47, 317–19. For more on Joseph F. Smith's and other prominent leaders' personal involvement in the defense and continuation of post-manifesto polygamy, see Quinn, "LDS Church Authority," 56–103.

28. Flake, *American Religious History*, 93–95.

29. Francis M. Lyman, quoted in ibid., 104.

30. "Tells of the Mormons," *Los Angeles Times*, February 26, 1907. Dr. Wishard had also stood as a key witness a few years earlier against B. H. Roberts when his House seat was rejected.

31. Reed Smoot to Allie Smoot, January 13, 1906, Smoot Papers. For more on this topic, see Merrill, *Reed Smoot*, 52.

32. Smith's testimony was published in the *Salt Lake Tribune* by the colorful former Utah senator and LDS excommunicant Frank J. Cannon. As Smith's testimony denied post-1890 plural marriages and downplayed the importance of revelation, priesthood authority, and the role of obedience in the church, Mormons at home were both confused and shaken. See Flake, *American Religious Identity*, 94–101, and Moyer, "Dancing with the Devil," 508–11.

33. Roberts, *Defense of the Faith*, 1:73–74.

34. Ibid., 1:73.

35. "Lutherans Fail to Act in Smoot Case," *New York Times*, September 12, 1903.

36. As a reminder of how emotion fit into nineteenth-century American cultural and religious history, historian of American religion John Corrigan noted that emotion had long been a "category of collective identity," one that had established cultural and religious boundaries and appeased collective anxieties. The use of emotion as a tool to establish support against Smoot and the church was apparent throughout the hearings. Corrigan, *Business of the Heart*, 251.

37. National newspapers throughout the Smoot hearings featured such provocative headlines as "Mothers Denounce Smoot," "Women Unite against Smoot," "W.C.T.U. Denounces Smoot," and "Signed by 1,000,000 Women."

38. Joan Smyth Iversen, *The Antipolygamy Controversy in U.S. Women's Movements, 1880–1925: A Debate on the American Home* (New York: Garland Publishing, 1997), 217; "Mormonism Scored," *Washington Post*, March 15, 1905.

39. "Congress at an End," *Washington Post*, April 23, 1905.

40. "Mormons a Menace," *Washington Post*, July 11, 1905.

41. "Another Smoot Protest," *New York Times*, March 1, 1903.

42. Smoot Hearings, 1:70.

43. Merrill, *Reed Smoot*, 38.

44. Smoot Hearings, 1:984, 42.

45. Taylor, *The Turner Thesis*, 44; Smoot Hearings, 1:984, 42.

46. Smith flatly denied that the church mixed its influence with the politics of the State, but that as an individual citizen, he claimed the right of political participation as had any minister of religion. When questioned by the committee, Smith denied that his authority as president

of the church was ultimate or absolute; that the First Presidency was necessarily made up of apostles ("they may or may not be apostles"); and that their access to divine inspiration was any different than that of other members of the church, including women, whom he spoke of as having "priestly authority." He continued this point by claiming that he himself as president of the church had "never pretended to nor do I profess to have received revelations" beyond the personal revelation that Mormonism is "God's divine truth." Concerning the principle of revelation in Mormonism and whether the words of the prophets are always divine, Smith responded with purposeful ambiguity: "When it is divine, it always is; when it is divine, most decidedly." In adding nuance to prophetic authority, Smith highlighted the value and acceptability of religious division and dissent within the church, and that being a "good Mormon" did not imply strict conformity and obedience, even to doctrines determined by the church to be fundamental to Mormonism and revealed by God. Smith made a special point to address the committee regarding the independence enjoyed by each citizen of Utah: "I should like to say to the honorable gentlemen that the members of the Mormon Church are among the freest and most independent people of all the Christian denominations. They are not all united on every principle. Every man is entitled to his own opinion and his own views and his own conceptions of right and wrong so long as they do not come in conflict with the standard principles of the church." Regarding polygamy, seen as an unquestioned revelation and command from God, Smith argued that only three to four percent of the Mormon membership followed "the principle," and "thousands" in the church rejected it as divine, yet "they were not cut off from the church." Indeed, when pressed by Senator Dubois, Smith responded, "I know that there are hundreds, of my own knowledge, who say they never did believe in it and never did receive it, and they are members of the church in good-fellowship." Smoot Hearings, 1:90, 98–99, 162, 188.

47. Ibid., 1:32.
48. In fact, "Mr. Smoot had, in his position in the church, done more to stamp out polygamy than any thousand other men, and yet you propose to punish him for this by expelling him from the Senate." From "Smoot is Championed," *Washington Post*, January 12, 1907.
49. Reed Smoot, Letter to John G. McQuarrie, December 16, 1902, in Merrill, Reed Smoot, 31.
50. Moyer, "Dancing with the Devil," 287–88, 443, 461–63.
51. Ibid., 293, 388, 517–19, 527–28; Flake, *American Religious History*, 100;

Milton R. Merrill, "Theodore Roosevelt and Reed Smoot," *Western Political Quarterly* 4, no. 3 (September 1951): 446–48.

52. Harvard S. Heath, "The Reed Smoot Hearings: A Quest for Legitimacy," *Journal of Mormon History* 33, no. 2 (Summer 2007): 73.

53. This fight proved similar to an earlier fight against Utah's quest for statehood, where non-Mormon ministers in Salt Lake City were accused in 1893 of being the main opponents. "Is Utah Fit for Statehood?"

54. Alexander, *Mormonism in Transition*, 257.

55. "Presbyterian Union in Sight," *New York Times*, May 29, 1904.

56. "Miss Anthony for Smoot," *New York Times*, January 27, 1903; see also Joan Smyth Iversen, *The Antipolygamy Controversy in U.S. Women's Movements, 1880–1925: A Debate on the American Home* (New York: Garland Publishing, 1997), 219.

57. "Want Smoot Unseated," *Washington Post*, October 28, 1905. By 1905, the Post claimed one million signatures: "Signed by 1,000,000 Women," *Washington Post*, November 26, 1905. By 1907, however, it had grown to two million: "Smoot Keeps Seat," *Washington Post*, February 21, 1907.

58. "Smoot Is Championed," *Washington Post*, January 12, 1907. "Good Luck Ladies," *Washington Post*, June 9, 1906.

59. "Defended by Mrs. Smoot," *Washington Post*, December 8, 1903; Moyer, "Dancing with the Devil," 527.

60. Theodore Roosevelt, *The Winning of the West* (New York: G. P. Putnam's Sons, 1906), 4:237.

61. Theodore Roosevelt, *Thomas Hart Benton* (Boston: Houghton, Mifflin, 1900), 15–19.

62. Johnson, *Hunger for the Wild*, 206.

63. Hofstadter, *The Progressive Historians*, 106–7; Putney, *Muscular Christianity*, 40.

64. George E. Mowry, *The Era of Theodore Roosevelt, 1900–1912* (New York: Harper and Brothers, 1958), 48.

65. Kathleen Dalton, *Theodore Roosevelt: A Strenuous Life* (New York: Alfred A. Knopf, 2002), 127, 233; xxxx.

66. Hine and Faragher, *Frontiers*, 198.

67. Theodore Roosevelt, *The Rough Riders* (New York: P. F. Collier & Son, 1899), 10–11, 13–15, 18, 22, 225.

68. Hine and Faragher, *Frontiers*, 200.

69. Dalton, Roosevelt, 127.

70. Flake, *American Religious Identity*, 12–13; Moyer, "Dancing with the Devil," 527–28.

71. Moyer, "Dancing with the Devil," 405, 466–69, 527.

72. "Reed Smoot Dines Negroes," *New York Times*, February 13, 1903. For more on this controversy, see Moyer, "Dancing with the Devil," 307.

73. Hutchison, *Religious Pluralism in America*, 85–88, 101–6, 175, 177.

74. Moyer, "Dancing with the Devil," 455–61.

75. Merrill, *Reed Smoot*, 28.

76. Milton R. Merrill, "Theodore Roosevelt and Reed Smoot," *Western Political Quarterly* 4, no. 3 (September 1951): 441; Flake, *American Religious Identity*, 144; Moyer, "Dancing with the Devil," 526. Reporting on the April 1905 Mormon conference, where Smoot did not sustain Taylor and Cowley, the *Washington Post* notes that, in the sustaining of the First Presidency and the Twelve, two negative votes came from the bishop's section of the Tabernacle, most likely against apostles Taylor, Cowley, and Teasdale. See "Revolt of Mormons," *Washington Post*, April 7, 1905. For more on this incident with Taylor and Cowley as related to Smoot and their dismissal from the Twelve, together with the growing animosity toward them from both within and outside the church, see Merrill, *Reed Smoot*, 57; Flake, *American Religious Identity*, 91–94, 106–8; Heath, "The Reed Smoot Hearings," 30–33, 57–59. With the death of Marriner W. Merrill the following February, the three apostolic vacancies were filled by George F. Richards, Orson F. Whitney, and David O. McKay. "Two Apostles Are Let Go," *Los Angeles Times*, April 9, 1906. Concerning the messiness of this issue, see Moyer, "Dancing with the Devil," 505–9, 523–25.

77. Flake, *American Religious Identity*, 12–13, 146, 162. See also Merrill, *Reed Smoot*, 92; "Riis Misled President, Says a Senator's Wife," *New York Times*, December 19, 1906.

78. "Smoot Is Assured of Victory To-day," *New York Times*, February 20, 1907.

79. Merrill, *Reed Smoot*, 37; "Dubois Attacks President," *New York Times*, December 14, 1906; "If Smoot Is Expelled," *Hartford Courant*, March 9, 1904; "President Is Assailed," *Washington Post*, December 14, 1906.

80. "Dubois Attacks President."

81. H. W. Brands, *The Selected Letters of Theodore Roosevelt* (New York: Cooper Square Press, 2001), 375.

82. As explained by his biographer Kathleen Dalton, young Roosevelt appeared to have been deeply influenced by this form of Christianity through statements by Trinity's pastor, Philip Brooks, that it was the concern for "one's self" that represented the "root of every cowardice." Dalton, *Theodore Roosevelt*, 62–63.

83. Putney, *Muscular Christianity*, 5.

84. Iversen, *The Antipolygamy Controversy*, 224–27. Regarding the trans-

formed sexual politics of the time that painted female reform groups as suspect, together with an examination of their underlining misogyny, see Flake, *American Religious Identity*, 162–64.

85. "Smoot Is Assured of Victory To-day"; see also "Riis Misled President."

86. H. W. Brands, *T. R.: The Last Romantic* (New York: Basic Books, 1997), 519.

87. Theodore Roosevelt, "Mr. Roosevelt to the Mormons," *Collier's*, April 15, 1911.

88. Albert Bushnell Hart, ed., *Theodore Roosevelt Cyclopedia* (New York: Roosevelt Memorial Association, 1941), 431; Roosevelt, *Benton*, 21.

89. Iversen, *The Antipolygamy Controversy*, 224–27.

90. "Menace of Mormonism," *New York Times*, February 1, 1904.

91. "Smoot Keeps Seat," *Washington Post*, February 24, 1907; "Senate Refuses to Oust Smoot."

92. Smoot Hearings, 1:161.

93. Moyer, "Dancing with the Devil," 494; Michael Harold Paulos, ed., *The Mormon Church on Trial: Transcripts of the Reed Smoot Hearings* (Salt Lake City: Signature Books, 2008), 558.

94. For a detailed social and political analysis of moral agency, see Mowry, *The Era of Theodore Roosevelt*, 50.

95. Smoot Hearings, 1:161.

96. "Controls Utah Politics," *Hartford Courant*, April 23, 1904.

97. Importantly, part of Thatcher's dissent from the Twelve and his inattendance at meetings with the Council of Fifty were at least partly owed to his disagreement with President John Taylor's increased centralization of power around himself after he was crowned king of the world. See Rogers, *Council of Fifty*, 353. Bitton, *George Q. Cannon*, 353–55, 412–13; Smoot Hearings, 1:1023–24; Kenneth W. Godfrey, "Moses Thatcher in the Dock: His Trials, the Aftermath, and His Last Days," *Journal of Mormon History* 24, no. 1 (Spring 1998): 67–73. For more in Thatcher's episode with the church and the Political Manifesto, see Thomas G. Alexander, "'To Maintain Harmony': Adjusting to External and Internal Stress, 1890–1930," *Dialogue: A Journal of Mormon Thought* 15, no. 4 (Winter 1982): 48–49; Edward Leo Lyman, "The Alienation of an Apostle from His Quorum: The Moses Thatcher Case," *Dialogue: A Journal of Mormon Thought* 18, no. 2 (Summer 1985): 67–91; Roberts, *Comprehensive History*, 6:330–36.

98. Letters between Moses Thatcher and Lorenzo Snow were reprinted in the Smoot Hearings, 1:1034–35.

99. Despite the testimony by Thatcher, the Political Manifesto of 1896 continued to be a problem in the Smoot hearings, as it was a prime example of political influence by the church and seemed to infer that no one in

the church could run for office unless they had permission, or "counsel," from church authorities. "Smoot's Moot Question Up," *Los Angeles Times*, December 12, 1906.

100. Quoted in Stanley S. Ivins, *The Moses Thatcher Case* (Salt Lake City: Modern Microfilm Co., n.d.), 9; Godfrey, "Moses Thatcher," 67–70.

101. Godfrey, "Moses Thatcher," 74; Smoot Hearings, 1:1042.

102. Smoot Hearings, 1:1035–37.

103. Ibid., 1:987, 1007–8.

104. Gail Bederman, *Manliness and Civilization: A Cultural History of Gender and Race in the United States, 1880–1917* (Chicago: University of Chicago Press, 1995), 44. See literary historian Ann Douglass, *The Feminization of American Culture* (New York: Doubleday, 1977), 327, on the new masculinization of American culture in reaction to growing concerns of an overly effeminate one. Revivalist Billy Sunday embodies this cultural shift in his depiction of Jesus as "the greatest scrapper that ever lived."

105. As reprinted in Smoot Hearings, 1:968–71.

106. Ibid., 1:727–28, 1038–50.

107. "Mothers Denounce Smoot," *New York Times*, March 18, 1905. Frank J. Cannon's indiscretions with prostitutes and alcohol while a young married man (monogamous) in 1885, were an "open secret" in Salt Lake City. See Nichols, *Prostitution, Polygamy, and Power*, 65, 138.

108. As reprinted in Michael Harold Paulos, "'I Am Not and Never Have Been a Polygamist': Reed Smoot's Speech before the United States Senate, February 19, 1907," *Utah Historical Quarterly* 75, no. 2 (Spring 2007): 105.

109. "An Address: The Church of Jesus Christ of Latter Day Saints to the World, April 5, 1907," in Clark, *Messages*, 4:143–55, particularly pp. 144 and 146. The Ministerial Association's letter was reprinted in full in Roberts, *Defense of the Faith*, 2:525–51. Interestingly, in response to the Ministerial Association's "Review," Roberts offered his own defense of the church's "letter to the world." Before an audience of between four and five thousand listeners at the Mormon Tabernacle, Roberts forcefully argued that the LDS "world letter" was "truthful" and was meant to be "conciliatory in spirit." Roberts opposed the Ministerial Association's accusations as "unjust; conceived in spite and vengeance; brought forth of malice; and nurtured by hate." Roberts also dismissed its representative ministers for being, "as a class, narrow, bigoted, intolerant, petty; and I say that in the very best of feeling." *Defense of the Faith*, 2:587, 605. For his entire lecture, see 2:552–605. The Ministerial Association had long been a stalwart enemy of Mormonism for theological reasons, and Smoot's seeming legitimation of it fueled the enmity. However, in proclaiming it to be not

so different from other Americans, the First Presidency letter provoked some in its claims of being not just another Christian denomination, but rather an example of "pure Christianity," which was not just American, but "the most distinctively American."

110. Roberts, *A Comprehensive History*, 6:438.

111. This view of the "higher law" was articulated before Congress by Senator William H. Seward (R–New York) more than fifty years earlier. As he explained before Congress: "The Constitution regulates our stewardship; the Constitution devotes the domain to union, to justice, to defense, to welfare, and to liberty. But there is a higher law than the Constitution, which regulates our authority over the domain, and devotes it to the same noble purposes." Quoted in Frederick W. Seward, *William H. Seward: An Autobiography from 1801 to 1834, with a Memoir of His Life, and Selections from His Letters, 1831–1846* (1877; rpt., New York: Derby and Miller, 1891), 126. Charles Taylor marks this recession of "higher times" as a move toward the "secular." See *A Secular Age*, 719.

112. Smoot Hearings, 4:3413.

## CONCLUSION

1. In demonstrating the broader relevance of these racial concerns over the meaning of what it means to be American and religious, historian David W. Wills argued against the idea that African Americans were "outsiders" in this earlier white evangelical story, but instead argued that they must be seen as "full Americans" and an integral part of a larger American narrative that has yet to be written. Black religious America was thus not to be a tool of this white "fairytale" narrative of American liberty and progress. David W. Wills, "The Central Themes of American Religious History: Pluralism, Puritanism, and the Encounter of Black and White," in *African-American Religion: Interpretive Essays in History and Culture*, ed. Timothy E. Fulop and Albert J. Raboteau (New York: Routledge, 1997), 10, 16–19.

2. The challenge, then, in our cautious redefining of an overall American experience inclusive of once-excluded minorities, is not to engage in simple "add-on" procedures to an earlier narrative of progress and liberty, but, as we are reminded by William Hutchison, to place such groups and all their contradictions to this narrative "side-by-side" with the "enormously dominant and influential Protestant establishment." There is no "overall American experience," but instead there are many. Hutchison, *Religious Pluralism in America*, 3. As Patricia Limerick argues, this is no simple revision of the historians' "shopping list," where forgotten items are merely added to the shopping cart. Instead, there needs to be recognition that there has never been one single story in which all others fit, but rather "everyone became

an actor in everyone else's play." Limerick, *The Legacy of Conquest*, 48–49, 292.

3. Inman and Cody, *Great Salt Lake Trail*, v.

4. Albert Bushnell Hart, *National Ideals Historically Traced, 1607–1907* (New York: Harper & Brothers, 1907), xiv, 37, 213–17.

5. For further examples of this historiographical trend, see Charles William Eliot, *American Contributions to Civilization: And Other Essays and Addresses* (New York: Century, 1907); Ernest Hamlin Abbott, *Religious Life in America: A Record of Personal Observations* (New York: Outlook, 1903); James Bryce, *The American Commonwealth* (New York: Macmillan, 1919 [1910]). Concerning secularism as a support of religious pluralism, Jacques Berlinerblau argues, "And if you fancy being able to think about God in any way you see fit, then once again, a little gratitude is in order. This type of freedom is secularism's essence. This is secularism's promise. This is the end to which all genuine secularisms aspire." *How to Be Secular: A Call to Arms for Religious Freedom* (Boston: Houghton Mifflin Harcourt, 2012), xvi.

6. Klaus J. Hansen, *Mormonism and the American Experience* (Chicago: University of Chicago Press, 1981), 211–14.

7. Yorgason, *Transformation*, 167. With degrees from prestigious universities like Harvard, Stanford, and the University of Chicago, Mormon historians such as Nels Anderson, Levi Edgar Young, Andrew Love Neff, and Leland H. Creer produced impressive regional histories, stressing economic, social, and geographic factors from within a "frontier history" worldview. Ronald Walker, David J. Whittaker, and James B. Allen, *Mormon History* (Urbana: University of Illinois, 2001), 42–44.

8. As quoted in Hansen, *Mormonism*, 206. In an invitation to church president Heber J. Grant to be the first speaker at the General Convocation on Scouting in the churches, Dr. James E. West, chief scout executive and editor of the Boys' Life magazine, wrote that such an honor was based on the fact that "the Church of Jesus Christ of Latter-day Saints was the first to give its official endorsement to Scouting." The "Mormon Church" also "leads all others in the high percentage of its boys and young men who have received Scout training. . . . You have gone further than any other church group in relating Scouting to the entire program of your church in its service to boys." As quoted in Heber J. Grant, "The President Speaks to Scouters," *Improvement Era* 39, no. 8 (August 1936): 461–62.

9. With significant parallels to this Mormon historiography and the Mormon appropriation of the Turnerian model, Terence Ranger comments that in colonial Africa, native populations embraced subjugating colonial models to such an extent that they were considered indigenous. Though becoming

a new and "invented tradition," these models served as an important entry point for Africans into the new colonial world. As written in his critique of Kenyan elites, Ngugi wa Thiong'o wrote in his Prison Diary, "The black pupils now do the same, only with great zeal: golf and horses have become 'national' institutions." As quoted in *The Invention of Tradition*, ed. Eric Hobsbawm and Terence Ranger (Cambridge: Cambridge University Press, 1997), 227, 261.

10. Eric Mazur represents a familiar example of how this story of Mormon transformation is understood devoid of these needs, where it was solely the work of the American government and the exercise of its "awesome power" that "eventually brought [Mormonism] into line." Though attributing this moment to Mormonism's conceding of "its foundation" (i.e., polygamy), Mazur implies that the doors were now swung open for an entirely different Mormonism to emerge—one that was both progressive and entirely American, thereby allowing Mormonism to fit within the prevailing historiography and historical narrative. Eric M. Mazur, *The Americanization of Religious Minorities: Confronting the Constitutional Order* (Baltimore: Johns Hopkins University Press, 1999), 92.

11. Chidester, *Savage Systems*, 219. For more on this adoption of the term "religion" for Native Americans following the closure of the frontier, see Tisa Wenger, *We Have a Religion*, 34–40, 184–88, and 237, where she explains that Pueblo Indians likewise adopted this term "religion" as a way of reclaiming power.

12. See Terryl L. Givens, *Viper on the Hearth*, 21–22.

13. Chidester, *Savage Systems*, xiv–xv.

14. Cavanaugh, *Myth of Religious Violence*, 179.

15. Masuzawa, *Invention of World Religion*, 268.

# BIBLIOGRAPHY

## NEWSPAPERS

*Atlanta Constitution*

*Brooklyn Eagle*

*Chicago Daily Tribune*

*Chicago Times*

*Crescent City (IA) Oracle*

*Daily Inter-Ocean* (Chicago)

*Deseret News* (Salt Lake City) (later *Deseret Semi-Weekly News*)

*Hartford (CT) Courant*

*Los Angeles Times*

*National Era* (Washington, DC)

*New York Daily Times*

*New York Times*

*St. Louis Post Dispatch*

*Sunday Herald* (Chicago)

*The Wasp* (San Francisco)

*Washington Post*

*Weekly Vincennes (IN) Gazette*

*Western Rural and American Stockman: A Weekly for the Farm, Field & Fireside* (Chicago)

## OTHER SOURCES

Abbott, Ernest Hamlin. *Religious Life in America: A Record of Personal Observations.* New York: Outlook, 1903.

Abd-Allah, Umar F. *A Muslim in Victorian America: The Life of Alexander Russell Webb.* New York: Oxford University Press, 2006.

Ahlstrom, Sydney E. *The American Protestant Encounter with World Religions. The Brewer Lectures on Comparative Religion.* Beloit, WI: Beloit College, 1962.

———. *A Religious History of the American People.* Vol. 1. New York: Image Books, 1975.

Albanese, Catherine L. "American Religious History: A Bibliographical Essay." *Currents in American Scholarship Series* (December 2002). Washington, DC: Department of State Bureau of Education and Cultural Affairs, Office of Academic Programs, 2002.

Alexander, James W. "The Holy Flock." In *The New York Pulpit in the Revival of 1858: A Memorial Volume of Sermons*, edited by Samuel Irenaeus Prime, 13–37. New York: Sheldon, Blakeman, 1858.

Alexander, Thomas G. *Mormonism in Transition: A History of the Latter-day Saints 1890–1930.* Urbana: University of Illinois Press, 1996.

———. "'To Maintain Harmony': Adjusting to External and Internal Stress, 1890–1930." *Dialogue: A Journal of Mormon Thought* 15, no. 4 (Winter 1982): 44–58.

———. *Utah: The Right Place.* Salt Lake City: Gibbs Smith, 2008.

Allen, James B., and Glen M. Leonard. *The Story of the Latter-day Saints.* 2nd ed. Salt Lake City: Deseret Book, 1992.

America, Banco de. *The War in Nicaragua as Reported by Frank Leslie's Illustrated Newspaper, 1855–1857.* Managua: Editorial San Jose, 1976.

Anderson, Benedict. *Imagined Communities: Reflections on the Origin and Spread of Nationalism.* Rev. ed. New York: Verso, 1991.

"Anti-Chinese Testimony." In *Living History America: The History of the United States in Documents, Essays, Letters, Songs and Poems*, edited by Erik Bruun and Jay Crosby, 497. New York: Tess Press, 1999.

Appel, John J. "From Shanties to Lace Curtains: The Irish Image in *Puck*, 1876–1910." *Comparative Studies in Society and History* 13, no. 4 (October 1971): 365–75.

Applegate, Debby. *The Most Famous Man in America: The Biography of Henry Ward Beecher.* New York: Doubleday Broadway, 2006.

Arrington, Leonard J. *Brigham Young: American Moses.* Urbana: University of Illinois Press, 1986.

———. *Great Basin Kingdom: Economic History of the Latter-Day Saints, 1830–1900.* Cambridge: Harvard University Press, 1958.

Arrington, Leonard J., Feramorz Y. Fox, and Dean L. May. *Building the City of God: Community and Cooperation among the Mormons.* Urbana: University of Illinois Press, 1992.

Asad, Talal. *Formations of the Secular: Christianity, Islam, Modernity.* Stanford: Stanford University Press, 2003.

———. *Genealogies of Religion: Discipline and Reasons of Power in Christianity and Islam.* Baltimore: Johns Hopkins University Press, 1993.

Bacon, Leonard Woolsey. "Polygamy in New England." *Princeton Review* 2 (July–December 1882): 39–57.

Bacon, Leonard. *Thirteen Historical Discourses, on the Completion of Two Hundred Years, from the Beginning of the First Church in New Haven, with an Appendix.* New York: Gould, Newman & Saxton, 1839.

Bagley, Will. *Blood of the Prophets: Brigham Young and the Massacre at Mountain Meadows.* Norman: University of Oklahoma Press, 2002.

Baird, Robert. *Religion in the United States of America; or, An Account of the Origin, Progress, Relations to the State, and Present Condition of the Evangelical Churches in the United States, with Notices of the Unevangelical Denominations.* New York: Arno Press & The New York Times, 1965 [1844].

————. *View of the Valley of the Mississippi; or, The Emigrant's and Traveler's Guide to the West.* Philadelphia: N.p., 1834.

Ballard, Henry. *Henry Ballard Journal, 1852–1885.* Vol. 1. Joel E. Ricks Collection of Transcription. Logan: Library of the Utah State Agricultural College.

Ban, Joseph D., and Paul R. Dekar, eds. *The Great Tradition: In Honor of Winthrop S. Hudson, Essays on Pluralism, Voluntarism, and Revivalism.* Valley Forge, PA: Judson Press, 1982.

Bancroft, Hubert Howe. *The Book of the Fair.* Chicago: Bancroft Company, 1893.

Barnes, Albert. *The Church and Slavery.* Philadelphia: Parry & McMillan, 1857.

Barrows, John H. *Christianity, the World-Religion.* Chicago: A. C. McClurg, 1897.

————. *Parliament of Religions at the World's Fair.* New York: Funk and Wagnalls, 1892.

————, ed. *The World's Parliament of Religions: An Illustrated and Popular Story of the World's First Parliament of Religions, Held in Chicago in Connection with the Columbian Exposition of 1893.* 2 vols. Chicago: Parliament Publishing, 1893.

Bauer, K. Jack. *The Mexican War, 1846–1848.* New York: Macmillan, 1974.

Bederman, Gail. *Manliness and Civilization: A Cultural History of Gender and Race in the United States, 1880–1917.* Chicago: University of Chicago Press, 1995.

Beecher, H. W. *Evolution and Religion.* Boston: Pilgrim Press, [1885].

Beecher, Lyman. "A Plea for the West (1835)." In *The Fear of Conspiracy: Images of Un-American Subversion from the Revolution to the Present,* edited by David Brion Davis, 85–94. Ithaca, NY: Cornell University Press, 1971.

Bell, Catherine. *Ritual: Perspectives and Dimensions.* New York: Oxford University Press, 1997.

Berger, Peter. *The Sacred Canopy: Elements of a Sociological Theory of Religion.* New York: Anchor Books, 1967.

Berlinerblau, Jacques. *How to Be Secular: A Call to Arms for Religious Freedom.* Boston: Houghton Mifflin Harcourt, 2012.

Bigler, David L. *Forgotten Kingdom: The Mormon Theocracy in the American West 1847–1896.* Logan: Utah State University Press, 1998.

Bigler, David L., and Will Bagley. *The Mormon Rebellion: America's First Civil War 1857–1858*. Norman: University of Oklahoma Press, 2011.

Billington, Ray Allen. *The Protestant Crusade 1800–1860: A Study of the Origins of American Nativism*. Chicago: Quadrangle Books, 1964.

Bitton, Davis. "B. H. Roberts at the World Parliament of Religion 1893 Chicago." *Sunstone Magazine* 7, no. 1 (January–February 1982): 46–51.

———. *George Q. Cannon: A Biography*. Salt Lake City: Deseret Book, 2004.

Boller, Paul F. *American Thought in Transition: The Impact of Evolutionary Naturalism, 1865–1900*. Chicago: Rand McNally, 1969.

Bond, Henry F. "Cuba and the Cubans." *North American Review* 79, no. 1 (July 1854): 109–37.

Bonney, Charles C. *World's Congress Addresses*. Chicago: Open Court Publishing, 1900.

Bowden, Henry Warner. *Church History in the Age of Science: Historiographical Patterns in the United States 1876–1918*. Carbondale: Southern Illinois University Press, 1991. First published 1971 by University of North Carolina Press (Chapel Hill).

Bowman, Matthew. *The Mormon People: The Making of an American Faith*. New York: Random House, 2012.

Bramen, Carrie Tirado. *The Uses of Variety: Modern Americanism and the Quest for National Distinctiveness*. Cambridge: Harvard University Press, 2000.

Brands, H. W. *T. R.: The Last Romantic*. New York: Basic Books, 1997.

———. *The Selected Letters of Theodore Roosevelt*. New York: Cooper Square Press, 2001.

Brooks, Juanita. *The Mountain Meadows Massacre*. Stanford: Stanford University Press, 1950.

Bryce, James. *The American Commonwealth*. New York: Macmillan, 1919 [1910].

Buchanan, James. *Great Speeches of the Honourable James Buchanan: Delivered at the Mass Meeting of the Democracy of Western Pennsylvania, at Greensburg, on Thursday, Oct. 7, 1852*. Philadelphia, 1852.

Bunker, Gary L., and Davis Bitton. *The Mormon Graphic Image, 1834–1914: Cartoons, Caricatures, and Illustrations*. Salt Lake City: University of Utah Press, 1983.

Burris, John P. *Exhibiting Religion: Colonialism and Spectacle at International Expositions 1851–1893*. Charlottesville: University Press of Virginia, 2001.

Bushman, Richard Lyman. *Joseph Smith, Rough Stone Rolling: A Cultural Biography of Mormonism's Founder*. New York: Knopf, 2005.

Bushnell, Horace. *Barbarianism the First Danger: A Discourse for Home Missions*. New York: William Osborne, 1847.

———. "Our Obligations to the Dead." In *Building Eras in Religion*. New York: Charles Scribner's Sons, 1910.

Butler, Jon. *Awash in a Sea of Faith: Christianizing the American People*. Cambridge: Harvard University Press, 1990.

Capers, Gerald M. *Stephen A. Douglas: Defender of the Union*. Boston: Little, Brown, 1959.

Cavanaugh, William T. *The Myth of Religious Violence: Secular Ideology and the Roots of Modern Conflict*. New York: Oxford University Press, 2009.

Cherry, Conrad, ed. *God's New Israel: Religious Interpretations of American Destiny*. Chapel Hill: University of North Carolina Press, 1998.

Chidester, David. *Authentic Fakes: Religion and American Popular Culture*. Berkeley: University of California Press, 2005.

———. *Savage Systems: Colonialism and Comparative Religion in Southern Africa*. Charlottesville: University Press of Virginia, 1996.

Christenson, Scott. *Sagwitch: Shoshone Chieftain, Mormon Elder 1822–1887*. Logan: Utah State University Press, 1999.

Clark, James R., comp. *Messages of the First Presidency*. 6 vols. Salt Lake City: Bookcraft Publishers, 1966.

Cleland, Robert Glass. *From Wilderness to Empire: A History of California*. New York: Knopf, 1960.

Colwell, Stephen. *The Position of Christianity in the United States, in Its Relations with Our Political Institutions, and Specially with Reference to Religious Instructions in the Public Schools*. Philadelphia: Lippincott, Grambo, 1854.

Compton, Todd. *In Sacred Loneliness: The Plural Wives of Joseph Smith*. Salt Lake City: Signature Books, 1997.

Cooper, William J., Jr., and Thomas E. Terrill. *The American South: A History*. 2nd ed. New York: McGraw-Hill, 1996.

Corrigan, John. *Business of the Heart: Religion and Emotion in the Nineteenth Century*. Berkeley: University of California Press, 2002.

Corrigan, John, and Lynn S. Neal, eds. *Religious Intolerance in America: A Documentary History*. Chapel Hill: University of North Carolina Press, 2010.

Cott, Nancy. *Public Vows: A History of Marriage and the Nation*. Cambridge, MA: Harvard University Press, 2000.

Crane, Paul, and T. A. Larson. "The Chinese Massacre." *Annals of Wyoming* 12, no. 1 (1940): 47–55; 12, no. 2 (1940): 153–62.

Craycraft, Kenneth R. *The American Myth of Religious Freedom*. Dallas: Spence, 1999.

Cross, Barbara M., ed. *The Autobiography of Lyman Beecher*. Cambridge, MA: Harvard University Press, 1961.

Cross, Gary, and Rick Szostak. *Technology and American Society: A History*. New Jersey: Prentice Hall, 1995.

Crowe, Charles, ed. *The Age of Civil War and Reconstruction, 1830–1900: A Book of Interpretive Essays.* Homewood, IL: Dorsey Press, 1966.

Crunden, Robert M. *Ministers of Reform: The Progressives' Achievement in American Civilization, 1889–1920.* New York: Basic Books, 1982.

Cruse, Laura. "American Republicanism as Shown through Mormon-Federal Conflict, 1846–1890." Master's thesis, Northeast Missouri State University, 1994.

Dalton, Kathleen. *Theodore Roosevelt: A Strenuous Life.* New York: Alfred A. Knopf, 2002.

Darwin, Charles. *The Descent of Man: And Selection in Relation to Sex.* 2nd ed. 2 vols. London: John Murray, 1888.

Davis, David Brion. *Images of Un-American Subversion from the Revolution to the Present.* Ithaca, NY: Cornell University Press, 1971.

———. "Some Themes of Counter-Subversion: An Analysis of Anti-Masonic, Anti-Catholic, and Anti-Mormon Literature." *Mississippi Valley Historical Review* 47, no. 2 (September 1960): 205–24.

Davis, William T., ed. *Bradford's History of Plymouth Plantation.* New York: Charles Scribner's Sons, 1920.

Daynes, Kathryn M. *More Wives Than One: Transformation of the Mormon Marriage System 1840–1910.* Urbana: University of Illinois Press, 2001.

Derr, Jill M., Janath R. Cannon, and Maureen U. Beecher. *Women of Covenant: The Story of Relief Society.* Salt Lake City: Deseret Book, 1992.

Doddridge, Joseph. *Notes on the Settlement and Indian Wars.* Pittsburgh: N.p., 1912.

Dorchester, Daniel. *Christianity in the United States from the First Settlement Down to the Present Time.* New York: Hunt and Eaton, 1889.

Douglass, Ann. *The Feminization of American Culture.* New York: Doubleday, 1977.

Douglass, Frederick. "What, to the Slave, Is the Fourth of July?" In *Lift Every Voice: African American Oratory, 1787–1901,* edited by Philip S. Foner and Robert Branham, 249–68. Rev. ed. Tuscaloosa: University of Alabama Press, 1997.

Dove, Patrick Edward. *The Theory of Human Progression, and Natural Probability of a Reign of Justice.* Boston: Sanborn, Carter and Bazin, 1856.

Dunn, Lewis A. "Past as Prologue: American Redemptive Activism and the Developing World." *World Politics* 27, no. 4 (July 1975): 612–27.

Dwight, Timothy. *Virtuous Rulers a National Blessing, A Sermon Preached at the General Election, May 12th, 1791.* Hartford: Hudson and Goodwin, 1791.

"Editor's Table: Providence in American History." *Harper's New Monthly Magazine* 17, no. 97 (June–November 1858): 694–700.

Eliot, Charles William. *American Contributions to Civilization: And Other Essays and Addresses*. New York: Century, 1907.

Etcheson, Nichole. *Bleeding Kansas: Contested Liberty in the Civil War Era*. Lawrence: University Press of Kansas, 2004.

Fessenden, Tracy. "Race." In *Themes in Religion and American Culture*, edited by Philip Goff and Paul Harvey, 129–62. Chapel Hill: University of North Carolina Press, 2004.

Firmage, Edwin B., and Richard C. Mangrum. *Zion in the Courts: A Legal History of the Church of Jesus Christ of Latter-day Saints*. Chicago: University of Illinois Press, 2001 [1988].

Fitzgerald, Timothy. *The Ideology of Religious Studies*. New York: Oxford University Press, 2000.

Flake, Kathleen. *The Politics of American Religious Identity: The Seating of Senator Reed Smoot, Mormon Apostle*. Chapel Hill: University of North Carolina Press, 2004.

Fluhman, J. Spencer. *"A Peculiar People": Anti-Mormonism and the Making of Religion in Nineteenth-Century America*. Chapel Hill: University of North Carolina Press, 2012.

Foster, Gaines M. *Moral Reconstruction: Christian Lobbyists and the Federal Legislation of Morality, 1865–1920*. Chapel Hill: University of North Carolina Press, 2002.

Foucault, Michel. *The Order of Things: An Archaeology of the Human Sciences*. New York: Parthenon Books, 1994. Originally printed 1971.

Franchot, Jenny. *Roads to Rome: The Antebellum Protestant Encounter with Catholicism*. Berkeley: University of California Press, 1994.

Franklin, John Hope, and Alfred A. Moss Jr. *From Slavery to Freedom: A History of African Americans*. 7th ed. New York: Alfred A. Knopf, 1994.

Furniss, Norman F. *The Mormon Conflict 1850–1859*. New Haven: Yale University Press, 1960.

Gaustad, Edwin S. *Faith of the Founders: Religion and the New Nation, 1776–1826*. Waco, TX: Baylor University Press, 2011.

Gaustad, Edwin, and Leigh Schmidt. *The Religious History: The Heart of the American Story from Colonial Times to Today*. Rev. ed. New York: HarperSanFrancisco, 2002.

Geertz, Clifford. *The Interpretation of Cultures*. New York: Basic Books, 1973.

Gilbert, James. *Perfect Cities: Chicago's Utopias of 1893*. Chicago: University of Chicago Press, 1991.

———. *Whose Fair?: Experience, Memory, and the History of the Great St. Louis Exposition*. Chicago: University of Chicago Press, 2009.

Gilchrist, Etta L. "The World's Fair." *Ashtabula News Journal*, May 23, 1893. Reprinted in *Woman's Exponent* 21, no. 24 (June 15, 1893): 177–78.

Givens, Terryl L. *The Viper on the Hearth: Mormons, Myths, and the Construction of Heresy*. New York: Oxford University Press, 1997.

Glaab, Charles N. "Historical Perspective on Urban Development Schemes." In *Social Science and the City: A Survey of Urban Research*, edited by Leo F. Schnore, 197–219. New York: Praeger, 1968.

Godfrey, Kenneth W. "Moses Thatcher in the Dock: His Trials, The Aftermath, and His Last Days." *Journal of Mormon History* 24, no. 1 (Spring 1998): 54–88.

Godkin, Edwin Lawrence. *Problems of Modern Democracy: Political and Economic Essays*. New York: Charles Scribner's Sons, 1896.

Goldfield, David, et al. *The American Journey: A History of the United States*. 2 vols. Upper Saddle River, NJ: Prentice Hall, 1998.

Gordon, Sarah Barringer. *The Mormon Question: Polygamy and Constitutional Conflict in Nineteenth-Century America*. Chapel Hill: University of North Carolina Press, 2002.

Gordon, Sarah Barringer, and Jan Shipps. "Fatal Convergence in the Kingdom of God: The Mountain Meadows Massacre in American History." *Journal of the Early Republic* 37, no. 2 (Summer 2017): 307–47.

Graebner, Norman, ed. *Manifest Destiny*. The American Heritage Series. Indianapolis: Bobbs-Merrill, 1968.

Graham, Stephen R. *Cosmos in the Chaos: Philip Schaff's Interpretation of Nineteenth-Century American Religion*. Grand Rapids, MI: Wm. B. Eerdmans, 1995.

Grant, Heber J. "The President Speaks to Scouters." *Improvement Era* 39, no. 8 (August 1936): 461–63.

Green, Arnold H. "Mormonism and Islam: From Polemics to Mutual Respect and Cooperation." *Brigham Young University Studies* 40, no. 4 (2001): 199–220.

———. "The Muhammad-Joseph Smith Comparison: Subjective Metaphor or a Sociology of Prophethood?" In *Mormons and Muslims: Spiritual Foundations and Modern Manifestations*, edited by Spencer J. Palmer, 111–33. Rev. ed. Provo, UT: Religious Studies Center at Brigham Young University, 2002.

Griffith, R. Marie. *Born Again Bodies: Flesh and Spirit in American Christianity*. Berkeley: University of California, 2004.

Grow, Matthew J., and Ronald W. Walker. *The Prophet and the Reformer: The Letters of Brigham Young and Thomas L. Kane*. New York: Oxford University Press, 2015.

Gunnison, John Williams. *The Mormons, or, Latter-Day Saints, in the Valley of the Great Salt Lake: A History of Their Rise and Progress, Peculiar Doctrines,*

*Present Conditions, and Prospects, Derived from Personal Observation, During a Residence Among Them.* Philadelphia: J. B. Lippincott, 1857.

Habermas, Jergen. *The Structural Transformation of the Public Sphere: An Inquiry into a Category of Bourgeois Society.* Translated by Thomas Burger. Cambridge: MIT Press, 1989.

Hafen, Leroy R., and Ann W. Hafen, eds. *Mormon Resistance: A Documentary Account of the Utah Expedition, 1857–1858.* Lincoln: University of Nebraska Press, 2005 [1958].

Hamburger, Philip. *Separation of Church and State.* Cambridge: Harvard University Press, 2002.

Hansen, Klaus J. *Mormonism and the American Experience.* Chicago: University of Chicago Press, 1981.

———. "The Political Kingdom of God as a Cause for Mormon-Gentile Conflict." *BYU Studies* 2, no. 2 (1960): 241–60.

Hanson, J. W., ed. *The World's Congress of Religions: The Addresses and Papers Delivered before the Parliament and an Abstract of the Congresses Held in the Art Institute, Chicago, Illinois, U.S.A., Under the Auspices of The Worlds Columbian Exposition, Profusely Illustrated.* Chicago: International Publishing, 1894.

Hardy, B. Carmon. *Solemn Covenant: The Mormon Polygamous Passage.* Urbana: University of Illinois Press, 1992.

Harper, Ida Husted. *The Life and Work of Susan B. Anthony.* 3 vols. Indianapolis: Bowen-Merrill Company, 1898.

Harris, Samuel. "The Millenarian Conference." *New Englander and Yale Review* 38, no. 148 (January 1879): 114–45.

Hart, Albert Bushnell. *National Ideals Historically Traced, 1607–1907.* New York: Harper & Brothers, 1907.

———, ed. *Theodore Roosevelt Cyclopedia.* New York: Roosevelt Memorial Association, 1941.

Hartzler, H. B. *Moody in Chicago; or, The World's Fair Gospel Campaign: An Account of Six Months' Evangelistic Work in the City of Chicago and Vicinity During the Time of the World's Columbian Exposition, Conducted by Dwight L. Moody and His Associates.* Chicago: Fleming H. Revell, 1894.

Hassard, John R. G. *Life of the Most Reverend John Hughes, DD: First Archbishop of New York.* New York: Appleton, 1866.

Hatch, Nathan O. *The Democratization of American Christianity.* New Haven: Yale University Press, 1989.

Heath, Harvard S. "The Reed Smoot Hearings: A Quest for Legitimacy." *Journal of Mormon History* 33, no. 2 (Summer 2007): 1–80.

Heise, Tammy. "Marking Mormon Difference: How Western Perceptions of Islam Defined the 'Mormon Menace.'" *Journal of Religion and Popular Culture* 25, no. 1 (Spring 2013): 82–97.

Henry, Caleb Sprague. *Politics and the Pulpit: A Series of Articles Which Appeared in the Journal of Commerce and in the Independent, During the Year 1850 . . .* New York: William Harned, 1851.

Hine, Robert V., and John Mack Faragher. *Frontiers: A Short History of the American West.* New Haven: Yale University Press, 2007.

Hobsbawm, Eric, and Terence Ranger, eds. *The Invention of Tradition.* Cambridge: Cambridge University Press, 1997.

Hofstadter, Richard. *The Progressive Historians: Turner, Beard, Parrington.* New York: Vintage Books, 1968.

———. *Social Darwinism in American Thought.* Boston: Beacon Press, 1955.

Horner, Joseph. "Christianity and the War Power." *Methodist Quarterly Review* 60 (April 1865): 165–86.

Hosmer, William. *The Higher Law, in Its Relations to Civil Government: With Particular Reference to Slavery, and the Fugitive Slave Law.* Auburn, NY: Derby & Miller, 1852.

Houghton, Walter R., ed. *Neely's History of the Parliament of Religions and Religious Congresses at the World's Columbian Exposition.* 3rd ed. Chicago: F. T. Neely, 1893.

Hubbard, William. *A General History of New England, from the Discovery to MDCLXXX.* 2nd ed. New York: Arno Press, 1972. First published 1848 by Little and Brown (Boston).

Hudson, Winthrop. *Religion in America: A Historical Account of the Development of American Religious Life.* New York: Charles Scribner's Sons, 1981.

Hutchison, William R. *The Modernist Impulse in American Protestantism.* Durham, NC: Duke University Press, 1992.

———. *Religious Pluralism in America: The Contentious History of a Founding Ideal.* New Haven: Yale University Press, 2003.

Inman, Henry, and William F. Cody. *The Great Salt Lake Trail.* Topeka: Crane, 1914.

Isaacs, Abram S. "What Shall the Public Schools Teach?" *Forum* 6 (October 1888): 207–8.

Iversen, Joan Smyth. *The Antipolygamy Controversy in U.S. Women's Movements, 1880–1925: A Debate on the American Home.* New York: Garland Publishing, 1997.

Ivins, Stanley S. *The Moses Thatcher Case.* Salt Lake City: Modern Microfilm Co., n.d.

Jackson, Samual M., ed. *Papers of the American Society of Church History: First Annual Meeting in Washington D.C., December 28, 1888.* Vol. 2. New York: Knickerbocker Press, 1889.

Jacobs, Wilbur R., ed. *Frederick Jackson Turner: The Frontier in American History.* Tucson: University of Arizona Press, 1986.

Jacobson, Matthew Frye. *Whiteness of a Different Color: European Immigrants and the Alchemy of Race.* Cambridge: Harvard University Press, 1998.

James, William. *The Varieties of Religious Experience: A Study in Human Nature.* New York: Simon & Schuster, 1997 [1902].

Johnson, Michael L. *Hunger for the Wild: America's Obsession with the Untamed West.* Lawrence: University Press of Kansas, 2007.

Kearney, Richard. *Strangers, Gods and Monsters: Interpreting Otherness.* New York: Routledge, 2003.

Kerstetter, Todd M. *God's Country, Uncle Sam's Land: Faith and Conflict in the American West.* Urbana: University of Illinois Press, 2006.

———. *Inspiration & Innovation: Religion in the American West.* Somerset, NJ: John Wiley, 2015.

King, Richard. *Orientalism and Religion: Postcolonial Theory, India and "The Mystic East."* New York: Routledge, 1999.

Kingsbury, O. A. "A Christian Daily Paper." *New Englander and Yale Review* 47 (September 1887): 182–188.

Kitagawa, Joseph. "The World's Parliament of Religions and Its Legacy." Eleventh John Nuveen Lecture. Chicago: University of Chicago Divinity School, 1983.

Knox, Thomas W. *Life and Work of Henry Ward Beecher: An Authentic, Impartial and Complete History of His Public Career and Private Life, from the Cradle to the Grave.* Kansas City, MO: S. F. Junking, 1887.

Lambek, Michael. "Provincializing God? Provocations from an Anthropology of Religion." In *Religion: Beyond a Concept,* edited by Hent de Vries, 120–38. New York: Fordham University Press, 2008.

Larson, Gustive O. *The "Americanization" of Utah for Statehood.* San Marino: Huntington Library, 1971.

Larson, J. Edward. *Summer for the Gods: The Scopes Trial and America's Continuing Debate over Science and Religion.* New York: Basic Books, 2006.

Laycock, Thomas. "Manhood and Womanhood." *Appleton's Journal: A Magazine of General Literature* 1, no. 10 (June 5, 1869): 311–21.

Lee, Erika. *At America's Gates: Chinese Immigration during the Exclusion Era, 1882–1943.* Chapel Hill: University of North Carolina Press, 2003.

Limerick, Patricia Nelson. *The Legacy of Conquest: The Unbroken Past of the American West.* New York: W. W. Norton, 1987.

Lincoln, Bruce. *Theorizing Myth: Narrative, Ideology, and Scholarship.* Chicago: University of Chicago Press, 1999.

Loewenberg, Bert J. "The Controversy over Evolution in New England 1859–1873." *New England Quarterly* 8, no. 2 (June 1935): 232–57.

Long, E. B. *The Saints and the Union: Utah Territory During the Civil War*. Chicago: University of Illinois Press, 2001.

Long, Kathryn Teresa. *The Revival of 1857–58: Interpreting an American Religious Awakening*. New York: Oxford University Press, 1998.

Lowell, James Russell. "Democracy" [1884]. In *Essays, Poems, and Letters*, edited by William Smith Clark II. New York: Odyssey, 1948.

Lyman, Edward Leo. "The Alienation of an Apostle from His Quorum: The Moses Thatcher Case." *Dialogue: A Journal of Mormon Thought* 18, no. 2 (Summer 1985): 67–91.

———, ed. *Candid Insights of a Mormon Apostle: The Diaries of Abraham H. Cannon, 1889–1895*. Salt Lake City: Signature Books, 2010.

———. *Political Deliverance: The Mormon Quest for Utah Statehood*. Chicago: University of Illinois Press, 1986.

MacKinnon, William, ed. *At Sword's Point, Part I: A Documentary History of the Utah War to 1858*. Norman, OK: Arthur H. Clark, 2008.

Madsen, Truman G. *Defender of the Faith: The B. H. Roberts Story*. Salt Lake City: Bookcraft, 1980.

Mandel, Ernest. *Late Capitalism*. Translated by Joris De Bres. London: Humanities Press, 1975.

Marquardt, H. Michael, ed. *Early Patriarchal Blessings of the Church of Jesus Christ of Latter-day Saints*. Salt Lake City: Smith-Pettit Foundation, 2007.

Marr, Timothy. *The Cultural Roots of American Islamicism*. New York: Cambridge University Press, 2006.

Marsden, George M. *The Evangelical Mind and the New School Presbyterian Experience: A Case Study of Thought and Theology in Nineteenth-Century America*. New Haven: Yale University Press, 1970.

———. *Fundamentalism and American Culture*. 2nd ed. New York: Oxford University Press, 2006.

Mason, Patrick Q. *The Mormon Menace: Violence and Anti-Mormonism in the Postbellum South*. New York: Oxford University Press, 2011.

Masuzawa, Tomoko. *The Invention of World Religion; or, How European Universalism Was Preserved in the Language of Pluralism*. Chicago: University of Chicago Press, 2005.

Mazur, Eric M. *The Americanization of Religious Minorities: Confronting the Constitutional Order*. Baltimore: Johns Hopkins University Press, 1999.

McCutcheon, Russell T. *Manufacturing Religion: The Discourse on Sui Generis Religion and the Politics of Nostalgia*. New York: Oxford University Press, 1997.

McDaniel, E. A. *Utah at the World's Columbian Exposition*. Salt Lake City: Press of the Salt Lake Lithographing Co., 1894.

McGreevy, John T. *Catholicism and American Freedom: A History.* New York: W. W. Norton, 2004.

McIntire, C. T. "Transcending Dichotomies in History and Religion." *History and Theory, Theme Issue* 45, no. 4 (December 2006): 80–92.

Mead, Sidney E. *The Lively Experiment: The Shaping of Christianity in America.* New York: Harper & Row, 1963.

———. "Timothy Dwight and Disestablishment." In *The Unfinished Experiment: Essays of Sidney E. Mead,* edited by Richard Wentz, 15–21. Tempe, AZ: Scholargy Custom Publishing, 2004.

Melville, Herman. *White-Jacket; or, The World in a Man-of-War.* London: Richard Bentley, 1850.

Mendenhall, J. W. "The Mormon Problem." *The Ladies Repository: A Monthly Periodical, Devoted to Literature, Arts, and Religion* 1, no. 4 (April 1875): 306–14.

Merrill, Milton R. *Reed Smoot: Apostle in Politics.* Logan: Utah State University Press, 1990.

———. "Theodore Roosevelt and Reed Smoot." *Western Political Quarterly* 4, no. 3 (September 1951): 440–53.

Miller, Randall M., Harry S. Stout, and Charles Reagan Wilson, eds. *Religion and the American Civil War.* New York: Oxford University Press, 1998.

Mode, Peter G. *The Frontier Spirit in American Christianity.* New York: MacMillan, 1923.

"Modern Millenarianism," *Princeton Review* 25, no. 1 (1853): 66–83.

Moore, John Bassett, ed. *The Works of James Buchanan: Comprising His Speeches, State Papers, and Private Correspondence.* Philadelphia: Washington Square Press, 1911.

Moore, Moses N., Jr. "Black Presbyterians and the Schism of 1837." *Union Seminary Quarterly Review* 54, nos. 3–4 (Spring 2000): 53–84.

———. "History and Historiography: Revisiting the Presbyterian Schism of 1837." *AME Church Review* (October–December 2005): 53–83.

Moore, R. Laurence. *Religious Outsiders and the Making of Americans.* Oxford, UK: Oxford University Press, 1986.

Moore, William E., comp. *The Presbyterian Digest of 1886: A Compend of the Acts and Deliverances of the General Assembly of the Presbyterian Church in the United States of America.* Compiled by the Order and Authority of the General Assembly. Philadelphia: Presbyterian Board of Publication and Sabbath Work, 1886.

Moorman, Donald. *Camp Floyd and the Mormons: The Utah War.* Salt Lake City: University of Utah Press, 2005 [1992].

Mowry, George E. *The Era of Theodore Roosevelt, 1900–1912.* New York: Harper and Brothers, 1958.

Moyer, Jonathan H. "Dancing with the Devil: The Making of the Mormon-Republican Pact." PhD diss., University of Utah, 2009.

Mulder, William. "Immigration and the 'Mormon Question': An International Episode." *Western Political Quarterly* 9, no. 2 (June 1956): 416–33.

National Woman Suffrage Association. "Declaration and Protest of the Women of the United States by the National Woman Suffrage Association." Philadelphia, July 4, 1876. Pdf. https://www.loc.gov/item/rbpe.16000300/.

Naylor, D. Keith. "The Black Presence at the World's Parliament of Religions, 1893." *Religion* 26, no. 3 (June 1996): 249–59.

Neilson, Reid L. *Exhibiting Mormonism: The Latter-day Saints and the 1893 Chicago World's Fair.* New York: Oxford University Press, 2011.

Nichols, Jeffrey. *Prostitution, Polygamy, and Power: Salt Lake City 1847–1918.* Urbana: University of Illinois Press, 2002.

Nichols, Roy Franklin. *The Disruption of American Democracy.* New York: Macmillan, 1948.

Niebuhr, H. Richard. *The Kingdom of God in America.* New York: Harper & Brothers, 1959.

Nietzsche, Friedrich. *The Birth of Tragedy and the Genealogy of Morals.* Translated by Francis Golffing. New York: Anchor Books, 1956 [1870–71] [1887].

Noll, Mark A. *America's God: From Jonathan Edwards to Abraham Lincoln.* New York: Oxford University Press, 2002.

———. *Civil War as a Theological Crisis.* Chapel Hill: University of North Carolina Press, 2006.

Novick, Peter. *That Noble Dream: The "Objectivity Question" and the American Historical Profession.* Cambridge: Cambridge University Press, 1989.

Oliphant, Laurence. *Patriots and Filibusters; or, Incidents of Political and Exploratory Travel.* Edinburgh: William Blackwood and Sons, 1860.

Ostler, Jeffrey. *The Plains Sioux and U.S. Colonialism from Lewis and Clark to Wounded Knee.* Cambridge: Cambridge University Press, 2004.

Parrington, Vernon L. "The Puritan Divines, 1620–1720." In *Cambridge History of American Literature*, 1:31–56. New York: G. P. Putnam's Sons, 1917.

Pastor, Robert A. *Not Condemned to Repetition: The United States and Nicaragua.* Cambridge, MA: Westview Press, 2002.

Paulos, Michael Harold. "'I Am Not and Never Have Been a Polygamist': Reed Smoot's Speech before the United States Senate, February 19, 1907." *Utah Historical Quarterly* 75, no. 2 (Spring 2007): 105–15.

———, ed. *The Mormon Church on Trial: Transcripts of the Reed Smoot Hearings.* Salt Lake City: Signature Books, 2008.

———. "Under the Gun at the Smoot Hearings: Joseph F. Smith's Testimony." *Journal of Mormon History* 34, no. 4 (Fall 2007): 181–225.

Paxson, Frederic L. *History of the American Frontier 1763–1893*. Boston: Houghton Mifflin, 1924.

Peabody, Andrew P. Review of *Samuel Eliot's History of Liberty, Part II*, by Samuel Eliot. *North American Review* 78, no. 2 (1854): 345–58.

Peterson, Charles S. *Take Up Your Mission: Mormon Colonizing along the Little Colorado River 1870–1900*. Tucson: University of Arizona Press, 1973.

Pfaelzer, Jean. *Driven Out: The Forgotten War Against Chinese Americans*. Berkeley: University of California Press, 2008.

*Picturesque Chicago and Guide to the World's Fair Issued by the Religious Herald, and Presented to Its Subscribers as a Souvenir of Fifty Years Publication of the Paper*. Hartford: D. S. Moseley, 1893.

Platt, Ward, ed. *Methodism and the Republic: A View of the Home Field, Present Conditions, Needs and Possibilities*. Philadelphia: Board of Home Missions and Church Extension of the Methodist Episcopal Church, 1910.

Pletcher, David M. *The Diplomacy of Annexation: Texas, Oregon, and the Mexican War*. Columbia: University of Missouri Press, 1973.

Pratt, Orson, ed. *Journal of Discourses, by Brigham Young, President of the Church of Jesus Christ of Latter-day Saints, His Two Counsellors, the Twelve Apostles, and Others*. London: Latter Day Saints' Book Depot, 1856.

Prime, Damuel Irenaeus. *The Power of Prayer: Illustrated in the Wonderful Displays of Divine Grace at the Fulton Street and Other Meetings in New York and Elsewhere, in 1857 and 1858*. London: Sampson, Low, Son, 1859.

Putney, Clifford. *Muscular Christianity: Manhood and Sports in Protestant America, 1880–1920*. Cambridge: Harvard University Press, 2001.

Quinn, D. Michael. "LDS Church Authority and New Plural Marriages, 1890–1902." *Dialogue: A Journal of Mormon Thought* 18, no. 1 (Spring 1985): 9–105.

———. *The Mormon Hierarchy: Origins of Power*. Salt Lake City: Signature Books, 1994.

Radke-Moss, Andrea G. "Polygamy and Women's Rights: Nineteenth-Century Mormon Female Activism." In *The Persistence of Polygamy: From Joseph Smith's Martyrdom to the First Manifesto, 1844–1890*, edited by Newell G. Bringhurst and Craig L. Foster, 263–97. Independence, MO: John Whitmer Books, 2014.

———. "'Truly Her Soul Rejoiced in Helping the Helpless': Emily Sophia Tanner Richards (1850–1929)." In *Women of Faith in the Latter Days. Vol. 3, 1846–1870*, edited by Richard Turley and Brittany A. Chapman, 131–45. Salt Lake City: Deseret Book Company, 2014.

Reavis, L. U. *The Life and Military Services of Gen. William Selby Harney*. St. Louis: Bryan, Brand, 1878.

Redpath, James. *The Public Life of John Brown*. Boston: Thayer and Eldridge, 1860.

Reed Smoot Papers. L. Tom Perry Special Collections, Harold B. Lee Library, Brigham Young University, Provo, UT.

Reeve, W. Paul. *Making Space on the Western Frontier: Mormons, Miners, and Southern Paiutes*. Urbana: University of Illinois Press, 2006.

———. *Religion of a Different Color: Race and the Mormon Struggle for Whiteness*. New York: Oxford University Press, 2015.

Reimers, David M. *White Protestantism and the Negro*. New York: Oxford University Press, 1965.

Roberts, Brigham H. "The Church of Jesus Christ of Latter-Day Saints at the Parliament of Religions: 'Christian Treatments of Mormons.'" *Improvement Era* 2, no. 10 (August 1899): 750–66.

———. *A Comprehensive History of the Church of Jesus Christ of Latter-day Saints, Century I*. 6 vols. Provo, UT: Brigham Young University Press, 1965.

———. *Defense of the Faith and the Saints*. 2 vols. Provo, UT: Maasai Publishing, 2002. Originally published 1907 and 1912 by Deseret News (Salt Lake City).

Rogers, Jedediah S., ed. *The Council of Fifty: A Documentary History*. Salt Lake City: Signature Books, 2014.

Rolle, Andrew F. *California: A History*. New York: Thomas Y. Crowell, 1969.

Roosevelt, Theodore. "Mr. Roosevelt to the Mormons." *Collier's*, April 15, 1911.

———. *The Rough Riders*. New York: P. F. Collier & Son, 1899.

———. *Thomas Hart Benton*. Boston: Houghton, Mifflin, 1900.

———. *The Winning of the West*. New York: G. P. Putnam's Sons, 1906.

Rossell, Garth M., and Richard A. G. Dupuis, eds. *The Original Memoirs of Charles G. Finney*. Rev. ed. Grand Rapids, MI: Zondervan, 2002.

Ruchames, Louis. "John Brown and the American Tradition." In *The Age of Civil War and Reconstruction, 1830–1900: A Book of Interpretive Essays*, edited by Charles Crowe, 209–14. Homewood, IL: Dorsey Press, 1966.

Said, Edward W. "Michel Foucault, 1926–1984." In *After Foucault: Humanistic Knowledge, Postmodern Challenges*, edited by Jonathan Arac, 1–12. New Brunswick: Rutgers University Press, 1988.

Sargent, Winthrop. "M. Gironiere and the Philippine Islands." *North American Review* 78, no. 1 (1854): 67–82.

Sarna, Jonathan D., ed. *Minority Faiths and the American Protestant Mainstream*. Urbana: University of Illinois Press, 1998.

Saxton, Alexander. *The Indispensable Enemy: Labor and the Anti-Chinese Movement in California*. Berkeley: University of California Press, 1971.

Schaff, Philip. *America: A Sketch of the Political, Social, and Religious Character of the United States of North America, in Two Lectures, Delivered at Berlin, with a Report Read before the German Church Diet at Frankfort-on-the-Maine, Sept., 1854.* New York: C. Scribner, 1855.

———. *History of the Apostolic Church: With a General Introduction to Church History.* Translated by Edward D. Yeomans. New York: Charles Scribner, 1853.

———. "Progress of Christianity in the United States of America." *Princeton Review* 2 (July–December 1879): 209–52.

Schlesinger, Arthur M., Jr., ed. *The Almanac of American History.* New York: Barnes & Noble Books, 2004.

Schmidt, Leigh E. *Restless Souls: The Making of American Spirituality, From Emerson to Oprah.* Berkeley: University of California Press, 2005.

Schultz, Kevin M., and Paul Harvey. "Everywhere and Nowhere: Recent Trends in American Religious History and Historiography." *Journal of the American Academy of Religion* 78, no. 1 (March 2010): 129–62.

Seager, Richard Hughes, ed. *The Dawn of Religious Pluralism: Voices from the World's Parliament of Religions, 1893.* La Salle, IL: Open Court Publishing, 1993.

———. "Pluralism and the American Mainstream: The View from the World's Parliament of Religions." *Harvard Theological Review* 82, no. 3 (July 1989): 301–24.

———. "The Two Parliaments, the 1893 Original and the Centennial of 1993: A Historian's View." In *The Community of Religions: Voices and Images of the Parliament of the World's Religions,* edited by Wayne Teasdale and George F. Cairns, 22–33. New York: Continuum, 1996.

———. *The World's Parliament of Religions: The East/West Encounter, Chicago, 1893.* Bloomington: Indiana University Press, 2009.

Sehat, David. *The Myth of American Religious Freedom.* New York: Oxford University Press, 2011.

Sewall, May Wright, ed. *The World's Congress of Representative Women: A Historical Resume for Popular Circulation of the World's Congress of Representative Women, Convened in Chicago on May 15, and Adjourned on May 22, 1893, Under the Auspices of the Women's Branch of the World's Congress Auxiliary.* Chicago: Rand, McNally, 1894.

Seward, Frederick W. *Seward at Washington, as Senator and Secretary of State: A Memoir of His Life, with Selections from His Letters, 1846–1861.* New York: Derby and Miller, 1891.

———. *William H. Seward: An Autobiography from 1801 to 1834, with a Memoir of His Life, and Selections from His Letters, 1831–1846.* New York: Derby and Miller, 1891.

Sharpe, Eric J. *Comparative Religion: A History.* La Salle, IL: Open Court, 1986.

Shea, William M. *The Lion and the Lamb: Evangelicals and Catholics in America.* New York: Oxford University Press, 2004.

Shipps, Jan. "From Peoplehood to Church Membership: Mormonism's Trajectory since World War II." *Church History: Studies in Christianity and Culture* 76, no. 2 (May 2007): 241–61.

———. *Mormonism: The Story of a New Religious Tradition.* Urbana: University of Illinois Press, 1985.

Shipps, Jan, et al. *A Preliminary Look Inside* Tragedy at Mountain Meadows*: A Panel Discussion.* Proceedings of Mormon History Association, Salt Lake City, Utah, 2007.

Smith, Christian, ed. *The Secular Revolution: Power, Interests, and Conflict in the Secularization of American Public Life.* Berkeley: University of California Press, 2003.

Smith, Henry Nash. *Virgin Land: The American West as Symbol and Myth.* Cambridge: Harvard University Press, 1975.

Smith, Jonathan Z. *Map Is Not Territory: Studies in the History of Religions.* Chicago: University of Chicago Press, 1993.

———. "Religion, Religions, Religious." In *Critical Terms for Religious Studies*, edited by Mark C. Taylor, 269–84. Chicago: University of Chicago Press, 1998.

Smith, Joseph, Jr. *History of the Church of Jesus Christ of Latter-day Saints.* Salt Lake City: Deseret Book Co., 1960.

———. *History of the Church of Jesus Christ of Latter-day Saints.* 7 vols. 2nd ed. rev. Salt Lake City: Deseret Book Co., 1972.

Smith, Joseph F. "Opening Address." *Seventy-Second Annual Conference of the Church of Jesus Christ of Latter-Day Saints*, April 1902, 1–3. Salt Lake City, UT: Deseret News, 1902.

———. "Opening Address." *Seventy-Seventh Semi-Annual Conference of the Church of Jesus Christ of Latter-day Saints*, October 1906, 1–10. Salt Lake City, UT: Deseret News, 1906.

Smith, Wilfred Cantwell. *The Meaning and End of Religion.* Minneapolis: Fortress Press, 1991.

Snodgrass, Judith. *Presenting Japanese Buddhism to the West: Orientalism, Occidentalism, and the Columbian Exposition.* Chapel Hill: University of North Carolina Press, 2003.

Stampp, Kenneth M. *America in 1857: A Nation on the Brink.* New York: Oxford University Press, 1990.

Starbuck, Charles C. "The Sects and Christianity." *New Englander and Yale Review* 49, no. 225 (December 1888): 416–24.

Stenhouse, T. B. H. *"Tell It All": The Story of a Life's Experience in Mormonism, An Autobiography.* Hartford: A. D. Worthington, 1975.

Strong, Josiah. *The New Era; or, The Coming Kingdom.* New York: Baker and Taylor, 1893.

———. *Our Country*, edited by Jurgen Herbst. Cambridge: Belknap Press of Harvard University Press, 1963 [1885].

Styers, Randall. *Making Magic: Religion, Magic, & Science in the Modern World.* New York: Oxford University Press, 2004.

Sullivan, Winnifred F. *The Impossibility of Religious Freedom.* Princeton: Princeton University Press, 2005.

Sweet, Leonard I. "'A Nation Born Again': The Union Prayer Meeting Revival and Cultural Revitalization." In Ban and Dekar, *The Great Tradition*, 193–221.

Sweet, William Warren. *The Story of Religion in America.* 2nd rev. ed. New York: Harper & Row, 1950.

Szasz, Ferenc Morton. *The Divided Mind of Protestant America, 1880–1930.* Tuscaloosa: University of Alabama Press, 1982.

———. *The Protestant Clergy in the Great Plains and Mountain West, 1865–1915.* Lincoln: University of Nebraska Press, 2004.

Szasz, Ferenc M., and Margaret Connell Szasz. "Religion and Spirituality." In *The Oxford History of the American West*, edited by Clyde A. Milner II, Carol A. O'Connor, and Martha Sandweiss, 359–91. New York: Oxford University Press, 1994.

Tambiah, Stanley J. *Magic, Science, Religion, and the Scope of Rationality.* New York: Cambridge University Press, 1990.

Taves, Ann. *Fits, Trances, & Visions: Experiencing Religion and Explaining Experience from Wesley to James.* Princeton: Princeton University Press, 1999.

Taylor, Charles. *A Secular Age.* Cambridge: Belknap Press, 2007.

Taylor, George Rogers, ed. *The Turner Thesis: Concerning the Role of the Frontier in American History.* Lexington: D. C. Heath, 1972.

Taylor, John. *An Examination into and an Elucidation of the Great Principle of the Mediation and Atonement of Our Lord and Savior Jesus Christ.* Salt Lake City: Deseret News Company, 1882.

———. *The Government of God.* Liverpool: S. W. Richards, 1852.

Tocqueville, Alexis de. *Democracy in America.* Translated by Henry Reeve. New York: Bantam Classic, 2000 [1835].

Towle, Nancy. *Vicissitudes Illustrated, in the Experience of Nancy Towle, in Europe and America.* Charleston, SC: James L. Burges, 1832.

Turner, Frederick Jackson. *The Frontier in American History.* New York: Henry Holt and Company, 1921.

———. *The Frontier in American History.* Tucson: University of Arizona Press, 1986.

Turner, James. *Without God, Without Creed: The Origins of Unbelief in America.* Baltimore: Johns Hopkins University Press, 1985.

Turner, John G. *Brigham Young: Pioneer Prophet.* Cambridge, MA: Belknap Press, 2012.

Tuveson, Ernest L. *Redeemer Nation: The Idea of America's Millennial Role.* Chicago: University of Chicago Press, 1968.

Twain, Mark. *The Innocents Abroad and Roughing It,* edited by Guy Cartwell. New York: Literary Classics of the United States, 1984.

Underwood, Grant. *The Millenarian World of Early Mormonism.* Urbana: University of Illinois Press, 1993.

U.S. Congress. *Enforcement of the Anti-Polygamy Act. Letter from the Secretary of the Interior, Transmitting Certain Petitions for Enforcing Anti-polygamy Act of 1862.* By Samuel J. Randall. 45th Cong., 3d sess. H. Doc. 58. Washington, DC: US Government Printing Office, 1879.

———. House Committee on the Judiciary. *Suppression of Polygamy in Utah,* by John Randolf Tucker. 49th Cong., 1st sess. H. Rept. 2735. Washington, DC: US Government Printing Office, 1886.

———. Joint Congressional Committee on Inaugural Ceremonies. *Inaugural Addresses of the Presidents of the United States: From George Washington to George W. Bush.* Washington, DC: US Government Printing Office, 1976.

———. *Message of the President of the United States to the Two Houses of Congress at the Commencement of the First Session of the Thirty-Fifth Congress, Vol. II.* 35th Cong., 1st sess. Cong. Doc. 2. Washington, DC: William A. Harris, 1858.

———. *Message of the President of the United States to the Two Houses of Congress at the Commencement of the Second Session of the Thirty-Fifth Congress.* 35th Cong., 2d sess. Cong. Doc. 1. Washington, DC: William A. Harris, 1858.

———. *Proclamation of President of United States to People of Territory of Utah,* by James Buchanan. 35th Cong., 2d sess. Cong. Doc. Vol. 2. Washington, DC: US Government Printing Office, 1858.

———. *Utah: Message from the President of the United States, Transmitting Information in Reference to the Condition of Affairs in the Territory of Utah,* by Lemuel G. Brandebury, Perry E. Brocchus, and B. D. Harris. 32nd Cong., 1st sess. Cong. Rept. 25. Washington: N.p., 1852.

U.S. Senate. Committee on Education and Labor. *Notes of a Hearing before the Committee on Education and Labor, United States Senate, May 7, 1886, on the Proposed Establishment of a School under the Direction of the Industrial Christian Home Association of Utah, to Provide Means of Self-support for the Dependent Classes in That Territory, and to Aid in the Suppression of Polygamy Therein,* by Henry W. Blair. 49th Cong., 1st sess. S. Rept. 1279. Washington, DC: US Government Printing Office, 1886.

————. Committee on Privileges and Elections. *Proceedings before the Committee on Privileges and Elections of the United States Senate in the Matter of the Protests against the Right of Hon. Reed Smoot, a Senator from the State of Utah, to Hold His Seat,* by Julius C. Burrows and Joseph Benson Foraker. 59th Cong., 1st sess. S. Rept. 486. Washington, DC: US Government Printing Office, 1906.

Wald, Kenneth D., and Allison Calhoun-Brown. *Religion and Politics in the United States,* 5th ed. New York: Rowman & Littlefield, 2007.

Walker, Ronald W., Richard E. Turley Jr., and Glen M. Leonard. *Massacre at Mountain Meadows.* New York: Oxford University Press, 2008.

Walker, Ronald, David J. Whittaker, and James B. Allen. *Mormon History.* Urbana: University of Illinois Press, 2001.

Walker, William. *War in Nicaragua.* Tucson: University of Arizona Press, 1985.

Webb, Richard D., ed. *The Life and Letters of Captain John Brown.* London: Smith, Elder, 1861.

Weinberg, Albert K. *Manifest Destiny: A Study of Nationalist Expansionism in American History.* Baltimore: Johns Hopkins Press, 1935.

Welling, James C. "The Science of Politics." *North American Review* 80, no. 2 (April 1855): 343–61.

Wenger, Tisa. *We Have a Religion: The 1920s Pueblo Indian Dance Controversy and American Religious Freedom.* Chapel Hill: University of North Carolina Press, 2009.

Wentz, Richard E. *The Culture of Religious Pluralism.* Boulder, CO: Westview Press, 1998.

————, ed. *Religion in American Life and Thought.* Tempe, AZ: Scholargy Custom Publishing, 2004.

White, Richard D., Jr. *Roosevelt the Reformer: Theodore Roosevelt as Civil Service Commissioner, 1889–1895.* Tuscaloosa: University of Alabama Press, 2003.

Whitman, Walt. *Drum-Taps.* New York: N.p., 1865.

————. *Passage to India.* Washington, DC: N.p., 1871.

Williams, J. D. "The Separation of Church and State in Mormon Theory and Practices." *Journal of Church and State* 9, no. 2 (Spring 1967): 238–62.

Williams, J. M. "Virtue, from a Scientific Standpoint." *New Englander and Yale Review* 43, no. 183 (1884): 759–64.

Wills, David W. "The Central Themes of American Religious History: Pluralism, Puritanism, and the Encounter of Black and White." In *African-American Religion: Interpretive Essays in History and Culture,* edited by Timothy E. Fulop and Albert J. Raboteau, 7–20. New York: Routledge, 1997.

Winthrop, John. *A Modell of Christian Charity (1630).* Collections of the Massachusetts Historical Society. 3rd series. Boston, 1838.

Woodruff, Wilford. *Wilford Woodruff's Journal, 1833–1898: Typescript.* 9 vols. Edited by Scott G. Kenney. Midvale, UT: Signature Books, 1985.

Worster, Donald. *Rivers of Empire: Water, Aridity, and the Growth of the American West.* New York: Oxford University Press, 1985.

Yorgason, Ethan. *Transformation of the Mormon Culture Region.* Urbana: University of Illinois Press, 2003.

Young, Ann Eliza. *Wife No. 19; or, The Story of a Life in Bondage, Being a Complete Expose of Mormonism, and Revealing the Sorrows, Sacrifices and Sufferings of Women in Polygamy, by Ann Eliza Young, Brigham Young's Apostate Wife.* Hartford, CT: Dustin, Gilman, 1876.

# INDEX

Page numbers in italic font refer to images.